Anti-Judaism and the Fourth Gospel

Anti-Judaism
and the Fourth Gospel

EDITED BY
R. BIERINGER, D. POLLEFEYT, AND
F. VANDECASTEELE-VANNEUVILLE

Westminster John Knox Press
LOUISVILLE • LONDON

Scripture quotations, unless otherwise indicated, are from the New Revised Standard Version of the Bible, copyright © 1989 by the Division of Christian Education of the National Council of the Churches of Christ in the U.S.A., and are used by permission.

Book design by Sharon Adams
Cover design by designpointinc.com

First edition
Published by Westminster John Knox Press
Louisville, Kentucky

A Deo title

This book is printed on acid-free paper that meets the American National Standards Institute Z39.48 standard. ∞

PRINTED IN THE UNITED STATES OF AMERICA

02 03 04 05 06 07 08 09 10—10 9 8 7 6 5 4 3 2

Library of Congress Cataloging-in-Publication Data
Anti-Judaism and the Fourth Gospel / edited by R. Bieringer, D. Pollefeyt & F. Vandecasteele-Vanneuville.—1st ed.
    p. cm.
    Includes bibliographical references and index.
    ISBN 0-664-22411-3 (alk. paper)
    1. Bible. N.T. John—Criticism, interpretation, etc. 2. Christianity and anti-Semitism. 3. Judaism (Christian theology)—History of doctrines—Early church, ca. 30–600. I. Bieringer, R. (Reimund) II. Pollefeyt, D. (Didier). III. Vandecasteele-Vanneuville, F. (Frederique)

BS2615.6.J44 A58 2001
226.5'06—dc21   2001023751

CONTENTS

CONTRIBUTORS

C. Kingsley Barrett, University of Durham, United Kingdom

Reimund Bieringer, Didier Pollefeyt, Frederique Vandecasteele-Vanneuville, Katholieke Universiteit Leuven, Belgium

James H. Charlesworth, Princeton Theological Seminary, New Jersey

Raymond F. Collins, The Catholic University of America, Washington, D.C.

R. Alan Culpepper, Mercer University, Atlanta, Georgia

Martinus C. de Boer, Vrije Universiteit Amsterdam, The Netherlands

Henk Jan de Jonge, University of Leiden, The Netherlands

James D. G. Dunn, University of Durham, United Kingdom

Jan Lambrecht, Katholieke Universiteit Leuven, Belgium

Judith M. Lieu, King's College London, United Kingdom

Stephen Motyer, London Bible College, United Kingdom

Adele Reinhartz, McMaster University, Hamilton, Ontario, Canada

Peter J. Tomson, Universitaire Faculteit voor Protestantse Godgeleerdheid, Brussels, Belgium

PREFACE

In the course of the development of the natural sciences, a number of well-known conflicts occurred that raised the question of the inerrancy of sacred scripture. We refer only to names such as Galileo Galilei and Charles Darwin. As mainstream Christian churches have gradually come to accept that the content of sacred scripture is theological and does not oblige Christians to accept its scientific worldview, another problem took center stage. The Bible was found wanting with regard to central ethical values. It became clear that the scriptures had been used to support and even to legitimate slavery, patriarchy, racism, and colonialism. The question arose whether the scriptures themselves or their misguided interpretation was responsible for such unethical phenomena.

At the Katholieke Universiteit Leuven (Belgium), a research program (1998–2001) funded by the Fund for Scientific Research, Flanders (FWO), studied the alleged anti-Judaism of the Gospel of John. This interdisciplinary research program is titled "The Gospel of John and Jewish-Christian Dialogue: An Interdisciplinary Investigation of the Theology of Jewish-Christian Relations Taking John 8:31–59 as Starting Point." In the context of this research, an interdisciplinary academic seminar was held in Leuven on January 17–18, 2000, in collaboration with the Netherlands School of Advanced Studies in Theology and Religious Studies and with the support of the Institutum Iudaicum, Brussels, and the National Catholic Commission for the Relations with Judaism, Belgium. Twenty-four leading scholars in the fields of Johannine exegesis and Jewish-Christian dialogue were invited to write papers and agreed to read one another's papers before the seminar began. The seminar sessions were devoted to scholarly discussion of the disputed issues. After the seminar, participants had the opportunity to rework and edit their contributions, which we are happy to present in this book. In dialogue with the views represented here, in our contribution we offer a hermeneutical framework for the analysis of the current debate and develop our own approach to the problem. We also provide a select bibliography on the topic.

At the end of this long and involved process, we are grateful to a large number of people. First of all, we thank the contributors who were willing to collaborate in this demanding process. Their work and their enthusiasm made this project possible. We are grateful to our students at the K. U. Leuven who were involved in the preparation of the seminar in classes and group discussion sessions. In a special way we thank Annemie Dillen, Barbara Focquaert, and Eva Gelper for their assistance with the editorial work. We are indebted to Frederik Glorieux and Isabelle Vanden Hove for their help in making the index and to Dr. Beate Kowalski for helping with the proofreading. The complete set of studies was published by Van Gorcum in Assen, The Netherlands, as volume 1 of the Jewish and Christian Heritage series. We are delighted that Westminster John Knox Press in Louisville, Kentucky, was willing to publish a selection of the papers in paperback. We are grateful to Dr. Carey C. Newman and Julie Tonini for their tireless support of the project.

Leuven, Belgium
January 27, 2001, Holocaust Memorial Day

Reimund Bieringer
Didier Pollefeyt
Frederique Vandecasteele-Vanneuville

ABBREVIATIONS

With the exception of the abbreviations listed below, all abbreviations used in this book can be found in the *SBL Handbook of Style* (Peabody, Mass.: Hendrickson Publishers, 1999).

AASF.DHL	Annales Academiae scientiarum fennicae. Dissertationes Humanarum Litterarum, Helsinki
ABPB	Aachener Beiträge zu Pastoral- und Bildungsfragen, Aachen
ACJD	Abhandlungen zum christlich-jüdischen Dialog, Munich
Ambrosius	*Ambrosius. Bolletino liturgico ambrosiano*, Milan
America	*America. A Catholic Review of the Week,* New York
Asprenas	*Asprenas. Organo dell'accademia ecclesiastica napoletana*, Naples
ATR.SS	Anglican Theological Review. Supplementary Series, Evanston, Illinois
BIS	Biblical Interpretation Series, Leiden–New York
BThSt	Biblisch-theologische Studien, Neukirchen-Vluyn
BU	Biblische Untersuchungen, Regensburg
CCARJ	*Central Conference of American Rabbis Journal*
CCSA	Corpus Christianorum: Series apocryphorum, Turnhout
Christliche Welt	*Christliche Welt. Evangelisches Gemeindeblatt für Gebildete aller Stände*, Leipzig

CSASE	Cambridge Studies in Anglo-Saxon England, Cambridge–New York
EHPR	Études d'histoire et de philosophie religieuses, Paris
EHS.T	Europäische Hochschulschriften. Theologie, Bern, Berlin, Brussels, Frankfurt a.M., New York, Vienna
EUS	European University Studies, Frankfurt a.M.
EWNT	*Exegetisches Wörterbuch zum Neuen Testament*
Expl.	*Explorations. Annual of Jewish Themes,* London
FS	Festschrift
GPM	*Göttinger Predigtmeditationen,* Göttingen
HCC	*Humanities, Christianity and Culture. International Christian University Publication IV-B,* Tokyo
HTCNT	Herders Theological Commentary on the New Testament, New York
JBTh	*Jahrbuch für Biblische Theologie*, Neukirchen-Vluyn
LTPM	Louvain Theological and Pastoral Monographs, Leuven
LuthBei	*Lutherische Beiträge,* Oesingen
MTSt	Marburger Theologische Studien, Marburg
NABPR	The National Association for Baptist Professors of Religion
NTDH	Neukirchener Theologische Dissertationen und Habilitationen, Neukirchen-Vluyn
NTE	New Testament Essays, Garden City, New York
NThT	*Nieuw theologisch tijdschrift*
NTLit	New Testament Literature, London
Orien.	*Orientierung. Katholische Blätter für weltanschauliche Information,* Zurich
PBTM	Paternoster Biblical and Theological Monographs, London
RC	Reich Christi

RHLR	*Revue d'histoire et de littérature religieuses,* Paris
RMT	Readings in Moral Theology
RQH	*Revue des questions historiques,* Paris
SBFA	Studium Biblicum Franciscanum Analecta, Jerusalem
SFNF	Studia Friburgensia, Neue Folge, Fribourg
SQEF	Synopse des quatre évangiles en français 3
SSA	Schriften der Sektion für Altertumwissenschaft
TEH	Theologische Existenz heute, Munich
ThDiss	Theologische Dissertationen, Basel
ThJb	*Theologisches Jahrbuch,* Leipzig
TW	Theologie und Wirklichkeit, Bern–Frankfurt
UTR	Utrechtse Theologische Reeks, Utrecht
VB	Verkenning en bezinning, Kampen
WdF	Wege der Forschung, Darmstadt
Worship	*Worship. A Review concerned with Problems of Liturgical Renewal,* Collegeville, Minnesota

INTRODUCTION

CHAPTER 1

Wrestling with Johannine Anti-Judaism: A Hermeneutical Framework for the Analysis of the Current Debate

Reimund Bieringer, Didier Pollefeyt,
Frederique Vandecasteele-Vanneuville

The Catholic cathedral of Brussels, in the heart of Europe, is known not only for its splendid architecture but also for its magnificent stained-glass windows of the sixteenth and nineteenth centuries. Some of these windows, however, represent a very unfortunate aspect of Jewish-Christian relations in the course of European history: the legend of host profanation. In 1370, some Jews in Brussels were accused of having stolen hosts and pierced them with knives. The legend goes on to claim that, as a result, the hosts began to bleed. For centuries to come, the cathedral was the place of pious devotion to this so-called miracle.

For more than a century, the presence of these stained-glass windows in such a prevalent place of Christian devotion and artistic heritage has been an element of controversy. Particularly in a post-Shoah context, the question must be raised of what to do with key elements of our cultural heritage that are contaminated with anti-Judaism. One option would be to purge all public life of the traces of past anti-Judaism, and thus to remove the stained-glass windows from the cathedral. Another option consists of providing information to the audience about the historical context and limitations of the story of the miracle, for example, the role it has played in misguided attempts to illustrate the doctrine of transubstantiation. Another option would be to ignore the problem and to hope that visitors will not perceive the anti-Jewish character of the windows. The leadership of the archdiocese of Malines-Brussels chose to draw attention to the legendary nature of the "miracle" by putting up a bronze plate with the following text: "In 1968, in the spirit of the Second Vatican Council, and taking note of historical research, the leadership of the diocese of Malines-Brussels has drawn . . . attention to the biased nature of the accusation and the legendary character of the 'miracle.'"

Scholars studying the Fourth Gospel are confronted with a similar challenge. This Gospel contains texts that shock the reader in the very first reading because of their anti-Jewish tendencies. The *locus classicus* of this problem is John 8:31–59, where, at the climax of the conflict, the Johannine Jesus refers to the Jews as children of the devil (8:44). The Gospel of John has shaped Christian history and culture more than any other New Testament text. We are thus confronted here with alleged anti-Jewish tendencies at the core of a central expression of the Christian faith, not just localized in one place of worship but with universal impact. Here the question becomes even more pressing: What must we do with such texts at the core of our Christian heritage? Some scholars have gone so far as to suggest leaving parts of John 8 untranslated or even removing them entirely from the Gospel.[1] Liturgically, this corresponds to the decision of the revised lectionary not to include John 8:43–50.[2] Another option would be to include an extensive footnote in the text, explaining the historical context that gave rise to this presentation of the conflict.[3] Liturgically, this means the Johannine text should never be read without a homiletic explanation. Finally, there are those who prefer to ignore the problem, hoping that the alleged anti-Judaism will be counterbalanced by positive presentations of Judaism in the Gospel of John (see 4:22).

The problem of anti-Judaism and the Fourth Gospel is a complex matter that has historical, sociological, and theological dimensions. It involves the study of the original texts, of their reception and effects throughout history, as well as of their ethical and theological implications in the perspective of Christian-Jewish dialogue after the Shoah.

In this chapter we develop a hermeneutical tool for understanding the current debate on John and anti-Judaism as represented in the contributions of this book.[4] We work out classifications and reading strategies that help structure and evaluate the great variety of positions defended in this area of Johannine research. Our hermeneutical tool is itself based on an analysis of the diversity of views that we encountered in the current scholarly debate. As such, it can hardly be a removed, objective presentation of the different positions in the debate. On the contrary, it reflects our own approach to the issues at stake. In this way, our own position will emerge.

---

1. See T. Pippin, "'For Fear of the Jews': Lying and Truth-Telling in Translating the Gospel of John," *Semeia* 76 (1996): 81–97.

2. In the post–Vatican II lectionary of the Roman Catholic Church, John 8:43–50 never occurs as a reading.

3. See chapter 2 by Dunn, p. 41 and chapter 12 by Charlesworth, p. 247.

4. References to contributions in this book are made by the name of the author and the page(s).

We are convinced that the discussion can be structured on five questions: (1) Is the Gospel of John anti-Jewish? (2) Who are "the Jews" in John? (3) How do we have to understand the presumed conflict between the Johannine community and "the Jews"? (4) Is John supersessionist? (5) What is the possible contribution of hermeneutics to reading John? For each question, we systematically map the different views found in this book.

Is the Gospel of John Anti-Jewish?

No one dares deny that anti-Judaism has found its way into the interpretation of the Gospel of John, but views vary with regard to where such anti-Judaism originated. In this section, we ask whether the intentions of the Fourth Evangelist themselves were anti-Jewish, or whether later readers (mis)used the Gospel of John for their own anti-Jewish purposes. Reading the literature on this question, we distinguish three—not mutually exclusive—levels on which scholars claim that anti-Judaism entered the "world"[5] of the Gospel of John: (1) the level of the interpreter(s) (*intentio lectoris*); (2) the level of the text (*sensus textus*); and (3) the level of the author (*intentio auctoris*).[6]

The Level of the Interpreter(s)

We Remember, the 1998 document of the Vatican Commission for Religious Relations with the Jews, quotes the words of Pope John Paul II: "In the Christian world—I do not say on the part of the Church as such—erroneous and unjust interpretations of the New Testament regarding the Jewish people and their alleged culpability have circulated for too long, engendering feelings of hostility towards this people."[7] Anti-Judaism is here ascribed to the level of the interpretation of the biblical text. It is unclear, however, whether the pope holds responsible individual readers "in" the Christian world or a more collective reading of the gospel "by" the

5. S. M. Schneiders, *The Revelatory Text: Interpreting the New Testament as Sacred Scripture* (San Francisco, 1991), pp. 97–179, speaks about the world behind the text, the world of the text, and the world before the text.

6. See "The Dogmatic Constitution on Divine Revelation *Dei Verbum*," in W. M. Abbott, ed., *The Documents of Vatican II: All Sixteen Official Texts Promulgated by the Ecumenical Council 1963–1965*, translated from the Latin (Chicago, 1966), pp. 111–28 (DV 12 on pp. 120–21); and T. Söding, *Wege der Schriftauslegung. Methodenbuch zum Neuen Testament* (Freiburg-Basel-Vienna), 1998, pp. 237–48.

7. "We Remember: A Reflection on the Shoah," *Catholics Remember the Holocaust*, No. 5-290 (Washington, D.C.: USCC, 1999), no. 3, footnote 8.

Christian world.[8] We are convinced that a distinction needs to be made between the individual reader and a collective reading of the gospel in the course of history (*Wirkungsgeschichte*).

Blaming the individual interpreter for an anti-Jewish reading of John's Gospel finds its classic expression in the commentary of Frédéric Godet: "The critic begins by decreeing what the Fourth Gospel must be, an anti-Jewish book. Then, when he meets an expression which contradicts this alleged character, he rejects it with a stroke of a pen. He obtains, thus, not the Gospel which *is*, but that which he *would have*."[9] This indeed points to a perennial problem of interpretation, namely, projecting one's own contemporary perceptions onto ancient texts. In a post-Shoah context, readers have become so sensitive to anti-Judaism that there is a danger of overinterpreting even the slightest (potentially) negative representation of Judaism. Nevertheless, the question must be asked whether, in the case of the Gospel of John, the anti-Jewish interpretation is a *creatio ex nihilo* or whether it is actualizing a dangerous potential that is present in the text itself. Few would deny that individual texts of John's Gospel permit anti-Jewish interpretations. At least some expressions are ambiguous enough to leave open the possibility of an anti-Jewish reading. The *Wirkungsgeschichte* is a clear illustration that the anti-Jewish interpretations of the Fourth Gospel cannot simply be ascribed to the whim of individual interpreters, but that a collective body of people in different places and at different times found consistent support in John for their anti-Jewish inclinations.

Therefore, instead of blaming the individual interpreter, some scholarly approaches ascribe the anti-Jewish reading of John to the *Wirkungsgeschichte* of the text. Moreover, they argue that this *Wirkungsgeschichte* produced "erroneous and unjust interpretations" (see *We Remember*) of John's Gospel. In this way, they show how the Gospel was "spoiled" by the later history of

---

8. Cf. *We Remember* 3: "Despite the Christian preaching of love for all, even for one's enemies, the prevailing mentality down the centuries penalized minorities and those who were in any way 'different.' Sentiments of anti-Judaism *in some Christian quarters*, and the gap which existed between *the Church* and the Jewish people, led to a generalized discrimination, which ended at times in expulsions or attempts at forced conversions"; *We Remember* 4: "But it may be asked whether the Nazi persecution of the Jews was not made easier by the anti-Jewish prejudices imbedded *in some Christian minds and hearts*. Did anti-Jewish sentiment among Christians make them less sensitive, or even indifferent, to the persecutions launched against the Jews by National Socialism when it reached power?"; *We Remember* 4: "We deeply regret the errors and failures of those *sons and daughters of the Church*" (i.e., of those "whose spiritual resistance and concrete action of other Christians was not that which might have been expected from Christ's followers"); *We Remember* 5: "At the end of this Millennium the Catholic Church desires to express her deep sorrow for the failures *of her sons and daughters in every age*. This is an act of repentance (teshuva), since, as members of the Church, we are linked to the sins as well as the merits of all her children." All emphases are ours.

9. F. L. Godet, *Commentaire sur l'évangile de Saint Jean* (Neuchâtel, 1864; 4th ed., 1902), vol. 1, p. 310 (English translation 1886; 4th ed., 1978, p. 429).

its reception, and they try to safeguard its original, innocent meaning by bypassing the problematic *Wirkungsgeschichte* that was "attached" to it. Against this strategy to neutralize the anti-Jewish character of John by relegating it to the responsibility of later interpretative groups, one can ask what the relationship is between the interpretation and the text itself. Does not the history of interpretation become part of the meaning of the text itself? Has the text not lost its innocence and become guilty? Moreover, while an individual "critic" might indeed misjudge the meaning of the text, it is much more difficult to defend that the mainstream in Christian tradition has created its anti-Jewish interpretations from nothing. Therefore, scholars continued their search for the source of Johannine anti-Judaism on the levels of the text and the author (see the following sections).

A specific variation on locating John's alleged anti-Judaism at the level of (collective) interpretation is the claim that the problem arose at the moment when the Fourth Gospel was incorporated into the canon. This position presumes that the word *the Jews,* which in the Fourth Gospel alone referred only to a limited group within Judaism (the Jewish authorities), took on a broader meaning under the influence of the other books of the canon where *the Jews* is assumed to refer to the entire Jewish people. But it is highly doubtful whether the problem of Johannine anti-Judaism can be limited to the meaning of the expression "the Jews," whether all the uses of the expression "the Jews" in John can be interpreted as having a limited meaning (see below), and whether the limited meaning is really totally absent in other books of the New Testament (cf. 1 Thess. 2:14–16 and Matt. 28:15).

The Level of the Text

We distinguish the level of the text from both the level of interpretation and the level of the author. In the contemporary discussion, some authors tend to make a distinction between the intention of the original author and the meaning of the text. The presupposition that one can find the meaning of the text exclusively through the intention of its author has been called the "intentional fallacy,"[10] since the meaning of the text and the meaning intended by the author are not automatically and completely the same. Paul Ricoeur, for instance, speaks about the "surplus meaning" that written texts acquire beyond the meaning intended by the author.[11] Writers of texts have

10. R. Barthes, *Image, Music, Text: Essays*, trans. Stephen Heath (London, 1977; 5th ed., 1987); see his chapter on "The Death of the Author."

11. P. Ricoeur, *Interpretation Theory: Discourse and the Surplus of Meaning* (Fort Worth, Tex., 1976). Cf. R. Bieringer, "The Normativity of the Future: The Authority of the Bible for Theology," *Bulletin Européische Theologie: Zeitschrift für Theologie in Europa* 8 (1997): 52–67.

come across the experience of being misunderstood by some of their readers, even if in a second reading they are able to recognize where their text
gave rise to an alternative understanding.

In the discussion on John's anti-Judaism, the distinction between text
and author is sometimes used to acknowledge the problems in John's text
but to deny the anti-Jewish intentions of the Evangelist himself. The
text itself can generate anti-Jewish prejudice, even if this prejudice was not
present in the mind of the author. Yet there is a major difference from
attempts to excuse the author for the *Wirkungsgeschichte* of his text (level
1). Focusing on the *Wirkungsgeschichte*, one stresses more the *subjective*
side of the process of interpretation, that is, anti-Jewish readers reading
John; whereas focusing on the level of the text, one stresses more the *objective* side of this process, that is, readers reading a text with anti-Jewish
"meaning producing dimensions."[12] In this context, new questions arise:
To what extent is the author responsible for the potential alternative
understandings that can emerge from a text? Is the possibility of alternative understandings the consequence of a fundamental existential ambiguity present in any text, or is this the result of the presence of "meaning
producing dimensions" for which the author is responsible? In short, to
what degree is the author responsible for the text and its effects? And ultimately, to the degree that the author can be held responsible for his own
text, is the outcome of his writing ethically and theologically acceptable?
These questions are central to the discussion among scholars who focus on
the level of the author.

The Level of the Author

If there is anti-Judaism in the Gospel of John, most people will agree that
the author[13] is in one way or another implicated. Much research has been
devoted to the question of the precise responsibility of the Fourth Evangelist. There is a great variety of positions, spanning from those, on the one
hand, who think that John's (negative) references to "the Jews" point only
to a very limited group of Jews, to those, on the other hand, who consider
John's theology to be intrinsically oppressive of the Jews. In this section we
present the whole range of views.

---

12. D. Patte, *Ethics of Biblical Interpretation: A Reevaluation* (Louisville, Ky., 1995).
13. In distinction from earlier literary-critical tendencies, in this book the majority of contributors start from the implicit working hypothesis that the Fourth Gospel is the result of the work of one
author.

Positions in Defense of the Author

One group of interpretations agrees that John depicts the relationship between Jesus and "the Jews" in a negative way but limits, relativizes, and even denies the anti-Judaism implied in it. An important aspect of the alleged anti-Judaism of John's Gospel is its frequent negative use of the term *the Jews*. Many authors are concerned with whom John has in mind when using this expression. They use historical, geographic, sociological, and/or theological criteria to limit the referent of "the Jews." In this way, they can argue that John is not anti-Jewish, since he does not intend to refer to all the Jewish social groups but only to the Jewish authorities (sociological); not to the Jews of all times but to first-century Jews (historical); not to all places but to Galilee and/or Judea (geographic); not to all Jews of all faith convictions but only to those who do not believe in Jesus (theological).[14]

Others are convinced that the conflict between Jesus and "the Jews" is part of an inner-Jewish, thus not anti-Jewish, conflict. This view is represented in this book by J. D. G. Dunn when he says: "This [portrayal of Jesus] is indeed 'anti-Jewishness' of a sort. But it is not 'anti-Judaism' as we understand it today. It does not presuppose two monoliths, Judaism and Christianity, clearly distinct and clearly separate in identity, denouncing each other in anathemas and open hostility."[15] In this way, Dunn does not deny the problem, but he warns us against an anachronistic understanding of the meaning of "anti-Judaism" in this context. Still others compare the Johannine polemics against "the Jews" with other Jewish (biblical and non-biblical) texts using the same literary strategy. We thus must learn to read the conflict in the Gospel of John in view of the literary conventions of the evangelist's time and religious tradition.

Critical questions can be raised with regard to these attempts to limit the anti-Jewishness of John. In this book, the strategy to limit the referent of "the Jews" (in a geographic, sociohistorical, and/or theological sense) is placed under severe criticism by R. A. Culpepper when he says: "Even if 'Ιουδαîοι once denoted Judaeans or Jewish authorities, the Gospel of John generalized and stereotyped those who rejected Jesus by its use of this term."[16] Along the same lines, A. Reinhartz argues: "The fact that the same word [*the Jews*] occurs numerous times and in a variety of contexts tends . . . to blur the fine distinctions and nuances implied by these contexts and to generalize the meaning to its broadest possible referent, that is, the Jews as

14. See the section below, "Who Are 'the Jews' in John?"
15. See chapter 2 by Dunn, p. 41.
16. See chapter 3 by Culpepper, p. 61.

a nation defined by a set of religious beliefs, cultic and liturgical practices, and a sense of peoplehood."[17]

The interpretation of the conflict between Jesus and "the Jews" as inner-Jewish has not been above criticism either. It is attacked for starting from the presupposition that the conflict cannot be anti-Jewish if it is inner-Jewish. One can call into question the very presupposition that John is describing an inner-Jewish conflict. Is the Gospel of John not a witness to the already irreversible separation between those who believed in Jesus and those who did not? And is the breach between those who did and those who did not believe in Jesus not deeper and more radical than the breach between any other conflicting parties in Jewish literature? If the latter question is to be answered in the affirmative,[18] then it becomes virtually impossible to uphold the thesis that the literary character of the polemic solves the problem of its anti-Jewishness.

No matter how successful they were, the above-mentioned attempts to limit the anti-Judaism expressed by the Fourth Evangelist could achieve only a reduction of the degree of the anti-Judaism, not its complete removal. Consequently, the residue of Johannine anti-Judaism is situated in its historical context. The intention is to make the position of the Evangelist understandable if not excusable. This context is the assumed fierce conflict between the Johannine community and the rabbinic Jewish synagogue in which the Christians were the victims and the Jews the perpetrators.

This line of reasoning presupposes the historical accuracy of the claim of John 9:22, namely, that "the Jews had already agreed that anyone who confessed Jesus to be the Messiah would be put out of the synagogue." Scholars assumed that Jews excommunicated Christians against their will from the synagogues. They tried to make this plausible for the Fourth Gospel by connecting the ἀποσυνάγωγος texts (9:22; 12:42; and 16:2) with the *birkat ha-minim*.[19] M. de Boer states, with unmistakable clarity, that the initiative for the exclusion came from "the Jews": "John's view is that 'the Jews' have forced a choice where none needed to be made. In light of that imposed choice, John has also been forced to agree that discipleship to Jesus is indeed incompatible with discipleship to Moses when, and only when, the latter adopts as a basic premise the rejection of Jesus as the Messiah."[20] De Boer thus claims that Jews considered the Christian faith

17. See chapter 10 by Reinhartz, p. 213.

18. The section below, "The Parting of the Ways," pp. 20–25.

19. In the form defended by J. L. Martyn, *History and Theology in the Fourth Gospel* (New York, 1968; 2d ed., Nashville, 1979), pp. 17–41, this view became almost universally accepted.

20. See chapter 7 by de Boer, p. 141.

incompatible with theirs, while Christians saw no fundamental incompatibility and would have desired to remain an integral part of the Jewish faith. In this position, any remaining traces of anti-Judaism must be understood within this historical framework of hurt and rejection. This contextual reading not only provides the mitigating circumstances for the harsh statements of the Fourth Evangelist; it is at the same time a stern warning not to export them to other situations where Christianity has become the majority and Judaism the minority. Within the narrow historical confines of the unilateral excommunication of Christianity by Judaism and the resulting "parting of the ways," the remaining Johannine anti-Judaism is therefore seen by some scholars as understandable, perhaps even ethically or theologically acceptable.

On the basis of recent research, however, the expulsion theory has come under criticism. A new scholarly consensus has emerged that accepts that the ἀποσυνάγωγος texts in John cannot be seen as evidence of "the parting of the ways" of Judaism and Christianity into separate religions.[21] For many, the ἀποσυνάγωγος texts refer only to a local conflict between the Johannine community and their Jewish neighbors. The conflict, while still being a conflict, is now seen on a much more local scale but can still function as a way to understand John's harshness against the Jews. A side effect of this position is that no longer is the entire Jewish religion seen as excommunicating all of Christianity by a formal decree. Thus, Judaism cannot be blamed exclusively for the rupture between Judaism and Christianity.

So far, the positions presented have in common that the exclusion from the synagogue, expressed in the ἀποσυνάγωγος texts, correctly reflects a historical reality, be it on a global or a local scale. Some raise the question, however, of whether the Fourth Gospel can truly be read as a historical witness to the expulsion of the Christian Johannine community by the synagogue.[22] A. Reinhartz points to John 11:1–44, which, in a two-level drama perspective, calls into question the expulsion theory: "John 11:1–44 . . .

21. R. Kimelman, "*Birkat Ha-Minim* and the Lack of Evidence for an Anti-Christian Jewish Prayer in Late Antiquity," in E. P. Sanders, ed., *Jewish and Christian Self-Definition* (Philadelphia, 1981), vol. 2, pp. 226–44, 391–403. Cf. also E. W. Stegemann and W. Stegemann, *Urchristliche Sozialgeschichte. Die Anfänge im Judentum und die Christusgemeinden in der mediterranen Welt* (Stuttgart-Berlin-Cologne, 1995), pp. 209–10; K. Berger, *Im Anfang war Johannes. Datierung und Theologie des vierten Evangeliums* (Stuttgart, 1997), p. 83: "Die Auseinandersetzung mit den nicht-christlichen Juden im JohEv . . . hat auch mit dem Achtzehnergebet rein gar nichts zu tun."

22. See chapter 10 by Reinhartz, p. 222: "There are sound reasons . . . to question the historicity of the notion that Johannine Christians were expelled from the synagogue"; and p. 223: "What complicates this picture and, in my view, undermines the expulsion theory itself is the presence of two passages [John 11:1–44; 12:11] that, when read on two levels according to this principle, imply a rather different relationship between the Jews and the Johannine Christians than that indicated in the expulsion theory."

describes the sisters Mary and Martha in mourning for their brother Lazarus. In a two-level reading of the Gospel, these sisters would represent Johannine Christians. Though apparently known to be 'beloved' of Jesus, these women have clearly not been excluded from the Jewish community, as evidenced by the fact that they are comforted in their mourning for Lazarus by 'many of the Jews' (11:19)."[23] Reinhartz uses this evidence to argue that the relationship between Johannine Christians and the Jewish synagogue was not exclusively characterized by expulsion but also included the possibility of ongoing community between them. In this view, attempts to excuse John on the basis of the presumed historical context lose almost all ground. This position stops short of defending that John's claims of expulsion from the synagogue are of his own making, for example, in order to hide the fact that it was not Jews who excluded Christians but rather Christians who withdrew from the Jewish community.[24] We pursue this question in the section "The Parting of the Ways," below, but it is already evident that it is no longer possible to use a clear-cut Jewish-Christian conflict as a foil to explain and defuse John's anti-Judaism.

To the degree, however, that John wrote within the context of a conflict, we would caution against excusing John's anti-Judaism on that ground too easily. Even within a conflict, the conflicting parties are bound to basic ethical principles. By excusing John on historical grounds, most of the exegetes seem to presuppose implicitly that such an "ethic for enemies"[25] does not exist.[26] Even in the most heated conflict, however, people are responsible for their actions and for the language they use, as well as for the implications their words and deeds may have for further generations. Even if the historical circumstances may make John's anti-Judaism understandable, they cannot make it acceptable from a moral point of view.

All the positions we have reviewed so far in this subsection try to excuse the Fourth Evangelist in one way or another, despite their acceptance of a certain measure of anti-Judaism at the level of the author. They try to pro-

23. See chapter 10 by Reinhartz.

24. A. Reinhartz, "John 8:31–59 from a Jewish Perspective," in J. Roth and E. Maxwell-Meynard, ed., *Remembering for the Future: The Holocaust in an Age of Genocide* (Hampshire, 2001), vol. 2, pp. 787–97.

25. D. W. Shriver, *An Ethic for Enemies: Forgiveness in Politics* (New York, 1997).

26. J. M. Lieu formulates a strong criticism against this presupposition, asking "whether the sociohistorical context is both a necessary and a sufficient explanation of the attitude to the Jews: given that context, was it inevitable that that response would ensue?" (See chapter 5, p. 109.) This critique implies that any sociohistorical explanation of why things happened the way they did, fails morally or theologically to legitimate this state of affairs. Lieu rightly insist on the fact that "if . . . the putative sociohistorical context is only one potential factor alongside others, further explanation or theological response is still demanded" (p. 110).

tect the author from ethical blame. A. Reinhartz saw this clearly: "New Testament scholars' efforts to limit the meaning of Ἰουδαῖος and to explain John's comments on Jews and Judaism as a response to Jewish exclusion are not primarily dispassionate academic interpretations but rather attempts to defuse the Gospel's anti-Judaism and make its expressions more acceptable to a post-Holocaust audience without undermining its status as an authoritative and sacred text."[27] It is true that John's anti-Judaism inevitably raises the question of the status of the biblical text. No matter how sophisticated the historical and exegetical nuances may be, they cannot escape this fact. Our reflection in the section "The Need for Hermeneutics," below, faces this issue.

Positions Accusing the Author

The second group of interpretations maintains that, despite all necessary nuances and distinctions, the author of the Fourth Gospel cannot be completely freed from responsibility. Even the most hesitant positions admit that the ambiguity in John's text leaves an opening for anti-Judaism. R. A. Culpepper sees the key of John's dangerous potential for anti-Judaism in the "transfer of hostility," in John's "connection between 'the Jews' who condemned Jesus and Jews known to the Christian community at a later time."[28]

There are also authors who admit that the Fourth Evangelist is responsible for anti-Judaism but condemn any anti-Judaism as a perversion of the overall message of the scriptures. This strategy establishes the core message of scripture as a measuring post against which the anti-Jewish texts can be gauged. For R. Burggraeve, this measuring post is "the Biblical wisdom of love." Whatever in the scriptures is in contradiction to love, including John 8:44, cannot claim any authority and needs to be rejected. Others refer us to Jesus' radical love, even of enemies, as the ultimate criterion that passes judgment on any anti-Jewish tendencies. In a 1996 publication, Culpepper reminds us of "the Fourth Gospel's declaration of God's boundless love for the world," which in his eyes "undermines its polemic against the

27. See chapter 10 by Reinhartz, p. 213.

28. See chapter 3 by Culpepper, pp. 61–66. The "transfer of hostility" presupposes the two-level drama technique. The question, however, is whether the two-level drama technique is itself (ethically and theologically) neutral or even acceptable. John's narrative identification of the opponents of his own time with the opponents of the earthly Jesus may be understandable from a sociohistorical point of view. Yet such identification initiates a potentially dangerous process of stereotyping and generalization because it does not take into consideration the historical particularity of the people involved and of the circumstances that caused the respective conflicts.

Jews."[29] The strategies we just surveyed admit that there is a problem, but they make an attempt to save the core message of the biblical text against the aberrations of individual authors or texts. In so doing, they admit that individual authors or texts may be contaminated by errancy or even sin, whereas the core of the biblical message is considered infallible.

The Dangers of Accusing the Author

As we just illustrated, in current exegesis those who hold the author of the Fourth Gospel responsible for Johannine anti-Judaism reject anti-Judaism and therefore put the Evangelist under criticism. History has demonstrated that recognizing anti-Judaism in the Gospel of John can also lead to unexpected consequences. Anti-Jewish and anti-Semitic movements within and outside Christianity have used the presence of anti-Judaism in John to give credence and authority to their pernicious claims. Both the Nazis and neo-Nazis made and make ample use of John 8:44 to discredit Jewish people. In 1945, the Nazi Julius Streicher, who had been the editor of the Nazi newspaper *Der Stürmer*, said at the Nuremberg trials in his defense: "Only the Jews had remained victorious after the dreadful days of World War I. These were the people of whom Christ said: 'Its father is the devil' [referring to John 8:44]."[30] To this day, neo-Nazis are using the same verse in support of their defamation of the Jewish people. Neo-Nazis quote this verse on the Internet in their lists of "what world famous men said about the Jews."[31] The honest attempt of critical scholarship to face up to the sinfulness present in biblical texts, in order to correct them, is here perverted and misused as an argument in support of vile and repugnant ideologies. Perhaps this is one of the implicit yet subconscious concerns underlying the immense efforts of many scholars to avoid at all cost the admission that the author or the text of the Fourth Gospel is contaminated by anti-Judaism. They are afraid that the results of their exegetical work might play into the hands of anti-Semites, who do not shy away from using the authority of revealed texts to defend their views.[32] This raises the question of the status

29. R. A. Culpepper, "The Gospel of John as a Document of Faith in a Pluralistic Culture," in F. F. Segovia, ed., *"What Is John?" Readers and Readings of the Fourth Gospel* (SBL Symposium Series 3; Atlanta, 1996), pp. 107–27, esp. p. 127.

30. *Trial of the Major War Criminals before the International Military Tribunal* (Nuremberg, 1945), vol. 12; and L. L. Snyder, *Hitler's Elite: Shocking Profiles of the Reich's Most Notorious Henchmen* (Berkeley, 1990).

31. http://www.stormfront.org/, 1 September 2000.

32. Cf. chapter 3 by Culpepper, p. 63: "Christian interpreters have been reluctant to recognize the anti-Jewish polemic of the Gospel of John. By denying that John condemned Jews or Judaism, Christian interpreters sought to remove one of the foundations of anti-Jewish rhetoric."

and authority of the biblical text and necessitates fundamental reflection on the theology of revelation. If divine authority is no longer attributed automatically to isolated texts or verses, it becomes impossible to misuse them to legitimate immoral goals; nor is it necessary any longer to defend their moral integrity at all cost.

In the course of this first section, we have shown the many ways in which critical studies have contextualized, nuanced, and frequently relativized Johannine anti-Judaism. Our analysis made clear, however, that it is not easy to ban anti-Judaism from the Evangelist's repertoire. While it is necessary to read the Gospel in its contemporary context, and while we should not confess any sins John never committed, the vindication of the Evangelist from all responsibility for anti-Judaism has proved difficult. The exact nature of this responsibility necessitates further investigation. The next sections explore questions such as: What do we mean by "the author of the Fourth Gospel," by "the Jews," and by "anti-"?

Who Are "the Jews" in John?

One characteristic feature of the Gospel of John that is central to the discussion of its alleged anti-Judaism is the frequent negative use of the expression "the Jews." The meaning associated with this expression has important implications for the question of the Evangelist's responsibility for anti-Judaism in the Gospel. The broader the meaning of "the Jews," the greater the responsibility of John for anti-Judaism. If, however, the meaning is narrower, John's responsibility diminishes. The Fourth Evangelist uses this expression roughly seventy times[33] (about half of these in a negative way), sometimes in places where Synoptic parallels use more precise language. In Mark 11:27–28, "the chief priests, the scribes, and the elders" (Luke 20:1–2; cf. Matt. 21:23: "the chief priests and the elders of the people") question Jesus' authority, whereas the Johannine parallel speaks of "the Jews" (see also Mark 15:1par. and John 18:28). The Johannine use of "the Jews" has baffled many of the recent readers of the Fourth Gospel and has stirred a vast amount of scholarly discussion.[34] In this book, M. de Boer put words to the question with which we are all confronted: "Why does John refer to

33. Cf. Matthew (five times), Mark (six times), and Luke (five times).
34. See U. C. von Wahlde, "The Johannine 'Jews': A Critical Survey," *NTS* 28 (1982): 33–60; and U. C. von Wahlde, "'The Jews' in the Gospel of John: Fifteen Years of Research (1983–1998)," *ETL* 76 (2000): 30–55.

those who are hostile to Jesus and his disciples as 'the Jews,' with the potentially misleading implication that Jesus himself and his (initial) disciples, as well as the Gospel's writer(s) and original, intended readers, were not themselves Jews?"[35] While the Fourth Gospel is the most Judeocentric of the Gospels and almost everyone we meet there is an ethnic Jew, there is a group among these Jews to whom the Evangelist refers as "the Jews." Scholars who are aware of this problem are spontaneously inclined to search for the historical referents of this expression. It is, however, not enough to identify the real people in history to whom the Evangelist is referring. Next to the reference of the expression "the Jews," we also need to investigate its sense, that is, the role the author assigns to the expression within the narrative itself.[36] The distinction between sense and referent is important because even a very limited referent can have a far-reaching sense in the narrative world of a text.

The Referent of "the Jews"

As we have seen above, scholars have tried to limit the group of people to whom the Fourth Evangelist might be referring when talking about "the Jews." We arrange the positions from those claiming the narrowest to those claiming the broadest referents.

In this volume, H. J. de Jonge defends the narrowest referent of the expression "the Jews," relying on the research results of B. W. J. de Ruyter.[37] He starts from the observation that in John 8:31ff., Jesus is speaking to "Jews who had believed in him" (πρός τούς πεπιστευκότας αὐτῷ Ἰουδαίους). De Jonge and de Ruyter assume that, on the level of the Johannine community, the people referred to are Christians who are not of Johannine persuasion and whose convictions are rejected by the Evangelist. In other words, the Gospel of John reflects an inner-Christian conflict. "The Evangelist uses the category of 'the Jews' as a watershed term to characterize fellow Christians who are anti-Johannine."[38] De Jonge sees this hypothesis confirmed in his assumption that the Evangelist does not know the historical Jews of his

---

35. See chapter 7 by de Boer, p. 149.

36. See chapter 3 by Culpepper, pp. 65–66: "Ashton perceptively lodges the complaint that neither Lowe nor von Wahlde distinguished between 'referent' and 'sense.' The 'referent' of Ἰουδαῖοι would be 'native or inhabitants of Judaea.' By 'sense' Ashton means the role the Ἰουδαῖοι play in the Gospel narrative. The distinction is essential. In the Gospel, historical persons become characters in a narrative in which the characters take on varying degrees of symbolic significance and characterize different responses to Jesus."

37. See chapter 6 by de Jonge, p. 121; B. W. J. De Ruyter, *De gemeente van de evangelist Johannes: Haar polemiek en haar geschiedenis* (Delft, 1998).

38. See chapter 6 by de Jonge, p. 134.

day.[39] The Evangelist is seen as having only vague ideas about Judaism. He uses the term *the Jews* to characterize a group of Christians whom he perceives as under strong influence of Judaism. This position is the only one in the scholarly discussion in this book that denies the referents of "the Jews" are truly Jews (in a religious sense). The consequences of this position are clear: if the Johannine Jesus is attacking Christians, there is no problem of anti-Judaism.

Among those who accept that "the Jews" refers to Jews who do not believe in Jesus as Christ and Son of God, the majority want to limit this referent further to include only the religious authorities in Jerusalem. U. C. von Wahlde defended this view with much conviction: "the term οἱ Ἰουδαῖοι (which could mean in Greek what English refers to as 'Jews' and also 'Judeans') refers to 'those in Judea', i.e., the religious authorities in Jerusalem with whom the Johannine community saw itself in conflict and who were ultimately responsible for the exclusion of the Johannine community from the synagogue."[40] While hardly anyone would deny that in certain passages the expression "the Jews," used with negative connotations, refers to the religious authorities in Jerusalem, it has proved virtually impossible to include all of them in this group (especially John 6:41 and 6:52).[41] Moreover, it seems that von Wahlde's distinction between the leaders and the people, which serves to excuse the (Jewish) people and to put all the blame with their leaders, overlooks the fact of "corporate personality"[42] at that time, which makes it impossible to separate too easily the leaders from the people. The obvious concern of scholars in limiting the referent of "the Jews" in this way is to point out its historical limits and to clear the Jewish people of any blame. The aim behind this is to make the "transfer of hostility" impossible. But does this strategy succeed?

The alternative is to accept that the expression "the Jews" does have in mind the broader group of all the Jewish neighbors of the Johannine community who did not become disciples of Christ. S. Motyer characterizes them in an even more specific way: "'the Jews' do indeed have a natural referent, namely, the scrupulous adherents of the religion of Judaea, those especially associated with the life of the Temple before 70 C.E., who were most particular about Temple purity and all that went with it, and who,

---

39. See chapter 6 by de Jonge, p. 123: "the Evangelist's depiction of the Jews in his story is so incongruent with actual traditional Jews that it is obvious they are actually strangers to him."

40. According to de Boer (p. 148), John uses "the Jews" "to designate certain authoritative, learned (Pharisaic) Jews who . . . rejected and opposed Jesus and his followers." John supposedly calls them "Jews" because they "claim to be the arbiters of a genuinely Jewish identity" (p. 155).

41. See von Wahlde, "The Johannine 'Jews,'" esp. pp. 49–54, who has to resort to a literary-critical solution in order to prove his point.

42. Cf. J. W. Rogerson, "The Hebrew Conception of Corporate Personality: A Re-examination," *JTS* 71 (1970): 1–16.

after the appalling loss of the Temple, by which they were especially affected, became leading lights of the movement that reemphasized a scrupulous Torah-centred lifestyle as the essential response to the disaster."[43] Even this position succeeds in diverting the blame for Judaism in general to a specific historical group. The way in which Motyer characterizes this group is historically uncertain, however, as more and more voices go up that call into question the traditional reconstructions of post-70 C.E. Judaism, which themselves have been suspected of being driven by implicit anti-Judaism.

Others have tried to limit the referent of "the Jews" not in time but in space. This geographic solution holds that the term οἱ Ἰουδαῖοι is exclusively used for Judaeans, that is, residents of Judaea.[44] If this could be shown to be correct, it would also make the "transfer of hostility" more difficult. The unfortunate thing for this hypothesis is, however, that there are instances where Galileans, most prominently Jesus himself, are called "Jews" (4:9, 22b; 18:35).[45]

Finally, some scholars explicitly oppose narrow and limited definitions of "the Jews." By using the general term *the Jews* instead of *chief priests, Pharisees,* or *scribes,* John uses an expression that has a variety of potential referents irrespective of time and space. As such, the expression is very convenient for the two-level drama technique. By using "the Jews," the Evangelist can refer to people at the time of the earthly Jesus, of the Johannine community, and of later generations. R. A. Culpepper is correct when he points out that the Gospel draws "a connection between 'the Jews' who condemned Jesus and Jews known to the Christian community at a later time. By means of this transfer of hostility, effected by the two levels of meaning Martyn found in the Gospel, the Gospel creates a dangerous potential for anti-Semitism."[46] By using the expression "the Jews" where the Synoptics mentioned the Jewish religious leaders, John suggests that those who do not believe in Jesus at the time of the Johannine community are the spiritual heirs of the people who entered into conflict with the

43. See chapter 4 by Motyer, p. 96.
44. See M. Lowe, "Who Were the Ἰουδαῖοι?," *NovT* 18 (1976): 101–30; von Wahlde, "The Johannine 'Jews'"; J. Ashton, "The Identity and Function of the Ἰουδαῖοι in the Fourth Gospel," *NovT* 27 (1985): 40–75.
45. See also A. Reinhartz's opposition to this position: "the term Ἰουδαῖοι does not refer narrowly to a resident of Judaea but rather denotes a member of a national, religious, cultural, and political group for whom the English word *Jew* is the best signifier. Hence the simple technique of using 'Judaean' or 'Jewish leader' as a translation of Ἰουδαῖοι does not work except (perhaps) for a small number of specific verses and should not be used to explain, or to explain away, the Gospel's hostile remarks about Ἰουδαῖοι" (see chapter 10 by Reinhartz, p. 218).
46. See chapter 3 by Culpepper, p. 66.

earthly Jesus and ultimately were responsible for his death on the cross. By implication, all future "unbelievers" are seen in the same light.[47]

The Sense of "the Jews"

Exegetes are rightly insisting that the meaning of the expression "the Jews" is not exhausted in determining its referent, that is, the extralinguistic entity to which it points. While discussing the meaning of the expression "the Jews," we may not forget its sense. Linguists mean by the sense of a word "its place in a system of relationships which it contracts with other words in the vocabulary." Sense "is to be defined in terms of relationships which hold between vocabulary-items." Therefore "it carries with it no presuppositions about the existence of objects and properties outside the vocabulary of the language in question."[48] The linguistic term *sense* was applied to the issue of "the Jews" in the Fourth Gospel in order to speak about a tendency that was strongly represented in the writings of R. Bultmann.[49] However, there are other ways to understand "the Jews" in the Fourth Gospel.

Focusing our attention on the sense in addition to the referent sharpens our awareness that the problem of the meaning of "the Jews" cannot be solved by limiting the concrete people to whom the expression refers (e.g., the Jerusalem authorities). In the Fourth Gospel, "the Jews" are characters within a narrative world and play a central role in its plot. For Reinhartz, Jesus and the Jews represent "two opposing poles of his [John's] Christology, his soteriology, and his narrative."[50] Even if "the Jews" has a very limited referent, its literary role in the narrative can be immense.

The Relationship between Referent and Sense

The assumption that the expression "the Jews" functioned in the Fourth Gospel as a symbol for the unbelieving world can also be used, implicitly

---

47. See chapter 10 by Reinhartz, p. 225: "While he was not specifically anticipating the impact that his writings might have on Jewish-Christian relations throughout the millennia, the universal tone of many of the discourses suggests the Evangelist did not exclude from his negative assessment those Jews in the future who would also reject the word of Jesus as conveyed in his Gospel, who would refuse to believe that Jesus is the Christ, Son of God, and, therefore, who would not attain life in his name"; and p. 217: "While the Gospel narrative is not historiography in our modern sense of the term, the Gospel makes historical claims (e.g., 'His testimony is true'; 19:35; 21:24). The fact that theological claims are not abstracted from the ostensible historical situation therefore raises the possibility that the negative comments about Jews reflect not only a symbolic use of 'the Jews' but also a negative assessment about the nonbelieving Jews as a historical group in the first century."

48. John Lyons, *Introduction to Theoretical Linguistics* (Cambridge, 1968; reprint, 1991), p. 427.

49. See Ashton, "Identity and Function," p. 59: "In a work of literature, especially one with as urgent a rhetoric as that of the Fourth Gospel, the important question concerns the role or function of the various characters: this is what I have called *sense*."

50. See chapter 10 by Reinhartz, p. 214.

or explicitly, to neutralize its anti-Jewish potential. If the Evangelist does not refer to concrete Jews, some argue, then what he says about them can hardly be used against concrete Jews. Too exclusive a focus on the sense, however, also runs the risk of making the expression "the Jews" a purely literary category and of obscuring the fact that there remains a connection with real people. In the words of Reinhartz: "the Fourth Gospel does not merely speak about 'the Jews' as a symbol for the unbelieving world but also sees the historical community of Jewish nonbelievers as children of the devil and sinners destined for death."[51] Moreover, using the expression "the Jews" to illustrate the disobedience and unbelief of the world does not dissolve the accusations leveled against concrete Jews but stigmatizes them as unbelievers par excellence. In this way, it contributes to the creation of stereotypes and prejudice against Jews of any place or time.

The Parting of the Ways

The New Testament, and the Fourth Gospel in particular, contains much evidence of a conflict between Jesus and certain groups among his own Jewish people, as well as between the later disciples of Jesus and those among the Jewish people who decided not to follow him. The assumption of such a conflict plays a central role in recent research on the allegedly anti-Jewish aspects of the Gospel of John. Historical-critical research has focused on the evidence in the Fourth Gospel and in contemporary extrabiblical literature that can help us in the effort of reconstructing the precise historical situation of the Evangelist's presentation of "the Jews." By pointing to the specific and unique situation of origin, historical critics contribute their part to the ongoing attempt of discouraging an anti-Jewish reading of the respective Gospel texts. They implicitly suggest that the harsh words against "the Jews" were situation bound and legitimate only, if at all, in their original context. They may not simply be universalized.

The consensus among recent scholarship goes only as far as agreeing that the Fourth Evangelist presents a conflict to have been at the origin of the allegedly anti-Jewish passages of John. Views differ, however, as to (1) the reality statute, (2) the parties, and (3) the nature of the conflict.

A Historical Conflict

Traces of a conflict are found in the numerous attempts of "the Jews" to kill Jesus, in the ἀποσυνάγωγος texts (9:22; 12:42; and 16:2), and in

51. Ibid., p. 225.

the texts that speak of the fear disciples of Jesus have of "the Jews" (19:38; 20:19, cf. 7:13; 9:22). Do we have sufficient evidence to assume a historical conflict to have been at the origin of these statements? The assumption of a conflict between Jesus and the Jewish religious leaders of his time is generally accepted among New Testament scholars. But can we safely assume that there was a conflict between some later disciples of Jesus, at the time of the Evangelist, and those who did not follow Jesus?

In this book, H. J. de Jonge rejects the idea that the conflict in the narrative world of the Fourth Gospel reflects a historical conflict in the real world of the Johannine community. He rather concludes that the conflict (which in de Jonge's perspective resulted in an excommunication of Christians from the synagogue) "is sufficiently and satisfactorily explained as a literary invention of the Evangelist, which he created in order to explicate why those who had actually come to believe in Jesus on account of his works did not openly profess their faith."[52] All the other contributors to this volume assume that the conflict of the Johannine narrative is a more or less accurate representation of a real historical conflict. It is usually assumed that a fierce conflict that led to a separation of disciples of Jesus from the Jewish synagogue preceded the composition of the Gospel. Views differ somewhat as to whether the conflict was past reality at the time when the Evangelist composed the Gospel, or whether the conflict was an ongoing reality even at the time of the Gospel's composition. Today, more and more scholars agree that the breach that was the result of the conflict was of a local nature and did not, at the time, mean the (beginning of the) "parting of the ways" of Judaism and Christianity as separate religions, which happened only much later, as the result of a gradual and very complex process. Culpepper nevertheless sees in the conflict that we encounter in John an important stepping-stone in this direction.[53]

The Parties of the Conflict

While most scholars agree that John refers to a historical conflict, positions vary greatly as to how this conflict is to be understood and the kinds of implications this has for the alleged anti-Judaism of the Fourth Gospel. The assumption of a spontaneous reading that the conflict and resulting breach

---

52. See chapter 6 by de Jonge, p. 139.
53. See chapter 3 by Culpepper, p. 63. See also below, p. 23.

are between Jews and Christians[54] has been called into question from two sides. Some scholars suggest that both sides of the conflict were Christian.[55] In this book, de Jonge states his view clearly: "the Fourth Evangelist ascribes the opposition that he himself was experiencing from the non-Johannine Christians to 'the Jews' of Jesus' time."[56] As we have already seen, one of the central arguments for this view is 8:31, a verse that identifies Jesus' interlocutors in the following verses (up to 8:47) as people who had come to believe in Jesus (πρός τούς πεπιστευκότας αὐτῷ ᾿Ιουδαίους). It is, however, by no means clear what the perfect participle of πιστεύω with the dative in 8:31 means, and whether the author has Christians in mind. Does the perfect have the meaning of a pluperfect and thus refer to people who had once believed in Jesus? Or does the dative express "limited belief"?[57] Or do the people referred to in 8:31 belong to a different group from the ones who want to stone Jesus in 8:59?

A second position sees the conflict, reflected in the Fourth Gospel, as inner-Jewish. This thesis is based on a trend in recent scholarship that warns against reading later historical developments into the text of John. From a radical historical-critical perspective, scholars insist that at the time of the composition of the Fourth Gospel, "the disciples of Moses" (cf. 9:28) and "the disciples of Jesus" did not yet form two separate religions. They point out that disciples of Jesus were still perceived, and probably even perceived themselves, as part of the Jewish religion, and therefore consider it to be anachronistic to speak about "Christians" at such an early period. Consequently, the conflict reflected in the Fourth Gospel is seen as an inner-Jewish conflict. In this book, J. D. G. Dunn expresses this view when he says: "John's language is more the language of *intra*-Jewish polemic than of *anti*-Jewish polemic. He seeks by it to warn *fellow Jews* not to follow what was emerging as the dominant view of 'the Jews.'"[58] M. de Boer further addresses the most difficult problems of the hypothesis of the inner-Jewish

54. The use of the term *Christian* in this context is problematic because Christianity proper did not yet exist at the time. Nevertheless, the term is used in the literature referring to those who had come to authentic faith in Jesus and were practicing this faith in their lives.

55. C. H. Dodd, "A l'arrière-plan d'un dialogue johannique (Jo 8,33–58)," *RHPR* 37 (1957): 5–17, esp. p. 8, who is convinced that "ces interlocuteurs représentent des Chrétiens 'judaïsants' plutôt que des Juifs en dehors de l'Église"; and p. 13: "en Jean 8 . . . nous rencontrons la controverse 'judaïque' dans l'Église primitive." (English translation: *Behind a Johannine Dialogue*, p. 42–47).

56. See chapter 6 by de Jonge, p. 122; cf. p. 125: "the nomenclature 'the Jews' sometimes represents the author's Christian opponents. These opponents did not share the writer's Christology but were nonetheless Christians. The evangelist called them 'Jews' because he took for granted that Jesus had lived and acted among Jews."

57. F. J. Moloney, *The Gospel of John* (Sacra Pagina Series 4; Collegeville, Minn., 1998), p. 277.

58. See chapter 2 by Dunn, p. 52. Cf. also de Boer, p. 156: "the peculiar Johannine use of the term *the Jews* probably emerged in a debate not *with* but *within* the synagogue."

conflict, namely, why, in an inner-Jewish conflict, one side (the Fourth Evangelist) calls the other side (the opponents of the Johannine community) "the Jews." De Boer needs to be credited with having found an intriguing and challenging answer to this virtually irresolvable question: "the Gospel's references to the Jewish scriptural authorities behind the decree of expulsion (9:22) as 'the Jews' is in the first instance *an ironic acknowledgment of their claim to be the authoritative arbiters of Jewish identity.*"[59]

The question can be raised whether de Boer's ingenious attempt to defend the hypothesis of an inner-Jewish conflict does not itself contain a strong counterargument. We suggest that what de Boer perceives as one group ironically distancing itself from another group of Jews is precisely an indication that a serious division has happened in the group. De Boer himself seems to acknowledge this when he continues, after the above quotation: "Being a disciple of Jesus was evidently no longer one of the ways in which a Jew could be a disciple of Moses."[60] The Gospel of John contains enough evidence that the Christology of the disciples of Jesus was an unparalleled challenge to unity within Judaism. Even the much earlier evidence from the Pauline letters contains proof of a fundamental incompatibility with "mainstream" Judaism of certain aspects of the christological confession. The fact that equally harsh polemic can be found in inner-Jewish controversies can help relativize the shock value of some Johannine texts, but it runs the risk of diverting attention from the actual problem.[61]

This brings us back to how commonsense reading interprets the conflict, namely, as a Christian-Jewish controversy. The position is stated clearly by R. A. Culpepper: "John marks the decisive separation of Christians from Jews, at least in one locality. It hardens the breach that has already occurred, and it probably contributed to the ultimate separation between Judaism and Christianity. Because John views the separation from Judaism as a past event with radical social and theological consequences, its position in relation to Judaism can no longer be regarded as an intra-Jewish debate."[62] According to P. Tomson, this is already reflected in the choice of words, that is, in the fact that the Fourth Evangelist most frequently uses the word *the Jews* but comparatively rarely *Israel.* For Tomson, "the Jews" is

---

59. See chapter 7 by de Boer, p. 142; emphasis ours.
60. Ibid., p. 155.
61. Cf. chapter 3 by Culpepper, p. 63: "differences between John and the hostile language of the scrolls should not be overlooked. Qumran carried on a debate with other Jewish groups while remaining within Judaism, whereas John stands early in the history of Christians who separated from Judaism. Nowhere in the scrolls do we find the authors writing about 'the Jews' as a people apart from themselves or referring to the Torah as 'your law' (John 8:17)."
62. See chapter 3 by Culpepper, p. 63.

an expression that non-Jews use to refer to Jews or that Jews use themselves when they speak with non-Jews. When Jews speak among themselves, they use the word *Israel*.[63] He concludes from this that the Fourth Gospel "is formulated in a non-Jewish setting, addressing non-Jews," and "portrays 'the Jews' as being hostile to Christianity."[64] Thus, the use of the expression "the Jews" in itself already characterizes the conflict as not inner-Jewish. According to other authors, the fact that in John we meet two clearly distinct groups is also reflected in the nature of the conflict, in the issues that divide the opposing parties. A. Reinhartz's description of the two camps stays more at a distance from the Johannine perspective: "Johannine Christians did not maintain their activities in or ties to the synagogue as a place of worship; Jews by definition did not believe in or follow Jesus."[65]

The Nature of the Conflict

On the basis of what we have seen so far, it is undeniable that how one sees the nature of the conflict that is reflected in the Fourth Gospel depends on how one reconstructs the conflicting parties. The defenders of an inner-Christian conflict assume that the dispute is about certain nuances of the Christian faith-conviction concerning Jesus, and ultimately about whether the Christian "Judaizers" are Christian enough. For those who claim the conflict to be inner-Jewish, the issue is rather to be seen from a Jewish perspective and comes down to whether the disciples of Jesus are still Jewish enough. If the conflict may justifiably be called Christian-Jewish, the nature of the conflict consists of the core problems that ended up dividing Jews and Christians into separate religions. Since J. L. Martyn, it had become a widespread assumption that the ἀποσυνάγωγος texts in the Fourth Gospel are evidence of the excommunication of the Johannine community by the official representatives of a monolithic Jewish religion by way of a formal decree (the twelfth benediction of the *birkat ha-minim*). As we have already seen above,[66] scholarship has become much more hesitant today to accept this hypothesis and thus to see in the Gospel of John a historical record of the beginning of Christianity and Judaism as separate and opposed religions. The critique of Martyn's position is based on the conviction that the "parting of the ways" was a much more complex and pro-

---

63. P. J. Tomson, "The Names 'Israel' and 'Jew' in Ancient Judaism and the New Testament," *Bijdr* 47 (1986): 120–40, 266–89.

64. See chapter 9 by Tomson, p. 211.

65. See chapter 10 by Reinhartz, p. 225.

66. Cf. pp. 8–15 in this chapter.

tracted process and that Martyn's reconstruction runs the risk of blaming the representatives of Judaism single-handedly for the separation. The alternative interpretation of the conflict that is gaining more and more ground today sees it as having a local nature, a first sign at the horizon of an approaching storm.[67] The assumption of a more local conflict opens the possibility of constructing the opponents as inner-Jewish, but it is still more plausible to see it as a Christian-Jewish conflict. In the Gospel of John, we happen to have a witness to a growing social and theological tension and distancing between the disciples of Jesus and those Jews who did not accept him. At the end of the first century, this conflict seems already to have reached a point of no return. In the Gospel of John, we catch glimpses of a complex process of separation at one locality at the end of the first century C.E., a process of which only later history was able to see the final result. The Fourth Evangelist created a theological interpretation and legitimation of this process, which is understandable under the circumstances but which needs to be subjected to evaluation, because it has (had) ethical implications. (Cf. an ethic for enemies.[68]) The Gospel of John leaves no doubt that the major issue of the conflict is expressed by John in christological terms. In 5:18;[69] 10:33; and 19:7, he lets "the Jews" voice their objection against Jesus, accusing him of making himself God (or Son of God). This brings us to the heart of the matter.

Supersessionist Christology in John?

As we have seen, the relationship of the Fourth Gospel with the Judaism (or Judaisms) of its time is complex and to some degree ambiguous. It seems, however, undeniable that the conflict has its roots in the core of John's message, in his Christology. It is to be expected that those who consider the Fourth Gospel to be anti-Jewish consider the Gospel to contain a supersessionist Christology, in which Jesus is seen as replacing Judaism. Those who do not accept that John is anti-Jewish also reject the idea of supersessionist Christology in this Gospel and suggest alternatives.

---

67. See chapter 3 by Culpepper, p. 63. See also above, p. 23.

68. See Shriver, *Ethic for Enemies*.

69. See H. C. Kammler, *Christologie und Eschatologie: Joh 5,17–30 als Schlüsseltext johanneischer Theologie* (WUNT 126; Tübingen, 2000); B. Lataire, "Jesus' Equality with God: A Critical Reflection on John 5,18," in T. Merrigan and J. Haers, eds., *The Myriad Christ: Plurality and the Quest for Unity in Contemporary Christology* (BETL 152; Louvain, 2000), pp. 177–90.

Johannine Christology Is Not Supersessionist

Some contributors to this book are convinced that Johannine Christology is not supersessionist and offer the "restoration of Israel" or "fulfillment" as alternative interpretive categories. These authors stress various degrees of continuity between Christianity and Judaism with regard to the person of Christ.

S. Motyer points to the post-70 situation and the Jewish discussion whether it was necessary to rebuild the Temple. He sees in this discussion the historical background for the so-called replacement motif in John. According to him, the Fourth Gospel in this regard "stands alongside R. Johanan ben Zakkai, who maintained, according to the famous exchange with R. Joshua, that it was not necessary to rebuild the Temple because 'we have another atonement as effective as this.' But whereas for R. Johanan ben Zakkai the alternative atonement was 'deeds of loving-kindness,' for the Fourth Gospel it is the death of Christ, whose body constitutes the locus of the glory of God (1:14), which is then destroyed and raised again, to become the place in which the people of God are reunited in worship and love."[70] Thus, according to Motyer, Johannine Christology must be understood in the context of the rabbinic discussion over *how* the Temple needs to be restored. So Jesus is not seen as a replacement of the Jewish Temple but as the "real meaning of the Temple and the cult—the one who fulfills and brings to reality their inner essence."[71]

In reading these attempts to defend John against the reproach of supersessionist Christology, different questions seem unavoidable. The first question is whether these positions are not based on a one-sided selection of texts in John. Authors who stress the importance of John 4:22, for example, frequently leave out of consideration John 8:44. Second, there is a need to determine further the relationship between "fulfillment" and "replacement." While we accept that fulfillment is not necessarily identical with replacement, history has proved dramatically that fulfillment all too easily turns into replacement. The question is whether this shift from fulfillment to replacement was caused only by the sinfulness of the actors of history or whether the concept of fulfillment already carries in itself a dangerous potential. It remains a challenge how fulfillment can be construed without implying the exclusion of those who refuse to accept this fulfillment. The type of fulfillment that some parts of Christian tradition have developed for centuries is not possible without replacement.

70. See chapter 4 by Motyer, p. 92.
71. Ibid., p. 91.

Johannine Christology Is Supersessionist

R. A. Culpepper is one of the authors in this book who explicitly admit that there are supersessionist dimensions to John's Christology. According to him, the problem of Johannine supersessionism is not solved but caused by the claim that Jesus fulfilled Judaism: "On the one hand, the Johannine retention of so many meaningful Jewish features is the highest compliment that the daughter faith could pay to the parent faith. On the other hand, apart from all that is fulfilled in Jesus, very little is left in Judaism. The Gospel of John, therefore, does not dispassionately set forth the truth of the Christian faith. It claims the fulfillment of Judaism, and in the process, it strips Judaism of the validity of its faith and practice."[72] Jews must experience the way in which John speaks about Jesus as the fulfillment of their religious aspirations as making Judaism deficient and inferior. As J. Lambrecht acknowledges in his study of anti-Judaism in the book of Revelation, "The fact that John so strongly denies that the Jews are genuine Jews implicitly proves that, in his opinion, the Christians are the true Jews. This seizure of the Jewish identity, its denial to the Jews and use for themselves, must have appeared to the Jews as 'anti-Judaistic' to the extreme."[73] For Culpepper, this rejection and condemnation of the Jews as a religious group is even "inherent in the Christology of John."[74] In a paradoxical way, this Christian exclusivism is, for the Evangelist, rooted in Jewish exclusivism: "For the Jews, loyalty to Yahweh made every other religion idolatrous and worthy only of reprobation. For John, this exclusivism means that apart from confessing Jesus as the Messiah there is no hope for the Jews."[75] Reinhartz refers to the same Johannine exclusivism when she states that "the christology of the Fourth Gospel does not include salvation for nonbelievers such as the Jews."[76]

Beyond Christological Supersessionism?

The preceding discussion of Johannine Christology and the issue of supersessionism raises serious questions with regard to the origin and core

72. See chapter 3 by Culpepper, p. 69.
73. See chapter 13 by Lambrecht, p. 288.
74. See chapter 3 by Culpepper, p. 72; see also p. 76: "The claim for the validity of Jesus' revelation of the Father carries with it in John a rejection of the claims of those who say they know God but do not accept Jesus. Given the Logos Christology of the Gospel, we may suspect that, for John, there neither has been nor could be any revelation of God apart from the revelatory role of the Logos."
75. Ibid., p. 73.
76. See chapter 10 by Reinhartz, p. 214.

message of Christianity. The central problem was formulated by Culpepper: "The critical theological issues, therefore, revolve around the question of whether supersessionism, with its attendant rejection of Judaism, is essential to Christianity."[77] It seems that Culpepper implicitly suggests a distinction between Johannine Christianity and Christianity in general. Concerning the Fourth Gospel itself, he seems to be in agreement with Reinhartz's charge "that anti-Jewish readings of this text are by no means distortions of the Gospel's meaning. This is not to say that the principal goal of the Gospel is to promote anti-Judaism. Rather, the Gospel's anti-Judaism is a by-product of the Evangelist's strong convictions regarding the identity and salvific role of Jesus, on the one hand, and his tendency to view not only attributes and actions but also communities in a polarized way, on the other."[78]

If one agrees with Reinhartz's assessment, the theological challenge for Christians is clear. We need to search for paths of expressing Christology that are not supersessionist and not simply exclusivist. In the words of J. Lieu: "How can the convictions of Christology, of the reality of good and evil, of divine sovereignty and guidance, be affirmed in a way that respects the 'otherness' of others? How can the church maintain its true identity when it has access to power as well as when it is oppressed?"[79] Depending on one's basic conviction about the presence of anti-Judaism in the Fourth Gospel, the task of developing a Christology and a Christian theology that is free from supersessionism either consists of ridding the Gospel of John of false interpretations[80] or calls for an alternative, hermeneutical approach to the Johannine text.

The Need for Hermeneutics

Those scholars who recognize the need for an alternative, hermeneutical approach to the problem acknowledge that classic historical-critical hermeneutics alone is not capable of solving the problem of anti-Judaism in the Fourth Gospel. In this section we first focus on attempts of historical-critical exegesis to come to terms with the problem of the alleged anti-Judaism of the Fourth Gospel. Second, we critique the theology of

---

77. See chapter 3 by Culpepper, p. 67.
78. See chapter 10 by Reinhartz, p. 225.
79. See chapter 5 by Lieu, p. 117.
80. For instance, Charlesworth points to the secondary nature of John 14:6, and Klappert interprets Johannine Christology along the lines of an eschatological approach to Synoptic Christology.

revelation underlying those hermeneutical strategies and fallacies. This leads us to a presentation of an alternative theology of revelation.

Hermeneutical Strategies

Explicitly or implicitly, all the authors who discuss the alleged anti-Judaism of the Fourth Gospel use certain reading strategies that allow them to safeguard the authority of the sacred text despite the presence of ethically problematic content. A well-known strategy that has driven much of historical-critical scholarship of the past two hundred years is to assume that only the earliest layer of the text has revelatory authority. Therefore, exegetes have made it their task to peel off the later accretions. In this book, this procedure is remarkably rarely used. It nevertheless has a strong representative in J. H. Charlesworth, who tries to prove that John 14:6b, which for him represents a major problem, is secondary, that is, un-Johannine: "We have discovered that a case—perhaps only a conceivable case—can be made for the possibility that John 14:6b is a later addition to the Gospel of John. In summation, John 14:6a has the character of tradition; that is, it may derive ultimately from Jesus—or may be a restating of his original message. In contrast, John 14:6b is redactional. It cannot be traced back to Jesus. It seems to reflect and thus derive from the problems and perspectives of the second generation of Jesus' followers."[81] A similar strategy is used by U. C. von Wahlde in his 1982 article, where he tries to prove that all the negative uses of "the Jews" in John refer to Jerusalem authorities. For the two texts (John 6:41, 52) where the expression "the Jews" refers to the common people, he takes his refuge in a source-critical solution.[82] This strategy, however, is not beyond criticism. First, exegesis is far from reaching a consensus with regard to the reconstruction of layers and sources in specific texts. Second, what are the criteria for the revelatory character of a biblical text? Can only those texts that have their demonstrable origin with Jesus or with the Evangelist claim revelatory authority? Does not Christian theology claim revelatory authority for the entire corpus of canonical writings? All these positions seem to have in common that they want to arrive at a text with which they can unconditionally agree. In the process, they remove all elements of the text

81. See chapter 12 by Charlesworth, p. 275.
82. von Wahlde, "The Johannine 'Jews,'" p. 44: "The *Ioudaioi* of 6.41, 52 are the only ones in the FG to appear outside Judea. . . . These *Ioudaioi* are also the only ones in the gospel to be identified with the common people. All of these features suggest not a distinction between signs source material and Evangelist, but between signs source material and an author whose usage was different from the Evangelist (i.e. a redactor). If this is true, the usage of *Ioudaioi* here would not be attributed to the original author—and an explanation is provided for the idiosyncratic usage in 6.41, 52."

that contain ethically or theologically problematic texts. The resulting reconstruction is considered not to be in need of further hermeneutical reflection. What is left, the core of Jesus' message, is to be taken as such. We are, however, convinced that this is a subtle form of biblical literalism. Not only the words of Jesus with which we do not agree but also those with which we do agree have to be read in hermeneutical perspective.

A different hermeneutical strategy, which is much more widespread in this book, makes use of the traditional rule of exegesis that the scriptures should be interpreted by means of the scriptures. Such a critical evaluation needs a norm, a measuring post. This hermeneutical strategy of critically evaluating certain biblical texts by means of other biblical texts is not only used in a holistic perspective, which tries to find the "inner coherence" of all the scriptures.[83] It is also applied on the level of the Fourth Gospel. Authors such as C. K. Barrett and R. A. Culpepper have tried to deconstruct the anti-Judaism of certain passages in the Fourth Gospel by pointing to the Jewishness of others.[84] In this way, 8:44 is usually deconstructed by means of 4:22. Culpepper refers to this strategy when he says: "There are elements in the Gospel that undermine or deconstruct the anti-Jewishness of its Christology. . . . The most obvious deconstructive element is Jesus' affirmation that 'salvation is from the Jews' (4:22)."[85] And a little further he states: "Providing us with at least a starting point for deconstructing its anti-Jewish *Tendenz*, therefore, the Gospel of John affirms the heritage of Israel as foundational to salvation, affirms that the Logos worked through Jews, and affirms a hope for the salvation of Jews along with all people."[86] We note, however, a tendency among authors not to subject 4:22 to an equally critical analysis as that applied to anti-Jewish texts. Could the expression "salvation is from the Jews" in 4:22 not also be intended in its context as a critique of the Jews who do not recognize the Savior, even though he comes from their own midst? Moreover, even if thorough exegetical research could demonstrate statements about the Jews to be positive (e.g., the declaration of God's boundless love for the world in John 3:16), we need to ask whether John's positive statements about the Jews undermine his anti-Judaism or

83. J. C. Beker, "The New Testament View of Judaism," in J. H. Charlesworth, ed., *Jews and Christians: Exploring the Past, Present, and Future* (Shared Ground Among Christians and Jews 1; New York, 1990), pp. 63–64.

84. Recently also in T. Söding, "'Was kann aus Nazareth schon Gutes kommen?' (Joh 1.46). Die Bedeutung des Judeseins Jesu im Johannesevangelium," *NTS* 46 (2000): 21–41; K. Scholtissek, "Antijudaismus im Johannesevangelium? Ein Gesprächsbeitrag," in R. Kampling, ed., *"Nun steht aber diese Sache im Evangelium . . ." . Zur Frage nach den Anfangen des christlichen Antijudaismus* (Paderborn, 1999), pp. 151–81.

85. See chaper 3 by Culpepper, p. 74.

86. Ibid., p. 75.

whether his anti-Judaism undermines the positive statements about the Jews.[87]

It may, therefore, be unavoidable to make use of a theological or even philosophical norm that comes from *outside* the scriptures. This issue is discussed under the name of *Sachkritik*. Henrix hesitantly asks whether such a procedure might be possible, because the theologians who might voice such a criticism are (in)formed by the text they are criticizing. The question comes down to whether the Shoah can provide that extrabiblical measuring post. Or to put the question more broadly: Does Christian-Jewish dialogue offer such an extrascriptural framework or set of rules, without which exegesis has become impossible or unacceptable today?

Two closely related and at the same time startling questions have called for our attention throughout this attempt to provide a hermeneutical framework for the study of John's alleged anti-Judaism. The first is: Can we further Christian-Jewish dialogue by denying John's anti-Judaism? P. Tomson introduces his contribution with a quote from R. E. Brown, who gives an unambiguous answer to this question: "It would be incredible for a twentieth-century Christian to share or justify the Johannine contention that 'the Jews' are the children of the devil, an affirmation which is placed on the lips of Jesus; but I cannot see how it helps contemporary Jewish-Christian relationships to disguise the fact that such an attitude once existed."[88] The second question that has arisen is situated at the other end of the spectrum but is not unrelated: Does the acknowledgment of Johannine anti-Judaism work in the hands of inner-Christian or extra-Christian anti-Semitism? This question can only be answered after reflecting on its presuppositions. If the revelatory character of the biblical text is understood as giving it undisputable, absolute authority even in cases where it clearly advocates immoral actions or attitudes, then Johannine anti-Judaism would have to be accepted as revealed and intended by God. In this way it would receive highest, unquestionable authority. Anti-Semitic people have tried to benefit, at least implicitly, from such authority, even if they did not believe in the "infrastructure" necessary to support such a claim (e.g., the existence of God). If, however, the revelatory character is not to be attributed to the biblical text in all its respects, and if the biblical text is subject

87. See chapter 10 by Reinhartz, p. 227: "In his call for an ethically responsible interpretation of John, R. A. Culpepper suggests that 'the Fourth Gospel's declaration of God's boundless love for the world undermines its polemic against the Jews.' My own, more pessimistic reading is that the Fourth Gospel's polemic against the Jews (minus the quotation marks) undermines its declaration of God's boundless love for the world."

88. R. E. Brown, *The Community of the Beloved Disciple* (London, 1979), pp. 41–42.

to critical evaluation according to ethical principles, then perpetrators of anti-Semitism will fall under the same verdict as the sinful aspects of the biblical texts. Johannine anti-Judaism would then have to be understood as revealing the sinfulness of the people responsible for the text.

Theology of Revelation

The discussion of the alleged anti-Judaism of the Fourth Gospel and the realization that it is very difficult to deny categorically all the charges has functioned as a reminder of some basic tenets of a theology of revelation that are easily overlooked in the face of inconspicuous scriptural texts. According to mainstream Jewish and Christian theology, biblical texts are God's Word expressed through human words. The human writers of the scriptures are authors in the full sense of the word, that is, they were not used by God as instruments of dictation. J. D. G. Dunn reminds us that "revelation comes through dirty hands and inadequate human language, and that the all-too-vigorous altercations of the first century were an integral part of Christianity's emerging identity and remain fundamental to its continuing self-understanding."[89]

At the end of this discussion, we have arrived at three convictions: (1) There are some dimensions in the way in which the Fourth Gospel treats Judaism and "the Jews" that we consider to be expressions of anti-Judaism (against those who propose escape routes). We find it impossible to relegate anti-Judaism to the marginal aspects of the text and to deny that, in one way or another, it reaches to the core of the Christian message. We find it hard to escape the conclusion that the anti-Judaism in the text of John is "intrinsically oppressive," that is, we are convinced that in these cases human sinfulness has in some way touched the core of biblical texts. The expression "intrinsically oppressive" is not intended to mean that the scriptures contain nothing but oppressive aspects. Rather, as we shall see, despite the all-pervasiveness of the consequences of human sin, we are convinced that the scriptures transcend their own intrinsically oppressive aspects. (2) We count the anti-Judaism that we find in the scriptures among the intrinsically oppressive dimensions and not among the revelatory dimensions, invested with divine authority. They are therefore totally unacceptable from a Christian point of view (against neo-Nazis). (3) Because of the all-pervasiveness of human sin, we do not find convincing any solutions that try to eliminate the anti-Jewish statements from scripture by ascribing

89. See chapter 2 by Dunn, p. 59.

them to later redactions (against literary-critical solutions). We reject attempts to create a canon within the canon by ascribing revelatory authority only to the words of Jesus or to the texts of the original writers (as eyewitnesses?) and none to the later redactors.

We thus affirm three convictions: (1) the Fourth Gospel contains anti-Jewish elements; (2) the anti-Jewish elements are unacceptable from a Christian point of view; and (3) there is no convincing way simply to neutralize or to remove the anti-Jewish dimensions of these passages in order to save the healthy core of the message itself. How can we affirm these three convictions at the same time? This is possible only if one can accept that even these problematic texts can have a place within the very process of revelation. But this calls for a review of our theology of revelation. Many approaches to the alleged anti-Judaism in the Gospel of John seem to continue to presuppose that revelation consists only in the imparting of the content of faith by the mediation of the scriptural text. This theology of revelation leads interpreters of the alleged anti-Judaism in the Gospel of John to defensive and apologetic reading strategies. An understanding of revelation as dialogical communication between God and the human person opens up new avenues in dealing with John's anti-Judaism.

Understanding revelation as shared life or loving communion between God and humanity has a number of important implications for our discussion. Revelation is not to be understood as simply coextensive with the content of the scriptural text. Rather, the scriptural text in all its dimensions (not only its content dimension) "constitutes a privileged possibility of revelation in the present."[90] In the process of present revelation, the scriptural text, as a human witness to God's self-communication in the past, is a privileged medium, but by far not the only medium, of God's loving self-gift in the present. More precisely, the scriptures are a witness to people's interpretation of God's self-communication to them. The scriptures themselves, and in particular the Gospel of John, do not claim to be the only place or the end of revelation. In the Fourth Gospel we find clear evidence that its writer presumed God's communication and shared life with the believers to continue in the community of those who come to faith through the word of the disciples (cf. 17:20). This is most striking in the "Farewell Discourses." The Johannine Jesus announces that the believers will do even greater works than Jesus (14:12). He also promises the Paraclete, the Spirit of truth who will guide them "into all the truth" and declare to them "the things that are to come" (16:13).

90. Schneiders, *Revelatory Text*, p. 46.

Since God enters people's lives in the historical conditions and limitations of real life, their interpretations are colored by these circumstances and shaped by their myopia and blind spots. The human authors of the scriptures are at the same time virtuous and sinful. The influence of sin on them was not rendered ineffective by God for the duration of their involvement in the writing of the scriptures.[91] When faith confesses the scriptures to be inspired, this confession does not imply that the scriptures are free from error but rather that God can write straight on crooked lines. In our conviction, this writing straight happens mainly in God's promise of and invitation to a new, alternative world. Even though this alternative world is also expressed under the conditions of the limitations of this world, it contains a new horizon that takes us beyond the conditions of this factual world. In the perspective of the future, we assume that God's alternative world has never been fully realized in the world. Christian faith confesses this alternative world to have been initiated in the coming near of the reign of God in Jesus Christ. But in the Christian faith, the expectation of Christ's second coming and the awareness of a future dimension of eschatology ("the eschatological reserve") serve as a reminder that there is more to come.

Moreover, in this world we know the alternative world of God only by approximation and in the light of our own interpretation. Therefore, error and selfishness continue to mar our vision of the future. For this reason, understanding God's dream of our future is an ongoing community effort. On its pilgrim journey through time, the people of God (in its various subgroups) is called to ongoing conversion with regard to the image it has formed for itself of God's future for humanity. In this process, the alternative world that the scriptures project plays a crucial role as a corrective. In its projected world, the text contains a truth claim, in the name of which the limitations and sinful dimensions of the text need to be corrected. This correction takes place in the process of the text's effective history, where both the world of the text and the imperfections of the world behind the text leave their traces. S. M. Schneiders comments: "This tradition is simultaneously purified by and purifying of the text."[92] She illustrates this position with the help of a basic idea of the American Declaration of Independence (1776): "All men are created equal." While it was certainly

91. J. Barr, *Beyond Fundamentalism: Biblical Foundations for Evangelical Christianity* (Philadelphia, 1984), p. 127: "The man of faith is sinful, and yet he is justified. Justification does not furnish him with perfection or infallibility. He still lives, and sees, and understands, and thinks, imperfectly. The Bible is the product of men of exactly this kind."

92. Schneiders, *Revelatory Text*, p. 8.

not the intention of its authors to include women, slaves, people of color, or children, by virtue of the qualifier *all* and of the possible inclusive meaning of the word *men,* the text unfolded an alternative world of all-inclusiveness that shaped its effective history and by which its effective history was shaped.

On the basis of these theoretical considerations, we return to the issue of anti-Judaism in the Gospel of John. Admitting anti-Jewish elements in the Fourth Gospel (or any scripture text) and evaluating them as unacceptable from a Christian perspective does not make impossible our faith conviction of the revelatory character of the scripture texts in question. Rather, the anti-Judaism is for us evidence of the fact that the human author of John, as well as the Johannine community, was a human person under the influence of sin. Anti-Jewish elements are expressions of their sinfulness that have found their way into the scriptural text. These are the crooked lines. But how does God write straight on them? The Fourth Gospel projects an alternative world; it contains the dimension of God's dream for the future of humanity. In John, God gives his only Son "so that everyone who believes in him may not perish but may have eternal life" (3:16). God sent the Son "in order that the world might be saved through him" (3:17). The Johannine Jesus says about himself: "I came that they may have life, and have it abundantly" (10:10).[93] God's ultimate concern is life and salvation for the world in an all-inclusive sense. We understand God's desire of salvation for all to be so strong that rejecting Christ as mediator of salvation is not necessarily a reason for excluding people from salvation. Johannine passages that, like 3:36, for example, explicitly or implicitly contain statements to the opposite were formulated under the influence of human sinfulness, because they can become an obstacle to the realization of God's alternative world, which the text projects.

John's intimation that the only possible reason for not accepting Jesus as mediator of God's salvation is moral corruptness (being murderers and liars; see 8:44–45 and 55) is unacceptable. In Romans 9–11, Paul shared John's view of God's desire for the salvation of all (see 11:26, 32). But with regard to the rejection by many Jews of Jesus as the Christ, he arrived at a very different conclusion. He suggested that it was a temporary reality in God's plan in order to incite early Christian missionaries to preach the gospel to the Gentiles (esp. 11:11, 25–26, 32). It is not moral corruptness but the deliberate, temporary hardening of the hearts of a part of Israel by God that, in Paul's view, keeps them from believing in Jesus. While this

93. A universalist perspective is also found in John 1:7; 6:39; 10:16; 11:54; 12:32.

view could be subjected to critical evaluation on a number of counts, we find in it an important testimony to the fact that John's perspective is not the only one in the New Testament. We do not consider either John's or Paul's explanation of Jewish unbelief in Jesus as the last word. In both texts we instead see God's will in the expression of God's concern for salvation of all as the ultimate horizon of the text. While it was not the intention of the original authors that all be saved independently of whether or not they accepted Christ as mediator of this salvation, we are convinced that this is the meaning that the text projects in the future.

In a final step, we make an attempt to apply this hermeneutic to John 8:31–59, the text that undeniably contains the most anti-Jewish polemic of the entire Gospel. We do not find convincing interpretations that use John 4:22 to deconstruct the anti-Jewishness of 8:44. For one thing, however positive the content of 4:22 might be considered, it cannot make 8:44 go away. Then we need to face the fact that 4:22 has a different focus and scope from 8:44 and therefore cannot neutralize it. Finally, more research is needed to clarify whether 4:22 is indeed as positive toward Judaism as many authors uncritically assume. The statement "salvation is from the Jews" in 4:22 might be used as a sharp reproach against "the Jews," accusing them of not recognizing and accepting Jesus although he is one of them and therefore should have easily been recognized by them. We find those positions more helpful that point out the expressions of inclusive love in John as deconstructing the expressions of exclusive hatred. But here we need to face the challenge of those who wonder whether, in John, it is not the other way around, namely, whether hatred does not deconstruct love. This is why we need to investigate whether "texts of terror" (in the words of Phyllis Trible) such as 8:31–59 do not project an alternative world, God's dream of all-inclusive love. The alternative world of 8:31–59 is one in which all know the truth that makes them free (8:32), in which all do what they have heard from the Father (8:38), in which all recognize God as their Father (cf. 8:41), in which all are from God and hear the words of God (8:47), in which all receive salvation and life and thus "never see death" (8:51). Both parties in the conflict between Jesus and "the Jews" ultimately agree that these are the goals of human longing and yearning. Neither of the parties excludes the other on principle from these goals. The Fourth Evangelist does not say anywhere that "the Jews" are excluded from them on "racial" or other unrelated grounds. Indeed, the specific reason there is a conflict at all is that the Johannine Jesus makes an attempt that is as passionate as it is desperate to include "the Jews" in reaching these goals. Despite John's positive inclinations toward the Jews in trying to include them in salvation, the fact that he condemns radically everyone who does not except Christ as mediator of salvation remains very problematic.

Our efforts to identify the projection of an alternative world in 8:31–59 that is different from the everyday reality of the Johannine community must not be misunderstood as an apologetic attempt to save the Johannine text. Our conviction of the presence in John 8:31–59 of a proposed world in no way mitigates or takes away the Evangelist's ethical responsibility for the real and the potential anti-Judaism of his Gospel. It does, however, raise the question of why there have not been more readers throughout the history of reading and interpreting John who allowed themselves to be touched by the text's alternative world.[94] Disappointing as it may be, the most effective eye-opener for the "world of the text" seems to have been the horror caused by the realization of the inhumanity and cruelty to which anti-Judaism can lead, and in fact did lead, especially in the twentieth century.

We cannot escape the recognition that there are anti-Jewish elements in the Fourth Gospel. But this may not lead us to reduce the Gospel to its anti-Jewish elements. For Christians, the Fourth Gospel is more than its anti-Judaism and its anti-Jewish potential. Even Jewish faith might be able to acknowledge that. Even if we cannot help but admit that the entire Gospel is affected by an anti-Jewish attitude, the text projects an alternative world of all-inclusive love and life that transcends its anti-Judaism. It is the world of the text, and not the world of the author, that is a witness to divine revelation.

94. Research is needed to bring to light those readings and interpretations throughout history that did engage the text's alternative world instead of allowing themselves to be infected by the anti-Jewish elements of the world of the author.

PART ONE

CHAPTER 2

The Embarrassment of History:
Reflections on the Problem of "Anti-Judaism"
in the Fourth Gospel

James D. G. Dunn

The present hermeneutical debate regarding how the New Testament should be used and read is particularly contentious when it focuses on John's Gospel. The range of views on the subject forms a kind of spectrum: from those at one end who see the document primarily, if not solely, as a witness to a particular stage in the historical development of earliest Christianity, to those at the other end who see it primarily, if not solely, as a document of Christian faith to be heard through the tradition of the Christian church and within the liturgy of Christian worship. Most views that seek to take account of or to give some place to both of these emphases, in differing measures, could position themselves at various points along such a spectrum. In principle, there need be no tension between the two ends or emphases of the spectrum. But in the event, there is. Among the topics increasing such tension over the past century have been the issues of Johannine "mysticism," sacraments, dualism, and Christology. But in the continuing reaction to the Holocaust, and particularly in the last twenty-five years,[1] it is the issue of John's "anti-Semitism," or more accurately, as most now agree, of John's "anti-Judaism,"[2] that has heightened the tension to, at times, an almost unbearable extent. The issue came home to me some years ago, when, after a week in which I had been reflecting on the question of anti-Semitism in the New Testament, I heard a sermon in Durham Cathedral in which John 8 (the Gospel reading for the day) was expounded straightforwardly as denouncing the Jews and Judaism, with little or no qualification.

1. The publication of R. R. Ruether, *Faith and Fratricide: The Theological Roots of Anti-Semitism* (New York, 1974), marked an increasing sensitivity on the part of Christian scholarship and recognition of the seriousness of the issue for students of the NT.
2. I discuss the problem of definition in J. D. G. Dunn, "The Question of Anti-Semitism in the New Testament Writings of the Period," in J. D. G. Dunn, ed., *Jews and Christians: The Parting of the Ways AD 70 to 135* (WUNT 66; Tübingen, 1992), pp. 177–211.

41

In my own view, it is simply impossible to do John's Gospel justice unless it is recognized to be a historical writing. By that I mean a writing that emerged at a particular period of history and that cannot properly be understood without reference to that period of history. This is not at all to deny that the Gospel has functioned from within a concept of the fourfold gospel since about the end of the second century, and from within the canon of the New Testament from some decades later. Nor is it to ignore the *Wirkungsgeschichte*[3] that has determined the Gospel's use within Christian history, which is certainly a major part of its continuing meaning and which inevitably influences our own reading of it today. My point is simply, in the first place, that as a document written (most probably) in the late first century, and written in the Greek of that time, we cannot begin to understand that document properly unless we recognize the language and idiom and imagery of the Greek of that time. New Testament scholars cannot go back, as it were, to a time before Erasmus and the first Greek New Testament (1516). We cannot deny or ignore the Renaissance fruits of critical philology. But that inevitably involves reading/hearing the Gospel, as far as is possible, within the context of that period of history. And it also involves giving at least some degree of priority to the findings of that "historical reading." Speaking philologically, we have to recognize that there is such a thing as a poor or a bad or even a wrong translation. And even if, should it prove to be the case, such a bad translation has been very influential through church history, it still has to be recognized as a misrendering of what the earliest retrievable text actually said. Should anyone respond that so to argue is to privilege a "historical reading" of the text inadmissably, whereas in principle all readings of the text should be accorded equal rights to be heard, I simply reply that the text has rights too, and that the primary right of a historical text such as John's Gospel is to be heard within the context in which and for which it was written.

The point could obviously be developed into a case for at least some degree of normativity to be accorded to a reading of the text within the historical context within which it originated, not simply the linguistic context but the ideological and sociological contexts as well. But this is not an essay in biblical hermeneutics, and it is unnecessary to pursue the point further here.[4] For one of the questions that cannot be ignored is whether the

---

3. I allude, of course, to H.-G. Gadamer, *Truth and Method* (London, 1975).

4. See further J. D. G. Dunn, "Historical Text as Historical Text: Some Basic Hermeneutical Reflections in Relation to the New Testament," in J. Davies, H. G. Harvey, and W. G. E. Watson, eds., *Words Remembered, Texts Renewed*, FS John F. A. Sawyer (JSOTSup 195; Sheffield, 1995), pp. 340–59.

straightforward translation of οἱ Ἰουδαῖοι as "the Jews" has proved to be a misleading translation over the centuries and particularly in the twentieth century. I therefore begin by restating my view of what the Fourth Evangelist was saying, and why he was saying it, within the historical context in which he was writing. In my conclusion, I take up the question of how such a historical reading should be correlated with the use of John's Gospel as Christian scripture.

John's Gospel in Historical Context

There is a large consensus in favor of the view that John's Gospel was written in the last decade of the first century, give or take a few years on either side. Where it was written and to whom is less clear but in the event less important, since the social setting of the Gospel can be largely deduced from the Gospel itself, even if particulars of locations of writer and recipients remain obscure. That some kind of dissension with Jews, or Jewish authorities, is reflected in the Gospel is also widely accepted.[5] In my own view, there are three important factors to be taken into account in any attempt to illuminate that dissension.

The Factionalism of First-Century "Judaism"

John wrote from within a movement that believed Jesus, crucified by Israel's Roman rulers with the approval of Israel's own priestly ruling class but raised by God, was Messiah. He wrote to persuade or confirm his readers in that belief (John 20:31). This messianic movement, focusing on this Jesus, emerged from within late Second Temple Judaism in the thirty years before the first Jewish revolt. In the course of that period, its opening to the Gentiles, particularly associated with the name of Paul, had begun to raise questions about the movement's continuing identity as part of Second Temple Judaism. In the years after the first Jewish revolt, these questions became more insistent, and the prospect of a "parting of the ways" between nascent Christianity and reconstituted Judaism became more and more of a real prospect—some would say, already a reality. It is precisely at this point of shifting and questioning identities that John wrote. To grasp the significance of this we need to fill out some more details.

5. J. L. Martyn, *History and Theology in the Fourth Gospel* (Nashville, 1968; 2d ed., 1979) has proved particularly influential here, even if the details of his reconstruction of the contemporary situation confronting John have been questioned.

There was a considerable degree of factionalism within Second Temple Judaism, particularly from the Maccabean crisis on.[6] We know of Pharisees and Sadducees from the New Testament texts themselves. Philo and Josephus have told us of Essenes, and Josephus later of Zealots, as well as of different figures who attracted followings in protest against Roman rule. Add the Old Testament Apocrypha and Pseudepigrapha, and we become aware of further dimensions of Second Temple Judaism in the Diaspora and of circles who cherished wisdom traditions and apocalyptic writings. But it is the Dead Sea Scrolls, firsthand evidence of the nearest thing to a Jewish "sect" in the modern sense, that have brought home to us how disparate were the emphases and priorities of different groups and factions within Judaism. This has helped us recognize that a movement that claimed a Jewish teacher from Nazareth was actually the Messiah would not have been so strange to the majority of Jews living near the eastern Mediterranean seaboard. Even the fact that this Jesus had been crucified, while off-putting for most Jews (1 Cor. 1:23), evidently did not disqualify such messianic Jews from functioning within Jerusalem and various Judaean towns and villages, if the witness of Acts is to be believed. Here we should also note that the ministry of Jesus himself, as recorded in the Synoptic Gospels, has been widely recognized in recent discussion between Christian and Jew as Jewish through and through. The arguments and conflicts that the Gospels refer to can be seen as similar to and even consistent with the kind and range of arguments and conflicts that characterized so much of the Judaism of Jesus' time.[7]

These observations help highlight one of our problems in talking about "the Judaism of Jesus' time." The problem is that the term *Judaism* suggests a homogeneous entity; all Jews practiced "Judaism." Until the discovery of the Dead Sea Scrolls there was the tendency, in both Jewish and Christian scholarship on the period, to assume that the Judaism of rabbinic tradition (e.g., the Mishnah) was simply "Judaism" (including Second Temple Judaism), that there was a concept and practice of what might be called rabbinic orthodoxy already operative in Second Temple Judaism. But to use *Judaism* in such an undifferentiated way does little or no justice to the factional picture indicated above. That major factors united all Jews, particularly what I have called elsewhere "the four pillars of Sec-

---

6. I have discussed this question and its ramifications in J. D. G. Dunn, "Pharisees, Sinners and Jesus," in *Jesus, Paul and the Law: Studies in Mark and Galatians* (London, 1990), pp. 61–88; also J. D. G. Dunn, "Judaism in the Land of Israel in the First Century," in J. Neusner, ed., *Judaism in Late Antiquity*, part 2: *Historical Syntheses* (Leiden, 1995), pp. 229–61.

7. Particularly E. P. Sanders, *Jesus and Judaism* (London, 1985).

ond Temple Judaism"[8] or what E. P. Sanders designated as "Common Judaism,"[9] need hardly be argued for. The point is that there were several, competing interpretations of what these common factors amounted to and how they should be lived out. And whether the term *Judaism,* hardly a common term itself at this stage,[10] was used to refer to the commonalities or, in effect, to refer to one or other of the competing interpretations[11] is by no means clear. Jesus and the earliest Christian congregations were, in effect, part of that ongoing debate over what it meant to be a Jew, what was involved in being Israel. Within the spectrum that was Second Temple Judaism, the Christian belief in Messiah Jesus, initially at least, was not much more than another element in the range of options that individual Jews might follow in practicing (their) "Judaism." The question, once again, for us is: Where and how do John and his Gospel stand within or in relation to this in-house debate, a debate in effect on what is Judaism and who belongs to it?

These reflections raise, in turn, the question as to how we should understand the key phrase in our discussion—*anti-Judaism.* At the very least, we should not assume that it means hostility to Judaism as a whole or to all Jews. At this stage we have to ask, "*Which* Judaism?" "*Whose* Judaism?" The question, it should be noted, arises not (simply) from any analysis of the term 'Ιουδαῖοι in John's Gospel. It arises from a historical recognition, in summary: (1) that the term *Judaism* was not much used, as far as we can tell, by Jews speaking of their religion; (2) that Second Temple "Judaism" was a more complex phenomenon than the single name implies, and that it may indeed be more accurate from a historical perspective to speak of multiple Judaisms for the period;[12] and (3) that there is a danger of superimposing our own twentieth-century, sociologically informed definition of Judaism onto our evidence. If, then, it should be concluded that there is "anti-Judaism" in John's Gospel, we still have to ask, "*What* Judaism?" "*Which* Judaism?" And even if later readings of John have encouraged an anti-Judaism on the way to anti-Semitism, it is only fair to the Fourth Evangelist to ask who the Fourth Evangelist thought he was attacking and why.

8. J. D. G. Dunn, *The Partings of the Ways between Christianity and Judaism* (London, 1991), chapter 2.

9. E. P. Sanders, *Judaism: Practice and Belief 63 BCE–66 CE* (London, 1992).

10. The term occurs only seven times in the literature of the period prior to John (2 Macc. 2:21; 8:1; 14:38 [twice]; 4 Macc. 4:26; Gal. 1:13–14 [twice]).

11. As I believe to be the case with Gal. 1:13–14; see J. D. G. Dunn, *The Epistle to the Galatians* (London, 1993), pp. 56–57.

12. See, e.g., those cited in Dunn, "Judaism," p. 230 n. 8.

If the situation within Second Temple Judaism—that is, properly speaking, up to 70 C.E.—was so complex in terms of factionalism, the failure of the Jewish revolt and the destruction of the Temple in 70 C.E. both simplified the picture and made it more complex. It simplified the picture in that several of the known factions seem to have lost power or influence, or indeed, virtually to have disappeared in the wake of the 70 C.E. disaster. I refer to the Zealots and the Sadducees but also to the Qumran community and probably the Essenes. Presumably this did not happen overnight, but the lack of any clear evidence that these groups remained major players in the subsequent shaping of Judaism is probably sufficient proof of their effective demise. At the same time, the successors to the Pharisees were evidently able to establish themselves as the chief custodians of the Pharisaic heritage and, more important, as the only effective political force in the land. Again, it did not happen overnight; on the contrary, it took many decades and even centuries for the rabbis to establish their interpretation of Judaism as the only authentic form of Judaism, to establish, that is to say, rabbinic Judaism as "Judaism."[13] In the meantime, other heirs of Second Temple Judaism, particularly in the Diaspora, and those with Jewish apocalyptic and mystical tendencies seem to have survived and flourished for some time at least, without making much, if any, impact on emerging rabbinic orthodoxy. The fact that their writings have been preserved within Christian rather than Jewish circles is probably enough to confirm that they influenced emerging Christianity more than they did emerging rabbinic Judaism.

This overview is, of course, far too brief and sketchy, and to make good the various conclusions on which it depends would require a much fuller essay than this. But I hope the overview will command sufficient consensus for the key corollary that emerges from it to be taken with due seriousness. The corollary I refer to is this: John's Gospel appeared from within the factionalism of Second Temple Judaism, and at a time when that factionalism had been completely disrupted by the disaster of 70 C.E.—disrupted but not dissolved or resolved. It appeared at a time when, with the benefit of hindsight, we can see only two substantive contenders for the heritage of Second Temple Judaism beginning to emerge from the pre-70 factionalism—Christianity and rabbinic Judaism. It is within this larger context that the question of John's "anti-Judaism" must be viewed.

---

13. See further P. S. Alexander, "'The Parting of the Ways' from the Perspective of Rabbinic Judaism," and M. Goodman, "Diaspora Reactions to the Destruction of the Temple," in Dunn, ed., *Jews and Christians*, pp. 1–25 and 27–38, respectively.

The Claim to Definitive Revelation

'The second factor that illuminates the dissension with "the Jews" in a historical reading of John's Gospel is recognition that the key issue of dispute with "the Jews" was the claim, embodied in John's Jesus, to definitive *revelation*. Here we need to recall that a passionate concern regarding divine revelation was, as far back as we can see, a defining characteristic of Jewish religion, characterized as it was by the central importance accorded to Torah, priest/Temple, and prophet. With the effective elimination of priest and Temple in 70 C.E., the interest in revelation seems to have been, if anything, intensified. The classic Jewish apocalypses (*4 Ezra* and *2 Baruch*) emerged in that period, not to mention the Apocalypse of John (Revelation). Ascents to heaven to acquire heavenly knowledge became almost commonplace—not just in the already long established speculation about Enoch but also concerning Adam and Abel, Abraham and Levi, Baruch and Isaiah.[14] *Merkabah* mysticism, inspired particularly by the chariot vision of Ezekiel 1, seems to have flourished. Yohanan ben Zakkai, who played the leading role in establishing the rabbis as the main power brokers within Israel and began the process of reconstituting Second Temple Judaism as rabbinic Judaism, was himself apparently very interested in the chariot chapter of Ezekiel 1 and probably practiced meditation on it (*t. Ḥagigah* 2.1ff. pars.).[15] And the "two powers heresy" is traced back to four sages (including rabbi Akiba) practicing *merkabah* mysticism in the period of John's Gospel or soon after, when one of them (Elisha ben Abuyah) mistook the glorious figure sitting on a heavenly throne as a second divine power, in some sense rivaling God (*m. Ḥagigah* 2.1; *m. Megillah* 4:10).[16] Wider speculation about heavenly wisdom and its source had already been resolved within Second Temple Judaism by identifying the figure of divine Wisdom with the Torah (Sir. 24:23; Bar. 4:1), no doubt to the satisfaction of Pharisees. This would have been still more satisfactory to the post-70 rabbis, since the Temple was gone and the various would-be prophets of the pre-70 years could inspire no confidence whatsoever.

It is precisely against this background that the emphasis on divine revelation in John's Gospel becomes so luminous. The central message of the Gospel is loud and clear and repeated in variation after variation. The Word, not the Baptist, is the light that enlightens every man (John 1:6–9); the polemical assertion sets the tone of many of the revelatory claims made for

---

14. Dunn, *Partings*, pp. 320–21 n. 49.
15. Ibid., p. 321 n. 57.
16. See particularly A. F. Segal, *Two Powers in Heaven: Early Rabbinic Reports about Christianity and Gnosticism* (Leiden, 1977).

Jesus. The Word, God's self-revealing word, became flesh in Jesus (1:14). Grace and truth came through this Jesus, more effectively, it is clearly implied, than through Moses and the Torah (1:17). "No one has ever seen God . . . the only Son . . . has made him known [ἐξηγήσατο]" (1:18). The vision of Jacob, of a ladder stretching to heaven (Gen. 28:12), which could have afforded the means of access to heaven, refers to Jesus the Son of Man, as the one who opens heaven to human gaze (John 1:51). The Pharisee, Nicodemus, comes to Jesus by night but has no idea how one can "see the kingdom of God," how it is possible to enter the heavenly realm (3:3, 5); he is unable to appreciate the "earthly things" that Jesus tells him, how much less the "heavenly things" (3:12); he has to be told, "No one has ascended into heaven except the one who descended from heaven, the Son of Man" (3:13). Only "the one who comes from above" (3:31–36), not Moses, not John the Baptist, is able to bear witness of the things of heaven (3:31–32). In John 6, the antithesis is extended: Jesus is not simply the prophet (6:14) but the Son of Man (6:27); Moses gave their fathers manna in the wilderness, and they died, but Jesus is the bread of God come down from heaven, and whoever eats of him will never die (6:30–58). The passage includes a further explicit claim that Jesus is the definitive revealer of God (6:45–46):

> It is written in the prophets, "And they shall all be taught by God." Everyone who has heard and learned from the Father comes to me. Not that anyone has seen the Father except the one who is from God; he has seen the Father.

We could continue, but that sample should be sufficient for present purposes.

To sum up: Probably the most consistent feature of John's Gospel is the emphasis on Jesus as the bearer of divine revelation. What he says has the stamp of heavenly authority, because as Son of God, sent by the Father, he speaks what he has seen and heard from the Father; as the Son of Man, he speaks with the authority of one who has descended from heaven; as one who is from above, his message outweighs in kind and quality anything said by him who is from below.[17] This feature is the basis of R. Bultmann's famous remark "Jesus as the revealer of God reveals nothing but that he is the revealer."[18]

But not only does Jesus bring revelation; he *is* revelation; he embodies revelation. This is where Bultmann mistakes the emphasis. It is not true that Jesus reveals nothing. On the contrary, it is precisely the point that he

17. John 1:17–18, 49–51; 3:10–13, 32; 7:16–18; 8:14, 28, 38; 12:49–50; 14:10; 15:15; 17:14.
18. R. Bultmann, *Theology of the New Testament,* 2 vols. (London, 1955), vol. 2, p. 66.

reveals *God*. He is God's own self-utterance in flesh (1:14); he "exegetes" God (1:18); he is the divine self-revealing "I am" (8:58), echoing God's self-revelation in the figure of divine Wisdom (6:51–58; 10:14; 12:8);[19] he who sees Jesus sees the one who sent him (12:45); he who has seen him has seen the Father (14:9). It is this testimony that is "heard" by Jesus' Jewish opponents in the Gospel as Jesus making himself to be equal with God (5:18), making himself God (10:33). For John, this is not a false assessment of Jesus but simply recognizes that Jesus' revelation of God is definitive.

The polemical note already observed in some of the texts referred to above also needs some emphasis. Jesus transforms the water of purification rites into the wine of rejoicing (2:1–11). The risen Jesus in effect replaces the Temple (2:19–22). The water he gives is far superior to the water from Jacob's well (4:10–14). He is greater than Moses or the prophet or the Baptist: Moses wrote of him (5:46); Isaiah saw his glory (12:41); and the Baptist bore witness to him (1:8, 20; 3:27–36; 5:33–35; 10:41). Of the Jews, the Pharisees are particularly picked out for criticism: Nicodemus, the teacher of Israel, is unable to appreciate heavenly things (3:10–12); those who honor Moses are accused by Moses because they do not believe his writings (5:45–46); the Pharisees profess to be able to see but are blind (9:40–41); they are the ones particularly in view when Jesus quotes the famous Isaiah passages about Israel's refusal to believe and hardness of heart (12:37–43).

Set against the background sketched above, it becomes hard to resist the conclusion that the Gospel was composed with a view to the post-70 concerns among Jews regarding revelation: how to understand God's will, how to understand God in the light of the failure of the first revolt, and where the authority now lay to speak in God's name, with God's voice. The Fourth Evangelist shared that concern and sought to answer these questions. And his answer focuses entirely on Jesus. In the face of traditional answers, and in forceful dialogue with, it would appear, the Pharisaic custodians and promoters of the rabbinic Judaism beginning to emerge at Yabneh, John had no hesitation in finding the answer in Jesus, the Word made flesh, the Son from the Father, the Son of Man now reascended to heaven—and exclusively in Jesus: "I am the way, and the truth, and the life. No one comes to the Father except through me" (14:6). As his wisdom predecessors had directed all those concerned to know the wisdom from God to the Torah, so now John directs all those concerned to know the wisdom of God and to know God to Jesus.

19. See further Dunn, *Partings*, p. 227.

These observations can be correlated with another feature of John's Gospel too little taken into consideration in discussion of John's "anti-Judaism." This is the fact that the key phrase, *the Jews,* is not at all so consistently negative in use as is sometimes suggested. In fact, about one-half of all the references are more accurately described as neutral. Most notable in this case are the references where *the Jews* clearly denotes the common people, the crowd.[20] Their function in the narrative is to represent the ambivalent middle ground in a process of sifting[21] and division[22] that John represents as taking place within the Jewish community throughout the middle period of Jesus' ministry. The motif is particularly prominent in chapters 7–12. Throughout chapter 7, "the Jews"/"the crowd"[23] debate back and forth the significance of Jesus, with many believing or responding positively (7:31, 40) but others skeptical (7:35); the end result is "a division [σχίσμα] among the people" (7:43). In chapter 8, the debate among "the Jews" continues, some believing (8:31) and others rejecting (8:48). Through chapters 9–10, the sifting process continues, causing some further "division among the Jews" (9:16; 10:19–21), with, once again, some rejecting (10:31–39) and many believing (10:41–42). And in 12:31–43, the sifting (κρίσις) process reaches its climax, between Jews who believe and bear witness to Jesus (12:11, 17–19) and those who refuse (12:37–40).[24]

Here, too, in the light of what has already been said, it is hard not to hear the Gospel as John's attempt to state his case, to preach his good news, within the context of a late-first-century Judaism uncertain of what God's will was for them and uncertain as to who could speak authoritatively for God. Many of "the Jews," particularly those endeavoring to establish themselves as the authoritative voice in continuing Judaism, evidently had already decided against John's message and were opposing the claims made for this Jesus; they are no doubt referred to in the famous ἀποσυνάγωγος texts (9:22; 12:42; 16:2). Moreover, the dualism and other features in John suggest something of the attitude of the "sectarian" who feels his group to be marginalized in relation to the larger body or in danger of being excluded by the parent body.[25] But equally evident, if we observe the pro-

---

20. John 6:41, 52; 7:11(?), 15, 35(?); 8:22, 31; 10:19, 24(?); 11:19, 31, 33, 36, 45, 54; 12:9, 11; 13:33(?); 18:20; 19:20–21.

21. κρίσις—"separation, judgment"—3:19; 5:22, 24, 27, 29, 30; 7:24; 8:16; 12:31.

22. σχίσμα—"schism, division"—7:43; 9:16; 10:19.

23. "The Jews"—7:11, 15, 35; "the crowd"—7:12, 20, 31, 32, 40, 43.

24. See more fully Dunn, *Partings*, pp. 156–57.

25. Cf. particularly the influential article of W. A. Meeks, "The Man from Heaven in Johannine Sectarianism," *JBL* 91 (1972): 44–72.

portion of negative/neutral uses of "the Jews," is that many Jews were not yet clear on the answers to their questions regarding revelation and authority; these were the Jews, including Nicodemus and the blind man of chapter 9, who had to be persuaded to come and take their stand fully within the light of the revelation of Jesus. If that is indeed the case, then here again we are reminded that the issue of "anti-Judaism" within John's Gospel needs to be much more carefully nuanced than a simple reference to John 8:31–59 would suggest.

The Language of Forthright Argument

One other factor should be taken into consideration. It is the brief reminder that the language of polemic and denunciation used by John in regard to "the Jews" should be heard initially with first-century ears before being condemned by twentieth-century sensitivities. We who would hesitate to start an action for heresy against a contemporary, and who would not even consider the possibility of burning someone at the stake for their beliefs, should hesitate for a long time before reacting to the fierceness of the vituperation evident in a chapter such as John 8. Times have changed, even in respect to interfactional political polemic, more than we sometimes care to admit. The temperate nature of most twentieth-century ecumenical or interfaith dialogue leaves us horrified by the outspokenness and crudity of, say, Reformation and Counter-Reformation polemic.

To hear John's polemic with first-century ears requires us to compare it with the factional polemic within Second Temple Judaism, or indeed the factional polemic within earliest Christianity. In the first case, we may instance the readiness, say, of the Psalms of Solomon to condemn other Jews as "sinners," bearing in mind just how serious a condemnation that was: sinners had no place within the covenant people, no acceptance by God, no hope of a place in the world to come.[26] Alternatively, we could cite the curses invoked in the covenant initiation ceremony into the Qumran community against "the men of the lot of Belial" (other Jews) and against those who make a false commitment to the community (1QS 2.4–18). Or in Christian factional polemic, we should bear in mind Paul's curses pronounced against the other (Christian) missionaries in Gal. 1:8–9 or equivalent denunciation of other missionaries as "false apostles, deceitful workers," and ministers of Satan (2 Cor. 11:13–15). Even Jesus is

26. See J. D. G. Dunn, "Jesus and Factionalism in Early Judaism: How Serious Was the Factionalism of Late Second Temple Judaism?" in J. H. Charlesworth and L. L. Johns, eds., *Hillel and Jesus: Comparative Studies of Two Major Religious Leaders* (Minneapolis, 1997), pp. 156–75.

recalled as rebuking Peter as Satan (Mark 8:33 / Matt. 16:23). Such identification with Satan of those with opposing views seems to have been characteristic of both Jewish and Christian polemic of the time. The
"diabolizing" of "the Jews" in John 8 (8.44—"You are from your father the
devil"), which we quite properly find so offensive when judged by today's
standards of disagreement and polemic, was evidently a standard topos in
the ancient Jewish/Christian rhetoric of vilification. What the real equivalent would be in the more consciously restrained and well-mannered
exchanges within Western intellectual circles or within today's more mutually respectful ecumenical and ecclesiastical circles is once again a question
too seldom posed, let alone answered.

The position is well summed up by the observations of two contemporary New Testament scholars who have taken seriously the issue of anti-
Jewish rhetoric in the New Testament. The Roman Catholic Luke Johnson
concludes his analysis of "The New Testament's Anti-Jewish Slander and
the Conventions of Ancient Polemic" with these words: "By the measure
of contemporary Jewish polemic, the NT's slander against fellow Jews is
remarkably mild."[27] And the Jewish scholar David Flusser, commenting on
Matthew 23, notes: "All the motifs of Jesus' famous invective against the
Pharisees in Matthew 23 are also found in rabbinical literature."[28]

Here again, then, the character of John's "anti-Judaism" needs careful
analysis and statement before it is straightforwardly described and
denounced as anti-Judaism. John's language is more the language of *intra*-
Jewish polemic than of *anti*-Jewish polemic. He seeks by it to warn *fellow
Jews* not to follow what was emerging as the dominant view of "the Jews."
By his portrayal of Jesus as the definitive revealer of God and of God's will,
in continuity with Israel's earlier claims to divine revelation but in opposition to other contemporary claimants within the Judaism of his day, John
still hoped to persuade the doubters and waverers to stand with the believers, still mostly fellow Jews, in Messiah Jesus.[29] This is indeed "anti-
Jewishness" of a sort. But it is not "anti-Judaism" as we understand it today.

27. L. T. Johnson, "The New Testament's Anti-Jewish Slander and the Conventions of Ancient
Polemic," *JBL* 108 (1989): 419–41, p. 441.

28. Cited by J. Koenig, *Jews and Christians in Dialogue: New Testament Foundations* (Philadelphia,
1979), p. 24.

29. It will be evident from this that I do not agree with the thesis of M. Casey, initially stated in his
From Jewish Prophet to Gentile God: The Origins and Development of New Testament Christology (Cambridge, 1991), that John belonged to "a group who had Gentile self-identification" (p. 27); see further
J. D. G. Dunn, "The Making of Christology: Evolution or Unfolding?" in *The Christ and the Spirit*,
vol. 1: *Christology* (Grand Rapids, 1998), pp. 388–404. The brief references to "certain Greeks" (7:35;
12:20) are probably included to remind his predominantly Jewish (or Jewish-oriented) readers that
Christianity had opened up to the Gentiles in a significant way.

It does not presuppose two monoliths, Judaism and Christianity, clearly distinct and clearly separate in identity, denouncing each other in anathemas and open hostility. Rather, it would be closer to historical reality to think of the situation presupposed in John's Gospel as reflecting the approaching breakdown of "ecumenical relations" between the two main bodies within post–Second Temple Judaism, the late phase of a forthright dialogue that was coming close to failure and not to be fully resumed until the Jewish-Christian dialogue of the twentieth century.

John's Gospel as Christian Scripture

What difference do the findings of this chapter make to the use of John's Gospel as Christian scripture? What difference *should* these findings make to the use of John's gospel as Christian scripture? If, in principle, a historical reading should be accorded at least some priority over other readings, what might or should that mean for the liturgical reading of John's Gospel? Can one respond with "Thanks be to God" without reservation when John 8 is read? What might or should it mean for John's status as *scripture*? Can one "hear the word of God" in such a passage without qualification? And how should such scriptures "play" in Jewish-Christian dialogue? Are they simply part of the problem and no part of its solution?

"Dynamic Translation"?

Part of the problem of using historical writings for modern purposes is that terms may have changed their meaning or scope of reference in the interval. In English versions of the New Testament, the decision by the King James translators to use *charity* (instead of Tyndale's *love*) in rendering 1 Corinthians 13 has been a matter of regret throughout most of the twentieth century. And the issue of whether γύνη should be translated "woman" or "wife" in several Pauline contexts has become a matter of major concern in the later decades of the twentieth century. Among the issues facing this book, the undifferentiated translation of οἱ Ἰουδαῖοι as "the Jews" has become unacceptable to many. How to deal with such issues?

One solution is the concept of "dynamic equivalence." John's text speaks consistently of οἱ Ἰουδαῖοι. As already noted, about half the uses are negative in character: for example, "The Jews were looking for an opportunity to kill him" (7:1); "The Jews said to him, 'Now we know that you have a demon'" (8:52); "the Jews had already agreed that if anyone should

confess him to be Christ, he was to be put out of the synagogue" (9:22
J.D.G.D.); "The Jews took up stones again to stone him" (10:31); "the
retainers [ὑπηρέται] of the Jews arrested Jesus" (18:12); "The Jews
answered him, 'We have a law, and according to that law he ought to die
because he has claimed to be the Son of God'" (19:7). But a strong case
can be made for seeing many of these references as directed against the Jewish *authorities* at the time of the Gospel's writing.[30] Should we then translate οἱ Ἰουδαῖοι in such instances as its dynamic equivalent, "the Jewish
authorities," rather than as "the Jews"? This is the policy followed by the
American Bible Society in their production of the Contemporary English
Version (1995). For example, the CEV renders οἱ Ἰουδαῖοι in the cases
cited above, in sequence, as "the leaders of the people," "the people," "the
leaders," "the people," "the temple police," and "the crowd." Alternatively,
or in addition, it can be argued that Ἰουδαῖος in these and other instances
retains its original geographical reference and should be translated more
accurately as "Judean."[31] This is the policy of *The New Testament: Judaean
and Authorized Version*,[32] which translates οἱ Ἰουδαῖοι as "Judaeans" or
"Hebrews" and "law" as "Bible." Alternatively, the more offensive passages
(offensive to Christian as well as Jewish sensitivities) could simply be
excluded from church lectionaries. N. A. Beck defends such policies as
follows:[33]

> Under the guidance of the Spirit of God in translations of the New Testa-
> ment intended for popular use, we will "prune" into footnote status its most
> viciously defamatory particles. In other instances, in which the polemic is less
> virulent, we will use circumlocution and translations according to the sense
> of the text in order to reduce emphasis upon the Jews, Judaism, and the Phar-
> isees. Third, we will be more selective in our choice of lectionary texts, pro-
> viding readings that are less blatantly anti-Jewish.

What the particular "particles" in view are is not specified at this point, but
in a footnote Beck defends the policy by referring to "the New Testament
material that has already been 'pruned' to footnote status in translations . . .
as a result of text-critical studies during the past three centuries."[34] In other
words, Beck puts the offensive "particles," whose textual authenticity is not

30. Particularly U. C. von Wahlde, "The Johannine 'Jews': A Critical Survey," *NTS* 28 (1982):
33–60. The matter is debated elsewhere in this book.
31. See particularly M. Lowe, "Who Were the Ἰουδαῖοι? *NovT* 18 (1976): 101–30 and the new
American edition of Bauer's lexicon (*BAGD*).
32. *The New Testament: Judaean and Authorized Version* (Jerusalem, n.d.).
33. N. A. Beck, *Mature Christianity: The Recognition and Repudiation of the Anti-Jewish Polemic of
the New Testament* (London and Toronto, 1985), p. 285.
34. Ibid., p. 286 n. 3.

in question, in the same category as the ending added to the Lord's Prayer in Matt. 6:13, the shorter and longer endings of Mark's Gospel, and the "Johannine comma" in 1 John 5:7-8. The boundaries of the canon become still more convoluted. And in lectionaries, the anti-Jewish passages will be excluded or at least bracketed to indicate that the read lection should omit these words or phrases or verses. The anti-Jewish passages of the New Testament should at best be treated like the imprecatory psalm passages of the Old Testament.

I confess that I am not at all happy with the first of these solutions. To extend the possibilities of textual emendation beyond that validated by text-critical considerations is essentially a retrograde step. Nor am I particularly happy with the third solution. The thought of thus "hiding" the character of the sacred text from the eyes or ears of the populace (Beck is talking about translations "intended for popular use") seems to reinforce the clergy-laity or professional-laity divide and has uncomfortable overtones of keeping the Bible from the people. As for the to date more popular second of Beck's solutions (translation by dynamic equivalent), I have serious reservations here too. Apart from anything else, such a policy makes it impossible for anyone working from such a modern translation to mount a coherent study of a motif in the New Testament documents having to do with "Jews."[35]

Here, too, I believe, we must fully respect the text, working from the eclectic Greek text provided for us by the consensus of text-critical scholars. We should therefore continue to translate οἱ Ἰουδαῖοι as "the Jews"; but we should always add or refer to a footnote explaining the historical context within which John was writing. Nor should we exclude difficult or disturbing passages from lections and liturgical readings; but no such reading should be without at least some explanatory comment. Only so can we preserve our status as both servants of the word and its interpreters.

The Necessity for Historical Criticism

More reflection is necessary on the need for better correlation among historical, canonical, and liturgical readings. In the present case in particular, we dare not forget Christianity's own sorry tradition of anti-Semitism. The extent to which this tradition has been inspired by or built upon anti-Jewish material in the New Testament is here not the issue. The point is that,

---

35. I have complained about the equivalent policies applied to Paul's concept of "flesh" in J. D. G. Dunn, *The Theology of Paul the Apostle* (Grand Rapids and Edinburgh, 1998), p. 70.

throughout the history of the church, the New Testament, or at least certain New Testament passages, has been read and heard as justifying, authorizing, even requiring anti-Jewish and subsequently anti-Semitic policies. Those who insist that the New Testament can be read only through the tradition or liturgy or properly heard only within the church need to remember that the virulent anti-Jewish polemics of John Chrysostom and Martin Luther are also part of the tradition,[36] bearing in mind both that the Eastern Orthodox still celebrate the liturgy of St. John Chrysostom and the incalculable influence of Martin Luther on Western Christianity.

Here again, I press for a fuller recognition of the priority that, within the range of possible readings, should be given to reading a historical text within its historical context. Such a reading, informed by knowledge of ancient philology and related texts, of the history and sociology, the philosophies and religions of the period, will by no means exclude debates about the text's meaning; but it will indicate the parameters within which meaning may legitimately be heard in the text and outside which any meanings heard may be faulted as illegitimate. This is also to affirm that that range of legitimate meaning should function as some sort of check on readings subsequently read from the text. The canonical normativeness of the text depends to a degree not sufficiently appreciated on reading a text such as John's Gospel first and foremost within its historical context.

One of the too little appreciated benefits of the history of Western Christianity stretching from Renaissance through Enlightenment is the recognition that the developments of the developing tradition had not always been for the best; that the canon has a corrective function within the tradition, *norma normans*; and that historical criticism is necessary if the scriptural text is to be heard in its historical meaning. Of course, the appropriation of this tripartite benefit has had a very checkered history. But at least we can see its outcome in the Western church's confession and criticism of its own anti-Jewish history. The critical perspective on tradition made possible or facilitated by recognition of the need to read the New Testament texts over against the tradition, to read them as historical texts, has played a significant part in awakening the Western churches to their anti-Semitic past. Vatican II's pronouncement on the Jews[37] well illustrates my point; that it came after the papal encyclical *Divino Afflante Spiritu* (1944) and the 1964

36. Chrysostom's *Homily against the Jews* is conveniently accessible in translation in W. A. Meeks and R. L. Wilken, *Jews and Christians in Antioch in the First Four Centuries of the Common Era* (Missoula, Mont., 1978), pp. 85ff. For Luther's *On the Jews and Their Lies,* see, e.g., M. Saperstein, *Moments of Crisis in Jewish-Christian Relations* (London, 1989), pp. 33–35.

37. In *Nostra Aetate* (Declaration on the Relationship of the Church to Non-Christian Religions), in W. M. Abbott, *The Documents of Vatican II* (London, 1966), pp. 666–67.

statement by the Pontifical Biblical Commission, validating a properly critical evaluation of the character of the biblical witness,[38] is no coincidence. And what Lutheran in the tradition of the Confessing Church would not be critical of Luther's diatribe against the Jews? Contrast the Orthodox churches of the East. In this case, it would appear that hearing the New Testament through the church and within the liturgy has not enabled a similarly critical and painful repudiation of the anti-Jewish elements in Christian history.

In short, the fact that anti-Semitism was able to grow and even to flourish within Christianity's living liturgical communities is a warning to us that historical exegesis is an important tool in the churches' equipment, a tool quite well fitted to provide some corrective or caution against ahistorical readings of the scriptural text that validated beliefs and acts of which the churches are now rightly ashamed. *Sachkritik* is most effective when it is also historical criticism.

Revelation in History

There is a further and important theological point to be made here. Properly to recognize the historical character of our texts is to recognize also the historical conditionedness of these texts. And to recognize the historical conditionedness of a scriptural text is to recognize also the historical conditionedness of the revelation that text embodies. This includes all the relativities and ambiguities of historical existence and language. If Jesus was a Jew living and working in the midst of Jews, then his actions and his teaching, the revelation he brought and embodied, were tied into the particularities of the history of that period. It could not be otherwise. The revelation was first and foremost to Second Temple Jews, and in terms adapted to their historical circumstances. This is precisely why a historical reading critically alert to these circumstances is so necessary. If we do not hear the revelation through and in Jesus first and foremost in its historical particularity, we are in serious danger of not hearing it at all. For the revelation cannot be separated from its historically conditioned form; it is not a timeless kernel that can be somehow extricated from a time-conditioned husk. There is no such thing as "pure" revelation. As the Word had to become "flesh" (cf. 1:13; 3:6; 6:63!) in order to reveal so fully the character of God's glory (1:14), so the revelation in Jesus had to become history for it to be heard.

---

38. See R. E. Brown, *Biblical Exegesis and Church Doctrines* (London, 1985), chapter 1.

In other words, the problem of "the Jews" in John is the problem of a "warts and all" portrayal of Christianity. We cannot solve the problem by simply excising the anti-Jewish passages from John; otherwise we may not hear the revelation conveyed through John in its givenness as revelation. We cannot disown the anti-Jewish passages in John without disfiguring the revelation he records. We must instead seek to hear the revelation through and in the light of the particularities of history within which and to which the word of Jesus came as revelation of the Word. Only so do we acknowledge the character of revelation in history. The ugliness of some of these particularities, as judged by twentieth-century standards, should not be thought to disqualify the revelatory significance that John claims for Jesus. To those who are all too conscious of the historical particularities and ambiguities of their own and their church's historical existence, such a recognition has liberating potential, even if it does not make any easier the task of interpreting the revelation that is the Fourth Gospel's Jesus to their own time.

The same point can be put in "canonical" terms. If certain texts continue to function as canonical, it is as historically conditioned texts that they do so. To declare a text canonical was certainly to indicate the (further) contexts (canon and church) within which Christians should read that text. But canonizing a text should not be seen as dehistoricizing that text; rather, the process of canonization served to identify those historical texts that were acknowledged from earliest days to represent and define Christianity.

In our present case, the inclusion of John's Gospel in the canon means that the dialogue between emerging Christianity and emerging rabbinic Judaism evident in John's Gospel was also included in the canonization process and in the resulting canon. The intra-Jewish debate about what belief in Messiah Jesus might/should mean in regard to Jesus and for those who believe in him is itself part of Christianity's canonical self-definition. Nascent Christianity's wrestling with its Jewish siblings in the attempt fully to appreciate their common Jewish heritage is a fundamental feature of Christianity's own identity. We could hardly have a starker reminder that Christianity cannot adequately understand itself except in relation to and in dialogue with its fellow heirs of Second Temple Judaism. "The Jews" of John still have a part in helping mark out Christianity's own heritage and boundaries.

In short, the problem of John's "anti-Judaism" will not go away, and Christian scholars should avoid attempting to solve the problem lightly, by disowning or denying it, by excising or hiding it, by ignoring or marginalizing it. On the contrary, the challenge that John's "anti-Jewishness" poses for the concept and use of Christian scripture should be taken up and worked through, partly because it reminds us of the still more virulent anti-Judaism and anti-Semitism of subsequent Christian tradition, and because a historical reading of John's Gospel (including his "anti-Jewish" passages) provides a check on and counter to that later anti-Judaism; and partly because it reminds us that revelation comes through dirty hands and inadequate human language, and that the all-too-vigorous altercations of the first century were an integral part of Christianity's emerging identity and remain fundamental to its continuing self-understanding.

Conclusion

The reaffirmation of John's Gospel as a historical text that must be read first and foremost in its historical context is strengthened by our ability to gain a surprisingly clear grasp of the historical circumstances in which John's "anti-Judaism" was articulated. In particular, we can recognize the historical relativities behind the composition of John, that is, the factionalism of late Second Temple Judaism, the mode of the divine revelation claimed, and the language of forthright argument. This historical contextualization of John's "anti-Jewishness" goes a long way to soften the problem of John's so-called anti-Judaism.

The reaffirmation of John's Gospel as primarily a historical text applies also to its role as scripture. Given John's status as Christian scripture, the problem of John's "anti-Jewishness" is not to be solved simply by eliminating the problem, through excision or translation by "dynamic equivalence." On the contrary, the historical text read historically can serve as a counter and rebuke to the anti-Judaism of later Christian tradition that was mounted upon John's anti-Jewish texts. Moreover, the recognition of the historical conditionedness of the revelation claimed by John provides a stark reminder of the unavoidably historical conditionedness of all revelation and claims to revelatory significance of historical individuals and words. More to the case in point here, the historical particularity of John's portrayal of the confrontations between "the Jews" and believers in Messiah Jesus is an indication of how fundamental to Christianity's own emerging identity was the dialogue with emerging rabbinic Judaism.

As a final thought, it is also important to recognize that the argument can be extended *mutatis mutandis* to the modern Jewish-Christian debate. This includes the recognition that even John's account of the insults and hurtful exchanges between "Jews" and believers in Messiah Jesus, as well as language that, when taken out of context, is easily heard as anti-Jewish in a later sense, is part of our common "warts and all" history. For in intra-Christian ecumenical experience, we have learned that we cannot ignore or lightly discard the wounding exchanges of earlier centuries, and that it is only by confronting them together in a deeper commitment to our common heritage that their point can be clarified and their poison counteracted. Perhaps the same lesson could be applied to the Jewish-Christian dialogue, ecumenical in a more profound way. In which case, John's Gospel, rather than being a stumbling block in the way of such dialogue, could actually provide a common agenda for Jews and Christians to study together, to explore and where possible to affirm what is the real extent of our common heritage, and to discover what common lessons, both positive and negative, we can both learn from the earliest stages of that dialogue.

CHAPTER 3

Anti-Judaism in the Fourth Gospel as a Theological Problem for Christian Interpreters

R. Alan Culpepper

Three decades ago, J. Louis Martyn proposed that the Gospel of John, especially John 9, is a two-level drama: on one level it describes Jesus' conflict with the Jewish authorities and on the other it reflects a conflict between the Johannine community and the synagogue at the time the Gospel was written.[1] Various features of Martyn's interpretation have been widely debated: the applicability of his two-level reading to other parts of the Gospel, the relationship between John 9:22 and the *birkat ha-minim* (or "blessing against the heretics," adopted at Yabneh),[2] whether John was written primarily to appeal to Jews and "secret believers" who remained in the synagogue or to encourage the community of believers, and whether the conflict with the synagogue was the primary concern at the time the Gospel was written or already lay in the community's past.[3] Although specific points continue to be debated, it is widely agreed that the Fourth Gospel reflects an intense and apparently violent conflict between Jews and Johannine Christians.[4] Joachim

1. J. L. Martyn, *History and Theology in the Fourth Gospel* (New York, 1968). A decade earlier T. C. Smith, *Jesus in the Gospel of John* (Nashville, 1959), p. vi, argued that "at a time after A.D. 70, when the antagonism of Jews to Christians had become acute, when the Jews were settling down more firmly than ever in the Torah, and when it was difficult to appeal to them with any other salvation than mitzvah salvation, a great Jewish Christian, the Evangelist, recognizing the desperate situation of the Jews wrote a Gospel designed to prove convincingly that Jesus was the Messiah, the Son of God."

2. See the careful study by W. Horbury, "The Benediction of the Minim and Early Jewish-Christian Controversy," *JTS* 33 (1982): 19–61, especially p. 52; and R. Kimelman, "'Birkat Ha-Minim' and the Lack of Evidence for an Anti-Christian Jewish Prayer in Late Antiquity," in E. P. Sanders et al., eds., *Jewish and Christian Self-Definition* (London, 1981), vol. 2, pp. 226–44.

3. P. N. Anderson, *The Christology of the Fourth Gospel: Its Unity and Disunity in the Light of John 6* (WUNT 2. Reihe 78; Tübingen, 1996), p. 218: "J. L. Martyn is correct to argue that this debate must have been especially intense within the Johannine Christianity, but he is wrong to assume this is the most acute debate at the time of the writing of John 6."

4. Dissenting voices keep the issue open. For example, M. Davies, *Rhetoric and Reference in the Fourth Gospel* (JSNTSup 69, Sheffield, 1992), p. 303, comments: "The Gospel does not give the impression that it is formed out of real disputes between Jews and Christians." J. Lieu, "Temple and Synagogue in John," *NTS* 45 (1999): 51–69, p. 51, agrees: "John's use of these narrative spatial-markers [synagogue, house, and Temple] . . . does not trace the separation of John's community from the synagogue, as often supposed."

Jeremias characterized the attitude of Jews toward non-Jews during this period as "uncompromisingly severe. . . . The dominant popular expectation eagerly awaited the day of divine vengeance, especially on Rome, and the final destruction of the Gentiles."[5]

Even a brief survey confirms the formative influence of this conflict on the composition of the Gospel. At least from the point of view of the Jews in the Gospel, the alternative is to follow either Moses or Jesus (9:28). Jesus implies that the Jews who were looking for a way to kill him are not Abraham's children (8:39–40), and they respond that they are not illegitimate (8:41). Jesus answers that the Jews are murderers and children of the devil (8:44). The Jews say that Jesus is a Samaritan and has a demon (8:48). Beyond the name-calling and language of invective, the Gospel describes a context in which steps are being taken to drive believers out of the synagogue (9:22). Some believe but will not confess Jesus openly "for fear of the Jews" (7:13; 19:38); parents even refer the authorities to their son (9:22–23); and believers gather behind locked doors "for fear of the Jews" (20:19). Jesus warns the disciples that "the world" will hate them just as it hated him (15:18–25), and "they will put you out of the synagogues" and "those who kill you will think that by doing so they are offering worship to God" (16:2). In response, Jesus washes the disciples' feet as a sign of his act of laying down his life for them and commands them to wash one another's feet. The footwashing was an example (ὑπόδειγμα—a term that designates an exemplary death).[6] Jesus' admonition "No one has greater love than this, to lay down one's life for one's friends" (15:13) takes on new meaning when understood in this context and in light of the community language at the close of 3 John: "The friends send you their greetings. Greet the friends there, each by name" (3 John 15).

The tragic conflict between the Johannine believers and the Jewish synagogue left an indelible mark on the Johannine community. While there is much that we do not know about the course of this conflict, the basic points are important and need to be recognized, difficult as they may be. Because of their new beliefs and practices, believers—those who would come to be known as Christians—were persecuted, put out of the synagogue, and perhaps even killed by the synagogue authorities. Separated from the synagogue, the Fourth Evangelist wrote a Gospel for the community of believers that appropriated much of their Jewish heritage and formulated aspects of their theology in response to this conflict.

5. J. Jeremias, *Jesus' Promise to the Nations* (Naperville, Ill., 1958), pp. 40–41.
6. See R. A. Culpepper, "The Johannine 'Hypodeigma': A Reading of John 13," *Semeia* 53 (1991): 133–52, especially pp. 142–43.

An Assessment of John's Anti-Judaism

The conflict between the Ἰουδαῖοι and Jesus and his followers in the Gospel has been interpreted in various ways. One approach has been to view John's anti-Jewish references as intra-Jewish polemic and set them in the context of references in the Old Testament, the Qumran scrolls, and the polemics employed by ancient schools.[7] The polemical language of the scrolls, especially the *Pesharim,* referring to the deeds of the "Wicked Priest," the corruption of the Temple, the "Man of Lies," and the "seekers after smooth things" is especially relevant. By contrast, differences between John and the hostile language of the scrolls should not be overlooked. Qumran carried on a debate with other Jewish groups while remaining within Judaism, whereas John stands early in the history of Christians who separated from Judaism. Nowhere in the scrolls do we find the authors writing about "the Jews" as a people apart from themselves or referring to the Torah as "your law" (John 8:17). John marks the decisive separation of Christians from Jews, at least in one locality. It hardens the breach that has already occurred, and it probably contributed to the ultimate separation between Judaism and Christianity. Because John views the separation from Judaism as a past event with radical social and theological consequences, its position in relation to Judaism can no longer be regarded as an intra-Jewish debate.[8]

Christian interpreters have been reluctant to recognize the anti-Jewish polemic of the Gospel of John.[9] By denying that John condemned Jews or Judaism, Christian interpreters sought to remove one of the foundations of anti-Jewish rhetoric. We can understand, therefore, when Bultmann interpreted the unbelieving Ἰουδαῖοι as "the representatives of unbelief (and thereby . . . of the unbelieving 'world' in general)."[10] Similarly, Raymond Brown observed: "For him [the Evangelist], the Jews belong to 'the world,' that is they are part of that division of men who are in dualistic opposition

7. See L. T. Johnson, "The New Testament's Anti-Jewish Slander and the Conventions of Ancient Polemic," *JBL* 108 (1989): 419–41.

8. Contra, for example: D. Rensberger, "Anti-Judaism and the Gospel of John," in W. R. Farmer, ed., *Anti-Judaism and the Gospels* (Harrisburg, Pa., 1999), pp. 120–57, especially p. 152; S. Motyer, *Your Father the Devil? A New Approach to John and 'the Jews'* (Carlisle, 1997); and S. Motyer, "Is John's Gospel Anti-Semitic?" *Themelios* 23:2 (1998): 1–4.

9. Portions of the following survey of interpretations of οἱ Ἰουδαῖοι in John and assessments of John's anti-Jewishness are drawn from my earlier essay, R. A. Culpepper, "The Gospel of John and the Jews," *RevExp* 84 (1987): 273–88, especially pp. 274–75 and 283–85, but this material is thoroughly rewritten and brought up to date here.

10. R. Bultmann, *The Gospel of John,* trans. G. R. Beasley-Murray, R. W. N. Hoare, and J. K. Riches (Philadelphia, 1971), p. 86.

to Jesus and refuse to come to him as the light. (John is not anti-Semitic; the evangelist is condemning not race or people but opposition to Jesus)."[11] If, for all their good intentions, these interpretations do not adequately recognize the extent of John's anti-Jewishness, they are at least correct in denying that the Gospel of John is in any sense racially anti-Semitic—the issue is strictly and solely religious.[12]

Other interpreters have diminished the force of John's anti-Jewishness by suggesting that the term οἱ Ἰουδαῖοι is more accurately translated by terms other than "the Jews." Many scholars have noted that whereas some references to the Ἰουδαῖοι in John are "neutral," describing Jewish religious customs, the land of Judaea, references to individuals, or "the King of the Jews," other references are "hostile" because they refer to a distinct group of people whose consistent characteristic is their hostility toward Jesus.[13] Urban C. von Wahlde surveyed ten previous studies and found that they agreed unanimously in identifying thirty-one instances of the hostile use of οἱ Ἰουδαῖοι in John.[14] On the basis of substantial support, von Wahlde adds seven other instances.[15] At least two of the ten studies agree in adding seven other verses to the list.[16] After reviewing these problematic verses, von Wahlde concludes that five represent the neutral use. John 8:31 and 10:19 present a mixture of features that von Wahlde

---

11. R. E. Brown, *The Gospel according to John* (AB 29, 29A; Garden City, N.Y., 1966), vol. 1, p. lxxii.

12. R. T. Fortna, *Theological Use of Locale in the Fourth Gospel* (ATR.SS 3; Evanston, Ill., 1974), p. 94. Similarly, J. N. Sevenster, *The Roots of Pagan Anti-Semitism in the Ancient World* (NovTSup 41; Leiden, 1975), p. 56, found not a single indication "that anti-Semitism in the ancient world used the theory of race as a weapon of attack." Instead, the basis for pagan anti-Semitism was the contempt of Jews for pagan religious practices, the autonomy and separation of Jewish communities, and the peculiarities of their religious practices (Sabbath observance, circumcision, and food laws).

13. J. C. O'Neill, "'The Jews' in the Fourth Gospel," *IBS* 18 (1996): 58–74, argues that the hostile references are scribal glosses. The Fourth Gospel presents "Jesus and the disciples as faithful Jews caught up in sharp dialogue with their fellow Jews" (p. 73). "Theories about John's Gospel that start from supposed hostility in that Gospel to the Jews as an organized body over against the church are probably based on a series of unfortunate late scribal corruptions" (p. 74).

14. U. C. von Wahlde, "The Johannine 'Jews': A Critical Survey," *NTS* 28 (1982): 33–60. The ten studies surveyed by von Wahlde are E. Grässer, "Die antijüdische Polemik im Johannesevangelium," *NTS* 11 (1964–65): 74–90; R. Schnackenburg, *The Gospel according to John,* trans. K. Smyth (New York, 1968), pp. 286–87; Fortna, *Theological Use of Locale*; R. G. Bratcher, "'The Jews' in the Gospel of John," *BiTr* 26 (1975): 401–9; R. Fuller, "The 'Jews' in the Fourth Gospel," *Dialog* 16 (1977): 31–37; G. J. Cuming, "The Jews in the Fourth Gospel," *ExpTim* 60 (1948–49): 290–92; G. Baum, *Is the New Testament Anti-Semitic? A Re-examination of the New Testament* (New York, 1965); Brown, *Gospel according to John,* vol. 1, pp. lxx–lxxiii; M. C. White, *The Identity and Function of Jews and Related Terms in the Fourth Gospel* (Ann Arbor, Mich., 1972); R. Leistner, *Antijudaismus im Johannesevangelium?* (TW 3; Bern–Frankfurt, 1974). These ten all identified the following as instances of the hostile use of οἱ Ἰουδαῖοι—1:19; 2:18, 20; 5:10, 15, 16, 18; 6:41, 52; 7:1, 11, 13, 15; 8:22, 48, 52, 57; 9:18, 22a, 22b; 10:24, 31, 33; 13:33; 18:14, 31, 36; 19:7, 31, 38; 20:19.

15. John 7:35; 8:31; 11:8; 18:12, 38; 19:12, 14. See the chart in von Wahlde, "Johannine 'Jews,'" pp. 39–40.

16. John 3:25; 8:31; 10:19; 11:54; 18:20; 19:20, 21a.

suggests may be the work of a redactor. The payoff comes when von Wahlde argues that, with the exception of John 6:41 and 52, all the hostile uses of οἱ Ἰουδαῖοι refer to the authorities, not to the common people. These are the only instances in which the Ἰουδαῖοι appear outside of Judaea, and von Wahlde attributes these verses to an author whose usage of the term was different from that of the Evangelist. Consequently, von Wahlde argues that "if the term refers only to authorities, it hardly provides evidence that the gospel is an attack on the attitudes of all Jews."[17] Malcolm Lowe restricts the meaning of οἱ Ἰουδαῖοι in a different way. Gathering evidence from ancient Jewish, Christian, and pagan writings, Lowe argues that while among "Gentile and Diaspora Jews the word had already a secondary religious meaning, . . . the primary meaning of Ἰουδαῖοι was geographical."[18] The term Ἰουδαῖοι designated "Judaeans" as opposed to people living in other areas. In the hostile references, therefore, the Ἰουδαῖοι are Judaeans, "either in references to the Judean population in general or (less frequently except after Jesus' arrest) to the Judean authorities."[19]

John Ashton responded to Lowe's work by distinguishing three related questions: (1) Who are the Ἰουδαῖοι? (2) What role or function do they fulfill in John? and (3) Why did the Evangelist regard them with such hostility?[20] Ashton reviews Lowe's thesis sympathetically, defending its plausibility but withholding judgment until more historical evidence is adduced. Groups of people were commonly identified by their place of origin or principal deity.[21] The religious and geographical meanings may, therefore, not have been sharply distinguished. Granting the difficulty of the references in John 6, Ashton accepts that "wherever Ἰουδαῖοι is used . . . these are natives or inhabitants of Judea. But to say this is to say very little: the nature and significance of the role they play is left undefined, and the reasons for assigning it to them unexplored."[22] Ashton perceptively lodges the complaint that neither Lowe nor von Wahlde distinguished between "referent" and "sense." The referent of Ἰουδαῖοι would be "natives or inhabitants of Judaea." By sense, Ashton

17. von Wahlde, "Johannine 'Jews,'" p. 33. See also R. Pereyra, "El significado de 'Ioudaioi' in el Evangelico de Juan," *Theologika* 3 (1988): 116–36; and G. Caron, "Exploring a Religious Dimension: The Johannine Jews," *SR* 24 (1995): 159–71.

18. M. Lowe, "Who Were the Ἰουδαῖοι?" *NovT* 18 (1976): 101–30, pp. 106–7. So also R. Pietrantonio, "Los 'Ioudaioi' en el Evangelico de Juan," *RB* 47 (1985): 27–41.

19. Lowe, "Who Were the Ἰουδαῖοι?" p. 128.

20. J. Ashton, "The Identity and Function of the 'Ioudaioi' in the Fourth Gospel," *NovT* 27 (1985): 40–75, p. 40.

21. Ibid., p. 45; W. A. Meeks, "'Am I a Jew?' Johannine Christianity and Judaism," in J. Neusner, ed., *Christianity, Judaism and Other Graeco-Roman Cults* (SJLA 12, 1; Leiden, 1975), p. 182.

22. Ashton, "Identity and Function," p. 55.

means the role the 'Ιουδαῖοι play in the Gospel narrative.[23] The distinction is essential.[24] In the Gospel, historical persons become characters in a narrative in which the characters take on varying degrees of symbolic significance and characterize different responses to Jesus.[25]

Even if 'Ιουδαῖοι once denoted Judaeans or Jewish authorities, the Gospel of John generalized and stereotyped those who rejected Jesus by its use of this term. Reginald Fuller succinctly attributes to the Evangelist three critical developments:

1. He altered the designation of Jesus' opponents in many places to the 'Ιουδαῖοι and introduced this new designation into his own composition.
2. He reinterpreted the issues between Jesus and his opponents in explicitly christological terms.
3. He gave the hostility between Jesus and his opponents a previously unparalleled bitterness.[26]

Perhaps even more important, the Gospel is the first document to draw a connection between "the Jews" who condemned Jesus and Jews known to the Christian community at a later time. By means of this transfer of hostility, effected by the two levels of meaning Martyn found in the Gospel, the Gospel creates a dangerous potential for anti-Semitism.

Douglas Hare defines the distinction between "anti-Judaism" and "anti-Semitism." Anti-Judaism is "that attitude which produces a clean break with Judaism theologically, either by thoroughly discrediting the Jewish tradition, as in Marcion's case, or by usurping the Jewish Bible and turning it against the Jews, as in the Epistle of Barnabas."[27] Similarly, Edward H. Flannery distinguished anti-Judaism, which is "purely a theological reality; it rejects Judaism as a way of salvation but not Jews as people," from anti-

23. Ibid., p. 57.
24. See R. A. Culpepper, *Anatomy of the Fourth Gospel: A Study in Literary Design* (Philadelphia, 1983), pp. 125–26.
25. See E. Krafft, "Die Personen des Johannesevangeliums," *EvT* 16 (1956): 18–32; R. F. Collins, "The Representative Figures of the Fourth Gospel," *DRev* 94 (1976): 26–46 and 95 (1976): 118–32; Culpepper, *Anatomy*, pp. 101–48; Davies, *Rhetoric and Reference*, especially pp. 290–315; D. A. Lee, *The Symbolic Narratives of the Fourth Gospel: The Interplay of Form and Meaning* (JSNTSup 95; Sheffield, 1994).
26. Fuller, "'Jews' in the Fourth Gospel," p. 35. So also J. T. Townsend, "The Gospel of John and the Jews," in A. Davies, ed., *Antisemitism and the Foundations of Christianity* (New York, 1979), pp. 72–97; and R. Kysar, "Anti-Semitism and the Gospel of John," in C. A. Evans and D. A. Hagner, eds., *Anti-Semitism and Early Christianity* (Minneapolis, 1993), pp. 113–27.
27. D. R. A. Hare, "Review of Three Recent Works on Anti-Semitism," *RelSRev* 21 (1976): 15–22, p. 16.

Semitism, "which must include a note of hatred or contempt of the Jewish people as such."[28] In *Faith and Fratricide,* a book that moved the discussion of anti-Judaism in the New Testament into a new era, Rosemary Radford Ruether prophetically declared, "There is no way to rid Christianity of its anti-Judaism, which constantly takes social expression in anti-Semitism, without grappling finally with its Christological hermeneutic itself"[29]—a challenge to which we turn in the second part of this essay. Norman Beck further refined the distinctions by identifying three types of anti-Jewish polemic in the New Testament: christological, which identifies Jesus with God; supersessionistic, which contends for the superiority of Christianity over Judaism; and defamatory, which is damaging to Jewish people and dehumanizing to Christians.[30]

These distinctions are useful in assessing the nature of anti-Judaism in the Gospel of John. Anti-Judaism may be implicit in confessions of the divinity of Jesus, but it is certainly not explicit or overt. Anti-Judaism becomes explicit, however, when the Gospel denies the continuing validity of Judaism. Christians can easily agree that defamation of Jews violates the spirit and ethic of the teachings of Jesus. The critical theological issues, therefore, revolve around the question of whether supersessionism, with its attendant rejection of Judaism, is essential to Christianity. The nuanced term *theological anti-Judaism* accurately describes the Fourth Gospel's language, tone, and attitude toward Jews and Judaism. Growing out of its historical context, the Fourth Gospel develops an anti-Jewish polemic motivated by theological concerns. In contrast, Janis E. Leibig and others who distinguish between the Fourth Gospel's intent and its effect rightly speak of the "anti-Semitic potential of the Fourth Gospel."[31] Its defamatory language fed hostility toward Jews and contributed to the development of anti-Semitism in later centuries. Indeed, Eldon Epp concludes that "the Fourth Gospel, more than any other book in the canonical body of Christian writings, is responsible for the frequent anti-Semitic expressions by Christians during the past eighteen or nineteen centuries."[32]

28. E. H. Flannery, "Anti-Judaism and Anti-Semitism: A Necessary Distinction," *JES* 10 (1973): 581–88, pp. 582–83.

29. R. R. Ruether, *Faith and Fratricide: The Theological Roots of Anti-Semitism* (New York, 1974), p. 116.

30. N. A. Beck, *Mature Christianity in the Twenty-first Century: The Recognition and Repudiation of the Anti-Jewish Polemic in the New Testament,* rev. ed. (New York, 1994), pp. 283–85.

31. J. E. Leibig, "John and 'the Jews': Theological Anti-Semitism in the Fourth Gospel," *JES* 20 (1983): 209–35, pp. 224–35.

32. E. J. Epp, "Anti-Semitism and the Popularity of the Fourth Gospel in Christianity," *CCARJ* 22 (1975): 35–57, p. 35, argues that "the attitude toward the Jews that finds expression in the Fourth Gospel . . . coacted with the extraordinary popularity of that gospel so as to encourage and to buttress anti-Semitic sentiments among Christians from the second-century C.E. until the present time."

In retrospect, the literature of the past two decades reflects a growing recognition of John's anti-Jewish polemic. Interpreters have moved from dismissing the problem (e.g., "Jesus and the disciples were all Jews" or "'The Jews' in John simply represent unbelief"), to minimizing it (e.g., "'The Jews' refers only to a certain group: Judaeans or the religious authorities"), to explaining it in terms of its historical context (e.g., "The Gospel of John reflects intra-Jewish polemic that was common among first-century Jewish groups and is no sharper than what we find elsewhere in Jewish writings"), to the confession that John is anti-Jewish in intent and anti-Semitic in its potential effect on later readers.

This sobering assessment of John's anti-Jewishness requires us to address a question that, to this point, we have been reluctant to voice: What influence, if any, does anti-Judaism in John have on its theology? Or, to sharpen an already disturbing question: Is Christian theology, to the degree that it is influenced by the Fourth Gospel, anti-Jewish in its inception?

A Reassessment of John's Theology in the Context of Its Anti-Jewish Polemic

To this point we have reviewed the historical context of the Gospel of John and its pervasive anti-Jewishness—ground that has been well traversed by others. Likewise, there are excellent surveys of John's theology, but they seldom hold it in dialogue with John's anti-Jewish polemic. The paradox that interpreters of the Fourth Gospel confront is, as C. K. Barrett put so succinctly, that "John is both Jewish and anti-Jewish,"[33] and as Wayne Meeks observed, "The Fourth Gospel is most anti-Jewish just at the points it is most Jewish."[34] This paradoxical situation can be recognized in each major area of John's theology. When we say that the Gospel is "Jewish," we mean that the Gospel originated in a context that was shaped by Judaism; the Evangelist sees the world and thinks in Jewish categories. The opposite of "anti-Jewish," therefore, would not be "Jewish" but "pro-Jewish." John is not anti-Jewish in a Marcionite sense; it affirms and appropriates the heritage of Israel. But it leaves no place for Judaism apart from Jesus. In John's dualism, all who reject Jesus are condemned, even those who believe in him, but secretly, and seek to remain in the synagogue.

At the outset, we should recognize that concentration on the "hostile" uses of οἱ Ἰουδαῖοι in John—though they are a clear indication of the

33. C. K. Barrett, *The Gospel of John and Judaism* (Philadelphia, London, 1975), p. 71.
34. Meeks, "Am I a Jew?" p. 172.

problem—does not adequately describe John's theological anti-Judaism. Paradoxically, both anti-Judaism and indebtedness to Judaism pervade the entire Gospel. In the separation and divorce between Christianity and Judaism, the Fourth Evangelist has gone through their common home and claimed all the valuables for Christianity: the witness of the Jewish scriptures, the significance of the Temple, the true meaning of the Jewish festivals, the authority of Moses, the instruction of Wisdom, self-understanding as "children of God," and the promise of salvation and resurrection to eternal life. By the end of the Gospel, therefore, the Jews "have no king but the emperor" (19:14–15; cf. 1:49). Nathanael is "truly an Israelite in whom there is no deceit" (1:47) because he comes to Jesus. "The true light . . . [that] was coming into the world" (1:9) was the revelation in Jesus. "True worshipers" worship "in spirit and truth" (4:23), not in Jerusalem or on Mount Gerizim. Jesus' flesh and blood are true food and drink. The true bread from heaven, therefore, was not the manna in the wilderness but the bread that Jesus gives. His judgment (i.e., his *mishphat,* משפט) is true, not that of "the Jews" (8:16), and he is "the true vine" (15:1), not Israel (cf. Psalm 80:8). On the one hand, the Johannine retention of so many meaningful Jewish features is the highest compliment that the daughter faith could pay to the parent faith.[35] On the other hand, apart from all that is fulfilled in Jesus, very little is left in Judaism. The Gospel of John, therefore, does not dispassionately set forth the truth of the Christian faith. It claims the fulfillment of Judaism, and in the process, it strips Judaism of the validity of its faith and practice.

Each of the following sections on John's Christology, doctrine of God, ecclesiology, and ethics develops a three-part argument: (1) the Jewishness of John's theology, (2) the influence of John's anti-Jewish polemic on its theology, and (3) the elements in John that deconstruct the influence of its anti-Jewish polemic on its theology.

Christology

Christology dominates the theology of the Fourth Gospel. Jesus is the central figure in the Gospel, and the Gospel clearly portrays Jesus in a way that sets the Gospel and its Christology apart from the other Gospels. The Jewishness of John's portrayal of Jesus is also clearly apparent. John draws heavily on the Wisdom tradition for the conceptual basis of its characterization

---

35. For this point I am indebted to W. E. Hull, whose response to an early draft of this essay was nearly as long as the essay itself and provided helpful correctives at a number of points.

of Jesus. As the Logos incarnate, Jesus is the one who was with God from the beginning and through whom the world was created (Prov. 8:22; Wisd. Sol. 9:1). Like Wisdom, Jesus is unique (μονογενής; John 1:18; 3:16; Wisd. Sol. 7:22). As wisdom incarnate Jesus also instructs the children of God and provides them with life.

The Gospel of John also uses the titles "Son of God" and "Son of Man" to characterize Jesus. Rather than explaining or justifying the confession "Son of God" by means of a birth narrative, John treats it as an outgrowth of Wisdom/Logos Christology. To put the matter sharply, Jesus did not become the Son of God by means of the virgin birth; he always was the Son of God. Although the title "Son of God" circulated elsewhere in early Christianity, quite separate from the Wisdom tradition and Logos Christology, John portrays a Son who was with the Father from the beginning and who does and says what the Father who sent him into the world gave him to do. Although the Jewish concept of the emissary (שליח, shaliah) charged with the authority of the sender no doubt lies in the background, in John the language of sending is closely tied to the portrayal of Jesus as the Son. Because the Son was sent by the Father, the Son can do nothing on his own authority (5:19). On the other hand, the Son does what the Father has given him to do. Like an apprentice, the Son does what he sees the Father doing, even raising the dead and giving life. A few verses later, the Son (i.e., Son of God) assumes the role of the expected Son of Man, judging the nations and raising the dead (5:25–27).

The distinctive feature of the thirteen references to the Son of Man in John is that they consistently deal with his descent to earth and his ascent to heaven (3:13; 6:62), his exaltation (3:14; 8:28; 12:34), and his glorification (12:23; 13:31). These are not unrelated; John presents a consistent picture of the Son of Man that is another facet of the Christology expressed by the Son of God sayings and the Wisdom/Logos Christology.

In the Wisdom tradition, Wisdom often speaks in the first person, but the figure of Wisdom does not use the "I am" formula. Nevertheless, the Wisdom tradition helps explain the use of the "I am" formula in John. When Jesus claims, "Very truly, I tell you, before Abraham was, I am" (John 8:58), the use of "I am" in the absolute sense has merged with the claim of preexistence in the prologue that arose from the influence of the Wisdom tradition on John's Logos Christology. In addition to the absolute "I am" sayings, John contains a series of "I am" sayings with complements. Most of the complements are drawn from the Old Testament, where they are often used as images for Israel. In the Gospel, these complements provide rudimentary images that further interpret Jesus' identity and functions.

None of the Synoptic parables appear in John, and the Johannine Jesus does not use parables to describe any reality beyond himself. Instead, the imagery of the Gospel serves a christological function also, and this imagery is thoroughly Jewish.

Jesus is the bread from heaven	Exod. 16:4, 15; Ps. 78:24
Jesus is the good shepherd	Ezek. 34; Ps. 23
Jesus is the true vine	Isa. 5:1–7; Ps. 80:8–13

Jesus not only speaks as Wisdom incarnate, but he continues to exercise the creative power of the preexistent Logos, changing water to wine, multiplying loaves, walking on the water, giving sight to the blind, and raising the dead. The signs that Jesus does are also fulfillments of the signs and wonders done by Moses, Elijah, and Elisha, or they develop prophecy and imagery rooted in the Hebrew scriptures:

John 2:1–11	changes water to wine	wine imagery: Eccl. 9:7; Zech. 10:6–7; Isa. 25:6; Joel 2:19, 24; 3:18; Amos 9:13
John 4:46–54	heals the official's son	1 Kings 17:21–24; 2 Kings 5:1–19
John 5:1–18	heals the lame	Isa. 35:6
John 6:1–15	feeds a multitude	Exod. 16; Num. 11; 2 Kings 4:42–44
John 6:16–21	walks on water	Job 9:8; Ps. 77:15–20
John 9:1–7	gives sight to the blind	2 Kings 6:17; Isa. 29:18; 35:5; 42:18; 61:1 (LXX)
John 11:38–44	raises the dead	1 Kings 17:17–24; Isa. 26:19

Other actions, if not actual signs, also fulfill an interpretive function in the Gospel:

John 2:13–22	drives the merchants out of the Temple	Zech. 14:21; Mal. 3:1; Ps. 69:9
John 12:12–19	enters Jerusalem riding on a donkey	Zech. 9:9; Ps. 118

In its conceptual basis (its use of Wisdom, Logos, preexistence, and fulfillment), its christological titles, its signs, and its "I am" sayings—all of its most distinctive features—the Christology of the Fourth Gospel is thoroughly Jewish. It is also disconcertingly anti-Jewish.[36] The influence of John's anti-Jewish polemic on the formulation of its Christology can be stated in three points, each more clearly anti-Jewish than the preceding one.

1. The Gospel of John advances two radically different claims: that Jesus was the Messiah who fulfilled the Jewish scriptures, and that apart from their fulfillment in Jesus, central elements of Jewish life and practice are invalid.

The statement that the Messiah came to "his own" and "his own" did not receive him (1:11) is not in and of itself anti-Jewish. To say that some Jews or Jewish religious leaders participated in the death of Jesus is not necessarily anti-Jewish. Neither is it anti-Jewish to say that Jewish scriptures and hopes for the Messiah were fulfilled in Jesus. Nevertheless, the axiom remains valid that the more Jewish the Christology, the more it is apt to be anti-Jewish. Claims of fulfillment easily mutate into claims of replacement, that is, that apart from its fulfillment in Jesus, Judaism is no longer valid.

Johannine scholars have often spoken of the "fulfillment and replacement" motif in John. Jesus fulfills and replaces the principal festivals. He is the prophet like Moses, the one who offers deliverance, and he is the true bread. Therefore, if the Jews believed Moses, they would believe Jesus (5:46). He is the new Temple (2:21); therefore the hour has come when the true worshipers will worship the Father in spirit and in truth (4:23), and neither on Mount Gerizim nor in Jerusalem (4:21).

The effect of this fulfillment/replacement motif is that the Gospel declares, by means of various specific illustrations, that Judaism apart from its fulfillment in Jesus has been rendered invalid by his coming. The scriptures that the Jews studied testify on Jesus' behalf (5:39), but the Torah is now "your law" (8:17). Jesus and the disciples never observe ritual purity. Food laws are not discussed. When Jesus goes to the Temple, it is to instruct his followers, not to offer sacrifices. The synagogue is mentioned only in passing (6:59; 18:20), and Sabbath observance is superseded by worship on the first day of the week (20:19, 26).

2. The Jews hope for life through faithfulness to the covenants with Abraham and Moses, yet no one can come to the Father except through Jesus (14:6).

The clearest evidence of the anti-Jewish polemic inherent in John's Christology is its claim of salvation exclusively through Jesus. Paradoxically,

---

36. M. de Jonge, "The Conflict between Jesus and the Jews, and the Radical Christology of the Fourth Gospel," *PRSt* 20 (1993): 341–55, argues (rightly, I believe) that "the Fourth Gospel's radical christology and its picture of the conflict between Jesus and the Jews are correlated. Both reflect the definitive separation between the group(s) of Johannine Christians and the local Jewish synagogue(s)" (p. 341).

this Christian exclusivism is rooted in Jewish exclusivism. For the Jews, loyalty to Yahweh made every other religion idolatrous and worthy only of reprobation.[37] For John, this exclusivism means that apart from confessing Jesus as the Messiah there is no hope for the Jews. The three principal covenants between God and the Jewish people were the Abrahamic covenant of sonship, the Mosaic covenant of deliverance and fidelity, and the Davidic covenant of kingship. Yet, by their actions, the Jews show that they are no longer children of Abraham (8:39–40). John claims that Jesus fulfills the role of Moses, that the Jews themselves do not keep the law (7:19), and that the Mosaic scriptures themselves testify to Jesus. Similarly, through his death, Jesus himself is exalted as the "King of the Jews" (19:19–22). Consequently, none of the covenantal bases for the Jews' relationship to God survive the coming of Jesus.

3. It is Jesus who uses the language of invective against the Jews, which means that another part of John's Christology is that Jesus is the one who condemned the Jews for their unbelief.

The higher the Christian claims for the authority of Jesus, the more serious it is that it is Jesus who declared that the Jews who did not believe in him were children of "the devil" (8:44). Inherent in the Christology of John, therefore, is the rejection and condemnation of the Jews as a religious group who maintain their life and practice while rejecting the messianic claims of Jesus. At this point, fulfillment that has become replacement all too easily leads to defamation. The principle that where John is most Jewish it is most anti-Jewish certainly applies, therefore, to its Christology.

The problem posed by the anti-Jewishness of John's Christology cannot easily be resolved precisely because the Christology is so Jewish. Core elements of John's characterization are at stake. Rejecting the Gospel's defamation of Jews may be a positive initial step, but it does not address the anti-Jewishness of John's supersessionism. One constructive alternative is to recognize that there are elements in the Gospel that deconstruct the anti-Jewishness of its Christology. Here we may take a page from current deconstructive criticism without necessarily subscribing to this school's view of texts and interpretation. In brief, deconstruction holds that texts do not yield to consistent, stable interpretations. In a text such as John, truth is often dialectical, and some elements of the text do not cohere neatly with the rest of it. Interpreters typically fill gaps and resolve tensions in order to produce a coherent interpretation, but there are always elements in the text that undermine the coherence of the interpreter's work and defiantly break

---

37. See R. Schwartz, *The Curse of Cain: The Violent Legacy of Monotheism* (Chicago, 1997).

free from the interpreter's grasp. Similarly, there are elements in John that undermine or deconstruct the anti-Jewishness of its Christology.

The most obvious deconstructive element is Jesus' affirmation that "salvation is from the Jews" (4:22). So contrary does it appear to the hostile references that pervade the Gospel that Bultmann declared it to be "completely or partially an editorial gloss. . . . It is not possible that the evangelist should have written it."[38] In the context of conversation with the Samaritan woman, Jesus affirms the historical primacy of Israel. The heritage and experience of Judaism are foundational to salvation. We can readily agree with Raymond Brown that this verse is a clear indication that John does not reject "the spiritual heritage of Judaism," and it is not a gloss.[39] The more difficult issue, however, is whether the next verse, "But the hour is coming, and is now here, when the true worshipers will worship the Father in spirit and in truth" (4:23), means that Judaism no longer has any special place, priority, or significance. Does the dawning of the new era in Jesus mean the end of the efficacy of Judaism? Or can the true worshipers, who worship the Father in spirit and in truth, come from Judaism as well?

The "but" (ἀλλά) at the beginning of 4:23 may imply a strong contrast to (1) the "neither . . . nor" in 4:21, to (2) the "you . . . we" of 4:22, or to (3) the statement that "salvation is from the Jews" at the end of 4:22. The first alternative can appeal to the repetition of "the hour is coming when" in 4:21 and 4:23. This interpretation can be used to argue that 4:22 is an aside or parenthetical comment, if not a later insertion or gloss. If we may judge from the omission of Luke 23:34 in some manuscripts, apparently by an anti-Jewish scribe, it is unlikely that a later scribe would have made such a pro-Jewish insertion. The third alternative is the weakest of the three, in spite of the fact that the "but" follows immediately after the end of 4:22. The best interpretation is the second: in the eschatological age that Jesus himself was ushering in, the divisions between worshipers and cults will be overcome. It will no longer matter that the Samaritans worship on Mount Gerizim while the Jews worship in Jerusalem, or that the Samaritans worship what they do not know while the Jews worship what they know. They will be able to worship together because cults and places of worship will no longer matter: all true worshipers will be able to worship in spirit and truth.

The preexistence of the Logos further deconstructs the anti-Jewishness of John's Christology. John 1:9, "The true light, which enlightens everyone, was coming into the world," is the most radically inclusive statement

38. Bultmann, *Gospel of John*, pp. 189–90 n. 6.
39. Brown, *Gospel according to John*, p. 172.

in the New Testament. Working since the creation as light enlightening every person, the Logos was active in the history of Israel and was confessed by her heroes: Abraham, Moses, and Isaiah. One who worships the God of Abraham, Isaac, and Jacob, therefore, worships the God revealed by the Logos, the same Logos that became flesh in Jesus. The Johannine Jesus who said, "No one comes to the Father except through me" (14:6), also said, "Before Abraham was, I am" (8:58). Christian claims for the exclusivity of salvation in Jesus, based on John 14:6, therefore do not do justice to John's testimony to the work of the cosmic Christ that is so distinctive of Johannine Christology.

Although John's view of the continuing validity of Judaism may be in some doubt, there is no doubt that John does not condemn the Jewish people as a people. Indeed, the Gospel holds forth the hope of universal salvation, at least in a general sense. Jesus is "the Lamb of God who takes away the sin of the world" (1:29), and when he is lifted up, he will draw all people to himself (12:32).

Providing us with at least a starting point for deconstructing its anti-Jewish *Tendenz,* therefore, the Gospel of John affirms the heritage of Israel as foundational to salvation, affirms that the Logos worked through Jews, and affirms a hope for the salvation of Jews along with all people.

Doctrine of God

There is the closest possible relationship between the Christology of the Gospel and its theology. We could not discuss the Christology of the Gospel apart from references to God, and any discussion of the Gospel's doctrine of God is necessarily an extension and outgrowth of its Christology. The Father sent Jesus, Jesus does only what the Father gives him to do and to say, and the Father bears witness to Jesus.

That the Johannine characterization of God is thoroughly Jewish hardly needs to be argued: God is the God of the Hebrew scriptures, God the Creator, the holy God, the delivering God, the judging God, and the gracious, loving God. By contrast, the anti-Judaism of John's doctrine of God is most critical at two points: (1) Do the Jews have a saving knowledge of God? and (2) Has God abrogated or nullified the covenants with Israel?

Jesus repeatedly challenges the Jews' contention that they know God (7:28–29; 8:19, 54–55; 15:21; 16:3; 17:25), saying that they do not know God because they do not know him (Jesus). In contrast, one who knows Jesus knows the Father and has eternal life (14:7; 17:3). In John, therefore, there is a conflict of concepts of God, a conflict of understandings of how

God is known (preeminently through Jesus or preeminently through the Torah), and a resulting conflict in commitments, self-understandings, and communities of faith. Jesus reveals a God who loves the world, including Samaritans and sinners (9:2–3, 34), and who values healing above strict observance of the Sabbath (5:16–17). The heart of the conflict between Jesus and the Jews in John, however, is less a matter of the nature and character of God than a difference in the locus of God's ultimate self-revelation. John says that no one has seen God, but Jesus has made God known (1:18). Consequently, Jesus' claims of preeminence over all prior revelation, claims that express the Christology of the church, are the point of contention.[40]

The claim for the validity of Jesus' revelation of the Father carries with it in John a rejection of the claims of those who say they know God but do not accept Jesus. Given the Logos Christology of the Gospel, we may suspect that, for John, there neither has been nor could be any revelation of God apart from the revelatory role of the Logos. Therefore, Jews who do not receive Jesus have missed the true revelation in their own tradition. In this way, John nullifies God's covenants with Israel, because the covenants have been superseded by the new basis for salvation through Jesus. Those who claim to be children of Abraham are not, because they do not receive God's promised Son. Those who claim to be disciples of Moses are not, because Moses bore witness to Jesus. And those who claim the covenant with the house of David ultimately avow no king but Caesar. To be precise, therefore, the Gospel of John does not say that God has abrogated the covenants but that the Jews have broken the covenants and therefore do not recognize Jesus as the Son of God. We may conclude from this discussion that the doctrine of God in the Fourth Gospel is thoroughly Jewish. It is also anti-Jewish in its claim that the revelation of Jesus supersedes not only the revelation of God in Israel but also God's covenants with Israel, so that salvation now requires believing that Jesus is the Christ, the Son of God (20:30–31).

Elements in the Gospel that deconstruct the anti-Jewishness of its doctrine of God are not readily apparent because most of what the Gospel says about God is a part of its characterization of Jesus. Two elements of John's Christology may be useful, however, in a theological critique of the influence of its anti-Jewish polemic on its view of God. First, John is distinctive among the Gospels in asserting the preexistence of Jesus as the Logos that was with God and was God (1:1); and second, John is distinctive in emphasizing incarnation in contrast to atonement. The incarnation, therefore, is

40. See Culpepper, *Anatomy,* p. 114.

a revelation of the redemptive love of God that has always been embodied in God's overtures toward Israel. The incarnation makes public and visible to the whole world what was concealed, or only partially revealed, in the heritage of Israel. The absence of any clear doctrine of atonement in the Johannine passion narrative becomes therefore all the more significant as John shades toward locating the salvific importance of Jesus in the incarnation rather than in his death.[41] While this balancing of atoning death with incarnate life can easily be misinterpreted, it nevertheless provides a secure basis for emphasizing that what God was doing in Jesus, God had been doing all along in the history of Israel. The God revealed in the incarnation, therefore, is the same God who called Abraham, Moses, and the prophets to faith and fidelity.

Ecclesiology

As with Christology and the doctrine of God, the Johannine doctrine of the church is both Jewish and anti-Jewish. Although the term ἐκκλησία does not occur in John, the church is reflected in the role of the disciples and in significant images and metaphors. The presiding metaphors for believers are relational, indeed familial.[42]

Two that appear in the prologue call for special attention. Some of the initial information given to the reader is the report that Jesus came to "his own," but his own did not receive him. Raymond Brown found here a reference to Exod. 19:5, "you shall be my treasured possession out of all the peoples."[43] The irony of the Gospel is that the Jewish Messiah came to Israel, but Israel did not receive him. Later, when Jesus gathers with his disciples at the beginning of John 13, the Evangelist reports that Jesus, "having loved his own who were in the world, . . . loved them to the end" (13:1). Because the Jews did not receive Jesus, they forfeited their place as "his own," and except in one aside (13:33), the Ἰουδαῖοι are not mentioned at all in John 13–17. The dualism here is between the disciples and the world, leading the reader to infer that because "his own" are now the disciples, the Jews are part of "the world." Other occurrences of τα ἰδία ("his own") in the Gospel seem to resonate with this technical use of the term as a reference to the community of believers. The shepherd leads "his

41. See R. A. Culpepper, "The Theology of the Johannine Passion Narrative: John 19:16b–30," *Neot* 31 (1997): 25–41.

42. See J. G. van der Watt, *Family of the King: Dynamics of Metaphor in the Gospel according to John* (Biblical Interpretation Series 47; Leiden, 2000).

43. Brown, *Gospel according to John*, 10.

own" out of the sheepfold (10:4), and the world loves its own just as Jesus loves those who are his own (15:19).

Similarly, the Gospel of John appropriates the phrase "the children of God" (1:12; 11:52) as a self-designation for the church. Although the phrase τέκνα Θεοῦ ("children of God") does not occur in the Hebrew scriptures, the concept is well established in relation to both the Davidic line and Israel as a whole. The relationship is conceived of in legal and moral, rather than primarily physical, terms and carries with it the obligations and promises of the covenants with Abraham, Moses, and David. Israel, like a child to its natural father, was to be subject to God, to receive his teaching, and to enjoy his lovingkindness. By claiming the designation τέκνα Θεοῦ, the Johannine community was identifying itself (and, perhaps more broadly, all Christianity) as the heir to a role and standing that Israel had abdicated by her failure to receive the Son of God.[44] Other metaphors and images of the church in John are also metaphors that were applied to Israel. Jesus is the good shepherd, and the disciples, who hear his voice, are his sheep (10:1–18, 26–27; 21:15–18; cf. Ezekiel 34; Num. 27:16–17). Jesus is the vine and the disciples are the branches (15:1–8; cf. Ps. 80:8–18; Isa. 5:1–7; 27:2–6).

At the same time that John's terms and metaphors for the church are thoroughly Jewish, they are decidedly anti-Jewish in that the church has taken the place of Israel as the heir to the promises made to Israel. The ecclesiology of the Gospel of John was molded in its conflict with the synagogue. As a result, the church is composed of those who are now ἀποσυνάγωγος ("out of the synagogue"). It is estranged from both the synagogue and the world, and hence the sectarian character of the Johannine community has been much discussed.

In this area also, therefore, it is evident that John's theology has been significantly shaped by its anti-Jewish polemic. The believers left or were driven out of the synagogue, carried with them terms and metaphors drawn from the Hebrew scriptures, appropriated these for their self-understanding, and defined themselves over against both the Jews and the world.

The Jewishness of John's images and metaphors for the church may also be turned deconstructively to undermine the anti-Jewishness of John's ecclesiology. If the church is the community of "his own" and "the children of God," then Gentile believers now belong to a community that began with and includes the Israelite "children of God." And if a new κοινωνία

---

44. These comments are drawn from summary statements in R. A. Culpepper, "The Pivot of John's Prologue," *NTS* 27 (1980): 1–31, which contains a full survey of the background of τέκνα Θεοῦ.

can be built on this shared experience of God's love as it has been revealed in the history of Israel and in the life of Jesus, then we may finally be able to bridge the chasm that has developed between Judaism and Christianity.

Ethics

The Gospel of John is distinctive in that it gives so little attention to specific ethical teachings. There is nothing in John like the Sermon on the Mount in Matthew or the lists of virtues and vices in Paul. The elements of a theological ethic are nevertheless clear: a dualistic worldview, the "new" commandment to love one another, and the model of Jesus.

John's dualism is rooted in the Jewish distinction between good and evil, but like the dualism of the Qumran scrolls, it may have been sharpened by Persian influences.[45] The most distinctive influence, however, is christological. The revelation in Christ has divided humanity into two clear categories. There is no need to wait for a future judgment; John declares: "This is the judgment, that the light has come into the world, and people loved darkness rather than light because their deeds were evil" (3:19). To this point, John's dualism differs from the dualism found in the scrolls only in its emphasis that the judgment is already present. It also differs, of course, in that for John the coming of the light has occurred in the incarnation. Jesus is the light, and the more clearly that light is seen, the more it separates humanity into two categories: those who believe and those who do not. The consequences follow predictably. Because the Jews do not believe, they belong to the darkness, their deeds are evil, and they are children of the devil. In the conflict between the Johannine community and the Jewish synagogue, John's ethical dualism served as a useful polemic for contrasting the alternatives starkly, wiping out any middle ground, and forcing a decision between the two communities. John's language thereby becomes an anti-language, establishing the community of believers while invalidating the values and claims of the rival community. Norman Petersen's analysis of Johannine language confirms Wayne Meeks's principle that John is anti-Jewish precisely where it is most Jewish. Petersen observes:

> The critical factor in this anti-language proves to be the image of Moses maintained by his "disciples," for many of the key terms in John's characterization of Jesus are derived from key terms in the image of Moses against

45. See J. H. Charlesworth, "A Critical Comparison of the Dualism in 1QS 3.13–4.26 and the 'Dualism' Contained in the Gospel of John," in J. H. Charlesworth, ed., *John and the Dead Sea Scrolls* (London, 1972), pp. 76–106.

which John reacts. The anti-language is "anti-" because its terms are derived from the image and transformed in contrastive and anti-structural ways.[46]

Similarly, John has taken up the command to love, which is grounded in God's love, and used it to strengthen the solidarity of the Christian community over against the synagogue and the unbelieving world. B. Gerhardsson comments that "in the Johannine writings, love has become the only ethical theme of significance."[47] The love command in Lev. 19:18 takes the form of (1) the imperative, "You shall love"; (2) the object, "your neighbor"; and (3) a qualifier, "as yourself." The Johannine love command follows the same formula but with significant alterations: (1) the imperative (a subjunctive following an epexegetic ἵνα); (2) the object, "one another"; and (3) a qualifier, "as I have loved you" (13:34; 15:12). Christian love thereby becomes the distinguishing sign of the Johannine community.[48] In scope it is limited to the community, just as "love your neighbor" was originally limited to the community of Israel, but in its Johannine form, the Jews are now excluded from the scope of the command. The command to love is limited to love for others within the community of believers.

Although John stops short of the reciprocal command to "love all the sons of light, each according to his lot in the Council of God; and . . . hate all the sons of darkness, each according to his fault in the Vengeance of God" (1QS 1.9–11),[49] the Gospel uses the language of light and darkness as ethical imagery (1:5; 3:19; 8:12; 12:35, 46). First John also instructs the community not to love the world or the things of the world (1 John 2:15). Hence, although there is no command to hate the Jews, the obligation of love is limited to the community of believers, and there is no explicit command to love those who remain in the darkness (12:35–36, 46).

In the new command, we can also see another principle of Johannine ethics: the καθώς ("just as") principle. In John, καθώς introduces both analogy and authority, first for Jesus, then for his followers. Jesus does nothing on his own (5:30). He judges just as he hears (5:30); he speaks as the Father instructs him (8:28; 12:50); and he does what the Father instructs him to do (14:31). Just as the Father knows him and he knows the Father, so he knows his own and his own know him (10:15). Just as the Father has loved him, he has loved the disciples (15:9). Similarly, just as Jesus lives

---

46. N. R. Petersen, *The Gospel of John and the Sociology of Light: Language and Characterization in the Fourth Gospel* (Valley Forge, Pa., 1993), p. 5.

47. B. Gerhardsson, *The Ethos of the Bible,* trans. S. Westerholm (Philadelphia, 1981), p. 98.

48. See S. van Tilborg, *Imaginative Love in John* (Biblical Interpretation Series; Leiden, 1993).

49. A. Dupont-Sommer, *The Essene Writings from Qumran,* trans. G. Vermes (Cleveland, 1961), p. 73.

because of the Father, so whoever eats him will live because of him (6:57), and just as Jesus has kept his Father's commandments, so if the disciples keep Jesus' commandments they will abide in his love (15:10). The disciples are to be one, just as Jesus and the Father are one (17:11, 21, 22). Jesus is the example: just as he washes the disciples' feet, they are to wash one another's feet (13:15). Just as he is not of the world, so the disciples do not belong to the world (17:14, 16). Just as the Father has sent the Son, so Jesus sends the disciples into the world (17:18; 20:21). The καθώς principle also plays a significant role in 1 John: "whoever says, 'I abide in him,' ought to walk just as he walked" (2:6), "purify themselves, just as he is pure" (3:3), and do what is right, "just as he is righteous" (3:7). The principle that believers are to live as Jesus lived takes us back to the influence of the anti-Jewish polemic on the characterization of Jesus in the Gospel of John. It can even be interpreted as giving explicit warrant for believers to engage in equally hostile and vitriolic relationships with Jews and condemn them for rejecting Jesus.

The result of our analysis of anti-Judaism and Johannine ethics is not encouraging. In each of its three major components—dualism, the love command, and the example of Jesus—the foundations of Johannine ethics are clearly anti-Jewish. The hostility between Jesus and the religious authorities of his day is thereby easily transmitted to Christian and Jewish communities today through unguarded interpretation of the Gospel of John for Christian theology and ethics, faith and practice.

If there is a deconstructive element in Johannine ethics, it may be found not in the example of Jesus but in the example of God, who sent his Son to "his own" (1:11). Moreover, an entirely different, and worthier, ethic emerges if we emphasize the inclusive love of God, who so loved "the world" that he sent his son (3:16). Such inclusive love would enlarge the circle of the command to love one another so that it includes the Jewish mothers and fathers, brothers and sisters of the Christian community.

Conclusion

This brief survey seems to confirm the observation that John is both thoroughly Jewish and trenchantly anti-Jewish. More to the point, the Fourth Gospel's anti-Jewish polemic played a significant role in shaping its theology and ethics. Anti-Judaism, however, is both an integral part of Johannine theology and a discordant element within it. It is therefore jarring for most Christians when they realize how profound and pervasive John's anti-Judaism is.

The hermeneutical challenge for Christian interpreters is to find a way to interpret the Gospel as a document of faith for contemporary Christian communities that recognizes its indebtedness to Judaism and responds to its anti-Jewish polemic.[50] Education and careful translation of the Gospel are certainly part of the solution,[51] but because anti-Judaism has influenced the formation of John's theology, progress toward meeting the hermeneutical challenge will require a serious engagement with theological aspects of the problem also. We have suggested here that a reassessment of Christian (and specifically of Johannine) anti-Judaism can begin by recognizing the influence of both the Jewish heritage and anti-Jewish polemic on Johannine (and therefore Christian) theology and by reasserting elements of John's theology that are discordant with its anti-Judaism and serve to deconstruct it. This is only a first step, but as an old Chinese proverb says, "Even the longest journey begins with a single step."

50. A. Reinhartz, "A Nice Jewish Girl Reads the Gospel of John," *Semeia* 77 (1997): 177–93, constructively contrasts compliant, resistant, and sympathetic readings of the Gospel. See also the essays in F. F. Segovia, ed., *What Is John? Readers and Readings of the Fourth Gospel* (Atlanta, 1996).

51. See especially T. Pippin, "'For Fear of the Jews': Lying and Truth-Telling in Translating the Gospel of John," *Semeia* 76 (1996): 81–97.

CHAPTER 4

The Fourth Gospel and the Salvation of Israel:
An Appeal for a New Start

Stephen Motyer

The title of this essay is deliberately ambiguous. First, it picks up the concern of the editors of this book in their search for "a new theology of Jewish-Christian relations." Second, this contribution makes something of an appeal for a new start in our approach to the "anti-Judaism" of the Fourth Gospel by, third, arguing that the Fourth Gospel itself functioned as an "appeal for a new start," addressed to late-first-century Judaism in the aftermath of the destruction of the Temple.

The "new start" is highly desirable. For over thirty years now, since the publication of J. Louis Martyn's epoch-making *History and Theology in the Fourth Gospel*,[1] the dominant consensus in Johannine scholarship has been that the Gospel arose out of hostility between a Jewish-Christian group and its parent synagogue. While Martyn himself helpfully maintained, "Yet the Conversation Continues" between the sundered groups,[2] subsequent studies, taking his work further, have been more ready to assume a complete severance of relations and an entrenched hostility, with the Christian group expropriating the sacred texts, language, and festivals of Judaism and regarding unbelieving Jews as "of the devil."

If this picture is true, then as Christians today, we will have to live with the uncomfortable realization that one of our sacred texts implicitly commends intercommunity hostility, and we will have to resort to a *Sachkritik* that excises this aberration in the name of a more fundamental command to love. If we have to live with this, so be it. But a case for a new start can be made, and this contribution attempts to outline it.[3]

---

1. J. L. Martyn, *History and Theology in the Fourth Gospel* (New York, 1968; 2d ed., Nashville, 1979).
2. One of his chapter-headings; see ibid., pp. 78–88.
3. The substance of the argument of this contribution rests on my monograph: S. Motyer, *Your Father the Devil? A New Approach to John and 'the Jews'* (Carlisle, 1997)—summarizing the argument of the book and in some respects taking it forward.

The contribution falls into four parts. The first section outlines the exegetical method on which the case rests. The second examines aspects of the resonance of the text within late-first-century Judaism, especially with regard to the issues of Temple and cult. Then we turn to "the Jews" in the Gospel and ask how our understanding of their identity is affected by the case presented thus far. Finally, we reflect hermeneutically on the implications of the argument for a new start today.

The Fourth Gospel as "Received" and "Heard"

My argument rests on the central contention that, if attention is diverted from reconstructing authorial concerns or delineating the historical origins of the text and instead is refocused on receiver concerns and on the rhetorical impact of the Gospel within the setting of late-first-century Judaism, then a wholly new perspective on its "anti-Judaism" emerges.

What is the justification for this methodological refocusing? It could ride simply on the recent literary interest in reading strategies, for it is not difficult to combine a narrative-critical interest in the "implied reader" with a historical interest in the reception of the text at any particular period, including the period of its initial circulation, as several have attempted to argue recently.[4] A reader- rather than author-centered approach to the Gospels has recently gained impetus, however, from the case argued by Richard Bauckham and others in the 1998 volume (edited by Bauckham) *The Gospels for All Christians*.[5] In the lead essay, Bauckham challenges the long-held assumption that the Gospels were written for distinct communities.[6] He argues, first, that the genre of the Gospels as (closest to) Graeco-Roman βίοι would lead readers to expect a general presentation of Jesus rather than a narrative with a particular reference to a single community,[7] and second (and chiefly), that the early Christians did not inhabit isolated, enclosed communities but engaged in extensive travel and contact, particularly involving their leaders, and that this creates a presump-

---

4. See Motyer, *Your Father the Devil?* chap. 4; also S. Motyer, "Method in Fourth Gospel Studies: A Way Out of the Impasse?" *JSNT* 66 (1997): 27–44; and M. C. de Boer, "Narrative Criticism, Historical Criticism and the Gospel of John," *JSNT* 47 (1992): 35–48.

5. R. Bauckham, ed., *The Gospels for All Christians: Rethinking the Gospel Audiences* (Grand Rapids, 1998).

6. R. Bauckham, "For Whom Were Gospels Written?" in Baucham, ed., *Gospels for All Christians*, pp. 9–48.

7. Ibid., pp. 27–30.

tion that the Gospels were written for general circulation.[8] A series of supporting essays strengthen the case, particularly those by Loveday Alexander and Richard Burridge, arguing respectively that techniques of ancient book production and distribution make it highly unlikely that the Gospels could have been meant for anything other than a general audience, and that the redaction-critical approach to the Gospels, by reinforcing their relatedness to a *Sitz im Leben* within particular communities, has obscured their clear commonality with the Graeco-Roman βίοι, a genre of writing that focuses on the presentation of a single-figure subject to a wide audience.[9]

The contributors to *The Gospels for All Christians* recognize that their general case has particular relevance for the Fourth Gospel, where a community-focused reading has been so highly influential. Bauckham criticizes J. Louis Martyn's "classic" use of the *birkat ha-minim* as an explanatory key on the grounds that, even if the case for this is granted, it is remarkable that Martyn assumed he had made a case for a crucial event in the life of a single Christian community, rather than for "a general process that, if he is correct, must have been going on in many Diaspora cities where Jewish Christians had previously attended synagogue."[10] Burridge criticizes both Martyn and Raymond E. Brown for the confidence with which they read the history of the Johannine community out of the Christology of the Gospel.[11] And Stephen Barton criticizes Wayne Meeks's influential essay "The Man from Heaven in Johannine Sectarianism," which built on the work of Martyn, for the assumption that sociological insights into the Johannine community can simply be "read off" the history of the Johannine Jesus, and for exaggerating the extent to which the metaphors of the Fourth

---

8. Ibid., pp. 30–44.

9. L. Alexander, "Ancient Book Production and the Circulation of the Gospels," in Bauckham, ed., *Gospels for All Christians*, pp. 71–111; R. A. Burridge, "About People. By People. For People: Gospel Genre and Audiences," in Bauckham, ed., *Gospels for All Christians*, pp. 113–45. See also R. A. Burridge, *What Are the Gospels? A Comparison with Graeco-Roman Biography* (SNTSMS 70; Cambridge, 1992).

10. Bauckham, "For Whom?" p. 23. Martyn's specific proposal about the *birkat ha-minim* has long since failed to command general consent. In 1985, Wayne Meeks declared it "a red herring in Johannine research" (W. Meeks, "Breaking Away: Three New Testament Pictures of Christianity's Separation from the Jewish Communities," in J. Neusner and E. S. Frerichs, eds., *To See Ourselves as Others See Us: Christians, Jews, "Others" in Late Antiquity* [Chico, Calif., 1985], p. 102), although Pierre Grelot still makes prominent use of it in his study *Les juifs dans l'évangile selon Jean. Enquête historique et réflexion théologique* (Paris, 1995). Grelot shows little awareness of English-speaking scholarship and does not refer to William Horbury's influential study that undermined Martyn's case about the *birkat ha-minim* by revealing the uncertainty of the date and textual details of the changes to the text of the Eighteen Benedictions (W. Horbury, "The Benediction of the Minim and Early Jewish-Christian Controversy," *JTS* 33 [1982]: 19–61).

11. Burridge, "About People," pp. 117–18.

Gospel form a private semantic world that could not have communicated to non-Christian readers.[12]

These substantial criticisms of the community reference of the Fourth Gospel give extra, historical impetus to a reception-based style of interpretation, which has much to commend it in any case, irrespective of the rightness or wrongness of the case made by *The Gospels for All Christians*. This reception-based approach was foreshadowed nearly twenty years ago by J. D. G. Dunn (though not described in these terms at the time), in his essay "Let John Be John," the significance of which has not been fully recognized or exploited.[13] Dunn argued that the key to the interpretation of the Fourth Gospel was to give it its proper historical location, thus avoiding the errors that arise from reading it against too late a setting, as a contribution to Nicene theology, or against too broad an environment, as a "stepping stone towards Gnosticism"[14] planted in a wide Hellenistic river, or against too early a background, judging its value simply by its faithfulness to the historical Jesus and the Gospel traditions. Instead, John must be allowed to settle and be read in its natural environment, which Dunn takes to be simply "the context of late first century Judaism."[15]

To read John in this context, Dunn proposes a method that involves taking a "preliminary fix" on the Gospel by looking for the "points of sensitivity . . . , the points at which an effort is evidently being made to clarify some confusion or to counter opposing views."[16] This method has something in common with that adopted by J. Louis Martyn in *History and Theology in the Fourth Gospel*, where he confesses how certain elements of the Johannine text became highlighted for him when he spotted correspondences with the Jewish background, most notably with the *birkat ha-minim*.[17] Rather than seek detailed references of this sort, however, a process fraught with the danger that attends all "mirror-reading," Dunn seeks to let the "points of sensitivity" emerge as the text is held up against the broad background of late-first-century Judaism, in all its complexity. He focuses on the Christology of the Gospel and attempts to see how this would have been a focus of dispute, particularly in the light of the mystical and apocalyptic traditions in this period. Then, having taken his preliminary fix, he returns to the Gospel

12. S. Barton, "Can We Identify the Gospel Audiences?" in Bauckham, ed., *Gospels for All Christians*, pp. 173–94 (here pp. 189–93, referring to W. A. Meeks, "The Man from Heaven in Johannine Sectarianism," *JBL* 91 [1972]: 44–72).

13. J. D. G. Dunn, "Let John Be John: A Gospel for Its Time," in P. Stuhlmacher, ed., *Das Evangelium und die Evangelien. Vorträge vom Tübinger Symposium 1982* (WUNT 28; Tübingen, 1983), pp. 309–39.

14. Ibid., p. 312.

15. Ibid., p. 318.

16. Ibid.

17. Martyn, *History and Theology*, p. xii.

for a closer look at the text, to see to what extent the wider narratives are il-lumined by the "location" he has proposed.[18]

This method contains much promise, and I believe that a fuller and more fruitful application of it is possible than Dunn is able to deliver within the confines of his essay.[19] The choice of late-first-century Judaism as the in-terpretative matrix hardly needs justification, in the light of the broad con-sensus that, in spite of its anti-Jewish features, the Fourth Gospel remains the most Jewish of the Gospels.[20] The distinctive features of this approach, in addition to the breadth of the proposed context noted above, are:

1. its focus on the hearing or reception of the text, rather than on its purpose or formation. It does not ask, 'How and why was this text written?' but 'How would it have been heard in its native setting?';

2. its open-endedness about who might have been doing this "hearing." By setting the Gospel against this broad background, the readership is left unspecified. It is not limited to a particular "community." In this respect, Dunn anticipates the argument and main conclusion of the essays in *The Gospels for All Christians.*;

3. its inductive quality. It allows the text to suggest its own "points of sensitivity" when read against the proposed background and allows these together to form (if possible) a coherent picture, before the rest of the Gospel is drawn in. In theory, the wider text can then falsify or confirm the overall proposals simply by their "fit."

When we apply this method to the Fourth Gospel, what emerges? For the purposes of this contribution, I explore two such points of sensitivity: (1) the emphasis on the Temple and the festivals, and (2) the prominence given to "the Jews" in the narrative. The second will lead naturally into our concluding reflections on how this approach enables us to reshape our understanding of the anti-Judaism of the Fourth Gospel.[21]

18. Dunn, "Let John Be John," pp. 325ff. The dangers of "mirror-reading" are well explored by J. M. G. Barclay, "Mirror-Reading a Polemical Letter: Galatians as a Test Case," *JSNT* 31 (1987): 73–93. Barclay helpfully formulates guidelines that apply fruitfully to the Fourth Gospel, specifying empha-sis, frequency, and unfamiliarity (the odd or surprising).

19. I have attempted to work this through in Motyer, *Your Father the Devil?*

20. One of the clearest indications of the overall rightness of the "Bauckham approach" (if we may call it that) is the way in which it can explain the long-observed conundrum posed by the juxtaposi-tion of explanations of the simplest Jewish terms and customs (e.g., 1:38, 41; 19:40) alongside unex-plained references to quite abstruse or complex Jewish phenomena, such as the title "Son of man" and the allusions to details of the Tabernacles ceremonies. The inconsistency of treatment points to an awareness of great potential variety in the readership.

21. Interestingly, neither of these is identified as a point of sensitivity by Dunn. He mentions par-ticularly John's "Son of God" Christology and the engagement with issues of revelation against the back-ground of the first-century Jewish interest in apocalyptic and *merkabah* mysticism.

The Gospel's Interest in the Temple and the Festivals

The Fourth Gospel's distinctive interest in the Temple and the festivals has often been noted. But far less often has this interest been brought into connection with the destruction of the Temple and the loss of the pilgrim festivals in 70 C.E.[22]

We suffer from historical longsightedness with regard to the period after 70. Viewing it from a longer-term perspective, we tend to read this period under the rubric "beginnings of rabbinic Judaism" and give prominence to the work of the Yabneh academy, which was clearly so significant for later Judaism. From this perspective, the significance of the destruction of the Temple is reduced to that of a vital historical catalyst. This was certainly its long-term significance; but for those who lived through this period, that description does not relate in the least to their experience. It was a period of immense suffering and deep confusion for Jews, both political and spiritual. Rival explanations of the disaster vied with rival proposals for the way ahead. In this period, supremely, the sheer variety of Judaisms is well illustratable.[23]

Against this background, there can be little doubt about how the Fourth Gospel would have been heard, both inside and outside the church. "Destroy this Temple, and in three days I will raise it up" (2:19): for Jewish readers anywhere, both Christian and not, these words could not fail to evoke the dreadful events surrounding the destruction of the Temple. Tragicomic irony is allied to an arresting expression of hope, which is immediately interpreted by the Evangelist so that it does not remain obscure. Jesus is presented as the rebuilt Temple (2:19), who had already played out the drama of destruction and rebuilding in his own body long before the house for which he was zealous unto death (2:17) was actually destroyed. The Evangelist advances the story of the "cleansing of the Temple" to the head of the narrative and attaches an interpretation to it, so that it can stand as a key to understanding the presentation of Jesus in the rest of the story. Raised from death, Jesus replaces the Temple as the focus of the wor-

---

22. The extent to which the relevance of the destruction of the Temple has been overlooked is staggering. For exceptions to the general rule, see G. A. Yee, *Jewish Feasts and the Gospel of John* (Zacchaeus Studies, New Testament; Wilmington, Del., 1989), pp. 25–26; C. R. Koester, *Symbolism in the Fourth Gospel: Meaning, Mystery, Community* (Minneapolis, 1995), pp. 81–85; and especially P. W. L. Walker, *Jesus and the Holy City: New Testament Perspectives on Jerusalem* (Grand Rapids, 1996), pp. 195–99.

23. I have tried to survey and summarize all this in Motyer, *Your Father the Devil?* pp. 74–104.

ship of God's people, so that the true significance of the festivals, especially the pilgrim ones, is found in him and not in Jerusalem.[24]

This presentation of Jesus as the essential Temple, the focus of the presence of God, the worship of Israel, and the atonement that brings them together, is at the heart of the Christology of the Fourth Gospel. After this identification with the Temple, Jesus is presented in turn as the one who incorporates the real meaning of the Sabbath (chapter 5), Passover (chapter 6), Tabernacles (chapters 7–10), and Dedication (chapters 10–12). The man born blind has pivotal significance in this process. Thrown out of the synagogue, he has worship restored to him as he bows before Jesus (9:38). He has been "led out" by the Shepherd of Israel (10:3). Pointedly, the verb ἐκβάλλειν is used both in 9:34, of his expulsion from the synagogue, and in 10:4, of the caring ministry of the shepherd.

The role played by Passover and Tabernacles in the narrative is widely recognized. But the thematic relevance of the festival of Dedication (10:22—the festival celebrating the rededication of the Temple in 164 B.C.E. after the Maccabean victory) is usually limited to the use of ἁγιάζειν in 10:36.[25] But the significance seems much greater than this. Not only do commentators generally miss the connection with 2:19–22 (Jesus is the renewed Temple), but they also fail to spot the evocative Maccabean imagery in 10:22–42 and in chapter 11. In seeking to take direct action against Jesus' blasphemy, the Jews stand in the tradition of the heroes who opposed Antiochus IV Epiphanes, the pagan king who also, being a man, made [himself] God (10:33). In contrast, Jesus is portrayed in Maccabean terms when Thomas declares "Let us also go, that we may die with him" (11:16); and as the story proceeds, the roles reverse. In their Maccabean zeal to preserve people and Temple from Antiochus's pagan successors (11:48), the Sanhedrin determine to kill Jesus; but it is his Maccabean self-sacrifice that will lead to the restoration of the people (11:51f.) and to their deliverance from a greater oppressor who already holds sway over them—death; signaled in the deliverance of Lazarus at the cost of Jesus' own life.

24. I maintain that the interpretive comment in 2:21 is meant to clarify the obscure saying about the raising of the Temple in 2:19, against John Ashton who argues that the whole passage is a "riddle" in which the uncomprehending Jews of verse 20 are identified with unbelieving Jews in the readers' environment (J. Ashton, *Understanding the Fourth Gospel* [Oxford, 1991], pp. 415–16.) But any unbelieving Jews, reading this narrative, would be left in no doubt that Jesus' resurrection is being made the equivalent of the rebuilding of the Temple. How this could be so, of course, remains unclear; but verse 22 assures readers that understanding on this point was not easy to reach and thus encourages them to persist with the narrative.

25. So, e.g., G. R. Beasley-Murray, *John* (WBC 36; Waco, Tex., 1987), pp. 173 and 177; R. E. Brown, *The Gospel according to John* (AB: London, 1966), p. 405.

Heard in the post-70 C.E. situation, this narrative would have resonated deeply with Jews, whether Christian or not. The irony of 11:48–52 is crushing: not just because the Sanhedrin's action against Jesus has manifestly failed—the Temple and nation have been destroyed—and not just because of Caiaphas's scornful "You know nothing at all!" his arrogant confidence made pathetic by events of which he is ignorant, but chiefly because, with a supreme twist, his role as high priest has been vindicated by words that had a much fuller meaning than he intended, so that in fact the Sanhedrin's action against Jesus has succeeded in saving the nation.[26] To "run with" this final irony, however, would be to accept the perspective of the Gospel that Jesus really is the rebuilt Temple in his own person, and attentive Jewish readers would certainly be aware of this. The message of the Gospel's Christology would not escape them.[27]

The implicit appeal of the narrative is carried forward in the next chapter. At the moment when many Jews are gathering in Jerusalem to purify themselves for Passover (11:55), Jesus becomes a focus of pilgrimage out of Jerusalem (12:9–11, 18–19), to the house in Bethany where he has undergone his own "purification" in preparation for his death (12:7). Rather than enter the Temple in the city, therefore, "the world has gone after him" (12:19)—a world consisting both of the Jews who seek him in Bethany and of the Greeks who arrive to see him (12:20). How will readers—especially Jews—respond to this? Having lost the Temple as one focus of pilgrimage, will they turn to the other and be "drawn," with the rest of the world, to the crucified Jesus (12:32)? The Jewish objection that a crucified man cannot be the Messiah is immediately voiced by "the crowd" (12:34),[28] and the reply provided by the narrative is not just Jesus' enigmatic saying in 12:35–36 but the following quotation from Isa. 53:1 (John 12:38). Scripture already speaks of a response of unbelief toward a dying messianic figure.

The narrative consistently disrupts the festivals and uses this disruption to further the presentation of Jesus. The process starts in chapter 5 with

26. See P. D. Duke, *Irony in the Fourth Gospel* (Atlanta, 1985), p. 87.

27. Because of passages like Ezekiel 37, there is a subliminal image connection between "resurrection" and "return from exile" that ties 11:52 into the preceding resurrection narrative. Lazarus thus becomes a token not just of Jesus' power to raise the dead but of the final restoration of Israel through the death of Jesus and through faith in him (11:25–27). Cf. N. T. Wright, *Jesus and the Victory of God* (London, 1996), pp. 255–56.

28. Here, as elsewhere in the Fourth Gospel, "the crowd" seems to be particularly the pilgrim crowd present in Jerusalem for a festival, rather than, more broadly, the *'am ha'aretz*. This reference is explicit in 12:12 and clearly implicit in 6:4–5 and 7:11–12, which creates a presumption that this is the reference of the term when we meet it within a "festival" narrative. This, in fact, covers all twenty occurrences of the term, except 11:42.

Jesus' high-handed flouting of the Sabbath Halakhah (possibly relating to the rabbinic distinction between private and public space). The flouting permits Jesus to claim that his relationship with God allows him to define what constitutes "work."

The process continues in chapter 6 with the Passover, which Jesus (in disobedience to the law)[29] does not attend. How will his disciples and "the crowd" respond to this? Will they stay with him in Galilee, where "living bread" is on offer, or leave him and continue up to Jerusalem for the memorial of the manna which "your ancestors ate . . . and they died" (6:49)? Some of the disciples leave (6:66). But the answer is clear for Peter: "Lord, to whom can we go? You have the words of eternal life. We have come to believe and know that you are the Holy One of God" (6:68f.). *Holy* is a word redolent with Temple and cult. So rather than go to Jerusalem, Peter and the rest of the Twelve remain with Jesus, who is now for them the way to eternal life, that which the cult had promised.

Similarly, Jesus refuses to attend Tabernacles (7:8). He goes to Jerusalem but does not participate in the festival,[30] until the last day, when he publicly appropriates the great Tabernacles images of water (7:37–39) and light (8:12) for himself. In the case of Dedication (10:22), W. D. Davies maintains that walking in Solomon's portico (10:23) implies that Jesus has distanced himself from the festival celebration.[31] And at the last Passover, not only does Jesus draw people out of Jerusalem, as we have seen, but when he eventually enters the city, events take place (12:13) that are typical not of Passover but of Tabernacles and strongly reminiscent of the founding of the festival of Dedication, as described in 2 Macc. 10:6–8.[32]

The purpose of all this disruption is clear: it serves the narrative program of presenting Jesus as the real meaning of the Temple and the cult— the one who fulfills and brings to reality their inner essence, understood on the basis of the founding scriptures that underlie and constitute them (except in the case of Dedication, where there are no scriptures but instead is a martyr tradition). Attention has often been drawn to this "replacement" or "substitution" motif in John but rarely to its historical resonance in the period after 70 C.E. Opinions were sharply divided in post-70 C.E.

---

29. Deut. 16:16; cf. Lev. 23:4–8.

30. This seems to be the significance of his going up "not publicly but . . . in secret" (7:10); see the discussion in Motyer, *Your Father the Devil?* pp. 125–27.

31. W. D. Davies, *The Gospel and the Land: Early Christianity and Jewish Territorial Doctrine* (Berkeley, 1974), pp. 292–93.

32. The waving of the *lulab,* the palm branch, and the crying of Ps. 118:25 are typical of Tabernacles. The original Dedication was likewise celebrated "in the manner of the festival of booths" (2 Macc. 10:6).

Judaism, ranging from those Jews who actually rejoiced in the destruction of the Temple, through those who accommodated themselves to its loss, to those who longed for its reconstruction, either miraculously by God or by human force.[33]

Within this spectrum, the Fourth Gospel stands alongside R. Johanan ben Zakkai, who maintained, according to the famous exchange with R. Joshua,[34] that it was not necessary to rebuild the Temple because "we have another atonement as effective as this." But whereas for R. Johanan ben Zakkai the alternative atonement was "deeds of loving-kindness," for the Fourth Gospel it is the death of Christ, whose body constitutes the locus of the glory of God (1:14), which is then destroyed and raised again, to become the place in which the people of God are reunited in worship and love.

This is the perspective on which the "Farewell Discourses" rest. Jesus is "the true vine" (15:1), where the description "true" could not fail to be heard as a polemical counterpart to Israel's self-conception as the "vine" of the Lord.[35] So the "branches," joined to him, together constitute the people among whom God makes his "dwelling" (ηονή, 14:23). These discourses are full of Temple imagery. James McCaffrey's detailed study fully explores the Temple symbolism of the opening sayings in 14:2–3[36] but does not carry that analysis through to a study of the same imagery in the following discourses. But clearly, (1) the "dwelling" motif in all its dimensions (including the indwelling of the Spirit/Wisdom of God); (2) the "purity" of the disciples through the word of Christ (15:2–3); (3) the emphasis on prayer offered in the name of Christ (14:13–14; 15:7; 16:23–26); (4) the language of "seeing," with its connotations of apocalyptic sight, especially associated with the Temple/sanctuary; and (5) particularly the "heavenly temple" connotations of the climactic 17:22–26[37] all build on the fundamental presentation of Jesus as the ηονή in whom God's glory rests and around whom Israel is "gathered into one" (11:52), with her worship restored and her identity secured.

These reflections illustrate our method. When internal literary prominence aligns itself naturally to prominent external events, a clear point of

---

33. See the survey in Motyer, *Your Father the Devil?* pp. 74–104.

34. *'Abot R. Nat.* A 4:5:2 (following Neusner's reference system): J. Neusner, *The Fathers according to Rabbi Nathan: An Analytical Translation and Explanation* (Atlanta, 1986), p. 41.

35. "Vine" is a frequent image for Israel in the literature of this period (as also in rabbinic literature: see Str-B 2:563f.): cf. Pseudo-Philo *Bib. Ant.* 12.8f.; 18.10; 23.12; 28.4; 30.4; 39.7; 4 Ezra 5:26; 2 Baruch 36:3ff., 39:7f. In *Bib. Ant.* 23.12 and 28.4f., it is associated with "flock" as a companion image.

36. "My father's house" (reminiscent of 2:16), "dwellings," "prepare a place," the unity implicit in "where I am, you will be also": J. McCaffrey, *The House with Many Rooms: The Temple Theme of John 14,2–3* (*AnBib*, 114; Rome, 1988).

37. I hope to explore all these in a further study.

sensitivity is revealed, and the impact of the text in its "home" environment becomes clear. Its relation to things Jewish suggests that, although readership could not be specified in advance, it would have been particularly among Jews, both Christian and non-Christian, that interest would have been sparked and copies requested, made, and distributed to friends and acquaintances.[38] In almost any community of Jews in the late first century, the text's relevance to the national and theological trauma associated with the destruction of the Temple would immediately have been clear— along with the essential "gospel" addressed to this need, namely, that Jesus Christ constitutes the theological essence of the Temple as the locus of the presence of God in Israel and the focus of the means of atonement, and that the company of those who believe in him experience that essential communion with God that the Temple symbolized, through the presence of the Paraclete in their midst.

Who, Then, Are "the Jews" in the Fourth Gospel?

The view that the Fourth Gospel could have functioned as I have proposed—to attract Jews to faith in Christ—has often been rejected on the ground of the hostility toward "the Jews" within the narrative. How could a narrative attract people by vilifying them? "The Jews" appear frequently (sixty-eight times, no less), notably as those who first "persecute" Jesus and plot to kill him (5:16–18), who call him demon-possessed (8:48) and throw his followers out of the synagogue (9:22), and who finally cry for his crucifixion (19:12). In return, Jesus calls them "from below," "of this world," "from your father the devil" (8:23, 44), and their identity with "the world" that hates both Christ and God is made clear (15:23–25).

It is easy to conclude from this hostile language that the Gospel is fundamentally anti-Semitic (defining *anti-Semitism* as the hatred of Jewish people on the ground of religion and race).[39] It would be far too quick a judgment if we simply identified this anti-Semitism with the later vile manifestations of hatred of Jews. At the very least, as many have noted, we are dealing with an argument within family, and with the use of language for which parallels can easily be found in the prophets and other Jewish

38. See the picture painted by Alexander in "Ancient Book Production," pp. 86–91, 99–105, drawing on the work of H. Y. Gamble, *Books and Readers in the Early Church: A History of Early Christian Texts* (New Haven, Conn.–London, 1995).

39. See the discussion of the definition of the term by G. Keith, *Hated without a Cause? A Survey of Anti-Semitism* (Carlisle, 1997), pp. 2–6. Keith provides an essential distinction between anti-Semitism (hatred of Jewish people) and anti-Judaism (theological disagreement with Jewish religion).

literature.[40] This seems to make it less serious: but if "hatred of Jewish persons" is the essence of anti-Semitism, then we must recognize that it can be exercised by Jews in reaction against their own race and past, and this is precisely the situation envisaged by the standard reconstruction of the Gospel's origins.

Various interpretive strategies have been adopted to limit the damage.[41] The chief strategy is to limit the reference of the term. If *the Jews* refers not to all who claim allegiance to Judaism (in whatever form) but to a smaller group within that broad definition, then the reason for the hostility cannot be simply Jewish religion and race. I suggest below that this is fundamentally the right approach, but there is currently no agreement about the right limitation of reference.

One of the most popular strategies is to identify "the Jews" as the Jewish authorities.[42] The comparison of 18:14 with 11:47–53 and the role of "the Jews" in 19:12–15 make it clear that there is at least overlap between them and the Sanhedrin. But we need to be cautious about suggesting a simple restriction of reference. There are clearly many references to "Jews" who are not leading Pharisees or members of the Jerusalem elite (e.g., 6:41–42; 11:31; 12:11), and the term is certainly sometimes used with a broad ethnic/religious denotation (e.g., 4:22; 11:55; 18:20).

Alternatively, several have defended the translation "the Judaeans" as a way of limiting the reference.[43] And again, the clear connection between "Judaea" and "the Jews" in 11:7–8 suggests that there is some truth in this view. But the fundamentally religious, rather than geographic, connotations of the term; the Galilean "Jews" in 6:41–42; and the broad usage noted above give pause before accepting a simple retranslation of the term.

Another strategy dehistoricizes the term, treating it as a blanket, catch-all expression with no exact referent, functioning in the narrative as a way of personifying the world's rejection of Christ.[44] This view can only rest on a prior judgment that, within a late-first-century Jewish environment, the Johannine "Jews" would have no clear referent, and this (I suggest) is highly questionable. But even if this were the case, the approach leaves us

---

40. See L. T. Johnson, "The New Testament's Anti-Jewish Slander and the Conventions of Ancient Polemic," *JBL* 108 (1989): 419–41. Even John 8:44 can be paralleled, for instance in *T. Dan* 5:6, "your ruler is Satan."

41. There is a survey and discussion of the options in Motyer, *Your Father the Devil?* pp. 46–57.

42. Most notably U. C. von Wahlde, "The Johannine 'Jews': A Critical Survey," *NTS* 28 (1982): 33–60.

43. Most notably M. Lowe, "Who Were the Ἰουδαῖοι'?" *NovT* 18 (1976): 101–30.

44. So, most notably, R. T. Fortna, "Theological Use of Locale in the Fourth Gospel," ATR.SS 3 (1974): 58–94, building on Bultmann's treatment of "the Jews" as "representatives of unbelief" (R. Bultmann, *The Gospel of John: A Commentary* [Oxford, 1971], pp. 86–87).

with our theological problem intact: for Jews can, with full justification, object to their blanket characterization as representatives of the world's rebellion against God.

I believe that the reception-based interpretive strategy we have employed helps us forward here. The first step is to recognize that the portrayal of "the Jews" is much more nuanced than is often allowed. It is not uniformly negative. In chapters 11–12 they are sympathetically pictured, coming to comfort Mary and Martha (11:19, 31—although a few verses earlier "the Jews" were trying to stone Jesus, 11:8), commenting warmly on Jesus' love for Lazarus (11:36), accepting that he really had opened the blind man's eyes (11:37), believing in him after the miracle (11:45), and welcoming him ecstatically into Jerusalem (12:9, 12f.).

Supremely, on the positive side of the picture, we have the remarkable confession on the lips of Jesus in 4:22 that "we worship what we know, for salvation is from the Jews." Since the whole point of chapter 4 is to create a dramatic platform for the Samaritan confession that Jesus is "the Savior of the world" (4:42), this originating of salvation from "the Jews" and the "we" that joins Jesus to the Jews here are striking indeed. They attest the Gospel's own awareness not just of the varieties of response to be found among "the Jews" but also of the foundational way in which the Jerusalem-centered issues of Temple, cult, Torah, and people feed into the salvation brought by Jesus. In 4:22, "the Jews" stand for all of that.

Of course, there is also irony in the statement that "salvation is from the Jews." The preposition ἐκ is unnecessary here if a statement of origin is all that is meant. Jesus has just withdrawn from Judaea, having experienced some success in the Judaean countryside (3:22) but not enough to disqualify the overall judgment that "no one accepts his testimony" (3:32). Nicodemus remained pointedly silent. In a moment, Jesus will testify that a prophet is not honored in his own πατρίς—meaning, I am sure, Judaea (4:44). So salvation is "from" the Jews also in the Acts sense, in that because the Jews have turned it down, it goes to others who will welcome it—in this case, first the Samaritans, then the Galileans (4:45).[45]

Nonetheless, Jesus persists in his ministry among "the Jews," returning to Jerusalem on at least three separate occasions after this point in the narrative. "Many" Jews believe in him at his final Passover (12:11), but "the Pharisees" bewail this fact (12:19), and the Evangelist's overall judgment is that "they" did not believe in him (12:37): here "they" seems to encompass

45. Note the pointed summary in 4:54, ἐλθὼν ἐκ τῆς Ἰουδαίας εἰς τὴν Γαλιλαίαν.

the generality of the crowd (12:34), the Jews, and the Pharisees. From then onward, the portrayal of "the Jews" is as uniformly hostile to Jesus.

Within the setting of late-first-century Judaism, would the Johannine usage of "the Jews" have appeared as mixed and confusing as at first sight it seems, or would a clear reference have been apparent? I concur with the view defended by John Ashton, proposed before him by (among others) Günter Reim and Wayne Meeks,[46] that "the Jews" do indeed have a natural referent, namely, the scrupulous adherents of the religion of Judaea, those especially associated with the life of the Temple before 70 C.E., who were most particular about Temple purity and all that went with it, and who, after the appalling loss of the Temple, by which they were especially affected, became leading lights of the movement that reemphasized a scrupulous Torah-centered lifestyle as the essential response to the disaster. Such Jews, of course, were around in abundance at the time of Jesus, but their religion had to re-form itself radically after 70.

While οἱ Ἰουδαῖοι could have a broad ethnic/religious reference, within the spread of "Judaisms" in the late first century the term could also designate this particular sort of Judaism, and the geographic connotations of the term make this easier. Josephus uses the term to refer either to "the Jews" in a general sense or to the inhabitants of Judaea. And although he does not use the term (as far as I can tell) to refer to the religious of Judaea in the sense proposed here, his descriptions of the Pharisees match what we have in mind (while making allowance for his adjustments to bring them into line with Greek norms).[47] Paul uses the term with exactly the reference we propose, in 1 Thess. 2:14–16. And although his description is concerned, negatively, with their persecution of Jesus and the churches in Judaea, we can read between the lines and discern the shape of his own preconversion history as a "Hebrew born of Hebrews; as to the law, a Pharisee" (Phil. 3:5, cf. Gal. 1:14). The Lukan portrayal of Paul as "a Jew" sent to Jerusalem, perhaps at quite an early age, to be "educated strictly according to our ancestral law" (Acts 22:3) fits with this sense of a particular religion that could not really be practiced in the Diaspora but only in the vicinity of the Temple.

Giving "the Jews" of the Fourth Gospel this reference allows the term the semantic overlap with "the Judaeans," the Pharisees, and the ruling elite

---

46. Ashton, *Understanding*, pp. 152–59; G. Reim, *Studien zum alttestamentlichen Hintergrund des Johannesevangeliums* (SNTSMS 22; Cambridge, 1974), pp. 142–43; W. A. Meeks, "'Am I a Jew?' Johannine Christianity and Judaism," in J. Neusner, ed., *Christianity, Judaism and Other Graeco-Roman Cults,* FS Morton Smith (SJLA 12; Leiden, 1975), vol. 1, p. 182.

47. E.g., Josephus *Ant.* 17:41; 18:12–15; *Life* 191.

that we have observed but also a distinct denotation that would have been clear, I believe, to any Jew or indeed well-informed Gentile of the period. And if, as is likely, Diaspora Jewish readers did not identify or sympathize with this type of Judaism—perhaps even blaming it for fomenting the Jewish War—then they might at least be open to sympathizing with the Jesus of the Fourth Gospel in his confrontation with "the Jews."

What about the hostility? Can the Fourth Gospel fairly be charged with hatred of these Judaean Jews who opposed Jesus and cried for his crucifixion? I believe the answer is no:

1. because of their dividedness. "The Jews" are not monochrome enemies of Jesus in the Fourth Gospel. Nicodemus, their "ruler" (3:1), is portrayed most sympathetically, commended for "coming to the light" (3:21), even if his faith falls short of that of the Samaritan woman. Similarly, the divisions in 9:16 and 10:19–21 sympathetically allow both positive and negative reactions to feature within the narrative, even though the narrative ultimately drives toward a positive response (20:28–31). One of the most moving exchanges in the Gospel is that between Jesus and the Pharisees in 9:40–41: these are Pharisees who are "with" Jesus,[48] not as critics but as puzzled learners. They are the "others" of 9:16b, who do not apparently object to Jesus' acceptance of worship from the man born blind and who ask anxiously if, in spite of all their learning, they are blind;

2. because of the positive portrayal of Jesus' Judaism. Jesus himself is identified as "a Jew" in 4:9 (cf. 4:22), and his portrayal in the Gospel, as we have seen, is consistently in terms of the great symbols and institutions so precious to "the Jews." The argument about Jesus' identity is carried on through the debate about the meaning of the scriptures.[49] The claim of the Gospel may well be deeply unacceptable to "the Jews" of the late first century, and indeed, of the twenty-first, because it involves a radical rereading of the events celebrated in the cult and of the covenant relationship expressed in and resting on the cult. But the starting point of this rereading is the recognition of Jesus as the prophet like Moses promised in Deut. 18:15, and the awareness, shared by all Jews in the late first century, that nothing could be the same again and that a radical new start of some sort was

---

48. μετ' αὐτοῦ, a phrase that elsewhere in the Gospel connotes discipleship or at least interested association: 6:66; 11:16; 12:17; 18:26.

49. To raise the issue of the use of the Old Testament in the Fourth Gospel is to touch on something beyond the scope of this contribution to deal with adequately.

inevitable. Into that theological vacuum, the Fourth Gospel projects the voice of the prophet like Moses;

3. because of the consistent appeal directed at these Jews. The Johannine Jesus is uncompromising. It is not enough to recognize him as a prophet, even as *the* prophet (3:2; 6:14; 7:40; 8:31). Only a radical transfer of allegiance from Moses to him will bring salvation. The exodus imagery in 8:12 makes this clear, connected to the frequent use of "light" as an image for the law. This, then, shapes 8:31–32, where Jesus issues a dramatic challenge: "If you continue in my word [as opposed to that of Moses], you will truly be my disciples [rather than his]; and you will know the truth, and the truth will make you free [previously you thought that the true freedperson is the one who perseveres in Torah, so that even in political slavery he is deeply free; but I tell you that I am the only source of freedom]."

Rejection of this dramatic challenge, according to 8:37ff., locks people into association with those who sought to kill Jesus because they "could not hear" his word (8:43). The alternatives are starkly contrasted, and no compromise between the two is apparently allowed. But through its presentation of the debate about the identity of Jesus, including both positive and negative arguments, the narrative seeks to lure readers into its perspective, and into accepting that he really is the raised Temple around which the scattered people of God can be gathered into one. The very care with which the narrative appeal is constructed forbids the conclusion that it is motivated by hatred.

Implications for Jewish-Christian Dialogue Today

Our circumstances are so different from those of the Fourth Gospel. The Evangelist, whoever he was, could look back on an appalling experience of suffering that he, too, had undergone, with all potential Jewish readers. The calamity was a shared physical, national, and ideational trauma, which left Judaism reeling for decades, and in that situation his presentation of Christ attempts to be "good news."

In contrast, we look back on an appalling experience of suffering that we have inflicted on Jews, or in which we are at least complicit. The question "How can we rightly conduct our relations with Jewish people in these circumstances?" is vital and testing. But two answers to it, I argue in conclusion, are not appropriate.

First, we should not distance ourselves from our own scriptures. *Sachkritik* can function in this way: it can offer an easy rationale for separating the "'acceptable" from the "unacceptable" within our sacred texts. I want to align myself with Stephen Fowl's vision of the "vigilant community" that is quick to criticize any use of scripture to reinforce and legitimate sinful practices—and with the notion of sensitivity to the voice of the Spirit, which, Fowl says, can prompt the vigilant community to distance itself critically from such sinful practices based on scripture.[50] This is a kind of *Sachkritik*, exercised by all of us when we state our united conviction that any use of Johannine texts to legitimate anti-Semitic hatred or practices is a misuse.

But it seems to me that this kind of Spirit-born(e) conviction needs to work with the texts as they really are. Fowl's "model for theological interpretation" moves away from historical criticism by resting itself on the contention that "texts don't have ideologies," only ideologically motivated interpreters, and so Christians need to take care that they are being motivated by the proper, legitimate concerns of Christian life, worship, and discipleship.[51] The problem is that, finally, it is our sacred texts that define for us the legitimate shape of our life and worship. If we cannot live in continuity with them in their historical particularity, then authentic Christian lifestyle will be finally impossible for us. So a Spirit-led conviction that anti-Semitic use is truly misuse will issue in the kind of patient rereading that this contribution has attempted: looking at the text afresh, alive to its inescapably historical claim, and seeking to rehear its voice in its "native" setting.

Second, we should not sink into silence. This response is understandable. We have lost all right to hold our convictions before Jews, this response asserts, because our conviction (that Jesus is the Christ) is irredeemably tainted by the long history of European anti-Semitism, climaxing in the Holocaust. In relation to Jews, therefore, the only response open to us is to hold conviction in abeyance, to renounce evangelism even in the form of dialogue, and simply to embody openness, acceptance, and support.[52]

But I believe that this response is wrong. For us, the basis of loving action is the revelation of God in Christ, and that conviction must be public if we are to live authentically. Of course, it would be quite wrong for us to

---

50. See S. Fowl, *Engaging Scripture: A Model for Theological Interpretation* (Oxford, 1998).

51. See especially ibid., pp. 62–96.

52. This is the stance taken, as I understand it, by the Sisters of Sion and (on the Protestant side) by the International Christian Embassy in Jerusalem.

act in imitation of the Fourth Gospel, proclaiming Christ as the "answer" and issuing a challenge to faith in the starkest possible way, based on John 8:31–36. Only those who have shared Jewish suffering have the right to speak like that. So the first calling for us is to share Jewish suffering—and Arab suffering and Christian suffering—in the name of the Jesus who experienced in his own body, even before it happened, the horror of the destruction of the "Temple," and who has risen again so that horror need not be the last word. In that context of shared suffering, let us then speak.

CHAPTER 5

Anti-Judaism in the Fourth Gospel:
Explanation and Hermeneutics

Judith M. Lieu

The fact that this collection of essays is gathered in a book on *Anti-Judaism and the Fourth Gospel* is sufficient evidence both of the importance of the topic and of a widespread sense that, however confident any individual might be about his or her own resolution of the problem, a consensus has yet to be achieved. In this chapter I explore some of the reasons surrounding the impasse and the hermeneutical challenges involved. There have been various "histories of scholarship" on the theme that I do not wish to repeat here. Although there are older studies,[1] the flourishing literature of the past quarter of a century evinces a number of major trends. In what follows, it is not my intention to assess the cogency of the arguments involved—that is done elsewhere in this book—so much as to assess the hermeneutical implications for the problem to be addressed.

John's "Jewishness"

Analysis of the Fourth Gospel serves as a paradigm of the "Hellenism versus Judaism" conflictual model of understanding early Christianity. While there have long been voices that recognized this as "the most Jewish" of all the Gospels, even tracing important exegetical and conceptual links,[2] the tide turned most decisively in the years following the publication of the Dead Sea Scrolls. This is not simply because of the discovery of parallels between traditions and language in the scrolls and in the Gospel but, more fundamentally, because our understanding of late Second Temple Judaism has become so much more dynamic and broad. Notable contributions are

---

1. See K. L. Carroll, "The Fourth Gospel and the Exclusion of Christians from the Synagogues," *BJRL* 40 (1957–58): 19–32.
2. H. Odeberg, *The Fourth Gospel* (Uppsala, 1989).

C. K. Barrett's *The Gospel of John and Judaism* and J. H. Charlesworth's *John and Qumran.*[3] They have been followed by a range of specialized studies that have shown that John presupposes Jewish exegetical traditions sometimes otherwise attested only contemporary with or later than the Gospel—for example the "bread-of-life discourse" of chapter 6, the Cain traditions behind chapter 8, and the allusions to the feast of Tabernacles in chapter 7.[4] At the same time, the centrality of Wisdom traditions not only for the Johannine "Logos" but, more broadly, for John's Christology has been demonstrated, so that concepts that previously were understood in radically "non-Jewish" terms, such as John's "high Christology" character-ized by the claim "I and the Father are one," have more recently been in-terpreted within the increasingly elastic boundaries of "Jewishness."[5] Thus, while not denying the validity of appealing to "parallels" within Greco-Roman thought, John's conceptual framework, his "culture," is unre-servedly "Jewish." In addition, passages such as 4:22 and perhaps 10:16 and 11:51 point to the primacy of the Jews in the pattern of salvation.

While details of this trend may properly be contested, its overall direc-tion would seem to be agreed. The consequences for our purposes are less straightforward. A simplistic assertion that the evidence of Jewishness dis-proves any anti-Jewishness is both naive and preempts the exercise of definition and investigation.[6] Instead, a number of further questions are implied. First, does the recognition of Jewishness bring us into the world of the readers or of the author only?—a question that can be asked of a number of early Christian writings. Would the readers recognize, and would they need to recognize, the multiple allusions and steps in the argu-ment? To ask this is to ask the relationship between the Gospel and its first audience—was it written for and from a community familiar with the tra-ditions with which it works?

Second, what is the function of this Jewishness within the overall con-ception of the Gospel? If, as is often argued, it serves a replacement theol-ogy, this may fit into our concerns in a different way than if it fits into a

3. C. K. Barrett, *The Gospel of John and Judaism* (London, 1975); J. H. Charlesworth, ed., *John and Qumran* (London, 1972).

4. See P. Borgen, *Bread from Heaven: An Exegetical Study of the Concept of Manna in the Gospel of John and the Writings of Philo* (Leiden, 1981); J. M. Lieu, "What Was from the Beginning: Scripture and Tradition in the Johannine Epistles," *NTS* 39 (1993): 458–77.

5. On Wisdom, cf. M. Scott, *Sophia and the Johannine Jesus* (Sheffield, 1992); on John's Christol-ogy, see C. A. Evans, *Word and Glory: On the Exegetical and Theological Background of John's Prologue* (Sheffield, 1993).

6. R. Leistner, *Antijudaismus im Johannesevangelium? Darstellung des Problems in der neueren Ausle-gungsgeschichte und Untersuchung der Leidensgeschichte* (TW 3; Bern–Frankfurt, 1974), moves in this direction.

theology of fulfillment: the former more categorically declares the redundancy of that which is replaced. There is, moreover, an important and frequently discussed theological question as to whether the early Christian conviction of scriptural fulfillment—and the same may be said even more of replacement—necessarily leads into "anti-Judaism"; and for our purposes, both the words I have highlighted, *necessarily* and *leads*, are important terms in the argument. "Jewishness" is undoubtedly to be found in the text itself, and thus it is the text that provokes the consequent questions. Yet the potential of the text to lead to the next stage obviously requires the interpreter if it is to be realized.

Third, and this forms a bridge to the next point, if we agree on the "Jewishness of John," what do we mean by *Jewishness,* and is the term being used in a way analagous to *anti-Jewishness*?

Debate about "Anti-Semitism," "Anti-Jewishness," "Anti-Judaism"

Most authors of contributions to this book have chosen to use the term *anti-Judaism,* although when forming the adjective, a minority opt for *anti-Judaic,* a majority for *anti-Jewish,* which could imply the substantive *anti-Jewishness.* Generally, *anti-Semitism* has been avoided, although the term is represented in the secondary literature.[7] It is not enough to protest that *anti-Semitism* is a post-Enlightenment term, presupposing now-discredited theories of race totally alien to a first-century context; those who wish to use the term of antiquity are well aware of this fact but still feel that it best expresses the animus they find in at least some of the sources.[8] More particularly, use of the term focuses our attention on the twenty-first century, specifically post-Holocaust, context within which we all work, especially within the framework of Jewish-Christian dialogue. Alongside the new awareness of the diversity of Second Temple Judaism, it is this context, and the recognition of the foundational role played by a long Christian tradition in making possible the Shoah, that has forced students of early Christianity to reexamine that tradition all the way back to its earliest texts. The

7. C. A. Evans and D. A. Hagner, eds., *Anti-Semitism and Early Christianity: Issues of Polemic and Faith* (Minneapolis, 1993); S. Sandmel, *Anti-Semitism in the New Testament?* (Philadelphia, 1978).

8. See J. G. Gager, *The Origins of Anti-Semitism: Attitudes towards Judaism in Pagan and Christian Antiquity* (New York–Oxford, 1983); J. N. Sevenster, *The Roots of Pagan Anti-Semitism in the Ancient World* (NovTSup 41; Leiden, 1975).

highly contentious questions of historical continuity and of a continuity of cause and effect cannot distract us here, yet the narrower one of a continuity of citation and interpretation has rightly become the concern of students of the New Testament and early Christian literature.[9]

At this point, it is noteworthy that contemporary studies of the rise of modern anti-Semitism rarely pay much attention to the New Testament sources; those that refer to the Christian theological tradition —and not all see this as determinative—tend to begin from the fourth century, with appropriate citations from John Chrysostom, Augustine, Jerome, and others.[10] In the context of Jewish-Christian dialogue, however, both on the literary level and, from my experience, on that of "oral" popular dialogue, the New Testament and specifically the Fourth Gospel do feature as significant areas of concern.

The distinction between *anti-Jewish/ness* and *anti-Judaic/Judaism* may seem to be a semantic quibble peculiar to the English language. To "English-hearing" ears, however, the latter speaks more of a system, the former more of a people, culture, and set of ideas. The question is thus focused on whether what we are assessing is the rejection of a system, even of "a religion," or the rejection of a people and their beliefs. Expanding this in one direction, as already noted, when we speak about the *Jewishness* of John, are we using the term in the same way as when we speak about the Gospel's *anti-Jewishness*? An easy answer would be to say that John affirms a certain literary and conceptual, even theological, tradition but rejects (some of) those who claim to represent that tradition in his own time. Whether we can effect so neat a separation between a tradition and its proponents may be questionable, but, more important, if this rejection is one of principle and to that extent not historically contingent—so that John could not envisage the possibility of "Jews who did not believe in Jesus" not being rejected—the hermeneutical dilemma is not solved.

Developing the underlying issue in another direction, we are forced to address the terminology of our sources. John does not know the term

9. "Never has a more terrible judgment been spoken against the so-called world Jewry as a demand for power than in the 'woe' of Jesus Christ in Matt. 23:15; never a more negative characterization of the Jewish religion as a religion of privilege than that found in John 8:40–44"; see G. Kittel, "Meine Verteidigung" (Nov.–Dec. 1946; unpublished), p. 7, quoted in R. P. Eriksen, *Theologians under Hitler: Gerhard Kittel, Paul Althaus and Emanuel Hirsch* (New Haven, Conn., 1985), p. 42.

10. See, for example, Y. Baer, ed., *Present-Day Antisemitism: Proceedings of the Eighth International Seminar of the Study Circle on World Jewry* (The Vidal Sassoon International Center for the Study of Antisemitism; Jerusalem, 1988); S. Almog, ed., *Antisemitism through the Ages* (The Vidal Sassoon International Center for the Study of Antisemitism, Oxford, 1988); A. S. Lindemann, *Esau's Tears: Modern Anti-Semitism and the Rise of the Jews* (Cambridge, 1997); K. MacDonald, *Separation and Its Discontents: Toward an Evolutionary Theory of Anti-Semitism* (Westport, Conn., 1998).

'Ιουδαϊσμός. Within the New Testament it is used only by Paul (Gal. 1:13–14); outside the New Testament it is used by 2 and 4 Maccabees, where it is evidently tendentious and set in implied opposition to Ἑλληνισμός or ἀλλορυλισμός.[11] Ignatius is similarly tendentious when he opposes it to his self-coined χριστιανισμός (Magn. 8.1; 10.3; Phld. 6.1). Yet, however suggestive these references might be, their real importance is their rarity throughout the early period. This again is not a semantic quibble: on the one hand, the more we become aware of the diversity of our period, the less confident are we in speaking of "Judaism," with its contemporary implications of a unitary religious system to be set alongside other analogous "-isms"; thus Shaye Cohen's recent study is titled The Beginnings of Jewishness.[12] On the other hand, how did our author or readers—without the benefits of these terms—conceptualize that which they rejected as well as that to which they were committed?

In the Fourth Gospel the debate has centered predominantly, if not entirely, on John's use of 'Ιουδαῖοι, which has been discussed widely, including by a number of authors of this book.[13] Such discussions focus properly on the developing and varying use of the term by Jewish and by Greco-Roman sources. Whether this resolves the dilemma of our own terminology is another question. Cassius Dio, who associates 'Ιουδαῖοι with 'Ιουδαῖοι, is frequently quoted: "I do not know when this label for them began, but it is also attached to all other people who are enthusiastic for their customs even if of other races [ἀλλοεθνής]" (Hist. Rom. 37.17.1). Having rejected the language of "race" that lies behind "anti-Semitism," even while acknowledging the growing use of γένος in the Maccabean literature and, before long, in "Christian" literature, with what are we to replace it?

John "from within" the Tradition:
A Prophetic or "Intrafamilial" Polemic

Students of the preexilic and exilic prophets are familiar with the debate as to whether those prophets saw only the inevitable judgment; or whether the apparent inevitability was but a form of urgency, demanding repentance before it was too late; or whether they anticipated a future restoration

11. Despite the nineteenth-century exploitation of the contrast, 'Ιουδαϊσμός (2 Macc. 2:21; 8:1; 14:38; 4 Macc. 4:26) does not appear alongside and in explicit contrast to ἀλλορυλισμός (2 Macc. 4:13; 6:24) or Ἑλληνισμός (2 Macc. 4:13).

12. S. Cohen, The Beginnings of Jewishness: Boundaries. Varieties. Uncertainties (Berkeley, 1999).

13. For a bibliography, see the "Select Bibliography" in this book.

beyond judgment, predicated on the return of the people to God. Might even the most intense condemnation be but a desperate plea for response, implying the certainty that such a response would be unconditionally accepted? Thus, to return to the terminological nuancing of the previous section, the polemic might not be "anti-Jews" but would be "anti-Judaism," or better, "anti-Judaism as previously interpreted by them, now seen as a denial of their true calling." Particularly if John's "Jewishness" is to be interpreted within a fulfillment framework, Jews, either directly or through the consequent activity of the Gospel's readers, are being invited to recognize in Jesus that fulfillment and not to follow the example of the (unbelieving) "Jews" of the narrative. The assumption is that since the intention behind such a strategy is a positive one, it in no way merits the rejectionist prefix *anti-*. In a twenty-first century context, however, the matter is rather more complex—and one should compare the tensions provoked in recent times for Jewish-Christian dialogue by organizations with an active proselytizing mission aimed at observant Jews, for example, at universities. In terms of the language of the Gospel, would those who responded continue to be Ἰουδαῖοι, and does it matter?

A slightly different but related solution is to appeal to the "internal" polemic found in other "Jewish" sources of the period; the most-quoted examples come again from the Dead Sea Scrolls, where the opponents of the community can be called "men of the pit or sin or Belial."[14] In the broader context, such apparently vituperative polemic was part of the rhetorical conventions of the day and would be recognized as such by all concerned. It is only a more courteous, and more libel-conscious, age that demurs at such language. Such rhetoric is not, of course, disinterested; if the community of the scrolls could rage, "Accursed without mercy for the darkness of your deeds—may God not be merciful when you entreat him" (1QS 2.7–8), it was because they saw themselves, and themselves alone, as the faithful keepers of the covenant in and through whom God's redemption would be effected. Scholarly interpretation of this as internal polemic, however, is shaped by Josephus's irenic account of the Jewish "sects" within a harmonious whole, an account that might not have been accepted by all those whom he described. In practice, who defines the boundaries between the "internal" and the "external" is a matter of perspective (and power) and is implicated in rather than independent of, the polemic of alienation: that is, to call someone "of the devil" is to make

---

14. See L. T. Johnson, "The New Testament's Anti-Jewish Slander and the Conventions of Ancient Polemic," *JBL* 108 (1989): 419–41.

them "outside" or "other," regardless of whether anyone else can recognize the crucial distinctions. It is precisely this process of "othering" that is our concern both historically and theologically: historically, in the problem of how what were to become "Judaism" and "Christianity" evolved in separation from each other; theologically, in the acts of definition of self and of other that were made in this process, acts that were constructed as divinely authored.

A further step in the line of argument traced here is that the use of this "prophetic" or "intrafamilial" polemical language by later interpreters "from outside" is a new step and not one envisaged by the author.[15] It was when Christian interpreters also no longer recognized "the Jews" as their sisters and brothers that the rhetoric of John unleashed a new potential that could sanction unconditional hostility without unconditional hope. It was, although this is equally applicable to the next line of interpretation, when the persecuted minority became a majority with absolute power that this potential could be translated into sanctioned acts of indescribable violence. This contextualization of a sense of election that also defines "those outside," not only in a specific historical setting but also in terms of access to power, is an important insight. It directs our attention away from the specific, isolated words to the speech acts in which they are effective; within a new set of relationships, the same terms and statements may function in totally different ways.

The Sociohistorical Context: Explaining the Sense of Alienation/Hostility

There are few interpretations of the Gospel, as well as specifically of its attitude to "the Jews," that do not appeal to a reconstruction of the situation and even prior history of the community it presupposes. While this is to some extent true of all New Testament writings, it is John that is peculiar in being constructed as a two-level drama, so that the narrative dynamic replicates the dynamic of recent historical experience for the community—which is here conceived as both generator and recipient of the tradition process, culminating in the Gospel as we have it. Particularly influential has been J. L. Martyn's *History and Theology in the Fourth Gospel,*

---

15. W. Rebell, *Gemeinde als Gegenwelt. Zur soziologischen und didaktischen Funktion des Johannesevangeliums* (Frankfurt-am-Main, 1987), p. 111, makes a similar contrast between origin and later use from a position of power, while adopting a position closer to those discussed in the section "The Sociohistorical Context" on pp. 107–10 below.

which has since been followed by many others;[16] a keystone in Martyn's reconstruction was the identification of the "exclusion from the synagogue" of John 9:22 (cf. 12:42; 16:2) with the formulation of the *birkat haminim,* or so-called Heretic Benediction, dated to the leadership of Gamaliel II in the mid-90s. According to this reconstruction, the Gospel evinces the hurt of the sense of exclusion and alienation consequent upon the Johannine Christians' expulsion from "the synagogue," within which the community had evolved; the "otherness" of the terminology of "the Jews," which for the most part ignores that Jesus and his disciples are themselves Jewish, reflects that alienation. One might say that "the Jews" have constructed themselves as such by the action they have initiated, whatever the extent to which that action was prompted by social (the inclusion of non-Jews) or theological (a high Christology) developments among the Johannine "Christians."

This simplistic presentation of the model has, of course, been refined by attention to the broader structures of Johannine thought, which have prompted the terminology of sectarianism to be applied to it.[17] Illumined by other studies of sectarianism,[18] this can shift the focus of attention from the action of "the synagogue" to the internal dynamics by which a group constructs and maintains its own separation either from the "mother" establishment or from "the world."[19] So, for example, the "demonization" of the previously held or alternative worldview can be seen as an expected strategy in the construction and maintenance of a new worldview, particularly one held by a beleagured minority. The emphasis remains, however, on a social or sociological interpretation of the "Johannine community" as explanatory of the Gospel's attitude to "the Jews."

Various issues are raised by this approach. There is the necessary fragility of the circle that argues from the hostility within the text, to a social context that might generate such hostility, and so back to a solution to

16. J. L. Martyn, *History and Theology in the Fourth Gospel* (New York, 1968); see also, for example, R. E. Brown, *The Community of the Beloved Disciple* (London, 1979); J. Painter, *The Quest for the Messiah* (Edinburgh, 1991).

17. See W. Meeks, "The Man from Heaven in Johannine Sectarianism," *JBL* 91 (1972): 44–72; S. Freyne, "Vilifying the Other and Defining the Self: Matthew's and John's Anti-Jewish Polemic in Focus," in J. Neusner and E. Frerichs, eds., *"To See Ourselves as Others See Us": Christians, Jews, "Others" in Late Antiquity* (Chico, Calif., 1985), pp. 117–43.

18. Most influentially, B. Wilson, *Patterns of Sectarianism* (London, 1976).

19. In this sentence a number of different elements and approaches are compressed that merit considerable analysis, including the common elision of concepts of the sect as constituted by opposition to the "church" (here Judaism/synagogue) and as constituted by its self-definition in relation to "the world."

the textual hostility. The text we are seeking to explain—the Fourth Gospel—is the only certain evidence for the history of the community, which in turn is held to explain that text. Indeed, it is because the Johannine epistles do not naturally fit within this history that they have to be assigned to a subsequent stage, even though, on purely internal and conceptual grounds, there are no compelling arguments to locate them later than the Gospel.[20] Moreover, within the narrative of the Gospel it is the Temple, and not the synagogue, that is the focus of action and conflict.[21] There is, furthermore, now considerably less confidence that we can date the *birkat ha-minim* to the 90s, assume that it was directed against (Jewish) Christians, equate what was a liturgical expression with a quasi-legal "exclusion," or imagine that it would have immediate effect even within the land of Israel, never mind in a Diaspora community such as Ephesus.[22] While all this must challenge confident assumptions about the dating of the Gospel, however, the general scenario envisioned may still function in such a reconstruction as representing a local situation specific to this "community."

A more pressing question is whether the sociohistorical context is both a necessary and a sufficient explanation of the attitude to the Jews: Given that context, was it inevitable that that response would ensue? For this explanation to be hermeneutically satisfying "without remainder," in the sense of providing a total solution to the problem, the answer would have to be affirmative; yet this subscribes to a highly functionalist understanding of sociological explanation, unlikely to be attractive to most New Testament exegetes with hermeneutical concerns! Moreover, it seems improbable that the Johannine "Christians" were alone in their experience of separation from "the synagogue"—a similar scenario has been envisioned for the Matthaean community—and yet the Johannine response is both distinctive and arguably more extreme. If, however, the putative sociohistorical context is only one potential factor alongside others,

20. This, too, is more contentious than the assertion acknowledges; see, however, K. Grayston, *The Johannine Epistles* (Basingstoke, 1984); and G. Strecker, *Die Johannesbriefe* (Göttingen, 1989), for attempts to reposition the epistles; also J. Lieu, *The Theology of the Johannine Epistles* (Cambridge, 1991), pp. 6–7.

21. See J. M. Lieu, "Temple and Synagogue in John," *NTS* 45 (1999): 51–69.

22. The literature is considerable; see W. Horbury, "The Benediction of the Minim and Early Jewish-Christian Controversy," *JTS* 33 (1982): 19–61 (republished in W. Horbury, *Jews and Christians in Contact and Controversy* [Edinburgh, 1998], pp. 67–110); S. Katz, "Issues in the Separation of Judaism and Christianity after 70 C.E.: A Reconsideration," *JBL* 103 (1984): 43–76; R. Kimelman, "*Birkat Ha-Minim* and the Lack of Evidence for an Anti-Christian Jewish Prayer in Late Antiquity," in E. P. Sanders, A. I. Baumgarten, and A. Mendelson, eds., *Jewish and Christian Self-Definition,* vol. 2: *Aspects of Judaism in the Greco-Roman Period* (London, 1981), pp. 226–44.

further explanation or theological response is still demanded.[23] In this case, the following trends may be appealed to as supplementary to this explanation.

Discussion of the Identity of the "Johannine Jews" and Their Role within the Gospel

To the twenty-first-century reader "Jews" are Jews, and in most European languages, the semantic link between the Ἰουδαῖοι and the land Ἰουδαῖοι is lost: thus both author and original readers would have "received" οἱ Ἰουδαῖα in the Gospel quite differently from readers some centuries later, and in this sense the interpreter necessarily contributes to the "meaning" of the text. Yet how is the sense as originally received to be understood? Under this heading there are two different approaches in recent scholarship. A narrative-critical approach, which is predicated on the final form of the text, will trace the developing picture of "the Jews" within the text itself, although some decision is always necessary as to what degree of prior knowledge readers would have brought with them; such an approach presupposes a relatively coherent, if developing, picture. A more diachronic approach starts from different sources or redactional layers arguably discernible within the text and is necessarily more alive to the differences or tensions that can be ascribed to such subsequent levels of tradition or redaction. In practice, both approaches will see certain usages or passages as primarily determinative for the distinctive (i.e., polemical) Johannine use of "the Jews."[24] Moreover, both rightly recognize that the Gospel is not a discursive treatise but a narrative; to ignore its narrative character in favor of a thematic, conceptual, or "theological" reading is to do violence to the specificity of the text, with its self-conscious, history-like quality.

Within such a framework, the all-encompassing negative overtone of the translation "the Jews" felt by the modern reader is deceptive both within a first- or second-century context and when proper close attention

23. Thus Rebell, *Gemeinde als Gegenwelt,* p. 112, suggests that John overplays the conflict and so prepares for the later theologically founded persecution of Jews; a similar position of historical contingency and theological responsibility is taken by W. Trilling, "Gegner Jesu—Widersacher der Gemeinde—Repräsentanten der 'Welt,'" in H. Goldstein, ed., *Gottesverächter und Menschenfeinde? Juden zwischen Jesus und frühchristlicher Kirche* (Düsseldorf, 1979), pp. 190–209.

24. Again, the bibliography is considerable; see U. C. von Wahlde, "The Johannine Jews," *NTS* 28 (1982): 33–60; also J. Ashton, "The Identity and Function of the 'Ἰουδαῖοι,' in the Fourth Gospel," *NovT* 27 (1985): 40–75. M. Lowe's attempt to retain "Judaeans" adopts a similar methodology: "Who Were the Ἰουδαῖοι?" *NovT* 18 (1975): 101–30.

is paid to the narrative dynamic of the text. Quite clearly, action predicated on "the Jews" at various points must be predicated on a delimited group, and contextual analysis indicates those with authority; such a framework also makes sense of the curious alternation with "the Pharisees," of the absence of other groups identified in the Synoptic tradition, as well as of the Johannine awareness of "the crowd." If we were to set the Fourth Gospel on stage, "the Jews" would be clearly distinguished by their appurtenances of authority from the no less "Jewish" Jesus, disciples, and individuals such as the blind man and his parents. Despite ongoing discussion of detail and of the compositional history implied, the approach here summarized is well established.

Equally well known are the consequences. First, there is the problem of translation, which has provoked a heated debate, perhaps particularly in North America.[25] This, it must be emphasized, is not the same as the problem of dynamic equivalence in translation, which addresses the temporal and cultural gap between text/original receptor and the new receptor; for what we have here is a consciously chosen authorial technique with few close parallels. Thus, second, we are driven back to ask both how this usage would have been received by the implied and/or intended audience and how it was intended by the author. Would the audience, familiar with the underlying narrative outline and focused on its evolution in the Gospel, have read or heard "the Jews" only within their textual role? And if so, for how long would this restricted reading have remained self-evident? If the author was aware of alternative possibilities—and of some, such as "rulers," he is aware—and perhaps even of those familiar from the Synoptic traditions, which he avoids, such as "scribes and elders," why did he choose to highlight "the Jews"? If the "traditional," more "historical," terminology would have been foreign to his readers, was the decision not to rely exclusively on more generalized leadership language ("rulers") deliberate, and if so, is it appropriate for subsequent translations to ignore that decision? What theories of composition, of the redaction of and of the failure to redact earlier layers of tradition, and of authorial intention are appropriate for understanding the surviving inconsistencies in the Gospel's nomenclature? Alternatively, if the perceived inconsistencies can be absorbed in a reading of the final form of the text according to which those forms that, in isolation or at an earlier stage of tradition history, might

25. See the American Bible Society's Contemporary English Version and Oxford University Press's *The New Testament and Psalms: An Inclusive Version.* D. Efroymson, "Let Ioudaioi Be Ioudaioi: When Less Is Better," *Expl.* 11 (1997): 5, supports the argument that the term should be left untranslated to alert readers to the problem.

appear neutral ("feast of the Jews") no longer do so in their final textual context, should we, after all, acknowledge the text's potential for determining interpretation—that is, a potential to generate a unitary meaning?

The "Jews" and the "World"

If the "Farewell Discourses" (John 13–17) most directly address the situation of the "Johannine community," the disappearance of "the Jews" in these chapters suggests that these various forms of "historical" readings do not totally explain the thought of the Gospel. So, most notably, the promise of being "put . . . out of the synagogues" (16:2) (literally "being made excluded from") belongs in a section that begins with the hatred of the world first for Jesus and then for his disciples (15:18). To what extent is the world focused in "the Jews" (7:7), or, alternatively, are "the Jews" a narrative cypher for "the world"? The second alternative forefronts the broader dualistic worldview of the Gospel, within which "being of the world" stands over against "not being of the world," and also fits within a range of oppositions that includes "above" versus "below," "from heaven" versus "from the earth," and "of God" versus "not of God" (cf. 8:47, where this is predicated on and spoken to "the Jews"). From this perspective, while on the narrative level "the Jews" might have a specific role in the drama being enacted, and/or while the past experience of the Johannine community may have found expression in the "othering" of the Jews, neither of these represents the function of the Jews in the final intention of the Gospel, an intention that is best articulated in theological terms. Such an approach, particularly associated with John Ashton's distinction between referent and sense,[26] can cohere well with a more Bultmannian reading of the Gospel, which emphasises the "timeless" significance of the rejection of God's revelation.[27]

Yet such an approach need not be tied to an existentialist individualism. It recognizes that there is a fundamental dualist structure to Johannine thought, which is found in a more thoroughgoing form in 1 John. It is the distinctive nature of Johannine dualism that sets it in relation to both

26. Ashton, "Identity and Function."

27. Thus R. Bultmann, *Theology of the New Testament* (London, 1955), vol. 2, p. 27, uses "the Jews" in quotation marks; "Taking the Jewish religion as an example, John makes clear through it how the human will to self-security distorts knowledge of God, makes God's demand and promise into a possession and thereby shuts itself up against God." J. Ashton, *Understanding the Fourth Gospel* (Oxford, 1991), sees Bultmann as a watershed in the interpretation of the Gospel.

apocalyptic and Gnostic thought-worlds, and yet, in contrast to both, the cosmic dimension has been reduced to God and "the devil" (John 8:44; 1 John 3:8–10). In the Gospel, "the Jews" are brought into this structure: within the restrictions of the narrative Gospel genre chosen by "John," they articulate the rejection of God. Yet they do so not merely by an act of the will but by the (predetermined?) location of their origin (8:47). The realized eschatology of the Gospel may only exacerbate the determinism implicit here. The "problem" of the Johannine Jews is thus generated by the symbiosis of "historical" tradition and dualist thought-world within the Gospel genre. To that extent, it derives from the Gospel's theological substructure, which shares some of the world-denying or world-hostile tendencies of both apocalypticism and Gnosticism. Yet perhaps the ultimate problem is the nature of the Gospel genre and its participation both in historical specificity and in redemptive "myth." All subsequent (re)interpretation of the Gospel that does not merely narrate but actively proclaims "redemption" participates in the same problem.

This discussion of the major trends in interpretation of the possible "anti-Judaism" of the Fourth Gospel does not suggest that they are necessarily mutually exclusive; rather, each can be used to address, to qualify, and/or to ameliorate the implications of the issue and the topics discussed in this book. Certainly, as has been indicated, the persuasiveness of the various solutions needs to be assessed within the critical framework of each, yet the continuing debate suggests that on their own they are unlikely to take us any further. Instead, as we have already begun to note, they provoke further questions, which in turn demand more close attention in the light of contemporary hermeneutical discussion.

The Problems of "Text," "Interpreter," and "Literary Means"

Recent developments in literary and hermeneutical analysis have made it much more difficult to think of the text as something that can be separated conceptually from its interpreters; in the same way, the idea of "authorial intention" as something accessible through a text, or even as the ultimate or only arbiter of its meaning, has also become highly problematic. Historical-critical analysis has long been seen as an attempt to preserve the integrity and "otherness" of the text and so to act as a defense against the subordination of the text to dogmatic interests or to inappropriate presuppositions. This ethos can be seen at work in attempts to describe John's use of "the Jews" as historically contingent in terms of the history either of the community or of the text. So doing intends to disqualify inappropriate absolutizing of assertions such as John 8:44; yet closer attention suggests that this interpretative endeavor may not be as neutral or as sufficient as claimed. First, there sometimes appears a tendency to blame the victim—the "Jews" excluded the "Christians." Second, there is the doubt already expressed above as to whether such explanations are not merely necessary but also sufficient. Third, there is the more general problem of the relationship between the historical contextualization and the interpretation of a "living" text, particularly one that has been given canonical status.

There is not space here to debate the virtues of the de facto displacement of the historical-critical method from the primacy it once claimed. Yet recent thought has given new emphasis to how the text functions as "text" only within a communicative relationship: text and interpreter are reciprocally interdependent—the interpreter needs and is constrained by the text, but the text becomes "meaning-full" only as it is interpreted. Inevitably, interpreters bring their own frameworks of understanding—it would be impossible to understand any text with a *tabula rasa*. John's use of "the Jews" and the Gospel's "Jewishness" are both clear examples of this, as they are also of our inability to recapture with certainty, and so to use as a restrictive criterion of meaning, the conscious or implicit frameworks either of the initial author or of the recipients.

Yet these features offer equally clear examples of the potential of a text to extend beyond the capacities of any, including the first, interpretative group: thus we cannot conclude that what the author or recipients might not have perceived is not part of the text. In this way John's decision to use Ἰουδαῖοι rather than "rulers," whatever the original reason, becomes part of the text's potential to be realized by interpreters at some future stage. One expression of this process is visible when that potential is developed through the redactional process, giving priority to the "final form" of the text; yet it also extends beyond the final form in subsequent contextualized interpretation. The peculiarly difficult hermeneutical question that has to be determined here is on what grounds any particular expression of that potential of the text is to be judged illegitimate.

Many would also argue that, given the inseparability of text and interpretation, the history of interpretation becomes part of the "meaning" of the text for subsequent interpreters. We cannot free ourselves from this or disregard it—and this must be particularly true of a text that has functioned

and continues to function as a canonical text. We operate within an interpretative tradition, and one that has not merely functioned as an intellectual topos but that has been articulated in practice, with destructive effect.

History, Literatures, and Ideology

The Gospel's avowed intention is "that you might believe," and this belief
is expressed in christological terms. In this John is no different from the
other Gospels. Indeed, it would be difficult to think of any ancient work
that, even if "historical" in genre, is not at the same time both literary and
ideologically shaped. The analysis developed above has highlighted particular aspects of the ideological shaping of John's Gospel. Fundamentally,
there is the conviction that John shares with most other early Christian
writers that the events played out in the story of Jesus and their own experience effectively fulfilled or replaced the experience of those among whom
they were enacted, "the Jews," particularly as the latter experience was expressed in scripture. Within such a conviction, Jesus appears as God's last
or ultimate Word, not to be superseded or equalled.

More specifically, in the Fourth Gospel this christological affirmation is
expressed through the medium of a dualist framework, which, whatever its
origins, demands a negative counterbalance. Perhaps this dualist framework proved congenial to the social experience of the author and his readers; more specifically, it can be seen as providing a hermeneutical solution
to the interpretative needs of the story of Jesus, not least of his (otherwise
perplexing) death. The dilemma of the Gospel genre lies in the tension
contained within it between the historical contingency of its narrative and
the conviction that the central figure and his life and death are not
"merely" historically contingent. Just as John's dualism articulates this conviction, so the problem of his "Jewishness" and of his "anti-Jewishness"
arises out of that dilemma.

To that extent, the problem of how we are to interpret the Fourth
Gospel belongs to the broader question of how, in the contemporary context—including that of Jewish-Chrisian dialogue—we are to respond to
the foundational Christian convictions of fulfillment and/or replacement.
So it is suggested that no (re)proclamation of the gospel can avoid this
dilemma. In contrast, not all early Christian literature goes as far down the
path of vilifying "the Jews" as does John, and this "excess" demands a response to the nature of and to the theological and hermeneutical problems
of the dualism characteristic of this Gospel.

All Interpretation Is "Responsible"

Another feature of the contemporary debate, and again one that is not limited to scriptural exegesis, is that all interpretation takes place within a specific context, and, moreover, that as such no act of interpretation is neutral but may (perhaps must) be used to sustain or challenge the status quo. If interpretation is necessarily perspectival, it must be consciously and responsibly so. This is (particularly?) true in the study of history, where, as has become sometimes painfully evident in recent years, the retelling of the past involves the exercise of power and can effect subjugation or liberation. It is therefore morally responsible and, in a Christian theological context, responsible to the Christian gospel. Recent examples, such as the retelling of the history of the peoples of South Africa or of the indigenous people of Australia, have shown that the threads of past action, of the conflict between what was experienced and what was intended as well as between socially and historically determined motivation and long-continuing consequences of continuity, inheritance, and disowning, are tied in a gorgonian knot.

For our concern, John and "the Jews," the present context in which our interpretation or retelling is carried out must be shaped by our awareness of the legacy of Christian anti-Judaism or anti-Semitism and of the role of the canon as a source of authority within this. I argue that this means a historical-critical or literary "solution" cannot be adequate but that the ideas of the canon and of the exegetical task become points of struggle.

History and the Power of the Text

The contribution of historical-critical analysis toward the attempt to delineate appropriate and inappropriate readings remains crucial. Theologically, it can be seen as consequent on a clear doctrine of the incarnation. So, conversely and perhaps surprisingly, the attempt to see the text as an expression of timeless or existential truths may at first glance appear to neutralize the specificity of the polemic of the Gospel as against "the Jews" yet is the more dangerous because in so doing it ignores not only the historical contingency of the text but, more specifically, the particular non-timeless and nonuniversal uses to which it can and has been put.[28] Yet, as the increasingly intense debate about the nature and parameters of the

---

28. So, forcefully, P. von der Osten-Sacken, *Grundzüge einer Theologie im christlich-jüdischen Gespräch* (Munich, 1982), pp. 178–80, who sees such a reading as theologically irresponsible and as a denial of the historical-critical position.

canon has demonstrated, historical-critical analysis has proved less success-ful in dealing with the continuing power of the text.[29] The argument of this essay is that neither of two possible solutions is acceptable, namely, ei-ther (1) to see the purportedly accessible, historically contextualized "meaning" as the only meaning, thus remaining tied to the past and dele-gitimating any developing or reapplied meaning, or (2) to reaffirm the authority of the text as a part of the canon and as such beyond critical analysis or judgment.

Within a Christian theological context, the continuing power of the text is the consequence not just of its de facto survival but because it has been consciously affirmed for the life, belief, and worship of the church. Yet this cannot be used to remove the text from the sphere of historical and theological critique. The problem of anti-Jewishness in John is but one ex-ample, albeit a powerful one, of why the ideas of revelation, canonicity, and authority can never be taken as self-evident but have to be continually reconceived. Perhaps a model more in tune with contemporary under-standing of the exercise of authority would be a dialogical model—instead of focusing on the "problem" of the authority of a text that might be judged as ethically (or otherwise) flawed, the Gospel invites us into an en-gagement with the intrinsic problems of Christian faith: How can the convictions of Christology, of the reality of good and evil, of divine sover-eignty and guidance, be affirmed in a way that respects the "otherness" of others? How can the church maintain its true identity when it has access to power as well as when it is oppressed? This is not to dissolve the particu-larity of John's Gospel into general truths but to affirm that all exegesis is carried out within a broader framework of commitment and—in a Chris-tian theological setting—of obedience to the gospel of Christ.

29. Feminist analysis has sharpened the dilemma particularly effectively. See E. Schüssler Fiorenza, ed., *Searching the Scriptures,* vol. 1: *A Feminist Introduction;* vol. 2: *A Feminist Commentary* (New York 1994).

PART TWO

CHAPTER 6

"The Jews" in the Gospel of John

Henk Jan de Jonge

The depiction of "the Jews" that arises in the Gospel of John is not a favorable image.[1] The Evangelist not only speaks frequently of "the Jews" as a group that is in vehement opposition to Jesus,[2] but he also treats this group repeatedly as a large, monolithic, indistinguishable mass.[3] The author often portrays "the Jews" *en bloc* as being opposed to Jesus, as if all the Jews of Galilee (2:18), or all the Jews of Judaea (7:1), or all the Jews of Jerusalem (5:18; 10:31–39; 18:31; 19:7) were completely and without exception hostilely antagonistic to Jesus.

A superficial reading of this Gospel can suggest that its author was led by anti-Jewish sentiments. Nonetheless, it is my view that the unsympathetic portrayal of the Jews in John is not attributable to an anti-Jewish inclination or to an anti-Jewish polemic on the part of the author. Instead, I believe this negative depiction is the unfortunate result of a combination of two very different intentions of the author. First, it is my opinion that the Fourth Evangelist did indeed write polemically in his Gospel, but this polemic was not aimed at non-Christian Jews; rather, it was targeted against contemporary Christians who refused to accept the particular christological understanding of the Johannine group.[4] Thus, the polemic of the Fourth Evangelist, as I hope to demonstrate, is aimed against

1. My interpretation of John's Gospel as a polemic against non-Johannine Christians and not against traditional, non-Christian Jews is based on the Ph.D. dissertation of my student Dr. B. W. J. de Ruyter, *De gemeente van de evangelist Johannes: Haar polemiek en haar geschiedenis* (The Community of the Fourth Evangelist: Its Polemics and Its History. With a Summary in English) (Delft, 1998). I wish to thank Dr. de Ruyter for his criticism and helpful suggestions.

2. E.g., 8:48–59.

3. E.g., 18:31, 36; 19:7.

4. This view is less novel than it may look. The thesis that John's Gospel reflects polemics against non-Johannine Christians is part of many scholars' theories on this Gospel. These scholars include E. L. Allen, "The Jewish Christian Church in the Fourth Gospel," *JBL* 74 (1955): 88–92, p. 92: "It is here suggested that John was aware of a Jewish Christian Church, still faithful to the Law but acknowledging Jesus as Messiah and prophet"; C. H. Dodd, "A l'arrière plan d'un dialogue johannique," *RHPR*

non-Johannine Christians, not against non-Christian Jews. Second, the author is committed to writing a story about the earthly ministry of Jesus. Because of this, he is forced to interweave his own polemical battle into the story of the life of Jesus. As a result, he projects the opposition of his contemporary non-Johannine fellow Christians (from the end of the first century C.E.) back on the opponents of Jesus (from around 30 C.E.). In this way, the Evangelist transmits the objections that the non-Johannine Christians raised against Johannine Christology (in the author's own time) into the mouths of the opponents of Jesus, who supposedly opposed him during his ministry (sixty years earlier). For the Evangelist, the opponents of Jesus during his earthly ministry were called "'Jews'" simply because the author considered it to be an historical fact that Jesus lived among the Jews. The result is that John portrayed "the Jews" in his Gospel as the spokespersons of the criticism that the non-Johannine Christians had against the Johannine Christology. In other words, the Fourth Evangelist ascribes the opposition that he himself was experiencing from the non-Johannine Christians to "the Jews" of Jesus' time. He projects the criticism of his contemporary opponents, who were Christians but not members of the (or of one particular) Johannine community, back on supposed Jewish opponents of the earthly Jesus.

This is my interpretation of John's treatment of "the Jews." If this interpretation is correct, then the polemic that is found in the Fourth Gospel is not anti-Jewish but is directed against Christians who refused to support the specific Christology of the Evangelist and his group. As such, the Fourth Gospel appears to be anti-Jewish, but it is in fact directed against non-Johannine Christians.

In justification of this perspective, I present two sets of evidence. In the first place, I demonstrate that whenever a breach takes place between Jesus and his opponents in chapters 5–12, the cause of the breach is not that the opponents reject Jesus completely but that they reject the main tenet of the Johannine Christology. This main tenet is that the earthly Jesus and the Father (God) are one. The Son and the Father are one in their work;

37 (1957): 5–17; C. H. Dodd, *More New Testament Studies* (Manchester, 1968), pp. 41–57; R. E. Brown, *The Community of the Beloved Disciple* (New York–London, 1979), pp. 71–88. According to Brown, John polemicizes against at least three different groups of Christians: "crypto-Christians," "Christians of inadequate faith," and "Christians of Apostolic Churches." See also M. de Jonge, *Jesus: Stranger from Heaven and Son of God* (Missoula, Mont., 1977), p. 99: "Johannine christology is developed not only in contrast with Jewish thinking but also with other christological views"; J. L. Martyn, *The Gospel of John in Christian History* (New York, 1978), p. 120: the Johannine community is "sharply differentiated and alienated from a group of so-called Christian Jews"; L. Schenke, "Das johanneische Schisma und die 'Zwölf' (Johannes 6.60–71)," *NTS* 38 (1992): 105–21. See also de Ruyter, *De gemeente*, p. 49 n. 67.

that is to say, they are functionally one. The Son does the work that the Father gives him to do; he does the work of the Father; he works in the very same way as the Father works. The Son is in the Father and the Father is in the Son. The point that repeatedly causes the breach between Jesus and his opponents is this Johannine claim that a solid, unique, and exclusive relation exists between the earthly Jesus and the Father. But this does not mean that those who refuse to accept this "high" Christology of John's Gospel reject Jesus entirely. It is very possible that they possessed an intensely positive appreciation of Jesus, even though they rejected the extremely high assessment of the earthly Jesus that is typical of John's Christology. What the opponents in chapters 5 through 12 are rejecting is the specifically Johannine claim of the functional unity of the Son and the Father. Based on this observation, it can be concluded that the Evangelist in fact polemicizes with non-Johannine Christian contemporaries, and not with Jews, even though he calls his contemporary opponents "the Jews" in his story of Jesus' ministry. With "real" (that is to say, traditional), non-Christian Jews, the discussion would have revolved around completely different subjects, namely, whether Jesus was someone sent by God at all, or whether it was even possible for him to be the definitive agent of God's eschatological salvation. These themes do surface in some places, but they never form the breaking point between Jesus and "the Jews." The breaking point is an intra-Christian issue: Was Jesus, who is acclaimed as prophet and Son of God, already one with God during his earthly ministry?

In the second place, I defend my view by examining the speeches in which the Evangelist has Jesus react to the objections of the opponents. These speeches are formulated in such a way that the opponents whom the Evangelist addresses can be seen as possessing a certain amount of positive appreciation of Jesus. The opponents who are being represented are apparently not non-Christian Jews but Christians who do not share the Johannine Christology.

I recognize that the two types of evidence I have just mentioned are perhaps not sufficiently compelling to make the interpretation of the Gospel as a polemic against other Christians necessary. Nonetheless, I prefer the interpretation that John's polemic does not reflect a dispute with traditional Jews; it reflects only a controversy with other Christians who maintain a different christological understanding from John's own group. The reason I prefer this interpretation is that the Evangelist's depiction of the Jews in his story is so incongruent with actual traditional Jews that it is obvious they are actually strangers to him. He speaks of them as a category of people with whom he has had no contact and whom he hardly even knows. The Evangelist's unfamiliarity with the Jewry of the first century is especially evident in the way in which he characterizes the Jews as a single, homogeneous ethnical group before Pilate in the passion account of chapters 18 and 19. The Evangelist depicts them in these chapters and elsewhere with a surprising ignorance and lack of nuance.[5] It becomes apparent from the unnuanced manner in which he speaks of "the Jews" in the passion story that he is unable to contrive a credible image of them for himself. He is no longer able to imagine them as real people of flesh and blood. They are an undifferentiated, foreign entity out of a relatively distant past, basically a fictional category. They are an *idée fixe*. The Evangelist speaks of them as strangers.[6] On the basis of this evidence, I am inclined to deduce that "the Jews" were no longer discussion partners for John. The Evangelist betrays his own attitude concerning "the Jews" when he has Jesus say, in 8:25: "'Why do I speak to you at all?'" John is no longer in dialogue with "the Jews" but with Christians who, although they did believe in Jesus in some manner, were not prepared to accept the Johannine Christology, and who therefore did not belong to the Johannine group.

I now attempt to substantiate my understanding of the Fourth Gospel by examining chapters 5–12. Due to the innate limitations of this contribution, it is inevitably necessary for the discussion to be concise. I have opted to discuss chapters 5–12 in this contribution because the Evangelist has Jesus manifest himself to the world here (chapters 1–12), and the confrontation between Jesus and "the Jews" begins with chapter 5. The Evangelist prepares the way for this confrontation in the preceding chapters. The relationship between Jesus and "the Jews" is already strained in 2:18, where they ask Jesus what gives him the right to act the way he does. In 3:11, Jesus makes the objection to Nicodemus: "'You [plural, referring to the Jewish teachers (3:10), the Pharisees (3:1), or "the Jews" (3:1) in general?] do not receive our [Jesus'] testimony.'" In 4:1–3, Jesus leaves Judaea and goes to Galilee because the Pharisees of Judaea were unfavorably inclined toward him on account of his growing popularity. But in chapter 5, the confrontation between Jesus and "the Jews" hardens. Now the Jews (of Jerusalem) "started persecuting him" (v. 16) and "were seeking . . . to kill him" (v. 18).

5. The Evangelist's ignorance is apparent in 18:3, "police from the chief priests and the Pharisees"; 18:12, "the Jewish police"; 18:13, "the high priest that year." A strange lack of knowledge also surfaces in 11:46, where the Jews go "to the Pharisees" to accuse Jesus; 11:47, "the chief priests and the Pharisees called a meeting of the council"; and 11:49, "Caiaphas, who was high priest that year." A peculiar lack of nuance is evident in John's use of the term *the Jews* in 18:31, 36, 38; 19:7, 12, 14, 31, 38; but also in 11:19, 31, 33, 36, 54, 55.

6. E.g., 19:40.

Before I begin my treatment of chapters 5–12, I make the observation that, in my opinion, many of the passages of the Gospel of John (as in the other Gospels) can carry more than one meaning. It is undoubtedly true that we are dealing exclusively with a text from the last decade of the first century. And yet many of the passages carry meanings on two different levels.[7] First there is the level of the narrated occurrence from the time of Jesus' earthly activity. On this level the text carries a kind of "literal," prima facie meaning. Thus, the reference to "the Jews" simply represents the Jewish contemporaries of Jesus, even though this category, with the reactions of "the Jews" to Jesus, is for the most part a construction of the Evangelist, which he invented himself. The hermeneutical context of this primary meaning is the world of Jesus during his time on earth as the Evangelist imagines it. But in many places the Gospel also carries another, even more important meaning that is determined by the hermeneutical context of the Evangelist's own world. On this second level the author wanted to infuse into the Gospel an actual meaning for his own contemporaries. On this level the Evangelist wages an indirect polemic against his opponents within a writing that is addressed to like-minded believers (the Johannine community). It is my contention that, on this level, the nomenclature "the Jews" sometimes represents the author's Christian opponents. These opponents did not share the writer's Christology but were nonetheless Christians. The Evangelist calls them "Jews" because he took for granted that Jesus had lived and acted among Jews. Thus, in one single passage, "the Jews" can refer to the characters in the biographical story of Jesus and at the same time represent a group of non-Johannine Christians with whom the author is engaged in a dispute.

John 5

In John 5, the story is related about how Jesus heals a man in Jerusalem who had been sick for thirty-eight years. The healing induces criticism from "the Jews" (5:10, 16, 18). At first, their objection appears to be grounded on the fact that Jesus "was doing such things on the sabbath" (5:16), whereby the Sabbath was being violated. But the motif of the violation of the Sabbath is only a prelude to the introduction of a more

---

7. The fact that it is often necessary to accept two meanings for one passage is explained by (along with other scholars) A. Boeckh, *Enzyklopädie und Methodologie der philologischen Wissenschaften* (Leipzig, 1886; reprint, Darmstadt, 1966), p. 91. This method is necessary when "der Wortsinn zum Verständnis nicht ausreicht." An extra ("übertragene") meaning must be postulated when "der Sinn des ganzen Werks und die gegenseitige Beziehung aller seiner Theile (es) verlangt."

important theme. According to the Evangelist, Jesus' work on the Sabbath is the work of his Father: "My Father is still working, and I also am working" (5:17). "Indeed, just as the Father raises the dead and gives them life, so also the Son gives life to whomever he wishes" (5:21). "The works that the Father has given me to complete, the very works that I am doing, testify on my behalf" (5:36). The central motif for the Evangelist here is that Jesus is one with the Father in his works. It is true that the Evangelist needed the introduction of the theme of the Sabbath to clarify his view of Jesus: just as God is still working on the Sabbath to prove his benevolence, so also may Jesus work benevolently on the Sabbath. But the crucial point is not the Sabbath but the confession of Jesus' functional unity with the Father. It is only when this last point has been made (5:17) that "the Jews" want to kill him, because, as the Evangelist has them say, he was "making himself equal to God" (5:18; 7:1). The essential problem the opponents have is actually this: the Johannine doctrine of the unity of Jesus and his Father.

On the level of the narrated occurrence, "the Jews" in this passage are traditional Jews. And yet, it is rather striking that the decisive objection these Jews raise against Jesus concerns the Johannine claim that he and the Father are one in their work. They acknowledge entirely that Jesus performed the miraculous healing (5:16). This raises the suspicion that, on the level of the communication between the Evangelist and his readers, "the Jews" are already thought of as people who rejected the Johannine Christology but not Jesus in general.

What is truly remarkable, however, is the discourse the Evangelist then places in Jesus' mouth in 5:19–47. The discourse is directed toward "the Jews" (5:19, αὐτοῖς, referring to "the Jews" in 5:18). But the speech is formulated in such a way that the recipients are considered to accept a priori the idea that Jesus is "the Son" of God the Father (5:19, 25). Those who are being addressed in Jesus' speech (i.e., "the Jews") are also considered to be familiar with the idea that God "sent" Jesus (5:23, 24, 30). These particular conceptions concerning Jesus are not subjects of discussion between the speaker (Jesus) and the recipients ("the Jews"). Even the question of whether Jesus is the apocalyptic Son of man who comes to judge (5:27) is not a subject of discussion. The only point for which the author argues is the notion that not only will Jesus appear and act as eschatological judge (i.e., as Son of man) in the future but that he had already appeared and acted in this way during his earthly ministry sixty years earlier: "the hour is coming, and is now here" (5:25). Finally, the opponents are expected to acknowledge, just as they did in 5:17 and 18, that Jesus has performed truly remarkable works.

But people who accept that Jesus is the Son of God, that he is sent by God, and that he is the Son of man must be Christians. Thus, when the Evangelist wrote the discourse of Jesus in 5:19–47, the opponents he had in mind were Christians but not Johannine Christians. The so-called Jews of chapter 5 are traditional, non-Christian Jews on the level of the narration, but on the level of the communication between the Evangelist and his readers, they represent non-Johannine Christians.

John 6

In the sixth chapter, John tells about the feeding of the five thousand and Jesus' walking on the water. These "signs" (6:14, 26) produce two reactions: the reaction of "the crowd" (6:2, 22, 24) and the reaction of "the Jews" (6:41, 52). After Jesus has spoken to "the Jews" in the discourse of 6:41–58, there is yet the negative reaction of "his disciples" (6:60–66) and the positive reaction of Peter.

The reactions of the crowd are typical responses of believers with inadequate faith. They profess that Jesus "is indeed the prophet who is to come into the world" (6:14; cf. Deut. 18:18–20), and they want to make him king (6:15). They look for Jesus (6:24, 26). But the Evangelist has Jesus rebuke them because they are hoping only to receive food that perishes, instead of food that endures for eternal life (6:27), that is, Jesus, who is the bread of God that has come down from heaven (6:33, 35, 38, 41).

From the perspective of John the Evangelist, the crowd consists of people who "do not believe" (6:36), but they are depicted in this way only because they do not share the high Christology of John. In actuality (that is, in the reality of the author's social world), they have quite a substantially positive appreciation for Jesus: they see him as a prophet like Moses (Deut. 18:15–18), as a teacher (6:25), and as the future ideal king of Israel (6:15); in other words, they see him as the "anointed of the Lord" or the Christ.

On the level of the narrated occurrence, the crowd is a group of Jewish disciples of Jesus who are not able completely to believe in Jesus with an adequate faith. On the level of the communication between John and his readers, the Evangelist is describing Christians who do not accept the Johannine Christology. In the speech that the Evangelist has Jesus deliver in 6:32–40, John polemicizes against Christians with non-Johannine convictions.

More important for our subject are the verses of the passage 6:41–59, because the reaction portrayed in these verses is identified as that of "the Jews." The Evangelist describes these "Jews" as raising only one objection against Jesus, namely, they object to the claim that he has come down from heaven as food that gives eternal life. Thus, "the Jews" protest only against the typical Johannine conception of Jesus, not against Jesus in general.

Moreover, in the speech the Evangelist has Jesus deliver to these Jews (6:43–58), they are considered to accept the following presuppositions: (1) that people must come to Jesus (6:44); (2) that Jesus was sent by the Father (6:44, 57); (3) that Jesus comes from God (6:46); (4) that Jesus is the Son of man (6:53); (5) that Jesus lives through the Father (6:57). These are all notions that are not justified or explained. The presumed hearers of Jesus' discourse are supposed to take them for granted.

In the context of the story of 6:41–59, "the Jews" are naturally thought of as traditional Jews. In the context of the author's message for his readers, however, verses 42–58 reflect a polemical rebuttal against Christians who do not share John's vision concerning Jesus.

Finally, John 6:60–66 relates how Jesus' speech about himself as the bread from heaven provoked exasperation from many of his disciples. They are indeed disciples, but they cannot accept the Johannine doctrine that Jesus is the bread from heaven that gives life. They have a different vision concerning Jesus; for instance, that he is the Son of man (6:62). But the Evangelist believes that if they do not share his radical Christology, they "do not believe" (6:64). He sees them as "turning away" from Jesus (6:66). On the narrative level, these people are disciples of Jesus whose faith in him is inadequate, and so they eventually desert him. In the context of John's message for his readers, however, he polemicizes here against contemporary Christians of a non-Johannine brand. The Evangelist typecasts them as unbelievers or apostates, but in their own opinion, they undoubtedly considered themselves to be Christians.

In general, then, it appears that the Evangelist is polemicizing against non-Johannine Christians not only in the passages about the crowd (6:1–40) and the disciples (6:60–66) but also in the passage about "the Jews" (6:41–59). On the narrative level, the crowd, the disciples, and the Jews are three distinct groups. On the level of the communication with his readers, however, the author uses these different groups to conduct one single polemic against one single group: it is a polemic against Christians who do not agree with his Christology.

John 7–8

Chapters 7–8 relate that Jesus goes from Galilee to Jerusalem, where he stays during the festival of Tabernacles. In the temple, he has discussions with various Jewish groups.

In the first scene (7:1–13), the writer observes that the Jews of Judaea want to kill Jesus (7:1). This is a resumption of 5:18. We have already seen that the cause of the Jewish opposition in 5:18 was the Johannine view of Jesus as the one who works like his Father (5:17). The antagonists are called "Jews" because they appear as characters in the social context of the earthly Jesus. But for the author of the Fourth Gospel, they represent at the same time the opponents of the Johannine community and its Christology. Although they maintained a positive appreciation of Jesus, they refused to acknowledge the functional unity of the earthly Jesus with God.

After Jesus' arrival in Jerusalem, it becomes apparent that the Jews in Jerusalem are in fact hostilely opposed to him (7:11, 13). This hostility receives no more explication than it does in 7:1; the explication has been given in 5:17–18, namely, that Jesus held the typically Johannine opinion that he was one with the Father. The Jews of 7:11 seem to be opposed not to Jesus but Johannine Christology.

In the second scene (7:14–30) Jesus meets "the Jews" in the Temple. Jesus knows that they want to kill him (7:19), but the crowd is not yet aware of this (7:20). The Evangelist has Jesus engage in a discussion with the Jews (v. 16, αὐτοῖς). In his report of the discussion, the Evangelist makes it clear once again that the anger of those who wish to kill Jesus is provoked by the claim that Jesus, just like God, works on the Sabbath (7:21, 23–24). The theme is the same here as in 5:18. The second scene is concluded with the sentence "Then they tried to arrest him [Jesus]" (7:30). It is not completely clear whether the antecedent of "they" in v. 30 is "some of the people of Jerusalem" (7:25) or "the Jews" of 7:1 (and 5:18). But for our purposes, it is irrelevant to ponder this matter too extensively. For in either case the remark in 7:30, "they tried to arrest him," immediately follows the words of Jesus in which, once again, the very typical Johannine Christology finds expression: "I have not come on my own. But the one who sent me is true, and you do not know him. I know him, because I am from him, and he sent me" (7:28–29). The opposition of 7:30 is directed against the Johannine claim that an exclusive bond existed between the earthly Jesus and God, whereby Jesus acted as the full envoy of God on earth.

It is only natural that those who wish to arrest Jesus within the story are Jewish contemporaries of Jesus. But the author also portrays them as opponents of the Johannine Christology, that is, as opponents of himself and his community. These adversaries possess a substantially positive appreciation of Jesus (7:15), but at the same time, John sees them as opponents of the Johannine Christology.

In the third scene (7:31–36), it is not "the Jews" (as in 7:11, 7:1, and 5:18) who want to arrest Jesus but the "chief priests and the Pharisees." In this case, their motivation is not an objection to the Johannine Christology but their irritation at the fact that "many in the crowd" believed in Jesus. Thus, their motive is jealousy, a motif that goes back to Mark 15:10 and that will return in 11:45–47 (see below). As a result, the "chief priests and Pharisees" of 7:32 are only characters in the narrative, not opponents of John. They are the Jewish leaders who will later arrest Jesus in the passion story (11:57; 18:3).

At the end of this scene, "the Jews" are once again introduced and characterized as being unable to comprehend Jesus. They are portrayed as being unable to understand what it means that Jesus will go where they cannot go. It is probable that the author understands "the Jews" here not only as characters in the story but also as representing Christian opponents of the Johannine community. For the author says that these "Jews" are "searching" for Jesus (7:34, 36) but that they do not find him, because they do not realize that Jesus is going to the One who sent him and to a place where they cannot go. These "Jews" search for Jesus; they probably belong to the "many in the crowd" who believed in Jesus (7:31); but they do not acknowledge that he is God's specific, exclusive envoy. When considered outside the parameters of the story, in the personal experience of the Evangelist, would they not actually be Christians of whom the Evangelist knows that they are in search of Jesus, but who do not share in the Johannine conception of Jesus?

The fourth scene (7:37–44) also concludes with the notation that some of the crowd "wanted to arrest" Jesus (7:44). In this case, there is no compelling reason to assume that John means any group other than the characters in the story. Their aggression against Jesus is incited by the positive reactions of some of the crowd toward Jesus (7:40–41a). The "division" of which 7:43 speaks corresponds with the contradistinction between the people who see Jesus as the prophet and the Christ (7:40–41a) and those who do not see him as the Christ (7:41b–42). All of this remains on the level of the narrative. The remark "some of them wanted to arrest him" can be sufficiently explained as a prelude, on the narrative level, to Jesus' arrest in the passion story.

In the fifth scene (7:45–8:20), the "chief priests and Pharisees" complain that their servants did not arrest Jesus. This passage is the continuation of 7:32, where the chief priests and Pharisees sent out their servants to arrest Jesus. We have already seen that these priests and Pharisees were motivated by jealousy (7:31–32). The opposition of the chief priests and

Pharisees must therefore be construed as an intranarrative theme and as a preparation for the arrest of Jesus (18:3, 12). Within the story, these characters do not represent Christian opponents of the Evangelist.

After Jesus' speech in 8:12, 14–19, the listeners, among whom the Pharisees (8:13) are mentioned, want to kill him, but they do not do this because Jesus' time had not yet come (8:20). It is possible that the Evangelist in 8:20 is alluding to the opposition of the Johannine Christology, for the message of 8:12–19 is clearly that Jesus and the Father are functionally one. Jesus' judgment is God's judgment (8:16), and Jesus' testimony is God's testimony (8:18). This theme reiterates the theme of 5:36.[8] Thus, it is possible that the opposition of 8:20 represents not only an element in the story of Jesus but also an element in the social context of the Evangelist. In this case, just as in chapter 5, it is the opposition of Christians against the Johannine group, because the criticism is directed against typical Johannine viewpoints and not against the appreciation of Jesus.

One cannot be entirely certain, however, that the opposition mentioned here is reflective of opposition on the level of the communication between the Evangelist and his readers. The resistance to Jesus alluded to in 8:20 can also be explained as nothing more than a narrative element within the literary context of the Gospel that serves only to prepare for the arrest of Jesus in chapter 18.

The sixth scene (8:21–59) records that Jesus tells "the Jews" that he speaks that which he has heard and learned from God (8:26, 28). As a result of his speaking, many come to believe in him (8:30). But it becomes quickly apparent that, according to the Evangelist, these believing Jews were not yet true disciples of Jesus (8:31). The writer tells us that Jesus discerns that they want to kill him (8:37, 40). The Evangelist even has Jesus tell them that they do not understand Jesus (8:43), that the devil is their father (8:44), and that they do not believe in Jesus (8:45). The contradiction between the claim that these Jews "believed in him" (8:31) and the statement of Jesus that they do not believe in him (8:45) is only superficial. In the story, they are Jews who believed in Jesus to a certain extent, but they did not accept all the Johannine refinements of the Christology that Jesus here assigns to himself. They are believers of inadequate faith. When they are referred to as unbelieving in 8:45 and 46, this is the judgment of the Evangelist, which he places in the mouth of Jesus. Their evaluation of Jesus is so inadequate that the Evangelist has Jesus say that they do not believe. From their own viewpoint, though, they would very much consider themselves to be believers.

8. de Ruyter, *De gemeente*, p. 67.

These believers of inadequate faith, however, do not play a role only within the narrated story. They also undoubtedly represent a group of Christian believers from the time of the Evangelist whom he rejects. He reproaches them because they do not sufficiently acknowledge that Jesus speaks and does what the Father has him say and do (8:38, 40). They are certainly believers, but they do not endorse the Johannine Christology, which maintains that the earthly Jesus appeared as God's envoy in the role of the apocalyptic Son of man and that he represented God already during his earthly ministry (8:28; see also 1:51, 5:27, etc.). Believers who do not accept this understanding of Jesus are considered by the Evangelist to be unbelievers. Nowhere is it so clear as it is here that "the Jews" (8:31, 48) against whom the author polemicizes are actually Christians with a non-Johannine persuasion.

In 8:48–59, the conflict between Jesus and "the Jews" escalates. The cause of the escalation is that Jesus insists that a unique relationship exists between him and God: Jesus glorifies God and is glorified by God (8:49, 54); the divine gift of eternal life is mediated through the word of Jesus (8:51, 52); and Jesus claims to be preexistent (8:58). These far-reaching christological claims cause "the Jews" to distance themselves from Jesus. And yet, these are the same Jews who had come to believe in Jesus (8:30) and who, to a large extent, had become his disciples (8:31). The breaking point between them and Jesus is now defined by the specifically Johannine view of Jesus. On the level of the narrative, these Jews who first followed Jesus and then fell away from him are just ordinary Jews. The fact that the breach becomes evident only when the notions of the typically Johannine Christology are introduced makes it plausible that, on the level of the Evangelist's message for his readers, he is polemicizing against a group of people who claimed to be Christians but who reject John's view of Jesus. In their own opinion they are Christians, but John considers them to be unbelievers. The Evangelist projects their rejection of the Johannine view of Jesus upon the attitude of the Jews toward the earthly Jesus.

John 9–10

This section begins by telling how Jesus heals, on the Sabbath, a person who was blind from birth. The Evangelist views this healing as a work of God (9:3) that is performed by Jesus (9:4). Jesus is here doing the work of the One who sent him (9:4). The work of God and the work of Jesus are the same.

Then the Evangelist records the reactions of two different groups: the reaction of the Pharisees (9:13–17) and that of "the Jews" (9:18–34). The reaction of the Pharisees is divided. Some of them declare that Jesus has not come from God due to the fact that he performed the healing on the Sabbath. We noted the same reaction in 5:18. According to the evangelist, this reaction demonstrates, in essence, that the Pharisees deny that Jesus, like God himself, is allowed to work on the Sabbath. They deny the functional unity between Jesus and God, which Jesus claims in 9:3–4. These Pharisees do not deny that Jesus has performed a miraculous healing. The only thing they reject is the Johannine view of Jesus, whereby Jesus is one with God.

In mentioning these Pharisees in the story, the Evangelist undoubtedly means nothing other than genuine Pharisees, contemporaries of Jesus. But the Evangelist portrays them as being critical of his Johannine Christology. For the Evangelist, then, these Pharisees represent opponents of the Johannine community. These adversaries do not reject Jesus in general, only the specifically Johannine Christology as it concerns the functional unity of Jesus and God. Thus, in the notion of the Evangelist, these people appear more as Christians who are against the Johannine Christology than as traditional Jews.

A justification for accepting the idea that these so-called Pharisees represent for the Evangelist a specific type of Christian can be found in his depiction of the other group of Pharisees. The other Pharisees argue with the first group of Pharisees. The second group of Pharisees reason that the signs that Jesus performs prove he is not a sinner (9:16) and that he comes from God. They accept that Jesus performs his signs on the Sabbath and, as such, that he works in the same way as the Father and that he works the work of the Father (9:4). On the level of the narrative, of course, these Pharisees are also genuine Pharisees. But on the level of the message of the Evangelist for his readers, they are conceived as people who recognize Jesus' miraculous acts as well as his unity with the Father; that is, they are conceived as Christians who possess, or who come near to possessing, the Johannine conviction.

Therefore, in the view that the Evangelist unfolds for his readers, the Pharisees of 9:16a as well as those of 9:16b stand for Christians: the first, for non-Johannine Christians, and the second, for Christians who come near to accepting the Johannine view of Jesus.

As far as "the Jews" of 9:18–34 are concerned, they also acknowledge that Jesus truly did perform the miraculous healing (9:19, 26). But like the first group of Pharisees (9:16), they consider Jesus to be a "sinner" (9:24).

In this chapter, there is no reason provided to support this opinion other than the violation of the Sabbath (cf. 9:16). Thus, these Jews also deny that Jesus, as is also true of God, may work on the Sabbath. Accordingly, they deny the unity of the work of Jesus and God, whereby they reject the Johannine evaluation of Jesus. But they do not completely reject Jesus. The Evangelist does not even have them deny that Jesus has come from God; they go no further than to say: "We do not know where he comes from" (9:29). The only thing they reject is the unity of Jesus and God.

In the plot of the story, there is no doubt that "the Jews" stand for actual Jews from the time of Jesus.[9] But insofar as the Evangelist wants to instruct his readers concerning what, in his opinion, the correct assessment of Jesus is, he employs the category of "the Jews" here as an illustration for non-Johannine Christians. After all, the only aspect of "the Jews" that the Evangelist discredits is the fact that they deny the unity of Jesus and God. But if this is the only basis for the Evangelist's condemnation of them, then they are Christians with a non-Johannine Christology, not non-Christian Jews. In the eyes of the Evangelist, however, Christians who do not share the Johannine Christology are unbelievers, even if they think of themselves as Christians. The Evangelist uses the category of "the Jews" as a watershed term to characterize fellow Christians who are anti-Johannine.

The parables of the shepherd and the thief (10:1–5), the gate (10:7–10), and the good shepherd (10:11–16) do not directly provide any support for our position. But the end of Jesus' speech (10:17–18) and the subsequent reactions of "the Jews" to the speech are rather enlightening. The Evangelist has Jesus claim that he can lay down his life and take it up again by virtue of a special mandate that he has received from the Father (10:18). Once again, an exclusive relationship between God and Jesus is being claimed here. This leads directly to a division among the Jews. Many of the Jews consider the claim of exclusive solidarity between God and Jesus to be unacceptable. Nonetheless, in their rejection they renounce nothing more than the Johannine view of Jesus; they do not reject Jesus in general. "Other" Jews are even able to accept the claim of the close relationship between God and Jesus on the grounds of Jesus' healing of the blind man (10:21).

Both groups of Jews in the narrative of 10:19–21 are real, traditional Jews. But at the same time the Evangelist uses these Jews in the framework of his communication with his readers. Within this framework, these people, whose only objection to Jesus revolves around the Johannine claim

9. This is why they are introduced in 9:22 and 34 as Jews who excommunicate the Christians from the synagogue.

of an exclusive relationship between Jesus and God, must be Christians. Otherwise, they would have objected to many other notions of Jesus, for example, the notion that Jesus was sent by the Father. But they only take offense at the claim that Jesus has received a special mandate concerning himself from God. If this is their only objection, then they are evidently conceived by the writer as Christians who reject the Evangelist's high Christology. The "other" Jews of 10:21 do not reject this Christology, in view of Jesus' healing of the blind man. Within the parameters of the message of the Evangelist, these other Jews are thus Christians who adhere to a view that is very near to that of the Johannine group. Therefore, on the level of the author's message for his readers, "the Jews" who reject John's Christology (10:20) are not directly traditional Jews; they are Christians whose view of Jesus does not coincide with the view of John. On the level of his communication with his readers, John typecasts the category of "the Jews" to play the role of Christian contemporaries who did not accept all, or perhaps only a portion, of John's Christology.

Although a period of approximately two months lies between Tabernacles (10:21) and the festival of the Dedication (10:22), the passage 10:22–39 belongs to the section 9:1–10:39. This is evident from the fact that 10:27–29 recalls the parables of 10:1–10. The debates between Jesus and "the Jews" that are recorded in 10:32–39 are the last in the series of discussions in Jerusalem that began in chapter 5. These last debates are particularly fierce.

The Evangelist tells his readers that "the Jews" once again want to stone Jesus (10:31).[10] This is the reaction of the Jews to Jesus' utterance "The Father and I are one" (10:30). Thus, the adversaries of Jesus are introduced again as being opposed to the specifically Johannine Christology. They are not entirely ill-disposed toward Jesus, for at the beginning of the debate (10:24) they are still able to ask Jesus, "How long will you keep us in suspense? If you are the Messiah, tell us plainly." It cannot be denied that they possess some form of interest or fascination for Jesus. But for the Evangelist, their appreciation of Jesus is much too little. He says simply that they "do not believe" (10:25, 26).

Within the narrative of chapter 10, "the Jews" of vv. 24–32 are Jewish contemporaries of Jesus. In the instructions that the Evangelist wants to transmit to his readers, however, these are people who do not reject anything except the Johannine Christology; otherwise, they exhibit a rather keen interest in Jesus. This is why the Evangelist has Jesus speak to these opponents as if Jesus can assume their acquiescence with the idea that he is

10. See also 8:59 and 11:8.

the Son of God (10:25) and that he has the right to act as the leader of a group of disciples (10:27). Thus, in the message of the Evangelist for his readers, "the Jews" of 10:22–31 represent people who are Christians but who do not accept the Johannine profession that Jesus and God are one. The Evangelist considers people like this to be unbelievers, even though they would consider themselves to be non-Johannine Christians.

At the end of chapter 10, "the Jews" persist in their rejection of Jesus. This is the Evangelist's preparation of the role "the Jews" will play in the passion story of chapters 18 (vv. 31, 36, 38) and 19 (vv. 7, 12, 14). In this passage we already see that "they tried to arrest" Jesus (10:39). On the level of the narrative, these Jews are ordinary Jews in the everyday life of the earthly Jesus. It is rather striking, however, that the objection of these "Jews" is directed against nothing other than the Johannine claim that the Father is in Jesus and that Jesus is in the Father (10:38). The opponents regard this evaluation of Jesus to be too much. And so this is the aspect that "the Jews" react against; but this is an objection against John, not against Jesus.

Thus, the Evangelist portrays "the Jews" as if they were critical of the Christology of the Johannine group. This points out the fact that the Johannine group itself was being confronted by such criticism toward the end of the first century—a criticism not of Jesus but of the Johannine Christology. But this critical attack must have emanated from a Christian source, for the discussion does not concern the significance of Jesus in general, only the typically Johannine profession that Jesus and God are one in their works. The Evangelist proceeds on the assumption that the opponents whom he has in mind share with him a positive evaluation of Jesus. He supposes that the opponents accept that "the Father has sanctified and sent [Jesus] into the world" (10:36) and that Jesus is the Son of God (10:38). The Evangelist pronounces these views without providing any justification or explanation. The opponents are considered to be in agreement with the Evangelist on these matters. Thus, the opponents are regarded by the Evangelist as Christians.

In short, the Evangelist portrays "the Jews" with the features of his own Christian opponents. The polemic of the Fourth Evangelist is directed here against Christian opponents, not against Jewish opponents.

John 11–12

The first half of John's Gospel, in which Jesus reveals himself to the world, is concluded with chapters 11–12. This section relates the reactions of several Jewish groups to Jesus, but none of these groups plays a role that transcends the narrative level of the story. They do not represent any opponents of the Evangelist. In this respect, chapters 11–12 prepare the way in which the Evangelist treats the Jews in the second half of the Gospel.

The resurrection of Lazarus provokes various reactions from the Jews. Many of them come to believe in Jesus (11:45). Others bring accusations against him before "the Pharisees" (11:46). The "chief priests and the Pharisees" now decide that Jesus must be arrested and put to death (11:53, 57). The belief in Jesus of the one group must be told (11:45) in order to make the hostile reaction of the other group (11:46) understandable. And this latter reaction must be told in order to make the animosity of the Jewish leaders toward Jesus comprehensible. In this way, all the actions and reactions of the Jewish groups in 11:45–57 can be perceived as fulfilling a specific, literary function within the narrative context of the Gospel, whereby preparation is made for Jesus' passion. They do not reflect the social relationships at the level of the author of the Gospel. The reason the Jewish leaders want to put Jesus to death is that Jesus is performing so many signs that countless people are on the verge of believing in him (11:48). The motivation of the Jewish leaders is thus determined by envy, a motif that already controls the plot of the passion story in the Gospel of Mark (Mark 15:10). Here, in 11:45–57, there is no record of a discussion between Jesus and the Jews, nor between the Evangelist and any kind of adversary. The Jews of chapter 11 are portrayed only as contemporaries of Jesus; they do not also represent opponents of the Evangelist.

The same simple representation is true for the chief priests who want to kill Lazarus (12:10) after the anointing of Jesus in Bethany (12:1–8). The motif here is also jealousy (12:9–11). These stories simply reflect the Evangelist's reconstruction of the events on a narrative level. There is no evidence at all of a discussion between the Evangelist and some kind of opponent.

The Pharisees who become angry after Jesus' entry into Jerusalem (12:19) are also motivated by jealousy. They are simply characters in the plot of the Passion, not representatives of some kind of opponent of the Evangelist.

In 12:37–43, the Evangelist sums up the final results of Jesus' preaching. The crowd in general ("they," i.e., the crowd mentioned in 12:29, 34) does not believe in him. This observation is astonishing, especially when one considers the supernatural signs and works that Jesus has performed. Such a failure to believe requires an explanation. And so the author offers two explanations.[11] The first is borrowed from tradition: the unbelief of the crowd is the effect of negative predestination (12:38–40). The other explanation is the invention of the Evangelist himself. Many of the leading Jews did believe in Jesus, but they believed in secret; they concealed the truth. As a result, the crowd was not able to confess belief in Jesus (12:42). It is necessary for the Evangelist to add the second explanation, because the explanation of negative predestination could provoke the reaction that the blind could not be held accountable for their unbelief. But from the perspective of the Evangelist, the actions of Jesus are definite signs that made it so overwhelmingly evident that he was divinely commissioned that everyone who had seen them should have believed in him. Thus, it is the Evangelist's task to explain the unbelief of the majority of the Jews, while maintaining the irrefutability of the works of Jesus. He accomplishes this by contending that the people who had seen Jesus' deeds had in fact come to believe in him but that they had concealed their faith (12:42),[12] so that many others did not come to believe.

But now the evangelist has a new problem: Why did the Jews who had actually come to believe in Jesus not publicly profess their belief? Why did they conceal their belief in Jesus? The Evangelist opts for the solution that they did not confess their faith for fear of excommunication (12:42). It is striking that the Evanglist uses the theme of excommunication in exactly the same way in 9:22. There, too, people are said to refuse to tell the truth about Jesus "because they were afraid of the Jews" who threatened to ban those who acknowledged Jesus as Messiah from the synagogue. The theme of excommunication serves simply to explain why people who had a correct knowledge about Jesus kept silent about him. Thus, the theme allows of an exclusively literary explanation, both in 9:11 and 12:42. It is unnecessary, therefore, to assume that in 16:2–4 the same theme has a more solid basis in historical facts, apart from the schism between the Johannine community and other Christian groups.

For the last thirty years, many exegetes have taken the excommunication of Christians from the synagogue, as it is mentioned in 12:42 (and 9:22; 16:2), as the historical starting point for the reconstruction of the origin of the Johannine community.[13] In my view, however, the mention

11. de Ruyter, *De gemeente,* pp. 113–15.

12. For the same motif, see 19:38; 9:22; and 7:13.

13. J. L. Martyn, *History and Theology in the Fourth Gospel* (New York, 1968; 2d ed., Nashville, 1979); J. L. Martyn, "Glimpses into the History of the Johannine Community," in M. de Jonge, ed., *L'Évangile de Jean* (BETL 44; Leuven, 1977), pp. 149–75 (reprinted in Martyn, *The Gospel of John in Christian History,* pp. 90–121). For a critique of Martyn's position, see de Ruyter, *De gemeente,* pp. 27–29.

of this excommunication is sufficiently and satisfactorily explained as a literary invention of the Evangelist, which he created in order to explicate why those who had actually come to believe in Jesus on account of his works did not openly profess their faith. And the silence of those who actually believed was the Evangelist's narrative construction to explain the general unbelief of the Jews.

All in all, chapters 11–12 do not reveal any reflection of a polemic of the Evangelist against his opponents. The behavior of the Jews in these chapters only fulfills a literary function within the narrative context of the Gospel; it serves as a preparation of the role played by the Jews in the Johannine passion story.

Conclusion

In many places in John's Gospel, Jewish people, groups, and leaders function only as literary characters within the parameters of the narrative. They do not represent contemporaries of the Evangelist with whom he is engaged in a dispute. This is true, for instance, in the case of the chief priests and the Pharisees of 7:32–36 and 7:45–8:20; the Jews of 11:19–57 and 12:9; the chief priests of 12:10; and the Pharisees of 12:19 and 12:42. Their role is repeatedly portrayed unfavorably by the Evangelist, but this role is the narrative, more or less fictional reconstruction of John. After one has examined the literary function of these groups within these passages of the narrative, the negative depiction of them can be put aside as historically unfounded and theologically irrelevant.

In many other cases, however, "the Jews" in John's Gospel are not only characters in the narrative but also, at the same time, people who represent Christian contemporaries of the Evangelist: Christians against whom he polemicizes. These people are Christians, but they do not share John's high Christology. They refuse to accept that the earthly Jesus was already one with God. In essence, they differ from John in terms of their view of eschatology. John asserted that eschatology had been realized with Jesus' appearance in the world: in Jesus, God had sent his representative to save and to judge the world. John's opponents, however, regarded the eschaton as not yet realized. Accordingly, they possessed a lower appreciation of Jesus. As a result, John views these less radical Christians as unbelievers. In his Gospel, he projects their unbelief on persons in the context of Jesus; inevitably, this projection falls on Jews surrounding Jesus. This does not mean, though, that John polemicizes against "Jews." His criticism is directed against Christians. He projects what he regards as the inadequacies of these Christians' faith, or what he regards as their unbelief, however, on the Jews figuring in his narrative about Jesus. This is perhaps an unfortunate technique. Nonetheless, when John practices this technique, he cannot be justifiably accused of being anti-Jewish. His polemic is elicited by and leveled against non-Johannine Christians. This is evident in John's treatment of the disciples in 6:60–66 and in his treatment of the Jews who believed in Jesus in 8:30–59. But the same interpretation applies to "the Jews" of Jerusalem in 5; 7:1–36; 9:18–34; 10:19, and 22–39; the crowd in 6:1–40; "the Jews" of Galilee in 6:41–59; and the Pharisees of Jerusalem in 9:13–16a and 40.

CHAPTER 7

The Depiction of "the Jews" in John's Gospel: Matters of Behavior and Identity

Martinus C. de Boer

"The Fourth Gospel is indeed one of the most Jewish of the early Christian writings," wrote Wayne Meeks in 1975, "even as it develops one of the most vehemently anti-Jewish polemics in the first century."[1] John Ashton responds to a similar comment by C. K. Barrett[2] with the observation that John is very Jewish with regard to "customs and ceremonies, turns of phrase and ways of thought,"[3] but anti-Jewish with regard to "a people or a nation." He goes on to ask: "Why does the evangelist, who never attempts to disguise the Jewishness of his hero, evince such hostility to his hero's people?"[4] The issue of anti-Judaism[5] in John thus comes to a focus, particularly in connection with the Gospel's references to and its depiction of "the Jews" (οἱ Ἰουδαῖοι).[6]

This essay makes some comments on (1) the nature of the charges leveled against "the Jews" in John[7] in connection with the problem of

---

1. W. Meeks, "'Am I a Jew?' Johannine Christianity and Judaism," in J. Neusner, ed., *Christianity, Judaism and Other Graeco-Roman Cults: Studies for Morton Smith at Sixty* (SJLA 12; Leiden, 1975), pp. 163–86. See also here, p. 185.

2. C. K. Barrett, *The Gospel of John and Judaism* (London, 1975; 3d. ed., 1983), p. 72.

3. Meeks, "Am I a Jew?'" p. 167—writes that an "impressively broad consensus exists today"—1975, but still true in 2001—that "the major ideas and symbols of Johannine Christianity derived from Judaism."

4. J. Ashton, *Understanding the Fourth Gospel* (Oxford, 1991), p. 131.

5. For a recent discussion of this issue in John, see K. Scholtissek, "Antijudaismus im Johannesevangelium? Ein Gesprächsbeitrag," in R. Kampling, ed., *"Nun steht aber diese Sache im Evangelium..."* *Zur Frage nach den Anfängen des christlichen Antijudaismus* (Paderborn, 1999), pp. 151–81; S. Pedersen, "Anti-Judaism in John's Gospel: John 8," in J. Nissen and S. Pedersen, eds., *New Readings in John: Literary and Theological Perspectives. Essays from the Scandinavian Conference on the Fourth Gospel in Århus 1997* (JSNTSup 182; Sheffield, 1999), pp. 172–93.

6. A survey of the discussion has been ably presented by U. C. von Wahlde, "'The Jews' in the Gospel of John: Fifteen Years of Research," with a bibliography (for the seminars on "Johannine Literature" and "Die Inhalte und Probleme der biblischen Theologie," SNTS Annual Meeting, Pretoria, South Africa, August 1999, published in *ETL* 76 (2000): 30–55). The term "the Jews" has been put in quotation marks since it often has a limited reference and peculiar meaning in John (see below).

7. In what follows, I shall use the traditional label "John" to refer to both the Fourth Gospel itself and its author or authors (one of these may well have been named John, but I leave that issue aside here).

141

defining the Gospel's supposed anti-Judaism (the problem is not "the Jews" as a group or a people but hostile, murderous behavior directed at God's Jewish envoy and his Jewish followers), and (2) the origin and significance of the designation "the Jews" for the opponents of Jesus (the epithet is probably an ironic acknowledgment of the claim on the part of Jewish authorities in the synagogue to be the authoritative arbiters of a genuinely Jewish identity).

"The Jews Were Seeking to Kill Him": Anti-Judaism in the Fourth Gospel?

Any discussion of anti-Judaism in the Fourth Gospel needs to be carefully circumscribed. There are statements with respect to "the Jews" in the Fourth Gospel that, on a first reading, can certainly be construed as maliciously and despicably anti-Jewish (most notoriously 8:44, often regarded as the most anti-Jewish statement of the New Testament), but only under the following conditions:

1. the literary or narrative contexts of such statements are ignored (on the narrative or literary level, the supposedly anti-Jewish statements occur as part of a debate between and among people who are all, ethnically speaking, Jews; one of those Jews is Jesus himself);
2. the historical context within which such statements initially functioned is not acknowledged (on any reading of the Gospel, the debate between Jesus and "the Jews" of John's narrative takes place in the first century C.E., not in the twentieth or twenty-first);[8] and
3. the charges made against "the Jews" in John (especially that they want to excommunicate followers of Jesus from the synagogue and to kill Jesus and his disciples) are deemed to represent not historically plausible actions on the part of (certain) Jews both within and out-

---

8. Even a narrative-critical or reader-response reading, which in principle brackets historical questions, must acknowledge that the setting of the story is that of the first-century Greco-Roman world, even if such a world never really existed outside the story. A historical approach assumes (on the basis of overwhelming evidence, both documentary and archaeological) that a first-century Greco-Roman world did once exist and can conclude (given the abundant material evidence) that there were actual people in the first century known as Jews; further, that there was someone named Jesus of Nazareth; that he had followers; and so forth. A historical approach can thus also assume, and perhaps must do so, that the actual historical context within which the Gospel was written and first read is relevant, indeed crucial, to its interpretation and continued use by Christians—and others.

side the narrative of this first-century work but the defamatory inventions of the Evangelist (such an appraisal of the evidence, though possible in principle, is surely implausible and improbable given the specificity of the charges, and would anachronistically make John an anti-Semite *avant la lettre*).[9]

In addition, and first of all, the claim made by Ashton (and others) that the Fourth Gospel expresses "hostility" toward "the Jews" of the story needs to be examined.[10] The Gospel's portrayal of "the Jews" arguably exhibits perplexity, exasperation, and annoyance[11] (with a strong undertone of sorrow and regret),[12] but neither Jesus in John nor the Evangelist in editorial comments counsels hatred or contempt for "the Jews" or their beliefs.[13] The only hating a Christian may do concerns his or her own life (12:25). The verb μισέω occurs elsewhere in John only in connection with hatred directed to Jesus and his followers (3:20; 7:7; 15:18, 19, 23, 24, 25; 17:14; cf. 1 John 3:13), usually by "the world." Disciples are, in fact, called on to spend their time "loving one another" and Jesus (13:34–15:17), not hating

9. It has sometimes been maintained that "the Jews" of the Gospel represent or symbolize the attitudes of (Jewish or other) Christians (for discussion, see Meeks, "'Am I a Jew?'" p. 183; see also now B. W. J. de Ruyter, *De gemeente van de evangelist Johannes: Haar polemiek en haar geschiedenis* [Delft, 1998] and chapter 6 by de Jonge). A much simpler and more plausible explanation is that of J. L. Martyn, *History and Theology in the Fourth Gospel* (Nashville, 1979), namely, that the formative version of John is a two-level drama testifying to a situation in which Johannine Jewish Christians were in conflict with Jews of the synagogue in the late first century. "The Jews" of the narrative in Martyn's hypothesis thus represent a particular group of synagogue Jews in John's own setting, not Jewish or Gentile Christians. See also M. C. de Boer, *Johannine Perspectives on the Death of Jesus* (Kampen, 1996), pp. 53–55, where I argue that the "point of correspondence between the two levels, or stages, of the Johannine drama is to be located primarily in the pervasive and bitter conflict of Jesus with 'the Jews'" (p. 55). In certain discrete passages (cf. 6:60ff.), the Gospel reflects a schism within the Johannine Christian community itself over the issue of Christology (see de Boer, *Johannine Perspectives*, especially pp. 63–71), but this conflict plays a subordinate role in the Gospel drama as a whole. The Christian Jews mentioned or alluded to in John 8:30–31; 12:42 belong to the primary setting in which the Gospel took shape, the conflict with "the Jews" of the synagogue.

10. See our opening paragraph (p. 141) for Ashton's comments (*Understanding the Fourth Gospel*). Cf. also P. J. Tomson, *If This Be from Heaven . . . : Jesus and the New Testament Authors in Their Relationship to Judaism* (The Biblical Seminar 76; Sheffield, 2001), p. 327. R. A. Culpepper speaks of their "vilification" in "The Gospel of John and the Jews," *RevExp* 84 (1987): 273–88 (e.g., p. 273), as does A. Reinhartz, *The Johannine Community and Its Jewish Neighbors: A Reappraisal*, in F. Segovia, ed., *"What Is John?"* Vol. 2: *Literary and Social Readings of the Fourth Gospel* (SBLSymS 7; Atlanta, 1998), pp. 111–38. Culpepper begins another article with the statement: "The Gospel of John contains some of the most hostile anti-Jewish statements in the Christian scriptures" (R. A. Culpepper, "The Gospel of John as a Threat to Jewish-Christian Relations," in J. H. Charlesworth, ed., *Overcoming Fear between Jews and Christians* (Shared Ground Among Jews and Christians 3; New York, 1992), p. 21.

11. See especially 5:39–47; 7:23–24; 10:37–38.

12. See John 1:11: "He came to his own home, and his own people received him not" (NRSV note).

13. Indeed, the respect for Jewish traditions and beliefs, including the Jewish scriptures, is everywhere apparent. See the works mentioned in the first paragraph, above. See also Martyn, *History and Theology*, pp. 102–4.

"the world" or "the Jews."[14] On the Gospel's own terms, moreover, there are good reasons for not being hostile to "the Jews" and to their beliefs and traditions: the Jewishness of Jesus himself is simply accepted and presupposed (cf. 4:9),[15] as is that of his disciples (at least on the narrative level). The titles of honor with which Jesus' identity and mission are summarized (especially, "the Messiah/Christ," "the Son of God," "the Son of Man") originated in contemporary Jewish traditions. The Old Testament is quoted or alluded to with respect, and its themes permeate the Fourth Gospel.[16] John assumes that "the Father" of Jesus, who "sent" him into the world, is the God of Israel (cf. 8:41–42) and that the scriptures of Israel bear testimony to Jesus as (this) God's authorized envoy (1:45; 5:46; 12:41). Jesus is "the king of Israel," that is, the Messiah (Christ) awaited and longed for by Jews (cf. 1:41; 12:14–15). The Johannine community or school (including the Evangelist or evangelists) was itself predominantly (and for quite some time exclusively) Jewish, that is, its members were Jews by birth and religious upbringing.[17]

The thoroughgoing Jewishness of this first-century work and of its writer(s) and first readers makes it rather unlikely that the Gospel's troublesome depiction of "the Jews" involves something ugly, a hatred of (first-

---

14. In 1 John 2:15, the Johannine readers are admonished not to love the world, which must not be turned into its opposite, hatred of the world; the admonition involves indifference toward the world and its values. Contrast 1QS 1:10: "hate all the sons of darkness" (trans. G. Vermes, *The Dead Sea Scrolls in English*, rev. and extended 4th ed. [London, 1995], n. 70.); only Rev. 2:6 comes close to such an attitude, and here evil actions, not people, are the objects of hatred: "you hate the works of the Nicolaitans, which I also hate." See Tomson, *If This Be from Heaven . . .* , p. 402.

15. In 6:42, Jesus is labeled "the son of Joseph" whose parents are known to "the Jews." Nine times in John, Jesus is addressed as ῥαββί (1:38, 49; 3:2, 26; 4:31; 6:25; 9:2; 11:8) or ῥαββουνί (20:16). See also 18:35 ("your own nation").

16. See C. K. Barrett, "The Old Testament in the Fourth Gospel," *JTS* 48 (1947): 155–68; M. J. J. Menken, "Observations on the Significance of the Old Testament in the Fourth Gospel," in *Neot* 33 (1999): 125–43.

17. Gentiles are only barely on the horizon (cf. 12:20; 17:21), and we can scarcely talk of an active, outward mission to the latter in connection with John. See Martyn, *History and Theology*, p. 65 n. 86: "It is a remarkable fact that, even in the completed Gospel as we have it, the Gentile mission plays no part in the Fourth Gospel as an issue, Jewish opposition to John's church is never presented as the result of the church's inclusion of non-Jews." See also J. L. Martyn, "A Gentile Mission That Replaced an Earlier Jewish Mission?" in R. A. Culpepper and C. C. Black, eds., *Exploring the Gospel of John: In Honor of D. Moody Smith* (Louisville, Ky., 1996), pp. 124–44. See also de Boer, *Johannine Perspectives,* pp. 190–91: "the Greeks" of John 12:20 are (1) not pagan Gentiles (they have come to Jerusalem to "worship" the God of Israel at "the feast" of Passover) or (2) the object of mission (they take the initiative, not Jesus or the disciples; they go to Philip and announce to him, in 12:21: "we wish to see Jesus"). The Greeks of John 12:20 thus probably represent God-fearers (Gentiles who worship the God of the Jews where Jews themselves do, in the Temple or the synagogue) who, in the contemporary Johannine setting, have become aware of Jesus of Nazareth in the course of their visits to the local synagogue and thus as a result of their attraction to Judaism. If so, they may well have regarded belief in Jesus as a form of Judaism (for a similar argument with respect to 7:35, which refers to "the Dispersion among the Greeks" and to "teaching the Greeks" about Jesus, see Martyn, "Gentile Mission," pp. 127–28).

century) Jews (by non-Jews), a hatred inevitably combined with a deep-seated contempt for their religious traditions, practices, and beliefs.[18] When Culpepper (like others) refers to John's hostility toward "the Jews," he lists passages that in fact depict "the Jews" of the story as the perpetrators of hostile, even violent behavior toward Jesus and his followers (5:16, 18; 7:1; 8:31, 37–38, 44, 47; 9:22; 16:2–3; 18:36; 19:38; 20:19).[19] In that light, the Fourth Gospel is anti-Jewish only in a very limited sense, and it is not obvious that the label "anti-Jewish" is even applicable here: the Gospel reproaches "the Jews" for their rejection of Jesus as "the Christ, the Son of God" (20:31, NRSV note). The Gospel's reproach of "the Jews" reaches an intense level, however, because "the Jews" of the story do not simply reject Jesus or the claims made by and for Jesus. They also actively plot to "arrest" (πιάζω: 7:30, 32, 44; 8:20; 10:39; 11:57) and to "kill" him (ἀποκτείνω: 5:18; 7:1, 19, 20, 25; 8:22, 37, 40; 11:53; 12:10; cf. 18:31). They make two attempts to "stone" him (8:59; 10:31, 32, 33; 11:8). They also drive Jewish believers in Jesus out of the synagogue (9:22; 12:42; 16:2), as a first step, and want to kill them (12:10; 16:2), as a second.[20] "The Jews" accuse Jesus of being demon-possessed (8:48, 52) and a blasphemer (10:33). They regard him as someone who, like a false prophet, "deceives the crowd," leading them astray from God (7:12, with 45–47; cf. Deut. 13:1–11).[21] At the end, they achieve their murderous aim with respect to Jesus, ironically effecting the crucifixion of their own king while trading him in for another, Caesar (18:33–19:22).[22] On the Gospel's

---

18. Thus those who see a particularly malicious form of anti-Judaism in John (a hatred or a vilification of Jews and of Judaism) misread the Fourth Gospel. Similarly, those who use the Gospel to support anti-Semitic propaganda and actions misuse the Gospel (see n. 35).

19. Culpepper, "Gospel of John as Threat," p. 21.

20. See John 16:2, where Jesus makes the twofold prediction (1) "They will put you out of the synagogues" and (2) "an hour is coming when those who kill you will think that by doing so they are offering worship to God." See Martyn, *History and Theology*, pp. 37–89; de Boer, *Johannine Perspectives*, pp. 55–63. The prediction envisages the situation of the disciples after Jesus' departure.

21. If it be granted that John is a two-level drama (at one and the same time the story of Jesus before Easter and the story of Johannine Christians after Easter), then the portrayal of the conflict between "the Jews" and Jesus reflects a conflict between Johannine Jewish Christians and Jews of the synagogue sometime after Easter: the two-level drama serves to make plain (for the original Jewish-Christian readers who were being persecuted by Jewish leaders and authorities in the synagogue) the correspondence and similarities between the story of Jesus and their own story. Cf. Jesus' words of farewell in 15:18, 20: "If the world hates you, be aware that it hated me before it hated you. . . . 'Servants are not greater than their master.' If they persecuted me [an echo of 5:16], they will persecute you." The case for John as a two-level drama was convincingly made by Martyn, *History and Theology*.

22. For John, there is a terrible irony in the fact that Jesus is confirmed as "the King of the Jews" for all the world to see in the successful campaign by "the Jews" to bring Pilate and the Romans to crucify Jesus. I explore this irony in "The Narrative Function of Pilate in John," in G. J. Brooke and J.-D. Kaestli, eds., *Narrativity in Biblical and Related Texts. La narrativité dans la Bible et les textes apparentés* (BETL 149; Leuven, 2000), pp. 141–58.

own terms, then, there are good reasons for Jesus' severe and pointed reproach of "the Jews."[23]

In view of such considerations, the Johannine reproach of "the Jews" can really be regarded as their vilification (false accusations motivated by hatred) only to the extent that the Gospel's depiction of their actions toward Jesus and his followers (whether before or after Easter) has little or no basis in history and is thus slanderous.[24] The conclusion that the Gospel is deeply and despicably anti-Jewish, perhaps even anti-Semitic, would then probably be inevitable and well founded. That certain Jewish leaders (both at Yabneh and beyond) sought to exclude Christian Jews from full participation in Jewish religious and social life in various places is historically plausible and probable, however, even if the link between the excommunication texts (John 9:22; 12:42; 16:2) and the *birkat ha-minim* is not as certain as Martyn had sought to demonstrate.[25] Furthermore, that certain Jews were

---

23. See n. 11, above. Add, e.g., 8:40. To be sure, in its focus on the role of "the Jews" in violent opposition to Jesus and his own (especially in chapters 5–10), the Gospel makes, in the narrative itself, "the Jews" into representatives of the unbelieving "world" in general. Cf. R. Bultmann, *The Gospel of John* (Philadelphia, 1971), pp. 86–87. It is important to recognize, however, that the term *the Jews* has a limited reference in these contexts (experts in scriptural interpretation and their followers among the rank and file) and that this symbolic role for "the Jews" was probably occasioned by (and cannot be removed from) the contemporary situation (persecution in the late first century C.E. by Jewish synagogue authorities and their followers, i.e., "the Jews") in which John was composed. In John's view, by rejecting Jesus as their king, "the Jews" have actually, astonishingly, and regrettably identified themselves with the (Gentile) world and its rulers (cf. 19:15b). In persecuting, even killing (16:2), Johannine Jewish Christians, "the Jews" who ran the synagogue in John's setting had (in John's view) joined "the world." John is horrified and saddened by this strange turn of events. See n. 22, above.

24. Obviously, no critical scholar would wish to maintain that the Fourth Gospel (or any other Gospel) is an objective historical report of the "facts." Where there is smoke, however, there is also fire. Some would wish to attribute the charges of exclusion and violent persecution (the two traumas mentioned in 16:2) to Johannine inventiveness. (In this view, John has retrospectively interpreted voluntary separation from the synagogue as involuntary expulsion and the experience of social alienation that followed the separation from the synagogue as intentional, violent persecution by synagogue authorities.) But this hypothesis fails to reckon with the fact that Jesus' crucifixion by the Romans, a historical fact if there ever was one, is retrospectively interpreted by John as Jesus' own sovereign departure from the world (cf., e.g., 10:17–18). On that analogy, it seems plausible, even likely, to assume that John has retrospectively interpreted actual experiences of involuntary expulsion and violent persecution as God's calling a new community into being and thus as a voluntary departure from the world of the synagogue (cf., e.g., 10:4, 14–16).

25. See W. D. Davies, "Reflections on Aspects of the Jewish Background of the Gospel of John," in Culpepper and Black, *Exploring the Gospel of John,* pp. 43–64, especially pp. 50–52. According to Davies, "whether or not the exact form of the Twelfth Benediction was changed with the addition of 'the Nazoreans' in order to explicitly include 'Christians' among the *minim,* it still seems to us historically probable that the Sages at Jabneh were aware of the 'menace' of the Christian movement and that among the *minim* whom they sought to exclude from the synagogues were Jewish Christians who were attending those synagogues" (p. 52). This conclusion is supported by P. S. Alexander's investigation of further rabbinic texts in "'The Parting of the Ways' from the Perspective of Rabbinic Judaism," in J. D. G. Dunn, ed., *Jews and Christians: The Parting of the Ways AD 70 to 135* (WUNT 66; Tübingen, 1992), pp. 1–25. We may also note that R. Kimelman, whose article is often cited as a convincing rebuttal of Martyn (R. Kimelman, "*Birkat ha-Minim* and the Lack of Evidence for an

hostile to Jesus and to his followers and played a significant role in bringing about his crucifixion by the Romans is widely attested in the New Testament, is also implied in Josephus (*Ant* 18.3.3 63–64) and rabbinic
literature (*b. Sanh.* 43a),[26] and is probably historically true (even if the
depictions of this involvement are tendentious).[27] The problem for John is
not "the Jews" as an ethnic group (John's writers and first readers themselves come from this ethnic group) or as a people with certain traditions
and beliefs (John's writers and first readers share and respect those traditions and beliefs)[28] but the hostile and finally murderous behavior that they
direct toward God's Jewish envoy and his Jewish followers.

The notorious John 8:44 must surely be read in this light. The Johannine Jesus here attacks the behavior of "the Jews" (8:22, 48, 52, 57), namely,
their desire to kill him (8:37, 40, 59).[29] That is, "the Jews" with whom Jesus
is here in conversation are not diabolical; rather, their murderous behavior
is diabolical (according to 8:44, the devil—not "the Jews"—has been "a
murderer from the beginning"). John 8:44 claims that the devil is the father

---

Anti-Christian Jewish Prayer in Late Antiquity," in E. P. Sanders with A. I. Baumgarten and A. Mendelson, eds., *Jewish and Christian Self-Definition*, vol. 2: *Aspects of Judaism in the Graeco-Roman Period*
[Philadelphia, 1981], pp. 226–44 and 391–403), concludes (contrary to what the title of his article
might suggest) that "the Palestinian prayer against the *minim* was aimed at Jewish sectarians among
whom Jewish Christians figured prominently" (p. 232). This observation actually supports Martyn's
case for a possible link. See further M. C. de Boer, "The Nazoreans: Living at the Boundary of Judaism
and Christianity," in G. N. Stanton and G. G. Stroumsa, eds., *Tolerance and Intolerance in Early Judaism
and Christianity* (Cambridge, 1998), pp. 239–62, especially pp. 249–52 on the *birkat ha-minim*. Aside
from the possible connection to the *birkat ha-minim,* Martyn's very careful grammatical and content
analysis of John 9:22 in its Johannine context (Martyn, *History and Theology,* pp. 38–42) needs careful
consideration.

26. See R. E. Brown, "The Babylonian Talmud on the Execution of Jesus," *NTS* 43 (1997): 158–59.
For further texts, see Alexander, "'The Parting of the Ways.'"

27. See R. E. Brown, "The Narratives of Jesus' Passion and Anti-Judaism," *America* 172 (1995):
8–12; R. E. Brown, *The Death of the Messiah: From Gethsemane to the Grave. A Commentary on the Passion Narratives in the Four Gospels,* 2 vols. (New York, 1994), vol. 1, pp. 372–97.

28. This is the case even if, as seems likely, Johannine Jewish Christians no longer observed certain
Jewish rituals or feasts, including those associated with the Temple, believing them to be (in some sense)
"replaced" by Jesus. The christological exclusivity of John is evident in such passages as 6:46 ("Not that
anyone has seen the Father except the one who is from God; he has seen the Father"); 14:9 ("Whoever
has seen me has seen the Father"); and 14:6 ("No one comes to the Father except through me"). Such
categorical statements were probably designed to exclude claims being made by (other) Jews on behalf
of Moses and the Law given through him as an independent "way" to God, i.e., as a way that attempts
to get around Jesus. But there is no rejection or repudiation of Jewish traditions and beliefs; rather, they
are absorbed into the Johannine Christology, i.e., redefined by the coming and the person of the revealer
of God (cf. 1:18; 5:37). One possible early motive for this process of absorption may well have been a
desire to bring fellow Jews to faith in Jesus (cf. 20:30–31). A major purpose of (the formative version
of) the Gospel was probably to defend and to expound the Johannine understanding of Jesus in the
face of objections coming from synagogue authorities as well as to appeal to hesitant or secret believers still in the synagogue to affirm their faith openly and publicly (see de Boer, *Johannine Perspectives,*
pp. 98, 162).

29. This group of Jews includes, according to 8:31, certain Christian Jews. See further on this in
n. 40, below.

not of "the Jews" as such but of their behavior. Furthermore, the Gospel probably does not have all "the Jews" (of Jesus' time or of John's) in view, since John can elsewhere use the term οἱ Ἰουδαῖοι to refer to Jews who are not hostile to Jesus at all (see, e.g., 11:19, 31, 33, 36, 45; 12:9, 11). In John 8, then, "the Jews" of the narrative represent a limited group of Jews, scriptural authorities in the synagogue and their followers among the rank and file who violently oppose the Johannine Jesus and his disciples.[30] The claim that the devil, a murderer *ab origine,* is the father of the murderous behavior of "the Jews" in John 8[31] can, I suggest, be read as an attempt to account for this behavior theologically. That is, both pained and perplexed by this behavior, John peers behind the stage of history and sees a mighty malevolent power at work, God's own opponent, the devil. "The Jews" have astonishingly become players in a cosmic drama between God and the devil, and they have been enlisted on the wrong side! Their inability to hear (8:43) the Johannine proclamation about Jesus as originating in the Truth (God) and their decision to kill him and Johannine Jewish Christians were, in John's considered theological estimation, not the result of personal or communal ill will or of some racial flaw but of a diabolical conspiracy in which "the Jews" of John 8 play no autonomous role at all. (They do, of course, play a role, but it is not autonomous.) How else, John seems to be asking, can one possibly explain their repudiation of Jesus as God's own Son (an incontrovertible fact for John) and their seeking to kill him (in the past) and his Jewish followers (in the Johannine present)? The attribution of diabolical agency (or paternity) can undoubtedly be used in despicable and dehumanizing ways, but that is not always or necessarily the case (cf. Mark 8:33).[32] Context and intention, one may perhaps assume, are important factors in the evaluation of such language.[33] John 8:44 is arguably John's considered theological assessment of an extremely perplexing and painful turn of events, the repudiation and violent persecution of the Jew-

---

30. See further in the section "'We Are the Disciples of Moses,'" pp. 149–57, on this definition of "the Jews" in John 8 and elsewhere.

31. Notice: The issue in John 8 is not simply the rejection of Jesus but the wish to kill him.

32. The import of John 8:44 is that the murder of one human being by another is the manifestation of a diabolical power at work in the world. The murder of Jews in subsequent centuries, and particularly in the Holocaust, can (following John 8:44) be characterized in a similar way, as diabolical—and thus in opposition to God's will and intention "from the beginning."

33. The attribution of diabolical agency in human affairs in antiquity and beyond deserves a fresh investigation. It is important to recognize that Christians could use the same language of other Christians (cf. 1 John 3:8, 10, 15!), just as Jews could of other Jews (the Dead Sea Scrolls). See the important article of L. T. Johnson, "The New Testament's Anti-Jewish Slander and the Conventions of Ancient Polemic," *JBL* 108 (1989): 419–41.

ish Jesus and his Jewish followers by those to and for whom (so John believes) Jesus was sent into the world by God, that is, the God of Abraham and Moses and Israel.

The conflict on display in John, then, is primarily between two groups of Jewish people (Johannine Jewish Christians and "the Jews") who were both nurtured by the scriptures and traditions of the synagogue.[34] The curious fact that needs explanation is why one group, the Johannine Jewish Christians, labeled the other group "the Jews" while rejecting (at least implicitly) this epithet for themselves as Jewish Christians. We here come up against the main interpretative issue with respect to the Johannine depiction of "the Jews." The interpretative issue is not why Jesus or the Evangelist is hostile toward "the Jews." (Neither, I believe, is.) Nor is the interpretative issue why John depicts "the Jews" as hostile to Jesus and his disciples. (The reasons for such a depiction are not arbitrary, irrational, or motivated by anti-Semitic impulses, since they are rooted in historically plausible and probable events.)[35] The issue is rather: Why does John refer to those who are hostile to Jesus and his disciples as "the Jews," with the potentially misleading implication that Jesus himself and his (initial) disciples, as well as the Gospel's writer(s) and original, intended readers, were not themselves Jews?[36]

"We Are Disciples of Moses": The Origin and Significance of the Designation "the Jews" in John

It is understandable that scholars who seek to understand John's portrayal of "the Jews" focus on what John or the Jesus of John says about them, both

---

34. These two groups compete for the allegiance of a wider group of Jews, often labeled "the crowd" (cf., e.g., 2:23; 7:12, 31; 11:45; 12:9–11). There is a group of Christian Jews who stand in the middle between the two groups but whom John regards as belonging to the group he labels "the Jews" (cf. 8:31; 12:42).

35. The despicable characterization of Jews in subsequent centuries as "Christ killers" partly on the basis of an appeal to John, in order to persecute and kill Jews, is another matter entirely. This sort of anti-Semitic defamation and distortion of the biblical record needs to be condemned at every turn. Let us be clear about this and shout it from the rooftops: there is no basis whatsoever in John (or elsewhere in the New Testament) for the persecution, maltreatment, or defamation of Jews (or others) who oppose, question, criticize, or simply do not share the faith of Christians.

36. In what follows, I take for granted as shared ground among the parties in the Johannine context the basic definition of *the Jews* given by Meeks when he writes that "there are numerous passages . . . in which the term must designate an organized religious community, with its 'festivals' and special customs, its 'rulers' and 'high priests,' centered in Jerusalem." He adds: "When pagan authors speak of Ioudaioi . . . the term denotes the visible, recognizable group with their more or less well-known customs, who have their origin in Judea but preserve what we would call their 'ethnic' identity in the diaspora" (Meeks, "'Am I a Jew?'" p. 182). See J. M. G. Barclay, *Jews in the Mediterranean Diaspora: From Alexander to Trajan (323 B.C.E.–117 B.C.E.)*, (Edinburgh, 1996), p. 408.

directly and indirectly, rather than on what they may say about themselves. The reason for this is clear: "the Jews whose opinion is expressed in the Gospel appear on a scene set by a Christian evangelist."[37] This crucial insight also applies to the ways in which "the Jews" refer (or are allowed to refer) to themselves in the Gospel.[38] The Gospel is not, and is not meant to be, an objective portrayal of first-century Jews and Judaism.[39] In one passage, however, "the Jews" who oppose Jesus and his disciples are allowed to define themselves in ways that can hardly be described as a misrepresentation of Jewish self-understanding: in 9:28, they declare themselves to be "disciples of Moses."[40] This self-designation finds a parallel in rabbinic sources. A *baraitah* in *b. Yoma* 4a refers to Pharisaic scholars in distinction from Sadducean ones as תלמידיו של משה, disciples of Moses."[41] Though there is scarcely (to my knowledge) any other attestation for the precise wording,[42] the (self-)affirmation of Jews in the first century as disciples of Moses is historically plausible and certainly no misrepresentation of Jewish self-understanding: "Moses *is* the normatively authorized figure of Judaism. . . . There is, then, nothing. . . which indicates a distortion of the

37. M. de Jonge, "Jewish Expectations about the 'Messiah' according to the Fourth Gospel," *NTS* 19 (1972–73): 246–70, pp. 247–48. Further, the Gospel (in its formative and final versions) was probably a book for "insiders," to deepen and strengthen the faith of Johannine Jewish Christians. See W. Meeks, "The Man from Heaven in Johannine Sectarianism," *JBL* 91 (1972); 44–72 (reprinted in J. Ashton, ed., *The Interpretation of John,* 2d ed. [Edinburgh, 1997], pp. 169–205).

38. B. Lindars, *John* (Sheffield, 1990), p. 37, writes that "John works like a playwright, who invents dialogue and speeches to convey the message of the play through the medium of drama." Also de Jonge, "Jewish Expectations," pp. 247–48. Lindars, like de Jonge (p. 263), nevertheless believes that the Johannine dramatic portrayals "carry the evangelist's treatment of the great issues of christology in the debate with the synagogue" (p. 56). These issues, in short, are not mere literary inventions.

39. Martyn writes: "It hardly needs to be said that John is not merely 'reporting' the opinions of his Jewish neighbors" (*History and Theology,* p. 103).

40. In John 8:33, there are certain Jews who make the claim "We are descendants of Abraham"; these are Christian Jews (8:31) whom John identifies with "the Jews" (in 8:22, 48, 52, 57) because they, like "the Jews" (in 5:18; 7:1, 19, 20, 25), seek to kill Jesus (8:37, 40). The "Jews who had believed in him" (8:31) probably represent Christian Jews in the Johannine setting who, still in the synagogue, found the high Johannine Christology as offensive as did other Jews (cf. 8:58–59; 10:31–33; 19:7). This is "the truth" that they do "not believe" (8:45). John 8:44 also, and perhaps especially, has these Christian Jews in view, because if the murderous reaction of "the Jews" demanded some sort of explanation, the murderous reaction of Christian Jews did so even more. John 8 indicates an intensification of the conflict in the contemporary Johannine setting beyond what is discernible in John 9. Martyn's insistence that the Johannine Christians underwent a double trauma (excommunication from the synagogue followed by violent persecution at the hands of synagogue authorities) is often insufficiently acknowledged and taken into account in the assessment of John's portrayal of the conflict between Jesus and "the Jews" (see 16:2; and nn. 9 and 20, above).

41. So C. K. Barrett, *The Gospel according to St. John* (Philadelphia, 1978), p. 362, relying on Str-B 2:535.

42. The particular formulation "disciples of Moses" may be dependent to some extent on the context (see below).

conversation."[43] The self-affirmation placed into the mouth of "the Jews" of John is undoubtedly a fundamental indicator of who Jews (or their spokespersons) understood themselves to be in the Johannine context. In chapter 9, these disciples of Moses live from the conviction that "God has spoken to Moses" (9:29). For this reason, Moses is the one in whom Jews have hoped (5:45) and whom they would wish to believe (5:46). To speak of Moses is to speak of that authoritative body of teaching revealed to Moses, namely, the Law: "the law indeed was given through Moses" (1:17; cf. 7:19) and "the law of Moses may not be broken" (7:23), including the law pertaining to the Sabbath (5:10; 7:23; 9:16). Moses' teaching is largely preserved in "the scriptures," primarily, if not exclusively, the Pentateuch.[44] Disciples of Moses thus "search the scriptures" with the conviction that "eternal life" is to be found there (5:39; cf. 7:52).[45] It will be the thesis of this section that the self-affirmation "we are disciples of Moses" in the context in which it occurs provides a crucial clue to the origin and significance of the epithet "the Jews" for the Jewish opponents of the Jewish Jesus and his Jewish followers.[46]

In John 9, Jesus' healing of a Jewish man who had been born blind does not lead immediately to an account of the man (or of others) coming to faith in Jesus[47] but to a "division" (σχίσμα) (9:16) among "the Pharisees" (9:13, 15). After an initial questioning of the healed man (9:13–15), some of these Pharisees said, "This man is not from God, for he does not observe the sabbath." Others among them pose a rhetorical question: "How can a man who is a sinner perform such signs?" (9:16). The implied answer would seem to be that a doer of such signs, such miracles, cannot be a sinner and must thus be "from God." If so, he may well be "a prophet,"[48] as

---

43. Martyn, *History and Theology,* pp. 103–4. In addition to the affirmation of Jews as disciples of Moses, Martyn lists six other items concerning Moses in the Fourth Gospel that he regards not only as "historically reliable" but as "representative of the very life nerve of Judaism" in the first century: e.g., the claim that God spoke to Moses (9:29) and the belief that Moses gave the Law to Israel (7:19). On the importance of Moses for Jews in the first century, see Barclay, *Jews in the Mediterranean Diaspora,* pp. 426–28.

44. In John 10:34 and 15:25, quotations from the Psalms are said to be written in "the Law."

45. There is nothing in these statements that represents a distortion of Jewish views as these are known from extra-Johannine texts and evidence. See Martyn, *History and Theology,* pp. 102–4.

46. Though perhaps wearisome, the repetition of the adjective *Jewish* in connection with Jesus and his disciples is an attempt to prevent the issue of John's depiction of "the Jews" from becoming a discussion about a conflict between "Judaism" and "Christianity," which would be anachronistic and misleading.

47. The man's embryonic faith only first becomes evident in 9:17 ("prophet"), then develops in 9:27–28 ("a disciple" of Jesus), and is moved to a new level in 9:35–38 ("Do you believe in the Son of Man?").

48. Perhaps "the [Mosaic] prophet."

the healed man suggests to them in response to their request to say what he thinks (9:17). The second group of Pharisees thus entertains the sympathetic view of Jesus attributed to Nicodemus, "a Pharisee [and] a leader of the Jews" (3:1; cf. 7:50), who came to Jesus and said to him: "Rabbi, we know that you are a teacher who has come from God; for no one can do these signs that you do apart from the presence of God" (3:2).

In what follows, however, the views of the first group of Pharisees prevail, and this group is strikingly referred to as "the Jews" (9:18, 22; cf. "some of the Pharisees" in 9:40).[49] The reader is informed that "the Jews did not believe that he [the man] had been blind and had received his sight until they called the parents of the man who had received his sight" (9:18). "The Jews" then interrogate his parents, who, like their son, are also Jews of the local synagogue. The parents confess ignorance of their son's healing because, according to John, "they were afraid of the Jews" (9:22). The reason for their fear, John informs the readers in a narrative aside, is that "the Jews had already agreed" to expel from the synagogue those Jews who had confessed Jesus to be the Messiah (9:22). "The Jews" of this narrative thus stand opposed to Jesus and to those (other Jews) who would believe him to be "the Messiah."[50]

The man is now called "a second time" (9:24–34), and the interrogators ('the Jews" of 9:18–23) ask him to "give glory to God," implicitly a request to see things their way.[51] Jesus, they claim, is a sinner (9:24); after all, he does not keep the Sabbath law (9:14, 16). The man confesses ignorance about the legal issues involved and immediately relativizes their importance in view of the healing he has experienced at the hands of Jesus: "I do not know whether he is a sinner. One thing I do know, that though I was blind, now I see" (9:25).[52] The interrogators now want to know how Jesus supposedly opened his eyes. The man responds that he had already told them, as he had (9:15), and then wonders whether they "also" wish to become "disciples" of Jesus (9:26–27). But that is not so. They revile the man and proclaim themselves to be "disciples of Moses," unlike the healed Jew, whom they typify as the disciple of someone else, not of Moses but of Jesus:

---

49. The two groups are also present in 12:42, where "the authorities" (i.e., secret believers or sympathizers such as Nicodemus and those "others" mentioned in 9:16) are afraid of "the Pharisees" (i.e., "the Jews" of John 9).

50. The term is used the same way in many other passages, including (I believe) 2:18, 20; 5:10, 15, 16, 18; 6:41, 52; 7:1, 11, 13, 15, 35; 8:22, 48, 52, 57; 10:24, 31, 33; 11:8, 54; 13:33; 18:12, 14, 31, 35, 36; 19:7, 12, 14, 20, 21, 31, 38; 20:19.

51. C. H. Dodd, *The Interpretation of the Fourth Gospel* (Cambridge, 1953), p. 81.

52. He thereby echoes, and answers in his own way, the rhetorical question posed by the second (sympathetic) group of Pharisees earlier, "How can a man who is a sinner perform such signs?" (9:16).

> "You [σύ] are his disciple,
> but we [ἡμεῖς] are disciples of Moses"
> (9:28)

They go on to explain why they are disciples of Moses and not of Jesus: "We know that God has spoken to Moses, but as for this man, we do not know where he comes from" (9:29). They may not know where Jesus is from, but they are certain that they know where he is not from—from God.

The man's view, which is John's view, is that "if this man were not from God, he could do nothing" (9:33). Since he did do something, namely, opened the eyes of a man born blind, something unique in human experience (9:32), he must be "from God." The interrogators then revile the man, a sinner from birth (9:34; cf. 9:2–3), for presuming to "teach" them and then throw him outside (9:34), putting into effect the already-existing decree of expulsion (9:22). They have sensed, rightly, that the man has indeed confessed Jesus to be the Messiah, that is, the miracle-working prophet-Messiah (cf. 9:16; 7:31). In John's view, "the Jews" thereby demonstrate that they, not the disciples of Jesus, are truly blind and that they, not Jesus or his disciples, are sinners (cf. 9:40–41; cf. 12:37–42).

About 9:28 within its context, the following may now be said. First, the fact that John allows "the Jews" to describe themselves as "disciples of Moses" is a clear indication that the term οἱ Ἰουδαῖοι cannot be translated "the Judaeans" (at least in chapter 9 and in many other passages). The interrogators define themselves not with reference to the region in which they live or originate, nor with reference to their ethnic identity, but with reference to Moses, that is, in religious terms. "The Jews" of the narrative thus understand themselves to be above all else "disciples of Moses," and it is as such that the Johannine Jesus repeatedly enters into debate with them (see 3:14; 5:39–47; 6:30–32; 7:19–24, 51–52; 10:31–39; cf. 1:17, 45).[53]

Second, then, it is apparent that the matter of Jewish identity is at stake in John 9:28.[54] "The Jews" present the formerly blind Jewish man (thus, *mutatis mutandis,* also other Johannine believers in Jesus, on both the

---

53. On the meaning of the term Ἰουδαῖοι in the ancient world, see S. J. D. Cohen, *The Beginnings of Jewishness: Boundaries, Varieties, Uncertainties* (Berkeley, 1999), pp. 69–106. "The end of the first century C.E.," according to Cohen, "witnesses for the first time the emergence [among Greek and Roman writers] of *Ioudaios* as a religious term, a designation for anyone who venerates the God of the Judeans" (p. 96). Cohen also argues, however, that this "religious" meaning of the term is first attested in the second century B.C.E., in 2 Macc. 6:6; 9:17 (p. 105).

54. Cf. Barclay, *Jews in the Mediterranean Diaspora*, p. 426: "If the law was the focal point of Diaspora Judaism, it was natural that Jews should find their *identity defined by Moses*" (emphasis added).

narrative and contemporary levels of John's two-level drama)[55] with a stark and uncompromising alternative that says, in effect:

"As disciples of Jesus, you have forfeited your Jewish identity;
as disciples of Moses, we (and not you disciples of Jesus) are truly the Jews."

Discipleship to Jesus and discipleship to Moses are presented as distinguishable, comparable, and incompatible modes of being Jewish.[56] John certainly does not entirely agree (cf. 5:39ff.): a disciple of Moses should believe in Jesus, for as the Johannine Jesus says, "he wrote about me" (5:46) and the scriptures "testify on my behalf" (5:39; cf. 1:45). In short, John's view is that "the Jews" have forced a choice where none needed to be made. In light of that imposed choice, John has also been forced to agree that discipleship to Jesus is indeed incompatible with discipleship to Moses when, and only when, the latter adopts as a basic premise the rejection of Jesus as the Messiah.[57] It is important to note that "the Jews" are here presented as the actors who both initiate and arbitrate the matter of Jewish identity.[58]

55. The blind man has not only obtained physical sight. More important for John, the man has obtained spiritual insight into the identity of Jesus. The gift of sight functions here as a symbol for salvation, obtained from the one whom John regards as "the light of the world" (9:5).

56. About 9:28, Martyn has written: "This statement is scarcely conceivable in Jesus' lifetime, since it recognizes discipleship to Jesus not only as antithetical, but also somehow comparable, to discipleship to Moses. It is, on the other hand, easily understood under circumstances in which the synagogue has begun to view the Christian movement as an essential and more or less clearly distinguishable rival" (History and Theology, p. 39). Cf. Pirke Aboth 5:19: "How do the disciples of Abraham our father [cf. John 8:53: 'our father Abraham'] differ from the disciples of Balaam [i.e., Jesus] the wicked?" The answer is that whereas the former are destined for salvation, the latter are destined for damnation. The former have "a good eye and a humble spirit and lowly soul," the latter "an evil eye, a haughty spirit, and a proud soul" (H. Danby, The Mishnah: Translated from the Hebrew with Introduction and Brief Explanatory Notes [Oxford, 1933; 16th ed., 1983], p. 458). The harsh words about Jesus and his disciples in this text (assuming Balaam stands for Jesus) are reminiscent of the attitude of "the Jews" toward Jesus and his disciples in the Gospel of John (though there is no indication of violent intentions in the Mishnaic passage, nor of excommunication as such). The dualism here is also a noteworthy parallel. (This dualism, like that of John, is apocalyptic, not Gnostic.)

57. Does John's noteworthy dualism have its origin (at least partly) in the alternative presented to the formerly blind man in John 9:28—one is either a disciple of Moses or a disciple of Jesus, one cannot be both? See end of n. 56, above. For John, as for "the Jews," there is finally no middle ground.

58. Note the title of L. H. Schiffman's book: Who Was a Jew? Rabbinic and Halakhic Perspectives on the Jewish-Christian Schism (Hoboken, N.J., 1985). Schiffman begins his study with the following words: "During the entire length of the Second Temple period, Judaism had tolerated sectarianism and schism. Yet by the end of the tannaitic period, Christianity was to be regarded as another religion entirely." Schiffman seeks to understand from the Jewish side of the conflict "why Christianity was not simply regarded as one of the sects, and why, when, and how Judaism sought to dissociate itself fully from Christianity" (p. 1). Interestingly, Schiffman's approach to "the parting of the ways" as it developed in the tannaitic period is congruent with the perspective of John (writing at the beginning of the tannaitic period), which is that it was Pharisaic Judaism that began to dissociate itself from "Christianity" rather than the other way around. In John, Jewish believers in Jesus do not dissociate themselves from the synagogue, but (certain) Jews have decided (for whatever reason) to dissociate themselves from Jesus of Nazareth and his Jewish disciples, a development painful to John (John 9:22; cf. Martyn's analysis of

This also suggests that they are experts in the interpretation of the Mosaic Law, who can be distinguished from "the crowd" (the common people) for whom they presume to speak and for whom they want to decide two closely related matters of importance:[59] (1) the validity of messianic claims made by Jesus (which are actually claims made by a Johannine preacher on behalf of Jesus in the contemporary situation)[60] and (2) the marks of a genuine "disciple of Moses" (see especially 7:14–24, 46–52). "The Jews" in John (who dramatically portray certain Jews in John's sociohistorical context) do not simply define themselves as "disciples of Moses"; they also define followers of Jesus as "not-disciples of Moses," that is, as "not-Jews."[61]

Third, given the first two points, the origin and significance of the peculiar and frequent epithet "the Jews" for those who, on the basis of their scriptural knowledge, reject and oppose Jesus and his disciples now come into focus: the Gospel's references to the Jewish scriptural authorities behind the decree of expulsion (9:22) as "the Jews" is in the first instance an ironic acknowledgment of their claim to be the authoritative arbiters of Jewish identity.[62] Being a disciple of Jesus was evidently no longer one of

---

this verse in *History and Theology*, pp. 37–62). Schiffman, however, locates the dissociation of Judaism from "Christianity" in the fact that the latter had, by the end of the tannaitic period, become overwhelmingly Gentile: the rabbis were confronted with "Gentiles who had converted to a religion which had rejected circumcision, the Jewish law of conversion, and the requirements of life under the halakha" (p. 76). Schiffman is at pains to point out along the way that a Jew (even a Christian Jew) could never be denied his or her Jewish identity: "Jewish status could never be canceled, even for the most heinous offenses against Jewish law and doctrine" (p. 51). However that may be, John 9:28 is not concerned with the canceling of Jewish ethnic identity (the ethnic marks of Jewish identity, e.g., circumcision and birth from a Jewish parent, cannot in the nature of the case be canceled), but it does involve the canceling of a Jewish religious identity. In John, furthermore, it is still anachronistic to speak of "Christianity" as an entity distinct from "Judaism"; in John, the parting of the ways involves a split within Judaism itself. (Gentile Christians are scarcely in the picture.)

59. This role of "the Jews" as the actors who initiate and arbitrate the matter of Jewish identity explains why the term οἱ Ἰουδαῖοι can also be used in John for the Jewish people as a whole, especially in connection with Jewish customs and feasts (cf. 2:6, 13; 4:9, 22; 5:1; 6:4; 7:2; 11:55; 18:20, 39; 19:3, 40, 42), and also for Jews who are potential or actual believers in Jesus (cf. 1:19; 3:1, 25; 8:31; 10:19; 11:19, 31, 33, 36, 45; 12:9, 11).

60. For John, there is no essential distinction, since the Paraclete (chapters 14–16) who speaks through a Johannine preacher is the substitute for Jesus in the post-Easter period and speaks for him (cf. 14:16–17, 26; 15:26; 16:7–11, 13–15). On the Paraclete and John's two-level drama, see Martyn, *History and Theology*, pp. 143–51.

61. This analysis is substantiated by the report in 9:22 (cf. 12:42; 16:2) that Jews accepting Jesus as Messiah were to be excluded from the fellowship of the synagogue, in effect an exclusion from Jewish religious and social life.

62. A modern (if somewhat imperfect) analogy may help clarify the usage: the *New York Times* carried a story in 1983 about the South African poet and dissident Breyten Breytenbach (D. Woods, "A South African Poet on His Imprisonment," in *New York Times Book Review*, May 1, 1983, pp. 3, 24–25). This Afrikaner, or Boer, was imprisoned for some time by his fellow Afrikaners for his protests against apartheid. "Mr. Breytenbach," the *Times* reported, "constantly refers to his warders as the 'Boere' (plural for Boer), explaining that this is prison terminology; he is aware of the irony whereby he, an Afrikaner or Boer himself, so describes them" (p. 24). Breytenbach's references to his persecutors as the

the ways in which a Jew could be a disciple of Moses. The Gospel is at pains
to reject this claim, as we noted above. For John, there is the deep and tragic
irony that it is actually "the Jews," the self-affirmed disciples of Moses, who
have forfeited their Jewish identity and heritage (cf. 19:15), because they
have rejected the Johannine proclamation of Jesus as the promised Messiah
of Israel: "Do not think that I will accuse you before the Father; your
accuser is Moses, on whom you have set your hope. If you believed Moses,
you would believe me, for he wrote about me. If you do not believe what
he wrote, how will you believe what I say?" (5:45–47). For John, Moses,
properly read and understood, stands on the side of Jesus and his disciples
and supports their claims. But the important point for our present purposes
is that the peculiar Johannine use of the term *the Jews* probably emerged in
a debate not *with* but *within* the synagogue (between Jews who embraced
Jesus as the expected Jewish Messiah and those who did not) about Jewish
identity, that is, about whether Christian Jews could properly be regarded
as genuine "disciples of Moses." The Christian Jews in the synagogue, who
were perhaps in the minority in the Johannine setting (though making
inroads),[63] were in a difficult situation, since "the Jews had already agreed
that anyone who confessed Jesus to be the Messiah would be put out of the
synagogue" (9:22), in effect declared no longer to be a Jew, a true disciple
of Moses. Pharisaic authorities (in the Johannine setting as elsewhere)
sought, after the destruction of the Temple by the Romans, to define what
it is to be a Jew (and thus to live like one) under new and threatening circumstances. At stake was not simply Jewish identity but Jewish survival, a
theme that finds its echo in John 11:47b–48: "This man is performing
many signs. If we let him go on like this, everyone will believe in him, and
the Romans will come and destroy both our holy place [the Temple] and
our nation."

The issue in John's use of "the Jews" to designate certain authoritative,
learned (Pharisaic) Jews who, with their followers among the synagogue
rank and file, rejected and opposed Jesus and his followers in the Johannine
context is thus identity—Jewish identity. "The Jews" are those who claim
to be the arbiters of a genuinely Jewish identity, and John acknowledges

---

"Boere" was in effect an ironic recognition of their claim to be the arbiters of Boer or Afrikaner identity. With his protests against apartheid, Breytenbach called into question both a cornerstone of Boer
identity and the presumption of the "Boere" to define that identity. Though Breytenbach remained a
Boer at the ethnic level, he did not remain one at the cultural/ideological level: to be a Boer and to be
against apartheid were not incompatible stances for him, as they were for "the Boere." Breytenbach's
protest caused him to be persecuted and to be excluded from the community of Boers through imprisonment and, subsequently, exile. See de Boer, *Johannine Perspectives,* p. 57.
    63. Note 11:45–48; 12:9–11, 19, 42.

this claim with the ironic (even sarcastic) epithet "the Jews." The end result (perhaps originally unintended) is that Johannine Jewish Christians came to abandon the term *the Jews* for themselves as Jewish disciples of Jesus, even as they sought in their own way to remain faithful to Moses and the scriptures of Israel.[64]

64. The Nazoreans (Jewish Christians) of a later time apparently did the same. According to Epiphanius (fourth century C.E.), the Nazoreans "did not keep the name Jews" (*Panarion* 29.7.1) even though they were "trained in the Law, in circumcision, the sabbath and other things" (*Panarion* 29.7.5). Epiphanius himself regarded them as "wholly Jewish and nothing else" (ibid.), since they differed only in their embrace of Jesus as Messiah (*Panarion* 29.7.1), though Epiphanius was not sure whether their Christology was high or low (see *Panarion* 29.7.6); according to Jerome, they believed Jesus to be the Son of God (see *Epist.* 112.13; *Tract. Isa.* 9.1–4; 11.1–3; 29.17–21; 31.6–9). For the relevant texts, see A. F. J. Klijn and G. J. Reinink, *Patristic Evidence for Jewish-Christian Sects* (NovTSup 36; Leiden, 1973). For the relationship between Johannine Christianity and the Nazoreans, see M. C. de Boer, "L'évangile de Jean et le christianisme juif (nazoréen)," in D. Marguerat, ed., *Le déchirement: Juifs et chrétiens au premier siècle* (Geneva, 1996), pp. 179–202. Since Johannine Christian Jews, like the Nazoreans later, no longer used the name Jews to describe themselves after their expulsion from the synagogue, it is appropriate to describe those who had been expelled as Johannine Jewish Christians, since for them faith in Jesus the Christ, rather than allegiance to Moses, had become central to their self-identity. After the expulsion, they began to use the term *the Jews* in an ironic sense for Jews of the synagogue community; the Law as read there then became "their law" (15:25) or "your law" (8:17; 10:34), which finds a parallel in *b. 'Abod. Zar.* 16b–17a, where a Jewish disciple of Jesus (his name is Jacob), in a midrashic discussion about Jesus with R. Eliezer, speaks to him of "your Torah." See now also J. Augenstein, "'Euer Gesetz'—Ein Pronomen und die johanneische Haltung zum Gesetz," *ZNW* 88 (1998): 311–13. On the useful distinction between Christian Jews (a group at home in the synagogue and accepted there) and Jewish Christians (a community distinguishable and socially apart from the synagogue fellowship), see Martyn, *History and Theology,* p. 66; J. L. Martyn, "Glimpses into the History of the Johannine Community," in *The Gospel of John in Christian History* (New York, 1978), p. 104. On the Law in John, see S. Pancaro, *The Law in the Fourth Gospel: The Torah and the Gospel, Moses and Jesus, Judaism and Christianity according to John* (NovTSup 42; Leiden, 1975).

CHAPTER 8

Speaking of the Jews:
"Jews" in the Discourse
Material of the Fourth Gospel

Raymond F. Collins

In the context of a book on "Anti-Judaism and the Fourth Gospel" it might be useful to consider the gospels as short stories about Jesus. Some three-quarters of a century ago it was suggested that John 1:6, "There was a man sent from God, whose name was John," was the original beginning of the Gospel according to John. These words have the air of the beginning of a narrative. They evoke in the mind of an Anglo-Saxon reader the classic "Once upon a time . . ." with which many of our stories begin.

Reading the Fourth Gospel as if it were a short story about Jesus is useful at the dawn of this millennium, just after narrative criticism has emerged as a methodology whose use yields various insights that contribute to an understanding of even ancient narrative texts. Each of the Gospels can be read as a short story about Jesus. Their plots are similar. Inasmuch, however, as the Fourth Gospel is richer in characterization[1] than are the Synoptics, the Fourth Gospel has a plot development somewhat different from that of the Synoptics. This intertwining of plot and characterization in the Fourth Gospel reveals something about its "anti-Judaism" or, as it is more commonly spoken of in the Anglo-Saxon world, its "anti-Semitism."

Dialogue is an element in characterization and in the development of a narrative plot. What the cast of characters have to say helps define who they are. What they say is often as important as what the narrator says about them. Their dialogue, moreover, serves to refine and develop the plot. From this perspective, it might prove useful to analyze what the various characters in the Fourth Gospel have to say about "the Jews."

A contemporary reader of the Fourth Gospel reads the prologue before he or she reads the story itself. As a kind of commentary on the Gospel, the

---

1. See, among other studies, R. F. Collins, "From John to the Beloved Disciple: An Essay on Johannine Characters," *Int* 49 (1995): 359–69.

prologue interprets the story of Jesus as the Word and light of God, who entered into the world and its darkness, where he was not received. Despite the lack of welcome, Jesus had the role of making God known within the context of the law given through Moses.

Jewish Time and Space

The narrative begins with the testimony of John the Baptist, who is engaged in a confrontational dialogue with a delegation sent by Jews from Jerusalem (1:19). The initial interaction indicates that the real issue in the confrontation and ultimately in the story itself is that of messianic identity. On the following day, John publicly and enigmatically testifies about Jesus that he is the Lamb of God. John does so with such conviction that two of his disciples leave him to become followers of Jesus. The story of Jesus' gathering a first band of disciples culminates in Jesus' discourse with Nathanael, which features a double identification. Nathanael is identified as "Son of God" and as "an Israelite" (1:47); Jesus, in turn, is identified as "King of Israel" (1:49). At this point in the narrative, the Jews remain a shadowy group of unknowns in Jerusalem who had the inquisitional delegation sent to John.

The story continues with two episodes that foreshadow what is to come: the account of the water made wine at Cana in Galilee (2:1–12)[2] and the report of the purification of the Temple (2:13–22). Each of these episodes anticipates the denouement of the story about Jesus, albeit in a different way. The first tells of the abundance of gifts offered by Jesus at the "hour." The second episode leads to the prediction of Jesus' resurrection. "The Jews" are present in each story as a point of reference, not as a focal point.[3] The Cana episode describes the vessels in which was contained the water soon to become wine as "six stone water jars for the Jewish rites of purification" (2:6). The Temple episode takes place as the "Passover of the Jews" (2:13) was drawing near.

Keeping "the Jews" in his narrative space and time as he does, the Evangelist allows the reader to understand that the story about Jesus, with its denouement, takes place in "Jewish" space and time. His story is to be a

---

2. Cf. R. F. Collins, "Cana (Jn. 2:1–12): The First of His Signs or the Key to His Signs?" in *ITQ* 47 (1980): 79–95 (reprinted in R. F. Collins, *These Things Have Been Written: Studies on the Fourth Gospel* [LTPM 2; Grand Rapids, 1989], pp. 158–82).

3. It could be argued that "of the Jews" (τῶν Ἰουδαίων) takes the place of an adjective that the Evangelist has chosen not to employ in 2:6 and 2:13. In this regard, it is interesting to note that the NRSV uses the adjective *Jewish* to translate τῶν Ἰουδαίων in 2:6 but uses a prepositional phrase with "of" in 2:13.

Jewish story. The use of the phrase "of the Jews" in 2:6 and 2:13 does more, however, than simply identify Jesus' story as a Jewish story. The usage allows the reader to gain a glimpse of the relationship between Jesus and Jewish space and time. The jugs that were available for the Jewish rites of purification are employed by Jesus as vessels in which Jesus makes available the abundance of first-quality wine that symbolizes the surfeit of gifts given at the (messianic) nuptials. In a sense, the traditional rites of purification of the Jews are to give way to the gifts that Jesus/the bridegroom gives.

In similar fashion, the location of Jesus' prophetic gesture of purifying the Temple on the Passover of the Jews is more than a merely temporal designation. The brief episode, strategically placed at the beginning of the Fourth Evangelist's narrative, continues the theme of the replacement of Jewish institutions. The destruction of the Temple is implicitly compared to the death of Jesus. Jesus' resurrection is compared to the reconstruction of the Temple.[4]

The Passover that was about to occur[5] was not merely one among several festivals of the Jews. The Passover recalls the slaughter of the firstborn of Egypt and the liberation and constitution of the people. These elements provide a meaningful context for the Evangelist's narrative of the story of Jesus. At this point in the narrative, there has been no confrontation between Jesus and "the Jews." Thus far, "the Jews" define Jesus' time and space and offer the reader a glimpse of the context in which the story will reach its climax.

The episode of Jesus' discourse with Nicodemus (3:1–21) brings the matter of "the Jews" into clearer focus. The Evangelist forges a link between the Pharisees and the Jews.[6] Nicodemus, the Pharisee, is characterized as "a leader of the Jews" (3:1). Elsewhere in the Fourth Gospel, Jesus dialogues only with the Pharisees or with the Jews. Here Jesus is engaged in a real dialogue with someone who is both a Pharisee and a leader of the Jews.

In 7:50, the Evangelist tells his readers that Nicodemus was "one of them." "They" are the Pharisees, described as those who search the law, in contrast with the masses, who are derisively derided as those who do not know the law (7:49). The crowd gathered for the festival was divided

---

4. Note that the destruction of the Temple was a past event for the readers of the Fourth Gospel. Jesus' resurrection was a past and very real event for his disciples!

5. Three times (2:13; 6:4; 11:55) in his narrative the Evangelist mentions that the Passover of the Jews was close. This triple mention has been exploited in various ways in the *Wirkungsgeschichte* of the Fourth Gospel—classically as an indication that Jesus went up to Jerusalem for three Passovers, with the inference that his "public life" extended for the greater part of three years; occasionally as an indication that the Fourth Gospel should be read as a Passover story or as one that had its literary origins in the Haggadic liturgical tradition. Less attention has been paid to the character of the feast itself.

6. Cf. 1:19, 24.

among themselves as to Jesus' identity. Some people thought that Jesus was the prophet (7:40; cf. Deut. 18:18). Others thought that he was the Messiah (7:41). Others thought that he could not be the Messiah. Jesus was from Galilee, not from Bethlehem as the scriptures had foretold (Micah 5:1). Cowering as they did in the face of the crowd, the Temple police did not arrest Jesus. When they reported to the chief priests and the Pharisees, the police were chastised. The crowds may have accepted Jesus, but the authorities did not accept him. The police should not have paid deference to the crowds. That accursed mass did not know the law.

Nicodemus's role in this short pericope is to affirm that Jesus should not be judged without a proper hearing. While advancing the plot of the Johannine narrative, the pericope serves to advance the Evangelist's characterization of Nicodemus as a Pharisee, a leader of the Jews, and a teacher of Israel.

John 4:1–42

After his account of the nocturnal meeting between Jesus and Nicodemus, the Evangelist continues his story with an episode in which Jesus meets a Samaritan woman (4:1–42). The Evangelist's portrayal of the woman contrasts sharply with his portrayal of Nicodemus.[7] Nicodemus is a Jew, a male, and a teacher. The nameless woman is a Samaritan, a woman, someone who does not know the gift of God (4:10). The contrast between these characters continues as they speak with Jesus. After his enigmatic dialogue with Jesus, Nicodemus, the teacher, is revealed as one who does not understand. He does not become a disciple. After a puzzling conversation with Jesus, the woman comes to know both the gift of God and who it was who was speaking to her (4:10, 15, 19, 25–26, 29). She becomes an evangelist-disciple.

The conversation between Jesus and the woman is readily divided into two sections, 4:7b–15 and 4:16–26. Each of the sections of the dialogue begins with a request by Jesus.[8] The verbs are in the imperative mood. Dialogue ensues as a result of what Jesus has told the woman to do, that is, to draw water for him (4:7) and to go and call her husband (4:16). The dialogue marks the first occasion in the Fourth Gospel where there is discourse about the Jews. Previously, mention of the Jews is found in the Evangelist's

7. See M. M. Pazdan, "Nicodemus and the Samaritan Woman: Contrasting Models of Discipleship," *BTB* 17 (1987): 145–48. Cf. H. Servotte, *According to John: A Literary Reading of the Fourth Gospel* (London, 1994), p. 22; and Collins, "From John to the Beloved Disciple," pp. 363–64.

8. In the Fourth Gospel, it is typically Jesus who initiates dialogue with his interlocutors, but there are exceptions to this pattern. Cf. 3:3; 4:7, 10; 5:19; 6:26; 7:16, 37; 8:12, 21, 31; 9:39; 13:31; 14:1–3; 16:16. For the exceptions, see 3:26; 4:31; 7:3; 9:2; 10:24; 12:21; 13:6.

narrative material. Now, for the first time in the Fourth Gospel, characters in the story broach the subject of "the Jews."

Ironically, perhaps, the first person who speaks about the Jews is the Samaritan. She identifies Jesus as a Jew (σὺ ᾽Ιουδαῖος ὤν, 4:9). This is the only place in the Fourth Gospel where Jesus is specifically identified as a Jew. Jesus is thus the first person in the Johannine Gospel who is specifically identified as a Jew by one of the narrative's speaking characters. His Jewish identity is revealed in a rhetorical question—a kind of "How dare you?" or "How can you?" rejoinder—whose purpose is to establish a distance between Jesus and the woman.[9] She has been twice identified as a Samaritan, once in the introduction to her question,[10] once in the Evangelist's aside. The explanatory comment[11] by the evangelist confirms that Jesus has done something that is not done by Jews by asking the woman to give him something to drink. "Jews," writes the Evangelist, "do not share things in common with Samaritans." Jesus' behavior is not characteristic of Jews, and to that extent, it is unseemly.

The motif of Jesus' identity is a major theme in the Evangelist's scene of Jesus' meeting the Samaritan woman. Once identified as a Jew, Jesus is described in a chain of christological titles. Jesus is "greater than our ancestor Jacob" (4:12). Jesus, the Jew, is "a prophet" (4:19), the Messiah (4:25), the Christ (4:29), and "the Savior of the world" (4:42).[12] In addition to what the woman and her neighbors say about Jesus, the pericope contains the first of the Gospel's 'ἐγώ εἰμι' sayings. The formula of self-identification is used when Jesus says to the Samaritan, "I am he, the one who is speaking to you" (ἐγώ εἰμι ὁ λαλῶν σοι, 4:26). The identification of Jesus has moved from the Samaritan's initial recognition of him as a Jew to his self-revelation as the revealer.

Subsequently, Jesus is identified as the "Savior of the world," a characterization that moves his role from that of the simple Jew to that of a world

9. J. E. Botha, *Jesus and the Samaritan Woman: A Speech Act Reading of John 4:1–42* (Leiden, 1991), p. 122, describes her utterance as "disputative." He comments, "The woman wants to get Jesus to desist in his socio-culturally unacceptable conduct. The author wants the reader to have positive feelings toward the woman and react negatively towards the conduct of Jesus."

10. The description of the woman as a Samaritan (ἡ γυνὴ ἡ Σαμαρῖτις, 4:9) in the introduction to the question is somewhat superfluous in view of the Evangelist's initial presentation of her as a woman from Samaria (γυνὴ ἐκ τῆς Σαμαρείας) in 4:7. The repetition clearly types her as a Samaritan and highlights the contrast between her, a Samaritan, and Jesus, a Jew.

11. On the parenthetical character of 4:9b, see G. Van Belle, *Les parenthèses dans l'évangile de Jean. Aperçu historique et classification. Texte grec de Jean* (SNTA 11; Leuven, 1985), pp. 210–35.

12. Cf. L. Schmid, "Die Komposition der Samaria-Szene Joh 4:1–42. Ein Beitrag zur Charakteristik des 4. Evangelisten als Schriftsteller," *ZNW* 28 (1929): 148–58, pp. 152–53; G. Segalla, *Volontà di Dio e dell'uomo in Giovanni (vangelo e lettere)* (RivBSup 6; Brescia, 1974), p. 189; van Belle, *Les Parenthèses*, pp. 231–32.

figure. From the perspective of those who are not Jews, Jesus is viewed as a Jew first and then he is seen as Savior of the World.

The λέγει αὐτῇ formula of 4:16, surprisingly without an expressed subject,[13] marks the juncture between the two parts of Jesus' dialogue with the Samaritan. The two parts of this dialogue are different from each other in form and in content. The first section (4:7b–15) has the form of a true dialogue, in which Jesus says something three times and the woman responds to each of his remarks. The second section (4:16–26) essentially consists of a monologue encompassed by a two-part confession of faith by the woman (4:19, 25). It culminates in Jesus' self-revelation (4:26).

The discourse in the first section of the dialogue concerns the gift of water, the gift of living water that Jesus is to give, in contrast to the water from the well that Jesus asked the Samaritan woman to give to him. The second section of the dialogue has worship as its content. The Samaritan speaks to Jesus about the mountain on which her ancestors worshiped. Jesus replies with a short discourse on worship in spirit and in truth (4:21–24).

The contrast between the subject matters of the two parts of the dialogue is underscored by personal references. In the first section of the dialogue, the conversation is essentially a person-to-person, one-on-one conversation. It concerns what Jesus wants to receive from the woman and what she might receive from Jesus. The second section of the discourse concerns a larger group of people. She speaks about her ancestors (4:20). Jesus speaks about true worshipers (4:23).

The shift to this broader human perspective appears in 4:20, where the woman uses a first-person plural to speak of herself and addresses Jesus in the second-person plural: "Our ancestors [οἱ πατέρες ἡμῶν] worshiped on this mountain, but you say [ὑμεῖς] that the place where people must worship is in Jerusalem." The use of the personal pronouns establishes a we-you contrast that underscores the difference between the Samaritans and the Jews previously expressed in the dialogue and narrator's comment in 4:9. The Samaritan woman's "you," in the plural, suggests that the contrast is ultimately a contrast between two peoples, the Samaritans and the Jews. She represents[14] the former, Jesus the latter. Despite her acknowledgment that Jesus is a prophet, the woman continues to situate him as a Jew.

---

13. Cf. 4:7b, 9, 11, 15, 16, 19, 21, 25, 26. The inferred subject of the verb in 4:16 is expressed in the NRSV translation, which renders λέγει αὐτῇ as "Jesus said to her."

14. On the representative character of the Samaritan woman, see further Collins, *These Things Have Been Written*, pp. 16–19.

The contrast between Samaritans and Jews highlighted in the woman's words continues in Jesus' response. He says, "You worship [ὑμεῖς προσκυνεῖτε] what you do not know; we worship [ἡμεῖς προσκυνοῦμεν] what we know, for salvation is from the Jews" (4:22). Speaking in the plural, Jesus speaks on behalf of others. The emphatic ἡμεῖς of 4:22b provides a sharp contrast with the emphatic ὑμεῖς of 4:22a. Jesus' use of an emphatic pronoun in the plural also contrasts with his use of the emphatic ἐγώ in the self-revelation formula of 4:26.

On whose behalf does Jesus speak? A reading of the Fourth Gospel in its entirety might initially suggest that Jesus is speaking as the spokesperson for the Johannine community. The Evangelist frequently uses a first-person plural in reference to his community.[15] Jesus' reference to the hour that is coming but that already is (νῦν ἐστιν, 4:23) indicates that the author's narrative future has entered into his narrative present. The slippage creates the possibility that Jesus might well be speaking on behalf of the Johannine community when he uses the first-person plural in 4:22. In 4:23–24, however, Jesus' discourse is expressed in the third person. The woman had spoken to him as a Jew (4:9) and as one among the Jews (4:20). Jesus speaks of true worshipers and of those who worship. With his use of the third person, Jesus distances himself from the Johannine community. His "we" in verse 22 implies that he is speaking on behalf of the Jews. By using the plural, Jesus acknowledges that he belongs to the Jewish people. It is as a Jew,[16] albeit a knowledgeable one, that Jesus says that salvation is from the Jews. Responding to the Samaritan's polarities, Jesus affirms that salvation is from the Jews.[17]

Jesus' remarkable utterance[18] is a powerful statement that has a singular place within the Fourth Gospel. It is one of only two instances in which the Johannine Jesus speaks about the Jews.[19] Within the Fourth Gospel, the utterance is particularly striking insofar as the logion speaks positively about "the Jews"[20]—a turn of phrase that elsewhere in the narrative is

---

15. Cf. 1:14, e.g.

16. Similarly, B. Lindars, *The Gospel of John* (NCB; London, 1972), p. 189; F. J. Moloney, *The Gospel of John* (SP 4; Collegeville, Minn., 1998), p. 128.

17. In this regard, Okure notes that salvation "is from the Jews" is what the Evangelist believes. See T. Okure, *The Johannine Approach to Mission: A Contextual Study of John 4:1–42* (WUNT II/31; Tübingen, 1988), p. 266, n. 91.

18. Brown comments, "This line is a clear indication that the Johannine attitude to the Jews cloaks neither an anti-Semitism of the modern variety nor a view that rejects the spiritual heritage of Judaism." Cf. R. E. Brown, *The Gospel according to John*, vol. 1: *Chapters i–xii* (AB 29; New York, 1966), p. 172.

19. Cf. 13:33.

20. This singular usage led Bultmann to consider that 4:22c was an editorial gloss. He holds that the statement is "impossible in Jn." See R. Bultmann, *The Gospel of John: A Commentary* (Oxford, 1971), p. 189 n. 6; cf. G. Friedrich, *Wer ist Jesus? Die Verkündigung des vierten Evangelisten dargestellt*

affected with negative or, at best, neutral connotations—and is found on the lips of Jesus, the unabashed hero of the narrative.

Jesus' utterance on salvation from the Jews has a rightful and meaningful place within Jesus' discourse with the Samaritan. The discourse has set the Jews over and against the Samaritans and clearly identifies Jesus as a Jew. It is Jesus the Jew who speaks as the revealer (4:26) and implicitly promises to give the Samaritan woman the living water, the gift of God that Jesus alone is able to give (4:10).

Having assumed the outsider's perspective of the Samaritan woman,[21] Jesus asserts that salvation comes from the Jews, of whom he is one. His "salvation is from the Jews" has a personal ring. It is more than a mere affirmation that salvation arises from God's promises to Israel[22] or that it was Israel's role to prepare for the coming of the kingdom of God.[23] Jesus' logion is an implicit claim to his own messianic status. He is the Jew who will give the messianic gifts. The living water of which he spoke enigmatically in 4:10—only to have the woman characteristically misunderstand— is a symbol of the never-ending life he will give.

Jesus' subsequent meeting and speaking with the inhabitants of the city (4:40–42) leads them to affirm that he "is truly the Savior of the world" (4:42). The only previous mention of salvation in the Fourth Gospel is in 3:17, where Jesus comments on the purpose of his mission. He affirms that God sent "the Son into the world . . . in order that the world might be saved through him." The Samaritans' confession of faith confirms and qualifies Jesus' own affirmation that salvation is from the Jews.[24] It is a confirmation insofar as it is a Jew, Jesus, who is acknowledged as Savior. It is a qualification insofar as salvation comes from the Jews but is for the world.

---

an Joh. 4,4–42 (Stuttgart, 1967), p. 43; S. Schulz, *Das Evangelium nach Johannes* (NTD 4; Göttingen, 1975), p. 76; E. Haenchen, *John,* vol. 1: *A Commentary on the Gospel of John. Chapters 1–6* (Philadelphia, 1984), p. 222. Thyen, Leidig, and O'Day argue, on the contrary, for the textual originality of 4:22c. See H. Thyen, "Das Heil kommt von den Juden," in D. Lührmann and G. Strecker, eds., *Kirche,* FS Günther Bornkamm (Tübingen, 1980), pp. 163–84; E. Leidig, *Jesu Gespräch mit der Samaritanerin und weitere Gespräche im Johannesevangelium* (ThDiss 15; Basel, 1981), pp. 103–33; G. R. O'Day, *Revelation in the Fourth Gospel: Narrative Mode and Theological Claim* (Philadelphia, 1986), pp. 69–70.

21. Dodd notes that, in the Fourth Gospel, Jesus' interlocutors essentially serve as foils. Their "interpolations," he writes, "do no more than provide the teacher with an occasion to elaborate his thought." See C. H. Dodd, *Historical Tradition in the Fourth Gospel* (Cambridge–New York, 1963), p. 318.

22. Thus Lindars, *Gospel of John,* pp. 188–89, who writes about the great messianic prophecies of Isaiah 9, 11, and 45.

23. Cf. F.-M. Braun, *Jean le théologien,* vol. 2: *Les grandes traditions d'Israël et l'accord des écritures selon le quatrième évangile* (Ebib; Paris, 1964), p. 208.

24. It is to be noted that both the noun σωτηρία (4:22) and the noun σωτήρ (4:42) are *hapax* in the Fourth Gospel. The related verb σώζω appears in 3:17; 5:34; 10:9; 11:12; 12:27, 47.

John 13:33

The dialogue between Jesus and the Samaritan woman, where mention of the Jews appears both on the lips of the Samaritan and on the lips of Jesus, is the only place in the so-called Gospel of Signs (John 1–12) where any specific mention of "the Jews" is found in the Evangelist's discourse material. The next time that Jews are spoken of by one of the characters in the Fourth Gospel is found in the first of the "Farewell Discourses" (John 13–14). Once again, it is Jesus who speaks of the Jews. He does so only once in his farewell address. When he does so, he implicitly identifies "the Jews" with the Johannine "Pharisees."

Jesus says to his disciples, "Little children, I am with you only a little longer. You will look for me, and as I said to the Jews so now I say to you, 'Where I am going, you cannot come'" (13:33). These words recall for the benefit of Jesus' disciples a pair of riddles that Jesus had pronounced on previous occasions. In 7:33–34, Jesus says, "I will be with you a little while longer, and then I am going to him who sent me. You will search for me, but you will not find me; and where I am, you cannot come." Later (πάλιν) he said, "I am going away, and you will search for me, but you will die in your sin. Where I am going, you cannot come" (8:21).

"The Jews" respond to the first riddle with characteristic misunderstanding.[25] They take Jesus' words as an indication that he might leave the land of Israel and go to the Dispersion, where he will teach the Greeks (7:35). The enigmatic saying of 8:21 is addressed "to them" (αὐτοῖς), arguably "the Pharisees" of 8:13. It, too, meets with misunderstanding. Jesus' interlocutors take his words as possibly meaning that he was about to kill himself (8:22).

As was the case with Jesus' logion on salvation being from the Jews (4:22), the words of Jesus in 13:33 are unique within the Gospel. One aspect of their singularity is that the words are spoken to the disciples, who are called "little children." The vocative τεκνία is *hapax* within the Gospel.[26] The diminutive form suggests not only a positive affective relationship between Jesus and his disciples; it also suggests that they have

---

25. Nicholson notes that in the Fourth Gospel, Jesus is "consistently misunderstood by the characters in the story known as the 'Jews.'" See G. C. Nicholson, *Death as Departure: The Johannine Descent-Ascent Schema* (SBLDS 63; Chico, Calif., 1983), p. 160.

26. Compare with the Evangelist's use of τέκνα in 1:12; 11:52. In contrast, the diminutive τεκνία is part of the characteristic vocabulary of the first Johannine epistle (1 John 2:1, 12, 28; 3:7, 18; 4:4; 5:21).

something to learn. There is some evidence that a Jewish teacher[27] might address his disciples as children.[28] As a form of address, "Little children" is particularly significant in a farewell discourse, a genre whose scenario features the departure of a parent.[29] That they have something to learn about Jesus' departure is evidenced in the misunderstanding represented by Simon Peter's naive question "Lord, where are you going?" (13:36).

In the Fourth Gospel, Simon Peter is spokesperson for "the Twelve,"[30] a group that does not figure prominently in the Evangelist's narrative.[31] Peter's misunderstanding of Jesus' words about his departure represents the misunderstanding of the entire group. His question images a naive view of discipleship, as if it were simply a matter of following Jesus, that is, accompanying the earthly Jesus as he goes about his travels. Peter does not understand that Jesus' departure is a matter of his return to the Father. Like "the Jews" to whom the utterances about Jesus' departure were addressed in 7:33–34 and 8:21, the Simon Peter of 13:36–37 has misunderstood what Jesus has to say. They took Jesus' words to be about his death; he takes Jesus' words to be about movement to another place, albeit one that might lead to his own death.

Ultimately, the misunderstanding of both the Jews and of Peter bears not only on the meaning of Jesus' revelation but also on their respective roles in the story of Jesus. The Jews speak of Jesus' death in 8:22. At that point in the narrative, they are seemingly unaware of the role that they themselves are to play in that death. Their naive misunderstanding of Jesus' words is an example of Johannine irony. So, too, is Simon Peter's misunderstanding. Brashly he speaks of his readiness to die for Jesus (13:37), unaware that at the decisive moment he will deny Jesus three times (13:38; cf. 18:27). He is also unaware that his following of Jesus will ultimately lead to his own death at the hands of others, as is indicated in the epilogue to the Johannine narrative, when the Evangelist adds a note on Peter's discipleship (21:18–19)[32] to Jesus' triple inquiry on the love of Peter, intended to correspond to and reverse Peter's triple denial (21:15–17).

---

27. Cf. 13:13–14.
28. Cf. Str-B 2:559.
29. The *Testaments of the Twelve Patriarchs* is a classic case.
30. Cf. P. Perkins, *Peter: Apostle for the Whole Church* (Studies on Personalities in the New Testament; Columbia, S.C., 1994), p. 95.
31. See Collins, *These Things Have Been Written*, pp. 78–86.
32. The "follow me" (ἀκολούθει μοι) that Jesus addresses to Simon Peter in 21:19 is one of only two occurrences (cf. 1:43) of the classic formulation of the call to discipleship in the Fourth Gospel. On the proverbial character of 18:19, see Collins, *These Things Have Been Written*, pp. 134–37.

Despite the similarities[33] between the exchanges in 7:33–36 and 8:21–24 on the one hand and 13:33–38 on the other, there are manifest differences between what Jesus said to the Jews and what, recalling that earlier exchange, he says to the disciples on the occasion of his farewell discourse. One obvious difference is that Jesus addresses the disciples as his "little children" and then speaks to them about the Jews. The direct address to the disciples contrasts with Jesus' third-person speech about the Jews. There is a personal relationship between Jesus and his disciples. "The Jews" are others about whom Jesus speaks. In a sense, they stand over and against the group constituted by Jesus and his disciples.

By this time in the story, the reader of the Johannine narrative already knows that this is indeed the case. There is a hostile relationship between Jesus and the Jews. The genre of the farewell discourse is such that the discourse is programmatic for the situation of those to whom the farewell discourse is apparently addressed. The tension between the "little children" and "the Jews," of which the term of endearment used by Jesus in addressing his disciples provides a narrative hint, reflects the real situation of the Johannine community.[34]

The second obvious difference between the two sayings of Jesus is that, in recalling his words to the Jews, in 13:33 the Johannine Jesus has omitted both the off-putting words "but you will not find me" (7:34) and the judgmental phrase "you will die in your sin" (8:21). It would have been inappropriate for Jesus to have addressed these words to his "little children" in the farewell discourse.

The disciples' search for Jesus would not lead to the same fate as would the Jews' search for Jesus.[35] The Jews will not find Jesus. Their search will be ineffective. They will remain in their sin, their lack of belief. The disciples cannot go where Jesus goes, but the Evangelist does not say that they will not find Jesus. Nor does he say that they will remain in their sin. In the time after his return to the Father, they will have the possibility of a new mode of relationship with Jesus. In the interim inaugurated by Jesus' departure, their mutual love will be the modality and instrument of his presence with them.

Jesus' departure meant life, not death, for his disciples. Although they, as their spokesperson showed, misunderstood Jesus' words, they were not in sin at the time that the Fourth Gospel was written. At that time, after

---

33. Cf. 6:67.
34. Cf. Nicholson, *Death,* pp. 161–62.
35. On the significance of the motif of the search for Jesus in 7:34; 8:21; and 13:33, see Collins, *These Things Have Been Written,* pp. 112–20.

the return of Jesus to the Father, they were a community of believers. The "sin" about which the Evangelist wrote was the sin of disbelief. Disbelief is the sin of the Johannine "Jews." The disciples may be weak and vacillating in their faith, but they are not unbelievers.

By speaking of "the Jews" as he does in 13:33, the Johannine Jesus has moved the Evangelist's narrative ahead in several ways. First, at the moment of his departure, Jesus has confirmed the Evangelist's narrative use of "the Jews." The Jews are "the Jews," and Jesus speaks openly about them. Second, "the Jews" of whom Jesus speaks are the Pharisees, and apparently the chief priests as well.[36] Third, Jesus associates "the Jews" with his departure and their search unto death for him. Finally, the fashion in which Jesus speaks about "the Jews" confirms the separation between the disciples whom he leaves behind and "the Jews."

John 18:33–38a

The third occasion in which discourse about "the Jews" is in the Fourth Gospel is in a series of related episodes during the Roman trial of Jesus, in which there is repeated talk about "the King of the Jews." To a large extent, the narrative focus of this trial scene is on "the King of the Jews."[37] The first episode is Pilate's interrogation of Jesus (18:33–38a). In the Johannine narrative, the scene takes place immediately after the Jews have handed Jesus over to Pilate with the expectation that he would be put to death.

Entering the praetorium, Pilate summons Jesus. His interrogation begins with the leading question "Are you the King of the Jews?" (18:33).[38] As an officer of the empire, Pilate was apparently seeking a political

---

36. The οὖν of 7:33 marks the narrative hiatus between the exchange between Jesus and the Jews in 7:33–36 and 7:32. John 7:32 serves as a somewhat independent transition between 7:25–31 and 7:33–36. Insofar as the transitional verse serves as an introduction to the exchange, it suggests that the Jews of verse 35 are the chief priests and the Pharisees, the group that had sent the Temple police to arrest Jesus.

37. See R. A. Culpepper, *Anatomy of the Fourth Gospel: A Study in Literary Design* (Foundations & Facets: NT; Philadelphia, 1983), p. 172. Culpepper notes that "the trial before Pilate spins this irony [that Jesus is the king of the Jews] into a fine and intricate tapestry."

38. As is the case in the Fourth Gospel, the title "King of the Jews," apart from Matt. 2:2, appears for the first time in all three Synoptics on the lips of Pilate (Matt. 27:11; Mark 15:2; Luke 23:3). Dodd notes that the title is in "a form which, we may safely say, is not likely to have been used by Jews, but which is natural enough in the mouth of a Roman" (Dodd, *Historical Tradition*, p. 88; cf. R. Schnackenburg, *The Gospel according to St John*, vol. 3 [HTCNT; New York, 1982], pp. 247–48). The title occurs six times in the Fourth Gospel but only three times in Matthew (27:11, 29, 37), five times in Mark (15:2, 9, 12, 18, 26), and three times in Luke (23:3, 37, 38).

justification for putting Jesus to death. Were Jesus as seditious as he might have appeared to be, were he to have claimed kingship over the Jews for himself, Pilate would have had sufficient warrant to order his death. Galilean uprisings took place often enough to suggest the possibility that the accused Galilean who stood before him was a leader of a group that sought to overthrow the political regime of which Pilate himself was the local representative.

According to the Johannine scenario, the questioning takes place in Pilate's judicial chambers.[39] To Pilate's question, Jesus responds with a question of his own. He asks about the source of Pilate's thinly veiled accusation (18:34). Pilate responds to Jesus' question with a rhetorical question about his own ethnicity. Then he interrogates Jesus directly by asking about the activity that had led to his having been handed over to the prefect for judgment (18:35). Jesus obviously does not answer the rhetorical question, whose negative form presumes a negative response. Neither does he answer Pilate's question about his activity. Rather, he speaks to Pilate about the nature of his kingship. He affirms that his kingship is not from this world, clearly implying that he is nonetheless a king.[40]

With respect to the Jews, Pilate is similar to the Samaritan woman in that he is an outsider. In their own words, Pilate (18:35) and the Samaritan (4:9) have identified themselves as individuals who are not Jews. Like the Samaritan, Pilate also identifies Jesus as belonging to the Jewish people. "Your own nation [τὸ ἔθνος τὸ σόν]," he says to Jesus, "and the chief priests have handed you over to me" (18:35; cf. 4:20). In contrast with his dialogue with the Samaritan woman, when he identified with Jews and served as their spokesperson, the Jesus who speaks to Pilate distances himself from "the Jews." Admitting that he is a king, Jesus does not acknowledge that he is "King of the Jews." Rather, his discourse about the Jews is in the third person. It is the "Jews" who have handed him over to Pilate (18:36). Jesus' "handed over" (παραδοθῶ) reprises the "handed over" (παρέδωκάν) of Pilate's immediately preceding remark. The Jews of

39. Questions can be raised as to the historical accuracy of Pilate's query. That the question is found in the four canonical Gospels is an argument (multiple attestation) in favor of its historicity. The Johannine narrative suggests that Pilate's interrogation of Jesus took place *in camera* and that it would have been a private affair. That "King of the Jews" is the title under which Jesus was put to death suggests that Pilate's query was plausible, to say the least. Brown concludes his study of the *titulus* by saying "I see no convincing objection to its historicity as the expression of the charge on which the Romans executed Jesus." See R. E. Brown, *The Death of the Messiah: From Gethsemane to the Grave. A Commentary on the Passion Narratives in the Four Gospels*, 2 vols. (ABRL; New York, 1994), pp. 962–68, especially p. 968.

40. Although Pilate's question "Are you the King of the Jews?" appears in all four canonical Gospels, the discourse that follows in John 18:34–38a is found only in the Fourth Gospel.

whom he speaks are presumably his own people, and their chief priests who handed him over to Pilate (18:35). By speaking of his followers (οἱ ὑπηρέται οἱ ἐμοί) as being in opposition to the Jews, Jesus' words about the Jews in 18:36 echo some of the nuances of his words about "the Jews" (οἱ Ἰουδαῖοι) in 13:33.

John 18:38b–40

The next episode in the trial of Jesus in which there is mention of the Jews takes place immediately after Pilate has concluded his questioning of Jesus with the dismissive "What is truth?" (18:38a). Pilate goes outside to meet the Jews. The prefect affirms that Jesus is innocent. "I find no case [οὐδεμίαν αἰτίαν] against him," he says (18:38). The term αἰτία used by Pilate is a technical term in legal usage. It designates grounds for action and, by extension, culpability or crime.[41] In essence, it affirms that he has not found Jesus guilty as charged. Jesus has not claimed to be king of the Jews and a potential leader of an uprising against the imperial regime.

In deference to the custom of pardoning a criminal on the occasion of the celebration of Passover,[42] Pilate offers to release the one whom he calls "King of the Jews" (18:39).[43] The Jews yell back,[44] "Not this man" (μὴ τοῦτον). Calling Jesus "that guy," they refuse to acknowledge him as king of the Jews. The only king whom they recognize is Caesar (19:15). They also have refused to accept him as the one to be released on the occasion of the feast. Instead of "that guy," they call out for the release of Barabbas.

In one of his characteristically terse but poignant comments, the Evangelist adds to the drama that "Barabbas was a bandit" (18:40). Barabbas was not a common thief; he was a violent brigand (λῃστής).[45] The

41. Pilate had previously used juridical language when he asked the Jews about the charge (κατηγορία, 18:29) that was being brought against Jesus. The Jews did not specify a charge; they simply implied that Jesus was an evildoer, without adducing any evidence whatsoever.

42. The Fourth Gospel stands alone in affirming that the custom was practiced on the occasion of the Passover festival (8:39; cf. Matt. 27:15; Mark 15:6). The precision is in keeping with the Fourth Gospel's emphasis on the Passover.

43. Cf. Mark 15:9. Neither in Mark nor in the Fourth Gospel is Jesus identified by name. He is simply designated as the "King of the Jews." Barrett indicates that it is not clear why Pilate describes Jesus as the "King of the Jews." He offers as possibilities the idea that Pilate has decided that Jesus is not a king in the ordinary sense of the word and that it was a description that would be little likely to commend Jesus to the Jews. See C. K. Barrett, *The Gospel according to St. John*, 2d ed. (Philadelphia, 1978), p. 539.

44. See Brown, *Death*, 2:808, who takes the πάλιν of 18:40 as "back" rather than "again," as if the Evangelist were digesting a longer account.

45. See C. Spicq, "Art. λῃστής," in *Theological Lexicon of the New Testament* (Peabody, Mass., 1994), 2:389–95.

Evangelist's sense of drama is such that he places the comment at the conclusion of the little scene. By doing so, he highlights the difference between violent brigandage and Jesus' kingship. Jesus and his companions were not given over to violence (18:36).

In sum, given the possibility of accepting Jesus as king of the Jews, "the Jews" refused to accept him. Jesus' kingship is confirmed as one that comes without recourse to violence.

John 19:1–3

It is commonly acknowledged that the Fourth Evangelist has carefully composed his account of Jesus' trial before Pilate in a sequence of seven dramatic episodes arranged in a chiastic pattern.[46] At the center of the chiasm is the scene in which the soldiers mock Jesus (19:1–3). The scene is different from the others in the Evangelist's dramatic arrangement insofar as the scene lacks a verb of motion indicating a change of locale on the part of the presiding judge, Pilate.

Striving to satisfy the Jews so that they will give up the idea of having Jesus put to death, Pilate has Jesus flogged. Then soldiers under his command[47] mock Jesus "the King." They plait a crown of thorns and place it on his head. They clothe him with a purple garment, reminiscent of the royal purple. The soldiers, presumably not Roman citizens but conscripts from conquered Roman territories, repeatedly[48] greet their buffoon with "Hail, King of the Jews." "King of the Jews" is in the nominative (with an article) rather than in the vocative.[49] The soldiers' derogatory remark is

46. A number of exegetes divide the trial scene (18:28–19:16) into seven episodes. The trial is dramatized by the Evangelist, who uses verbs of motion to shift the scene from outside to inside to outside and so forth. The scenes are (1) the handing over of Jesus to Pilate by the Jews (18:28–32); (2) the interrogation by Pilate (18:33–38a); (3) the declaration of innocence (18:33b–40); (4) mockery by the soldiers (19:1–3); (5) a second declaration of innocence (19:4–8); (6) a second interrogation (19:9–12); (7) the handing over of Jesus for crucifixion (19:13–16). The first, third, fifth, and seventh scenes take place outside. The second, fourth, and sixth take place inside. See, for example, D. Senior, *The Passion of Jesus in the Gospel of John* (The Passion Series 4; Collegeville, Minn., 1991), pp. 68–69; Brown, *Death*, 1:757–59.

47. This is the first time that soldiers under Roman command appear in the Fourth Gospel. Cf. 19:23 (two times), 24, 32, 34.

48. Note the use of the imperfect, ἤρχοντο and ἔλεγον, in 19:3.

49. Matt. 27:29 and Mark 15:18 use the vocative in their versions of the incident. Lindars, following Moulton, who identifies "descriptiveness" as the note of the articular nominative, says that the nominative "retains the idea of 'so-called King' without admitting that Jesus has a right to the description." See J. H. Moulton, *A Grammar of New Testament Greek* (Edinburgh, 1906), 1:70–71; Lindars, *Gospel of John*, p. 565; cf. Brown, *Gospel according to John*, 2:875.

equivalent to "Hail, 'you king of the Jews.'"[50] Their taunting drips with irony.[51]

The scene of the soldiers adorning Jesus with mock royal attire serves as a preface to the following dramatic scene, in which Pilate goes out to face the Jews. For a second time he affirms Jesus' innocence. Then Jesus appears before the Jews. Pilate presents Jesus as "the man." Once again, for a third time, Pilate affirms that there are no grounds to whatever accusations have been made against Jesus.[52]

The flogging of Jesus serves Pilate's purpose insofar as it is intended to satisfy the Jews' thirst for vengeance without his having to inflict the death penalty on someone whom he has found to be innocent of the charge of sedition. The repeated verbal taunts of the soldiers trivialize the very idea that Jesus is king of the Jews. They do not take it for real that Jesus is king of the Jews. Ironically, they confirm Jesus' denial that he was king in any political sense. Once again, however, it is non-Jews who seem to recognize the Jewishness of Jesus and call him, albeit with ironic mockery, "the King of the Jews."

John 19:19–22

Once the chief priests were successful in moving Pilate's agenda on the kingship of Jesus to their claim that the Roman emperor was their king (19:15), the cowardly Pilate[53] gave in to their demands. Jesus was handed over to be crucified. Carrying a cross by himself, Jesus went to Golgotha where he was crucified.

The final scene in the Fourth Gospel in which there is discourse about "the Jews" is the episode of a controversy over the indication of the charge under which the prisoner was to be put to death. According to Roman custom, a tablet with some indication of the crime of which he had been accused and found guilty was hung around a prisoner's neck or carried before him as he was led out to execution. Identification of the condemned person's crime served as a warning to those who saw him being led out to

---

50. Cf. Brown, *Death,* 1:868.

51. With regard to the dramatic irony of the scene, see J. Blank, "Die Verhandlung vor Pilatus Jo 18:28–19:16 im Lichte johanneischer Theologie," *BZ* 3 (1959): 60–81, pp. 73–74; P. D. Duke, *Irony in the Fourth Gospel* (Atlanta, 1985), pp. 131–32; I. de la Potterie, *The Hour of Jesus: The Passion and Resurrection of Jesus according to John* (Slough, 1989), pp. 101–3.

52. Pilate's words in 19:4 and 19:6 are almost identical with his earlier affirmation of Jesus' innocence (18:38).

53. In his study of the Fourth Evangelist's characterization of Pilate, Culpepper states that "Pilate represents the futility of attempted compromise" (Culpepper, *Anatomy,* p. 143).

execution. They knew that they would suffer a similar fate were they to commit a similar crime. In the case of Jesus, the title was "Jesus of Nazareth, the King of the Jews" (19:19).[54]

Attested in all four canonical Gospels,[55] the title is the subject of controversy only in the Fourth Gospel (19:19–22). Moreover, it is only the Fourth Gospel that uses a formal term, *title* (τίτλος),[56] to designate the inscribed placard that gave "the King of the Jews" as the reason for Jesus' execution. Use of the formal expression provides another flourish in the Johannine dramatization of the trial and its conclusion, as does the Johannine indication that the charge was written in three languages—surely of greater symbolic than historical value.[57]

A controversy took place between the chief priests of the Jews and Pilate over the words that the prefect had written on the placard. The chief priests of the Jews did not want the prefect to acknowledge Jesus' kingship. "Do not write," they said, "'The King of the Jews,' but, 'This man said, "I am King of the Jews."'" (19:21). This time Pilate did not acquiesce. Pilate's confirmation of the title, "What I have written, I have written" (19:22), has echoed down the ages.

That the Evangelist identifies Pilate's antagonist as "the chief priests of the Jews" highlights the difference between them and Pilate as well as the opposition between them and Jesus. As leaders of the Jews, the chief priests reject the designation of Jesus as "the King of the Jews." It is Pilate, someone who is not a Jew, who has identified Jesus as "the King of the Jews." The chief priests do not ask Pilate to omit "the King of the Jews" from the title. What they ask is that Pilate have inscribed that Jesus had made a claim to be the king of the Jews. Neither the Fourth Gospel nor any of the Synoptics records such a claim.[58] Nonetheless, it was important for the chief priests of the Jews to distance themselves from the one identified as king of the Jews. In their efforts to get rid of Jesus,[59] the chief priests claimed that

54. Haenchen implausibly suggests that the inscription "serves to honor Jesus . . . the charge against him is not mentioned" (Haenchen, *John*, 2:192). In fact, Pilate's question to Jesus in 18:33 suggests that a charge of potential sedition is implied in a claim to kingship. Pilate denies the grounds for the accusation but he allows the execution of Jesus in order to curry favor with "the Jews."

55. Cf. Matt. 27:37; Mark 15:26; Luke 23:38.

56. From the Latin *titulus*; cf. 19:19, 20.

57. Brown sees in the placing of the trilingual title on the cross "a world-wide proclamation of enthronement" (Brown, *Gospel according to John*, 2:919). Similarly, Culpepper (*Anatomy*, p. 172) and Moloney. The latter finds in the use of the "cultured languages of the Roman empire" an indication that "the kingship of Jesus is proclaimed universally" (Moloney, *Gospel of John*, p. 502). On the implausibility of the soldiers' having used three languages for the *titulus*, see Brown, *Death*, 2:965–67.

58. Moreover, it has not served as a confession of Christian faith.

59. See 11:49–50.

they had one king, the Roman Caesar (19:15). In the end, they had to submit to the authority of his local representative.

Conclusion

The confrontation between Jesus and the chief priests over the penal title is the last mention of "the Jews" in the discourse material of the Fourth Gospel. The Roman trial that led to the crucifixion of Jesus focused on Jesus as "the King of the Jews." Five of the six occurrences of the messianic title are found on the lips of the dramatis personae who appear in the series of dramatic episodes. Pilate twice speaks of "the King of the Jews" (18:33, 39). The soldiers repeatedly taunt Jesus with the same words (19:3). Twice (19:21) the chief priests of the Jews talk about "the King of the Jews." Only once does the enigmatic title appear in narrative material, that is, in 19:19, where it appears as the inscription that Pilate had written and placed on the cross.

The dialogue about the king of the Jews represents a new development in the Fourth Gospel's discourse material that speaks of "the Jews." Neither of the previous conversations about the Jews provided any indication that, in dying, Jesus would be identified as king of the Jews. They did, however, prepare for the attribution of Jewishness to Jesus by non-Jews and for the rejection of Jesus the Jew by the chief priests of his people. Ironically, the salvation that was to come from the Jews (4:22) was realized in the death of the one whom the chief priests refused to acknowledge as "the King of the Jews," the one whom "the Jews" could not find. Some time later an anonymous editor would comment, "He came to what was his own, and his own people did not accept him" (1:11).

CHAPTER 9

"Jews" in the Gospel of John as Compared with the Palestinian Talmud, the Synoptics, and Some New Testament Apocrypha

Peter J. Tomson

> It would be incredible for a twentieth-century Christian to
> share or justify the Johannine contention that "the Jews" are
> the children of the devil, an affirmation which is placed on
> the lips of Jesus; but I cannot see how it helps contemporary
> Jewish-Christian relationships to disguise the fact that such
> an attitude once existed.
> R. E. Brown, *The Community of the Beloved Disciple*

From a form-critical viewpoint, a Gospel is the creation of the community
in which it is celebrated, even if it is presented as the incorporation of
the tradition from its revered teacher. Hence a Gospel may be read as an
etiology of its supporting community. In a sense, Jesus' suffering and death
are at the roots of the community's existence. All Gospels tell us that his
execution was an injustice, if not a judicial murder. This information is
bound to generate a feeling of hostility against the perpetrators. Now, as
the community evolved in time, it experienced its own persecution—
among others, from Jewish authorities. At that moment, the identification
with its persecuted Lord may very well have caused the community to
identify its own enemies with his. This, we may suppose for weighty reasons, is what happened with the Fourth Gospel.

One preliminary comment may be appropriate. Delving into these matters fixes our attention on one particular aspect of the Gospel and may
obscure others. The following is not intended to deny the treasures of
insight that the receptive reader may find in this Gospel, nor the inspiration it continues to give to the community of believers.

176

The Johannine Trajectory

On the one hand, the text surface of the Fourth Gospel is marked by a fair number of bumps and cracks, "aporias"[1] that do not fail to incite one's curiosity about the history of the Gospel.[2] It is only natural to see this in relation to the conflicts of which the Johannine epistles speak. On the other hand, the Johannine Gospel and the letters as a whole evince the characteristic language of a closely knit and fairly isolated community. Thus, in the Gospel, the impression one gets is of being confronted with the cherished text of a community of elect that lived through external duress and inner conflict, a literary document that has grown into a record of the community's eventful history. Or, to use the image introduced by J. Louis Martyn, the Gospel text is like a "tell," one of those characteristic mounds found in the Middle East and consisting of "a stratified deposit from what archeologists would call a single, continuous occupation."[3]

Thus some sort of a consensus developed in which the "trajectory"[4] of the Fourth Gospel is studied, attention being paid not just to its literary history but to its literary and social history viewed together. After the Second World War, interest in the literary history was intensified by Rudolf Bultmann's hypothesis of an anterior "Gospel of Signs,"[5] while his theory of a "Gnostic Redeemer myth" as being the religious-historical background of the Gospel passed in rather obscure isolation.[6] After the war—that is to say, after the Shoah, that watershed event that today conditions all our utterings and movements—it was Martyn who led the way in viewing together "history and theology" when analyzing the Gospel's development.[7]

1. See R. T. Fortna, *The Gospel of Signs: A Reconstruction of the Narrative Source Underlying the Fourth Gospel* (SNTSMS 11; Cambridge, 1970), pp. 2f., on this term.

2. For bibliography, see G. Van Belle, *Johannine Bibliography 1966–1985: A Cumulative Bibliography of the Fourth Gospel* (BETL 82; Leuven, 1988), 405–7, "'Jews,' Antisemitism, Anti-Judaism."

3. J. L. Martyn, "Glimpses into the History of the Johannine Community," in M. de Jonge, ed, *L'évangile de Jean. Sources, rédaction, théologie* (BETL 44; Gembloux, 1977), p. 149.

4. See P. J. Lalleman, "The Acts of John: A Two-Stage Initiation into Johannine Gnosticism" (Ph.D. diss., Groningen, 1998), on the term in this connection.

5. R. Bultmann, *Das Evangelium des Johannes* (KEK 2; Göttingen, 1941; 21st ed. 1978), p. 78. The thesis is developed by Fortna, *Gospel of Signs,* and reviewed by G. Van Belle, *The Signs Source in the Fourth Gospel: Historical Survey and Critical Evaluation of the Semeia Hypothesis* (BETL 116; Leuven, 1994), with emphasis on Bultmann's prominence.

6. R. Bultmann, "Die Bedeutung der neuerschlossenen mandäischen und manichäischen Quellen für das Verständnis des Johannesevangeliums," in R. Bultmann and E. Dinkler, eds., *Exegetica. Aufsätze zur Erforschung des Neuen Testaments* (Tübingen, 1967), pp. 55–104. In less extreme form, the theory was also supported by Walter Bauer, *Das Johannesevangelium* (HNT 6; Tübingen, 1933), p. 245.

7. J. L. Martyn, *History and Theology in the Fourth Gospel* (New York, 1968; 2d ed., Nashville, 1979); and J. L. Martyn, *The Gospel of John in Christian History: Essays for Interpreters* (Theological Inquiries; New York, 1978); O. Cullmann, *Der johanneische Kreis. Sein Platz im Spätjudentum, in der*

In this constellation, the fundamental importance of the relationship to the Jews became obvious. Though without stressing the "trajectory," C. K. Barrett wrote that "the investigation of the relation between the Fourth Gospel and Judaism is in no sense pure antiquarianism, but a necessary element of exegesis," and for him, this includes the anti-Jewish attitude of the Gospel.[8] A crucial element recognized by many is the very frequent and often negative use made of the name Jew. Indeed, the Johannine Ἰουδαῖοι is a "unique, idiosyncratic terminology"[9] that expresses "the polemic attitude of the Fourth Gospel towards Judaism."[10] Again, the Gospel's textual complications and its social vicissitudes are simultaneously implicated here. While the religious connotations of the name Jews are evident, so is its immediate social reference. Even when a symbolic meaning is being stressed, how could any reader or listener in antiquity ever miss the reference of "the Jews" to a well-known and clearly identifiable religious-ethnic group?

But the Johannine trajectory comprises not only a negative relationship to the Jews. Its beginnings can only be thought of somewhere within incipient Judeo-Christianity, most probably in a fairly isolated group. If we imagine some primitive Johannine Gospel tradition, as Bultmann and his followers made explicit in their hypothesis of the Signs Gospel, it must have borne the marks of such a group. We would not be surprised to find Judeo-Christian features in the Gospel, and indeed, elements of Jewish tradition.[11] It seems clear, however, that the Gospel text also contains a later

---

Jüngerschaft Jesu und im Urchristentum. Zum Ursprung des Johannesevangeliums (Tübingen, 1975; simultaneous French edition: *Le milieu johannique. Étude sur l'origine de l'évangile de Jean* [Neuchâtel–Paris, 1975]); R. E. Brown, *The Community of the Beloved Disciple: The Life, Loves, and Hates of an Individual Church in New Testament Times* (London, 1979); K. Wengst, *Bedrängte Gemeinde und verherrlichter Christus. Der historische Ort des Johannesevangeliums als Schlüssel zu seiner Interpretation* (BThSt; Neukirchen-Vluyn, 2d. ed.,1983; 4th ed. 1992); J. Zumstein, "La communauté johannique et son histoire," in J.-D. Kaestli, J.-M. Poffet, and J. Zumstein, eds., *La communauté johannique et son histoire* (Le Monde de la Bible; Geneva, 1990), pp. 359–74; and J. Zumstein, "Zur Geschichte des johanneischen Christentums," *TLZ* 122 (1997): 417–28 (*Entwicklungslinie* for trajectory/*trajectoire*). On the Johannine letters, see below.

8. C. K. Barrett, *Das Johannesevangelium und das Judentum* (Delitzsch Lectures; Münster, 1967); ET by D. M. Smith, *The Gospel of John and Judaism,* (Philadelphia; London, 1975; 2d ed., 1980), p. 6 and pp. 70ff. He obscures the anti-Jewish character by concluding that John is purposefully "both Jewish and anti-Jewish," as he uses "Gnosis and anti-Gnosticism" and combines "apocalyptic with non-apocalyptic material." See n. 10, below.

9. M. Hengel, *The Johannine Question,* trans. John Bowden (Philadelphia: Trinity Press, 1989), p. 119.

10. R. E. Brown, *The Gospel according to John* (AB 29; Garden City, N.Y., 1966), p. lxxi. See also C. J. A. Hickling, "Attitudes to Judaism in the Fourth Gospel," in de Jonge, ed., *L'évangile de Jean,* pp. 347–54 (p. 354, criticizing Barrett for rejecting the trajectory approach); Brown, *Community of the Beloved Disciple,* pp. 40–43, 66–69; R. T. Fortna, *The Fourth Gospel and Its Predecessor: From Narrative Source to Present Gospel* (Edinburgh, 1989), pp. 294–314; Wengst, *Bedrängte Gemeinde,* p. 37.

11. Martyn, "Glimpses," pp. 151–60; "The Early Period." Brown, *Community of the Beloved Disciple,* pp. 27–31, following Martyn's basic hypothesis, finds common Jewish messianism in John 1:35–51 and in the "signs" material.

stratum that addresses a Gentile Christian audience.[12] As in Mark 7:2f., John 2:6 explains Jewish purity ritual to readers who need this information. Somewhere along the line, we must locate the banishment from the synagogue to which the unique ἀποσυνάγωγος testifies (see below). It is very important to relate all these developments to the upheavals that reshaped the landscape of first-century Judaism, and especially to the impact of the destruction of the Temple in Jerusalem. Most probably, the strata of the Gospel that presuppose the synagogue ban and the Gentile Christian audience must be dated after 70 C.E.[13] Finally, while attaining its extant form, during the last stretch of its trajectory, the Gospel must have begun to include a larger Gentile Christian audience which at that moment was moving in two opposite directions: one toward Gnosticism and the other toward apostolic "orthodoxy."

Before I focus on the phenomenon of the name Jew, these introductory observations lead me to some methodological implications. First, an adequate approach to the Fourth Gospel and the role it assigns to "the Jews" is possible only if we also take the sociohistorical implications into account. Mere "text-immanent" studies of this problem that fail to do so ignore an important aspect of this Gospel's text.[14] Second, the name Jew having the immediate social reference indicated, the scope of its meaning can never be limited to the Gospel itself. Studying "who the Jews are in John" in isolation from other sources runs the risk of operating on a slanted perception and of producing a trivializing analysis. Third, since, on the one hand, the Gospel trajectory includes a Judeo-Christian stratum and, on the other, "Jews" are so prominently involved, study of this name as used in ancient Jewish texts is necessary. For one thing, this will teach us that using the name Jew does not in itself imply an anti-Jewish stance.

The Dual Usage of "Israel" and "Jew"

The sources impose a fourth desideratum of method. Even a cursory look into the ancient Christian and Jewish texts reveals to the perceptive reader that it is necessary to study the name Jew in conjunction with the other

---

12. See Brown, *Community of the Beloved Disciple*, p. 55; and esp. M. Hengel, *Die johanneische Frage. Ein Lösungsversuch* (WUNT 67; Tübingen, 1993), pp. 298–306.

13. Thus also Hengel, *Die johanneische Frage*, p. 299.

14. Admirably, Caron postulates that "*in the text*, not outside it or behind it, both the sense and the reference of the term are to be found" yet with many scholars refuses "to empty the expression of its historical referent." See G. Caron, "Exploring a Religious Dimension: The Johannine Jews," *SR* 24 (1995): 159–71, p. 162.

name involved, Israel. This is obvious in the Gospel of John. Why does the narrator call Nicodemus "a leader of the Jews" while, within the narrative, Jesus calls him "a teacher of Israel" (John 3:1, 10)? Comparative study of ancient Jewish texts is both imperative and most instructive here.

In his 1996 monograph, Graham Harvey unfortunately made the mistake of not addressing this simultaneous dual usage.[15] He made separate semantic analyses of each of the three names, Jew, Hebrew, and Israel, in sources ranging from the Old Testament to Justin Martyr. His findings are that the three names have distinct semantic ranges that nevertheless partially overlap. "Jew" originally related to the territory of Judah and became the most general and fundamentally neutral name, though it acquired a negative connotation in early Christian sources. By using the seemingly ancient name "Hebrew," the sources emphasize the positive value of Jewish tradition. And "Israel" is used when "the community of Israel" are addressed by God or by their teachers. We can leave the name Hebrew aside, since it does not occur in John and it was not implicated in later polemics. Left with the names Israel and Jew, it is necessary to ask why many Jewish sources once in a while interrupt their habitual use of "Israel" and mention a "Jew," and why the Gospel of John does the opposite.

Since they concern group appellations with an immediate social impact, do such interruptions not imply a shift in social perspective? This is what I proposed in 1986, linking up with the 1938 *TWNT* article by Karl-Georg Kuhn.[16] From the start however, Harvey rejects this possibility as a "mistake."[17] He does not make it clear why, but in any case the result is that he cannot explain the dual usage. Especially the case of the marriage and divorce formulas quoted in the Mishnah and Tosephta, which, as I pointed

15. G. Harvey, *The True Israel: Uses of the Names Jew, Hebrew and Israel in Ancient Jewish and Early Christian Literature* (AGJU 35; Leiden, 1996).

16. K. G. Kuhn, "Ἰσραήλ, Ἰουδαῖος, Ἑβραῖος in der nach-at.lichen jüdischen Literatur," *TWNT* 3 (1938): 360–70. See other studies in P. J. Tomson, "The Names Israel and Jew in Ancient Judaism and in the New Testament," *Bijdr* 47 (1986): 12–40, 266–89, pp. 121f. S. Zeitlin, "The Names Hebrew, Jew and Israel: A Historical Study," *JQR* 43 (1952–53): 365–79, while offering interesting details, does not address the dual usage and is replete with enormities such as, "We never find the term Israel denoting the people of Judaea in the entire tannaitic literature" (p. 369); "To counteract the contention of the Christians, the Judaeans-Jews now assumed the name Israel" (p. 375). See also below, n. 48.

17. Harvey, *True Israel*, pp. 6f. Kuhn is not mentioned; the objection is against Tomson, "Names"; and J. D. G. Dunn, "Judaism in the Land of Israel in the First Century," in J. Neusner, ed., *Judaism in Late Antiquity*, vol. 2: *Historical Syntheses* (HO 1: Der Nahe und der Mittlere Osten, Leiden, 1995). Dunn bases himself on Kuhn but does not mention Tomson, "Names." On p. 235 he writes that " 'Israel has no defining antonym," although since Old Testament times the obvious antonym is גוים or גוי. But J. D. G. Dunn, "Who Did Paul Think He Was? A Study in Jewish-Christian Identity," *NTS* 45 (1999): 174–93, pp. 187f., accepts the dual usage as developed in Kuhn and Tomson, especially in the case of the Mishnah (below), as against Harvey.

out, evince a remarkably promiscuous use of the two names,[18] induces him
to confront the phenomenon. Harvey has no more to say than that "the
Tosefta discussion evidences no difficulty with the use of 'Jews'" and that
the Mishnah "does not suggest any problem with the name."[19] Still he notes
differentiation: "יהודי was much more ordinary, mundane or everyday than
'Israel'; . . . 'Israel'. . . suggests something more exceptional: a community
addressed by God . . . through Moses and . . . the sages."[20] Again this begs
the question: Why does the Mishnah use ישראל to denote Jews over 170
times, and only twice יהודי?

The explanation proposed by Kuhn and myself is that of a socially distinct usage, dependent on what sociolinguists call the "speech situation."
This allows us to understand "Jew" as the external name used in the Greco-
Roman period[21] in speech situations that include non-Jewish listeners, and
"Israel" or "Israelite" as the name used in inner-Jewish speech, such as
prayer, law, or narrative, which by nature does not assume a non-Jewish
audience. As a result, the same Jew may be called or call himself either "Jew"
or "Israelite," according to the speech situation. This explains why a Jewish text uses "Israel" as the appellation for Jews, except when a non-Jewish
speech situation is introduced and "Jew" is used. A shift to the other usage
within such a text indicates an exception to its standard speech situation,
as when interaction with non-Jews occurs. This seems to be the case in the
Mishnah. While this is an inner-Jewish text that normally uses "Israel(ite),"
the two occurrences of "Jew" can be understood as relating to interaction
with non-Jews.[22] Conversely, interaction between Jews within a text otherwise assuming a non-Jewish speech situation will exceptionally introduce
"Israel(ites)."

The language used does not prejudice preference for either name.[23]
Decisive are the implied speech situations, especially that of the author or
final redactor as distinct from his dramatis personae.[24] This is eloquently
demonstrated by the book of Esther. In its Hebrew text, it features "Jews"

18. Tomson, "Names," pp. 268–72, taking in also archaeological evidence.
19. Harvey, *True Israel,* pp. 101f. He does not display expertise in rabbinic studies when expressing wonder over my reliance on "two pre-eminent MSS: Kaufmann and De Rossi 138" and quoting
the translations (!) by Danby and Neusner against the reading involved.
20. Ibid., p. 103. Here and four more times on pp. 102f., יהודה is printed while יהוד is meant.
21. Another flaw in Harvey's study is that he does not distinguish systematically between pre- and
postexilic usage, which involved the rise of יהודי as a universal religio-ethnic appellation.
22. *m. Ketubot* 7:6; *m. Nedarim* 11:12. See n. 18, above.
23. As proposed by Y. M. Grintz; see Tomson, "Names," pp. 121f.
24. Harvey, *True Israel,* p. 7, does not seem to realize that "speech of a writer's dramatis personae" (Tomson, "Names," p. 123) does not mean their *ipsissima verba* but the writer's presentation
of these.

only. This defines the non-Jewish speech situation that lends this thoroughly Jewish narrative its atmosphere of estrangement: the Hebrew Esther does not identify as an inner-Jewish text. The Greek editors, however, inserted additions containing, among other materials, Jewish prayers and other inner-Jewish interactions, and here "Israel" is used.[25] By these interruptions, the composers of the Greek text, while maintaining the overall external view on the Jews, allowed glimpses into inner-Jewish life. Thus, their text, like the Hebrew Esther, is not at all anti-Jewish. It merely portrays the Jews from the outside and consequently calls them "Jews," except for the intermezzi where they are called "Israel." This is the characteristic Jewish dual usage, but in opposite proportion to the Mishnah. It is only when "Jew" acquires an intrinsically negative charge, as in early Christian texts, that we can no longer speak of a dual usage.

A remarkable domain of the dual usage was subjected to a fresh analysis by David Goodblatt. Accepting the socially distinct application of the names, he addressed the enigmatic self-appellation "Jews" that is used by the Hasmonaean rulers not only in their diplomatic correspondence, which naturally assumes an external speech situation, but, anomalously, also in the inner-Jewish documents, such as their dynastic coins bearing the Hebrew, inner-Jewish legend חבר היהודים, "the council of Jews." Moreover, this strikingly contrasts with the self-designation ישראל of the coins minted by the leaders of the two great Jewish wars against Rome. Goodblatt's wide-ranging documentation does not allow explanations beyond what I offered in an appended footnote, that is, "the external hellenization of the Hasmonean court."[26] I submit the additional specification that this seems to reflect the intricacies of Jewish identity in the Greco-Roman world, as in the Persian Empire. When presenting themselves as respectable subjects of the larger empire, the Hellenized Hasmonaean leaders seem to have opted for the appellation "Jews," but in defense of their religio-ethnic specificity, they would call themselves "Israel." This explanation is of limited value, however, as long as we do not possess documents of the initial Maccabean insurgents themselves.

Following Thomas S. Kraabel's insistence that Judaism in antiquity was "extremely varied and diverse," Ross Kraemer reinvestigated the forty-four Greek and Latin inscriptions that bear the name Jew, searching for geo-

25. LXX Esth. 4:17c, d, i, k, m (add. C, D); 10:3f, k (add. F). See Tomson, "Names," p. 133. On the Greek editions, see K. M. L. L. De Troyer, *Het einde van de alpha-tekst van Ester. Vertaal- en verhaaltechniek van MT 8,1–17, LXX 8,1–17 en AT 7,14–41* (Leuven, 1997), and for research on the additions, esp. pp. 267–75.

26. Tomson, "Names," p. 130 n. 36a. Kuhn offered no explanation.

graphical and other meanings than just "Jew." Her findings were that mostly these concern proselytes or non-Jews otherwise attracted to Judaism. In other words, a non-Jewish audience is co-implied in these cases. There was no actual evidence for the geographical connotation. Kraemer paid much attention to a Roman epitaph that to my knowledge, is the only one to use "Israelite" as an ethnicon: ειρηνη τρεζ / πτη προσηλυ / τος πατρος και / μητρος ειου / δεα ισδραηλιτης . . . The grammatical clumsiness is moving, but even so, the meaning remains undecided.[27] But clearly the notion of "proselyte" introduces a dual social perspective, which then can be seen as explaining the odd juxtaposition of the names Jewess and Israelite. Otherwise, the ancient Jewish inscriptions use "Israel" only in liturgical acclamations, which of course imply an inner-Jewish speech situation.[28]

"Israel" and "Jew" in the Palestinian Talmud

The Yerushalmi or Palestinian Talmud is an interesting source for us, since it is a large inner-Jewish text in Hebrew and Aramaic that contains multiple cases of daily-life interaction with non-Jews and also a fair sprinkling of Greek. It was not covered in my 1986 study for lack of technical means, but the concordance, a CD-ROM, and partial translations have now made it possible to make up for that lacuna.[29] The relatively late date of redaction of the Yerushalmi is no objection to the extent that it conforms to the usage found in earlier Jewish documents.

The following survey lists the passages where "Jew" occurs in the Yerushalmi in its various spellings: יהודי, יהודאי, יהודיי, יהודיי, יודאי or in one case the foreign derivative יהודאיק. In three cases, "Israel" appears close by. This is interesting since it directly demonstrates the Jewish dual usage. The hundreds of cases where "Israel" appears alone as the appellation for Jews establish the rule for this document, but including these would be senseless. The survey does not include quotations from the book of Esther,

---

27. R. S. Kraemer, "On the Meaning of the Term 'Jew' in Greco-Roman Inscriptions," *HTR* 82 (1989): 35–53, does not mention Kuhn's article and is silent on the phenomenon of the double Jewish usage.

28. Tomson, "Names," pp. 130f. For "Jew" in the ancient inscriptions, see the exhaustive survey by H. Solin, "Excursus 'Iudaeus,'" in *ANRW* 2.29.2, 648–51.

29. I have used the Davka Judaica Classics CD-ROM, which unfortunately is marred by many typos and by reliance on the *textus receptus* and its page division. The translations edited by P. Schäfer in *Übersetzung des Talmud Yerushalmi* (Tübingen, 1975–) are usually reliable, but not always, and they integrate helpful text-critical notes. Otherwise, I refer to the Venice *editio princeps*.

where "Jews" abounds,[30] or from the two passages in the Mishnah where "Jews" occur,[31] or names.[32]

We must recall that in Middle Hebrew the collectives יִשְׂרָאֵל, "Israel," and גּוֹי, "nation," have become generic names that also can designate a single person: "Israelite" and "Gentile." Incidentally, גּוֹי is often replaced by עכו"ם in the manuscripts, many of which date from medieval Europe. This is an acronym for "idolaters," which would supposedly be less offensive to a Christian censor.

"Jew" in Actual or Implied Interactions with Non-Jews

1. *y. Berakot* 2, 5a. "A certain Jew" (חַד יְהוּדָאי) was at work in the fields when an Arab[33] passed by and called out:

> Jew, Jew [בַר יוֹדָאי, בַר יוֹדָאי],[34] untie your oxen, untie your plow, for the temple is destroyed. . . .

2–3. *y. Berakot* 5, 9a

> R. Hanina and R. Yoshua ben Levi passed before the אַנְטִיפּוֹטָא[35] [ἀνθύ–πατος, i.e., proconsul] of Caesaraea, and when he rose to his feet before them the people said to him: Before those Jews [אִילֵין יְהוּדָאי] do you stand up?! He said to them: I saw the faces of angels.
>
> R. Yona and R. Yose passed before אַרְסְקִינָס [Ursicinus] in Antiochia,[36] and when he saw them and rose to his feet before them, the people said to him: Before those Jews [אִילֵין יְהוּדָאי] do you stand up?

4. *y. Berakot* 9, 13a

> It happened that Rav was walking up from Hammat Tiberias. He encountered some Romans [רוֹמָאי] who asked him: From whose domain are you?

30. Eleven times: *y. Berakot* 1, 2c = *y. Yoma* 3, 40b; *y. Megilla* 2, 73a–c. Cf. *b. Megilla* 12b–19b (see Tomson, "Names," p. 275).

31. *y. Yebamot* 15, 14d = *y. Ketubot* 4, 29a, citing the phrase from *m. Ketubot* 7:6, דַת מֹשֶׁה וִיהוּדִית / וִיהוּדָאי; *y. Nedarim* 1, 36d = 11, 42d bottom; *y. Sota* 1, 16d, quoting *m. Nedarim* 11:12, נְטוּלָה אֲנִי מִן הַיְּהוּדִים (see Tomson, "Names," pp. 268–70).

32. Yehudi, a biblical name: Jer. 36:14.

33. Alternatively, an inhabitant of Orvi or Arvu: *ed. princ.* חַד עַרְבִי; Geniza version (L. Ginzberg, *Yerushalmi Fragments from the Genizah*, vol. 1, [*JTS* 1909; reprint, Jerusalem, 1969], p. 9), חַד עוֹרְבִי. See M. Jastrow, *A Dictionary of the Targumim, the Talmud Babli and Yerushalmi and Midrashic Literature*, 2 vols. (Philadelphia, 1903 and reprints), s.v. עוֹרְבִי; and cf. *b. Ḥullin* 5a.

34. Ginzberg, *Yerushalmi Fragments:* בַר יְהוּדָאי.

35. Geniza version (Ginzberg, *Yerushalmi Fragments,* p. 16). Ed. princ., אַנְטִיפּוֹתָא.

36. Cf. *y. Šebiit* 4, 35a: R. Yona and R. Yose permitted baking bread for Ursicinus on *shabbat*; see Y. Feliks, ed. *Talmud Yerushalmi, Tractate Shevi'it, Critically Edited, Provided with Commentary, Introduction, Diagram, and Pictures* (Jerusalem: Zur-Ot Press, 1979), 232f.

He said: That of Sofianos [סופיינוס].[37] Then they turned their back on him. At night they came to him [Sofianos] and said: How much longer will you bear with those Jews [אילין יהודא׳]? He asked them: Why? They said to him: We came across one whom they called a Jew [יהודא׳] and asked him . . .

5. *y. Berakot* 9, 13b. "A ship of non-Jews on which there was a Jewish boy" (תינוק אחד יהודי) came in bad weather, and everyone prayed to his gods, but to no avail.

They said to this Jew [אותו יהודי]: Stand up my son, and call to your God. . . .[38]

6. *y. Peʾa* 3, 17d

Two brothers in Ashkelon had non-Jewish neighbors [מגורין נוכראין]. These said: When those Jews [אילין יהודאין] are going to Jerusalem we shall take all their belongings. But when [the brothers] were gone the Holy One blessed be He ordained angels who came in and went out in their likeness in their stead. [So nothing was stolen, and when the brothers came back and the neighbors understood what had happened] . . . they said: Blessed be the God of the Jews [בריך אלההון דיהוא׳]!

7–11. Similarly, in *y. Baba Mesiʾa* 2, 8c, in four successive stories in which Jews return lost objects to non-Jews, and in *y. Baba Batra* 3, 17c, when R. Yohanan surprises his Roman neighbor by his courteous behavior, the non-Jews exclaim every time:

Blessed be the God of the Jews [בריך [הוא][39] אלההון דיהודא׳]!

12. *y. Demai* 2, 22c, line 50[40] = *y. Sebiit* 9, 39a.[41] R. Yoshua ben Levi ordered his pupil to buy greens only from "the garden of Sisera," who as a non-Jew was exempt from observing the seventh year.

Then the One remembered in Praise [Elijah] stood by him and said: Go tell your master: The garden is not Sisera's. It was a Jew's [דיהודיי], but he

---

37. See Jastrow, *Dictionary*; S. Krauss, *Griechische und lateinische Lehnwörter in Talmud, Midrasch und Targum*, 2 vols. (1898–99; reprint, with additions by I. Löw, Hildesheim, 1964); cf. *Yalk Yoel* 537, פופיינוס, i.e., Vespasian or Severus.

38. The story recalls Jonah, of course, and interestingly, Jonah presents himself as an עברי in conversation with the non-Israelite sailors (Jonah 1:9).

39. Escorial MS in the first story: *y. Baba Mesiʾa* 2, 8c.

40. The story (ibid., l. 38) does not belong here: for דיהודא׳ we must apparently read יהי ודא׳. See manuscript evidence adduced by G. A. Wewers and F. G. Hüttenmeister in Schäfer, ed., *Übersetzung des Talmud Yerushalmi*.

41. These appear to be two independent versions.

killed him and took it from him. And if you want to be more severe on your-self [and refrain from eating from that garden], permit[42] it to others.

13. *y. Sebiit* 4, 35a–b = *y. Sanhedrin* 3, 21b.[43] R. Abba bar Zemena, who was working as a tailor with someone [חד בר נש][44] in Rome, was given nonkosher meat to eat, but he refused, even when the man said he would kill him.

> He said, if you want to kill me, kill me, for I will not eat non-kosher meat. He said: How did you know that I was going to kill you if you would eat? — Either as a Jew being a Jew, or as an Aramean being an Aramean [או יהודיי יהודיי או ארמאי ארמאי].[45]

14. *y. Sebiit* 9, 38d. R. Shimon ben Yohai assisted in purifying Tiberias from corpse impurity—

> One Samaritan saw him and said: Shall I not go and make this Elder of the Jews [הדין סבא דיודאי] stumble? He took a corpse and hid it. . . .

15–16. *y. Maaser Seni* 4, 25b–c. Two cases from a long series of dream inter-pretations by R. Yose ben Halafta and his son R. Yishmael:

> A man [חד בר נש] came before R. Yishmael be-R. Yose and said to him: I saw in my dream, someone swallowed a star. He said to him: May that man breathe out his spirit! he killed a Jew [יהודאי], for it is written, He trod a star from Jacob (Num 24:17). . . . A Samaritan [חד כותי] said: I shall go and make this Elder of the Jews [הדין סבא דיודאי] stumble. He went to him and said: I saw in my dream . . .

17. *y. Sabbat* 6, 8d. An astrologer saw two disciples of R. Hanina go out to pick fodder and foretold they would not return. But when an old man begged them for something to eat, they gave him half of their loaf of bread, and in gratitude he prayed for their well-being. They returned safely and people asked the astrologer how he explained this. He exclaimed:

---

42. Following *y. Demai,* אישתרי, as against *y. Sebiit,* אשתווי. If the garden were a Jew's, the seventh-year laws would apply, but since this is a past situation, their application would be only an "extra" sever-ity.

43. The text of *y. Sanhedrin* is somewhat better here.

44. *y. Sanhedrin*; *y. Sebiit* has the doubtful variant חד ארמאי.

45. The juxtaposition "Jew/Aramean" is also found in *Bereshit Rabba* 63,7 (J. Theodor and C. Albeck, *Midrash Bereshit Rabba: Critical Edition with Notes and Commentary,* 3 vols., [2d ed., with addi-tional corrections by C. Albeck, Jerusalem, 1965], p. 686); *b. Sabbat* 139a; *b. Pesahim* 8b; *b. Baba Batra* 21a. It is equivalent to Ἰουδαῖος—Ἕλλην in Acts 14:1; 18:4; 19:10; Rom. 1:16; 2:9f.; 10:12; 1 Cor. 1:22ff.; 9:20; 10:32; 12:13; Gal. 3:28; Col. 3:11. The relative spread in both cases indicates a common phrase; hence the usage in Paul and Acts may reflect Greco-Jewish parlance. See Tomson, "Names," pp. 276, 284.

But what could this man do, for the God of the Jews [אלההון די יהודאי] can be appeased with half a loaf!

18. *y. Sukka* 5, 55b. Trajans wife said to him:

Before you are going to subdue those barbarians [ברבריים], subdue the Jews [יהודים] who arose against you.

19. *y. Sanhedrin* 2, 30d.

R. Hizkia was walking on the road. He encountered a Samaritan who asked him: Are you a Master of the Jews [רבהון דיהודאי]? He said: Yes. He said: Look what is written . . .

20. *y. 'Aboda Zara* 2, 41a

A certain proselyte [חד גיור] was a barber and he was an astrologist [איצטרולוגוס],[46] and he saw in his astrology that the Jews [יהודאי] were shedding his blood—but they were only making him a proselyte! Now if a Jew [יודאי] would come to him to have his hair cut, he would kill him. . . .

"Israel" and "Jew" Side by Side in the Mouths of Jews

21. *y. Mo'ed Qatan* 3, 83b, on tearing one's clothes upon hearing the holy name profaned, as King Hezekiah did when hearing the words of the envoy of the Assyrians, Ravshakia (2 Kings 18:37–19:1):

But does one tear them upon profanation by a gentile [גוי]? If you suppose Ravshakia was a gentile, you must tear them [in other cases as well]; but if you suppose he was a Jew [יהודי], not [i.e. this would imply no obligation for the case of a gentile]. However R. Hoshaya teaches: Both when one hears profanation by an Israelite [ישראל] and when one hears profanation by a gentile, one is obliged to tear ones clothes. . . .

R. Hoshayas halakhah supposes an inner-Jewish speech situation; hence "Israel." But the consideration of Ravshakia's status uses "Jew," because it implies a supposed non-Jewish situation.

22. *y. Gittin* 1, 43b. In the course of a discussion on deeds of divorce carrying signatures not recognizable as being Jewish, a tannaitic tradition is quoted:

46. Cf. the same case introduction in *y. Sabbat* 6, 8d (eleven lines after the story quoted here as no. 17).

"Deeds of divorce from overseas though signed with foreign names are valid, for Israelites outside the Land [ישראל חוצה לארץ] carry names like gentiles."... [that is,] provided it was written in a *yudaïki* [יהודאיק, i.e., ἰουδαϊκή]; if there is no *yudaïki*, in a synagogue [בית כנסת]; if there is no synagogue . . . even in the shop of Israelites [בחנותן של ישראל].

Again, within inner-Jewish speech, a non-Jewish situation is introduced that causes a compound of the word *Jew* to be used. The word ἰουδαϊκή used within the Hebrew text is interesting; seemingly, it is a local usage from the Diaspora. It must indicate some Jewish legal body.[47] The contrast with "Israelites outside the Land" and "the shop of Israelites" in the preceding and the following is striking.

23. *y. Sanhedrin* 7, 25d

R. (E)liezer, R. Yoshua and Rn. Gamliel travelled to Rome. They came to a certain place where they found little children who [in their play] made small piles [of stones?] and said: This is how those in the land of Israel do: they say, "This is heave offering, this is tithe." [The sages] said: It appears there are Jews [יהודאין] here. . . .

"The land of Israel" signals inner-Jewish speech,[48] next to the sages coming across "Jews" in non-Jewish Rome.

"Jew" without Actual Non-Jews Being Implicated

24. *y. Demai* 1, 22a = *y. Ta'anit* 3, 66c top.[49] A difficult narrative about Rabbi (Yehuda the Prince) who wanted to annul the seventh year, while R. Pinhas ben Yair would not agree. Rabbi then invited R. Pinhas to come and have "a little bite" at his place, which he accepted.

---

47. Krauss, *Griechische und lateinische Lehnwörter*, s.v., proposes to supplement συναγωγή; Jastrow, *Dictionary*, s.v., also ἀγορά, where a Jewish court would meet. Levy, however, sees a derivation from *judicium, judicatus*—"Gerichtsamt" (J. Levy, *Neuhebräisches und chaldäisches Wörterbuch über die Talmudim und Midraschim*, 4 vols. [Leipzig, 1876–89]). בית כנסת is mentioned just afterward, which would seem to rule out Krauss's proposal. It could be, however, that in this particular local usage ἰουδαϊκὴ [συναγωγή] stands for "community" and בית כנסת, more limited, for "prayer house," προσευχή (see Hengel, *Johannine Question*, on both Greek terms). Cf. Josephus, *Ant.* 18:83, πᾶν τὸ Ἰουδαϊκόν for "the whole Jewish community."

48. Similarly, Matt. 2:20f. Hence Zeitlin, "The Names Hebrew, Jew and Israel," p. 372, errs when stating that the name was introduced after the Bar Kokhba defeat.

49. The text of *y. Demai* is rather more corrupted. Cf. also the elaborate legendary parallel *b. Hullin* 7b.

When he went away, he saw the prosperity of Rabbi's mules[50] and said: Are Jews able to feed all these [כל אילין יהודאי זיינין]!?[51] It is possible that my countenance will not be seen [here anymore]. . . .

If correctly interpreted, this saying evokes an outside perspective on the "Jews" involved, which indicates distance.

25. y. Seqalim 5, 49a = y. Bikkurim 3, 63c[52]

It is written: "And everyone stood at his tent door and looked after Moses until he went into the tent" (Exod 33:8)—two interpreters:[53] one explained it negatively and the other positively. The one who interpreted negatively said: [They said] look at those legs, look at those knees, look at that flesh— he eats off the Jews [מן דיהודאי], he drinks off the Jews, all that he has is from the Jews! And the one who interpreted positively . . .

This midrash appears in two different preredactional contexts, which suggests a certain popularity. The "interpreter" involved is an אמורא, *amora*, also called תורגמן, *turgeman*, a "loudspeaker" who interprets to the audience what the teacher says in a low voice or what is written in the difficult Hebrew scriptures. The obvious anachronism implied in the use of the name Jews in Moses' day brings out that contemporary "Jews" vilifying their elders are meant.

These two passages are most remarkable. While in the "'Jew' in Actual or Implied Interactions with Non-Jews" and "'Israel' and 'Jew' Side by Side in the Mouths of Jews" sections, an actual non-Jewish perspective can always be understood to be implied, this is not the case here. Both appear to be ironic sayings, reminiscent of popular proverbs that project a non-Jewish perspective and that are quoted elsewhere in Amoraic literature.[54]

---

50. מולוותא, "mules"; similarly Jastrow, *Dictionary,* and Levy, *Neuhebräisches und chaldäisches Wörter-buch,* s.v.; Wewers and Hüttenmeister in Schäfer, ed., *Übersetzung des Talmud Yerushalmi,* translates "Gläubiger," i.e., "debtors." "Mules" are also mentioned in the parallel *b. Hullin* 7b.

51. Implying that they must be ignoring the seventh year or other agricultural laws. Pnei Moshe explains from *b. Hullin* 7b, where the white mules represent (the angels of) death. The (less valuable) Vatican MS has קנין for זיינין (Ginzberg, *Yerushalmi Fragments,* p. 356): "All these do Jews buy!?"

52. *y. Bikkurim* 3, 63c has the two examples in inverted order; its text is shorter and more corrupt. A Babylonian parallel is found in *b. Qiddusin* 33b.

53. A frequent expression; cf., e.g., *y. Sukka* 5, 55d top.

54. Two sayings in *Leviticus Rabbah* 13,4 (M. Margulies, *Midrash wayyikra Rabbah: A Critical Edi-tion Based on Manuscripts and Genizah Fragments with Variants and Notes,* 2d ed., 5 parts in 3 vols. [2d ed., Jerusalem, 1972], p. 281); the second appears, in a rather different wording, at *b. Hagiga* 9b; cf. Tomson, "Names," p. 275. Remarkably, instead of "Jews," the first saying is quoted with "Israel" and the second, in R. Akiva's name, with "Jacob's daughter" in *Leviticus Rabbah* 35,5 (Margulies, *Midrash wayyikra Rabbah,* p. 824) and *Pesiqta de Rab Kahana* 14,3 (B. Mandelbaum, *Pesikta de Rav Kahana*

They also resemble the curious estrangement created by the exclusive use of the name Jew in the Hebrew Esther. The *amora* in the last passage seems to be inculcating respect of the elders by portraying the envious Israelites as rabble estranged from their community. Similarly, R. Pinhas's saying seems to distance itself from Jews who raise mules, especially during the dearth of the seventh year.

To sum up, the Palestinian Talmud shows the socially distinct Jewish dual usage also found in other rabbinic sources. It is an inner-Jewish text that uses the self-appellation "Israel" as a rule but switches to "Jews" when interaction with non-Jews, and hence a non-Jewish speech situation, is introduced. This happens in twenty-three passages, twenty of which concern simple interactions with non-Jews as discussed in "'Jew' in Actual or Implied Interactions with Non-Jews." "'Israel' and 'Jew' Side by Side in the Mouths of Jews" contains three interesting examples where the use of "Israel" is juxtaposed with "Jew," so that a switch is indicated from inner-Jewish interaction to (implied) interaction with non-Jews; here we have the Jewish dual usage exemplified. Finally, the two cases in "'Jew' without Actual Non-Jews Being Implicated" demonstrate the effect of estrangement a Jewish speaker can attain with this mechanism.

The Synoptic Gospels: "Israel" and "Jews"

The earliest Christian documents are best approached on the assumption that, like the Gospel of John, they embody a trajectory that started in Judeo-Christian surroundings. Socially, this means an inner-Jewish situation. That again would make it likely that the dual usage typical of Jewish texts is found, "Israel" being used as the normal appellation by Jews but "Jews" in interactions with non-Jews that occur within the narrative.

This is what we find in the Synoptic Gospels, with two or three exceptions. I review this briefly for the sake of comparison with the Gospel of John and further refer to my 1986 study.[55] In two of the exceptions, the Evangelists address an explanatory remark mentioning "Jews" to their audi-

---

according to an Oxford Manuscript with Variants from All Known Manuscripts, 2 vols. [New York, 1962], pp. 241f.). A mixed form is found in *Midrash haGadol Leviticus* 26:3 (M. Margulies, *Midrash haGadol,* ed. A. Steinsalz [Jerusalem, 1976], p. 728), with the first saying mentioning "Israel" and the second one, in name of R. Akiva, "Jews."

55. Tomson, "Names," pp. 279–81.

ence. Mark 7:3 states that "the Pharisees, and all the Jews," observe purity rules, which clearly is an explanation for non-Jewish readers. Matt. 28:15 reports that the rumor of the theft of the body of Jesus "is still told among Jews to this day," which not only is a late redactional remark but has an anti-Jewish slant; it must be part of the final stratum of Matthew, which also on other grounds should be termed anti-Jewish.[56] It is not necessary to read the explanation of Jewish purity rites in Mark 7:3 in the same vein, and therefore we should not do that. The meaning of a third passage is ambiguous. "Joseph . . . from the Jewish town of Arimathea" (Luke 23:51) may be addressing the readers, in which case it parallels the other two exceptions; but it may also cite a regional usage referring to a mixed population and may thus be no exception. Otherwise, "Jews" are found only in communications with non-Jews that are part of the narrative,[57] while the "Israel" of inner-Jewish communications forms the majority of appellations.[58] Especially enlight ening is the duality of Pilate and his soldiers addressing Jesus as "King of the Jews"[59] and the Jewish chief priests calling Jesus "King of Israel."[60]

We can conclude that the extant Synoptic Gospels on the whole have preserved the socially distinct use of the appellations "Israel" and "Jew" that must have characterized their Judeo-Christian substratum. Of the exceptions, only in the remark at the end of Matthew does "Jew" acquire a negative charge and the Jewish speech duality become impossible. This is not the case in Mark 7:2f. and Luke 23:51.

John: "Jews" and "Israel"

The opposite situation to the Synoptics is found in the Fourth Gospel (henceforth simply John): "Jews" are mentioned all over, "Israel" only by exception.[61] The implications are widely divergent, and we approach them one by one.

56. U. Luz, "Anti-Judaismus im Matthäusevangelium als historisches und theologisches Problem," *EvT* 53 (1993): 310–27; and U. Luz, "Das Matthäusevangelium und die Perspektive einer biblischen Theologie," in D. R. Daniels ed., *'Gesetz' als Thema Biblischer Theologie* (JBTh 4; Neukirchen-Vluyn, 1989), pp. 233–48; D. Flusser, *Judaism and the Origins of Christianity* (Jerusalem, 1988), pp. 552–60, "Two Anti-Jewish Montages in Matthew."

57. Matthew, four times; Mark, five times; Luke, four times.

58. Matthew, ten times; Mark, one time; Luke, twelve times.

59. Matt. 27:11, 29, 37; Mark 15:2, 9, 12, 18, 26; Luke 23:3, 37f., 51. Similarly the μάγοι from the East, Matt. 2:2.

60. Matt. 27:42; Mark 15:32.

61. Cf. Tomson, "Names," pp. 281–83.

A Non-Jewish Setting

The name Jew occurs throughout John and with extraordinary frequency: seventy times in all.[62] There are three sections where it does not occur: the prologue (1:1–18), the extended farewell discourse (14–17), and the final chapter (21). These are easily seen as belonging to a later stratum, but the question of what all this implies must wait. The extremely frequent mention of "Jews" generates a non-Jewish speech situation for the Gospel as a whole, somewhat like the book of Esther. The question that must now be addressed is how this works out in the case of John. As we saw, in spite of the frequent use of "Jews," Esther is by no means an anti-Jewish text. On that level, the use of "Jews" in John implies no more than an intended non-Jewish readership. This becomes clear in the ten cases where the Evangelist explains Jewish rites and customs to the reader (as in Mark 7:3): "Jewish rites of purification" (2:6); "the Passover of the Jews" (2:13; 11:55); "a festival of the Jews" (5:1; 6:4; 7:2); various other customs "of the Jews" (4:9; 19:40, 42); and Nicodemus being "a leader of the Jews" (3:1). The frequency and spread of these explanatory remarks indicate that the final text, as a whole, is framed in a non-Jewish setting. This is a first difference from the Synoptics. But as said, it is still neutral usage analogous to Mark 7:2, not per se hostile like Matt. 28:15.

Intermezzi with Jewish Dual Usage

Nevertheless, like the Synoptics, the beginnings of the Johannine tradition must be sought in Jewish and Judeo-Christian settings. Thus we would expect that this text, though re-edited in a non-Jewish speech situation, contains episodes framed in an inner-Jewish speech situation. Such indeed is the case. In four pericopes, "Israel" is used in speech among Jews. The most striking of these is John 1:31, where John the Baptist, on seeing Jesus, gives his witness concerning him and pronounces: "I myself did not know him; but I came baptizing with water for this reason, that he might be revealed to Israel." It is not immediately clear whom he is addressing, but the context mentions only Jews: Jesus in the first place (1:29); preceding him, Pharisees (1:24); and in the continuation, John's disciples (1:35). This

---

62. The seventy-first time, John 3:25—ζήτησις . . . μετὰ Ἰουδαίου [Ἰουδαίων] περὶ καθαρισμοῦ—is hardly correct. The verse is embedded in the parallel narratives about Jesus' and John's baptismal activities, and the conjecture μετὰ [τῶν] Ἰησοῦ deserves serious consideration.

is the more remarkable since the pericope is introduced with the phrase we shall address below, that "the Jews sent priests and Levites from Jerusalem" (1:19). There is not necessarily a special, elevated significance in the use of the name Israel here. All who are indicated by it are Jews, and this is simply inner-Jewish speech.

The other instances are self-evident. When Jesus sees Nathanael approaching, he pronounces, "Here is truly[63] an Israelite in whom there is no deceit," and in amazement over Jesus' perspicacity, Nathanael responds: "Rabbi, you are the Son of God! You are the King of Israel" (1:47, 49). Similarly, the crowd of Jews who welcome Jesus to Jerusalem on the eve of Passover call out: "The King of Israel" (12:13). Just as in the Synoptics, this neatly contrasts with the title given to Jesus by Pilate and other non-Jews, "King of the Jews" (on which, see below). The remaining passage was already mentioned and finds a simple explanation now. When Nicodemus is elaborately introduced to the readers as "a Pharisee . . . a leader of the Jews," this recalls the Aramaic expressions "master of the Jews" and "elder of the Jews" encountered in the Yerushalmi—both on the lips of Samaritans, as it happens (see nos. 14 and 19, above). But when Nicodemus does not understand Jesus' words, the latter asks him in inner-Jewish speech, though not without a tinge of irony: "Are you a teacher of Israel, and yet you do not understand these things?" (3:10). "Teacher of Israel" is the inner-Jewish equivalent of "master of the Jews." Although these uses of "Israelite" and "Israel" acquire a special effect in the midst of a text replete with "Jews," it is again not necessary to suppose that the Evangelist inserted them on purpose, departing from his standard usage. It is simplest to suppose these are fragments of the Judeo-Christian stratum displaying the dual Jewish self-appellation.[64]

Confirmation is found in the story of the Samaritan woman. In their conversation, she asks Jesus: "How is it that you, a Jew, ask a drink of me, a woman of Samaria?" (4:9). Apart from the immediate redactional comment that "Jews do not share things in common with Samaritans,"[65] this little scene could have been taken from any Jewish narrative, as we learned from the two Yerushalmi stories involving Samaritans. Most remarkable in the framework of the Fourth Gospel as a whole—but quite understandable

63. ἀληθῶς, not ἀληθὴς Ἰσραηλίτης; see below, n. 66.

64. Brown, *Gospel according to John*, pp. 427f., notes the different role of "Jews" in John 11–12 and ascribes this section to a later addition by the Evangelist himself. Brown explains 12:13, "Israel," as stemming from Zeph. 3:15 (pp. 432). Following his theory of continuous composition by the same Evangelist, this need not contradict my proposal.

65. The comment is lacking in ℵ and some other manuscripts but is found in the papyri and all other manuscripts. Hence it is more likely that it was omitted by (near) *homoioteleuton*.

if we hypothesize a Judeo-Christian residue—are Jesus' famous words further on in the conversation, "We worship what we know, for salvation is from the Jews" (4:22). *This confirms the nonspecific use made of "Israel(ite)" in John.* Were the Evangelist to have been pressing "Israel" as the special name of the true elect, as many commentators have it in the case of Nathanael,[66] he should have used it here: "Salvation is *from Israel.*" But he did not write that, I suggest, since in this and other passages he left the dual usage of his Judeo-Christian source in place, using "Jew" in situations involving non-Jews and "Israel" in inner-Jewish scenes.

So far, so good. The extant Fourth Gospel as a whole is set in a non-Jewish speech situation, while it preserves remnants of an earlier Judeo-Christian Gospel retaining inner-Jewish dual usage. Up to now, this is not unlike the Greek Esther, which speaks of "Jews" throughout, except in the inserted prayers and conversations between Mordecai and his cousin. But there is much more to be observed.

Conflict with "the Jews"

In quite a number of other cases, the name Jew is used in a curiously redundant and contradictory way. Thus, right at the start, after the prologue, the authorities send "priests and Levites from Jerusalem to investigate" John the Baptist. Only it does not say "the authorities" but "the Jews sent . . ."—as though these priests and Levites and John himself were not all Jews! Similarly, in 9:22, the parents of the man born blind dare not speak out about Jesus "because they were afraid of the Jews"—upon which Brown comments that "to have the Jewish parents of the blind man in Jerusalem described as being 'afraid of the Jews' (9:22) is just as awkward as having an American living in Washington, D.C., described as being afraid of 'the Americans.'"[67] Another scholar even writes that such uses of "Jew" are "pointless additions to the narratives" that, in view of some manuscript evidence, must be seen as "a series of unfortunate late scribal corruptions."[68] That would be too simple a way out, of course, and it is not practicable either. It would also underestimate the seriousness of the situation.

---

66. Brown, *Community of the Beloved Disciple,* p. 42: "Nicodemus may be a ruler of the Jews (3:1); but. . . he cannot be a teacher of Israel"; Brown, *Gospel according to John,* pp. lxxii–lxxiii: Israel in John is a "favorable term describing the real succession to the OT heritage"; Martyn, *History and Theology,* p. 164, believing Jews "cease even to be 'Jews' and become instead—like Nathanael—'truly Israelites.'" On the latter expression, see above, n. 63.

67. Brown, *Community of the Beloved Disciple,* p. 41.

68. J. C. O'Neill, "The Jews in the Fourth Gospel," *IBS* 18 (1996): 58–74.

These cases, to which more could be added,[69] teach us that the Evangelist felt the need to supplement the designation "Jews" even in many scenes where all participants were Jews. In so doing, he created a distance between the protagonists, with whom his reader is supposed to sympathize, and "the Jews"—even though the protagonists themselves are Jews. Indeed, I think this is what has given generations of Bible readers the idea that Jesus was no "Jew" himself. The explicit indications to the contrary in 4:9, 22 apparently were not sufficient to correct that idea.

The seemingly redundant addition of the term *Jew* must be understood as stemming from the situation of the Evangelist and his community. Brown remarks, "What has happened . . . is that the vocabulary of the evangelist's time has been read back into the ministry of Jesus."[70] Many have pointed out that the Evangelist's own situation seems to be reflected in the threefold reference to the synagogue ban.[71] The third one is blatantly anachronistic, since it is part of Jesus' farewell discourse: "They will put you out of the synagogues" (16:2). Although our sources do not allow us to decide exactly how, this must relate to the rephrasing of the *birkat ha-minim,* the section of the main prayer imploring the downfall of heretics, and possible to other measures to disqualify both Judeo-Christians and other Christians that were reportedly initiated by Gamaliel the Younger.[72] Indeed, by this time, the internal government of the Jews had fallen to the Pharisees, since the leading position of the Sadducees had gone down with the Temple.[73]

Pharisees, Chief Priests, and "Jews"

In light of this, it is important to observe that in a number of cases, the Jewish leaders opposing Jesus are identified as "the Pharisees." But we must immediately add that in other passages directly related to these, the same

---

69. E.g., 3:1, "A Pharisee named Nicodemus, a leader of the Jews"; 11:19, "Many of the Jews had come to Martha and Mary to console them about their brother"; 11:33, "When Jesus saw her weeping, and the Jews who came with her also weeping . . ."

70. Brown, *Community of the Beloved Disciple,* p. 41.

71. John 9:22; 12:42; 16:2.

72. Martyn, *History and Theology,* pp. 38–62, 156; Martyn, "Glimpses," pp. 161f.; Wengst, *Bedrängte Gemeinde,* pp. 48–61. Cf. the reservations in Hengel, *Die johanneische Frage,* pp. 288f. To the literature there indicated add G. Alon, *The Jews in Their Land in the Talmudic Age,* 2 vols. (Jerusalem 1980–84), pp. 288–307; Flusser, *Judaism and the Origins of Christianity,* pp. 635–44; R. Kimelman, "Birkat Ha-Minim and the Lack of Evidence for an Anti-Christian Jewish Prayer in Late Antiquity," in E. P. Sanders, ed., *Jewish and Christian Self-Definition,* vol. 2: *Aspects of Judaism in the Graeco-Roman Period* (London, 1982), pp. 226–44.

73. For some elaboration in relation to Luke-Acts, see P. J. Tomson, "Gamaliel's Counsel and the Apologetic Strategy of Luke-Acts," in J. Verheyden, ed., *The Unity of Luke-Acts* (BETL 142; Leuven, 1999), pp. 585–604.

persons can be called "the Jews."[74] This seems to reflect a subsequent shift in social orientation. A simple example is in 8:13, where "the Pharisees" reproach Jesus for giving testimony about himself. But in 8:22 we hear, without an apparent transition, "Then the Jews said . . ." More problematic is the complex pericope at 7:31–52. It is about "the Pharisees" and their guards, who are to arrest Jesus, with a scene about Jesus' preaching "on the last day of the festival" being inserted in 7:37–44. When the guards are sent, Jesus retorts with an enigmatic saying about his "going," to the amazement of "the Jews" (7:35). It is not clear who these are. They may be the guards, who in 7:45 report to the Pharisees. They may also be the crowd present where Jesus speaks, in which case the intermezzo starts already with Jesus' saying in 7:33. The hostile initiative is with the "Pharisees," except "one of them" (7:50), Nicodemus, who in 3:1 was introduced as "a Pharisee. . . a leader of the Jews." Hence, on one level, Jesus' enemies are the Pharisees, but on another, they can also be indicated as "the Jews." This is more clearly the case in the pericope about the man born blind. In 9:13, 15, 16, it is "the Pharisees" who incriminate the new believer, but in 9:18, they are called "the Jews." And while in 9:22 the man's parents fear "the Jews," who threaten them with the synagogue ban, in 12:42, the reader learns that it was "the Pharisees" who issued the ban. The latter is a more exact piece of information, as we have seen, and this confirms the impression of an eventual shift from "Pharisees" to "Jews" as denoting the Gospel's opponents.

There also seems to be an intermediate stage. In 7:31–52, the acting leaders are called "Pharisees," except when their guards are mentioned; then they are called "chief priests and Pharisees" (7:32, 45).[75] This expression is also found in other places, each time concerning justice and police action. Elsewhere, however, it is again replaced with "the Jews." Thus, in 11:47, 57, "the chief priests and the Pharisees" convene a Sanhedrin and, at Caiaphas's proposal, decide to kill Jesus. This detail is referred to in 18:14 as Caiaphas's proposal to "the Jews." Again, in 18:3, "the chief priests and the Pharisees" send their guards to arrest Jesus, but in 18:12, these are called the guards of the Jews.[76]

The combination of chief priests and Pharisees is not found in Mark and Luke, but it appears twice in Matthew, in what seem to be parts of a rather

74. Cf. Caron, "Exploring a Religious Dimension," pp. 163f.
75. Text uncertain in 7:32. The spread of variants is considerable, but a case can be made for the simple reading καὶ ἀπέστειλαν ὑπηρέτας, the "upper priests and Pharisees" being added parallel to 7:45. See below.
76. Similarly Brown, *Community of the Beloved Disciple,* p. 41.

late text stratum (see below). Historically, the combination is problematic, since in our main sources, Acts and Josephus, these two groups almost always appear in fundamental opposition to each other.[77] There is evidence, however, that the extreme circumstances of the war against Rome provoked all kinds of unusual coalitions and oppositions, among which was a violent inner-Pharisee clash of Shammaites and Hillelites; so the otherwise unlikely alliance of Shammaite, zealot Pharisees and high-priestly circles cannot be excluded.[78] Indeed, as signaled recently by Urban von Wahlde, the combination of chief priests and Pharisees is found three times in Josephus, and all of these refer to the war period.[79] Hence it is likely that the Johannine tandem of chief priests and Pharisees, which, like its Matthean counterpart, is so hard to fit in our image of pre-70 circumstances, somehow preserves the extraordinary war setting.[80] The rephrasing of the *birkat ha-minim* that ensued under Pharisaic guidance after the war has been mentioned already. It will not have mitigated anti-Pharisaic sentiment in Johannine and Matthean circles.

The Johannine "Jews"

If the case of John resembles that of Matthew, there is also a big difference. In John, unlike Matthew, the shifting entity of "Pharisees" and "chief priests and Pharisees" can just as well be designated with the blanket term *Jews*. It becomes clear now that this must reflect an all-out conflict between the Gospel's community and the Jews after 70 C.E. In the framework of this conflict, the Pharisaic-rabbinic opponents of the Johannine community were apparently generalized into "the Jews" as being the enemies of Jesus

77. Here Martyn, *History and Theology*, p. 84 is right. See especially the comparative survey by S. Mason, "Chief Priests, Sadducees, Pharisees and Sanhedrin in Acts," in R. Bauckham, ed., *The Book of Acts in Its Palestinian Setting* (Carlisle–Grand Rapids, 1995), pp. 115–77; and cf. Tomson, "Gamaliel's Counsel."

78. Josephus, *War* 2:409f., mentions Ἐλεάζαρος υἱὸς Ἀνανία τοῦ ἀρχιερέως as leader of the uprising. In rabbinic sources, he is a leader of the zealot Pharisee school of Shammai. For this and other information, see Tomson, "Gamaliel's Counsel," pp. 588f., and literature there cited.

79. Josephus, *War* 2:411 (just after the mention of Elazar ben Ananias!); Josephus, *Life* 21; ibid., 190–93.

80. U. C. von Wahlde, "The Relationships between Pharisees and Chief Priests: Some Observations on the Texts in Matthew, John and Josephus," *NTS* 42 (1996): 506–22, notes the exceptional circumstances in footnotes 34 and, especially, 43. The last line of n. 43 can be supplemented: yes, there is evidence that Pharisees and chief priests worked together only on such occasions. Ἀρχιερεῖς, גדולי כהונה, consist of a few high-priestly clans mentioned very critically t.Men 13:18–21; t.Zeb 11:16f; b.Pes 57a. Abba Shaul ben Botnit lived to see the Temple and can certainly be viewed as a Pharisee. See M. Stern, "Aspects of Jewish Society: The Priesthood and Other Classes," in S. Safrai and M. Stern, eds., *The Jewish People in the First Century: Historical Geography, Political History, Social, Cultural and Religious Life and Institutions* (CRINT I/2; Assen, 1976), pp. 561–630, especially pp. 603f.

and his followers.[81] It clearly is an anachronism by which the Evangelist projects his own situation into the narrative about Jesus. These are the hard-to-define, almost spectral Johannine "Jews."

One problem is caused by the fact—how fortunate for later critical scholars!—that the Evangelist did not carry this generalization through systematically but continued to work as evangelists do: patchwork editing of received material. This produced the multiple meaning of the name Jew that is so confusing, and which, when read synchronically, is so utterly contradictory.[82] Jesus is a "Jew" who pronounces "salvation is from the Jews" (4:29), yet at the same time he can reprimand "the Jews who had come to believe in him" along with "the Jews" in general and say they are "from the Father-Devil" (8:31, 44, 48 P.J.T.). If we do not want to reiterate the historical anomaly of this text being "both Jewish and anti-Jewish,"[83] the only way I see to make sense of it is by thinking in terms of a historical trajectory.

Not unlike Martyn and others, one could roughly hypothesize three stages.[84] The first stage is represented by the isolated Judeo-Christian Gospel remnants where the Jewish dual usage is found. It seems preserved in the stories of Nathanael, Nicodemus, the Samaritan woman, and the entry into Jerusalem. The second stratum is characterized by the conflict with the Pharisaic leaders and the synagogue ban. Here, the narrative of the plot against Jesus, his arrest and trial—in Mark and Luke, the work of the "chief priests, scribes, and elders"—is rephrased as a hostile campaign by "the Pharisees" or, echoing the extreme social tensions during the Roman war, the "chief priests and the Pharisees." The last stage is represented by the consolidation of the Johannine community in its extra-Jewish social and religious situation. It was at this point that the successive clashes recorded in the Gospel were lumped together into one single conflict with "the Jews." The last stratum became predominant in the narrative, and it

81. Brown, *Community of the Beloved Disciple,* p. 41 n. 65, calls John "guilty of offensive and dangerous generalizing," even though 1 Thess. 2:14f. was a first step on this road. See also Brown, *Gospel according to John,* pp. lxxi–lxxii: "Jews" is an anachronism, "almost a technical title for the religious authorities, particularly those in Jerusalem, who are hostile to Jesus," in parallel to Matt. 28:15.

82. Similarly, R. Kysar, *John: The Maverick Gospel,* rev. ed. (Louisville, Ky, 1993), p. 70. I agree with those who emphasize that John 4:22 is genuine Johannine tradition, but I cannot get away from the towering evidence of the denunciatory use of "Jews" in the final redaction of the Gospel.

83. Barrett, *Das Johannesevangelium;* see above, n. 8. He modifies his position somewhat in his contribution to this volume (chapter 11), now speaking more generally of "New Testament duality." In my estimation, there is a vast difference, however, between Luke-Acts (and Paul), where this is an adequate term, comprising both common and disputed ground with the Jews, and the Johannine (and Matthean) *contradiction* between inner-Jewish and anti-Jewish statements.

84. Martyn, "Glimpses"; J. L. Martyn, *The Gospel of John in Christian History: Essays for Interpreters* (Theological Inquiries; New York, 1978), pp. 90–121; Brown, *Community of the Beloved Disciple.* Fortna, *Gospel of Signs,* pp. 294–314, runs an analogous trajectory under the heading "Theological Locale: Jesus' Itinerary and 'the Jews.'"

involves all those disputes of Jesus with "the Jews" as a general category. But as noted, this re-editing was not fully rigorous, and earlier stages of the Gospel remained intact in places.

A major problem for exegetes and homilists is that these spectral opponents, representatives of a "pseudo-Judaism," as it has been called,[85] are designated by the name that, in spite of all "spectralization," keeps singling out a well-defined group of people: the *Jews without quotation marks,* the real Jews.[86] However one turns it, the Johannine anti-"Judaism" is also an anti-Judaism without quotation marks. One cannot be anti-American without hatefully intending the Americans.[87] The point is that hatred by nature is a generalization, a projection of one's negative feelings onto the other without respect to his or her actual person. Therefore, it has of necessity a positive correlate. History teaches that anti-Semites cannot do without their Jewish token friends.

The Jews in the Passion Story

"Jews" appear particularly frequently in the Johannine passion narrative—twenty-one times in chapters 18 and 19. Of these occurrences, nine concern customs "of the Jews" and the king "of the Jews."[88] These as such have a neutral significance. Others have a bizarre effect, such as 19:21, "the chief priests of the Jews." In 18:20, Jesus, addressing the high priest, speaks of "the temple, where all the Jews come together." This is a clear departure from the Jewish usage we would expect here.[89] In the remaining cases, it is "the Jews" who tenaciously see to it that Jesus is delivered to Pilate for crucifixion.

A further comparison with the Synoptics is indicated. In Mark and Luke, the Jews who have Jesus arrested and condemned are designated as "chief priests and scribes" or as "chief priests, scribes, and elders."[90] No Pharisees are mentioned, except the students who, in Mark, are sent to ask Jesus the question about the imperial tax and return in "amazement" at his

85. Caron, "Exploring a Religious Dimension," p. 170.
86. Thus the thrust of Adele Reinhartz's contribution to this volume (chapter 10).
87. S. Pedersen, "Anti-Judaism in John's Gospel: John 8," in J. Nissen and S. Pedersen, eds., *New Readings in John: Literary and Theological Perspectives. Essays from the Scandinavian Conference on the Fourth Gospel in Århus 1997* (JSNTSup 182; Sheffield, 1999), pp. 172–93, is probably correct in stating that "the Jews" are not being called children of the devil (8:44) *because* they are Jews, but he overlooks that the massive dualist denunciation of the Jews as Jesus' adversaries *results* in their effective diabolization.
88. John 18:33, 35, 39; 19:3, 19, 21, 21, 40, 42.
89. The same happens in 13:33, where Jesus reminds his disciples of what he has "said to the Jews."
90. Mark 11:27; 14:1, 10, 43, 53; 15:1, 11; Luke 19:47; 20:1, 19; 22:2, 66; 23:4, 10, 13.

answer (Mark 12:13, 17). This disposition squares with Acts, where the action against Jesus' apostles in Jerusalem is always taken by the chief priests, elders, and scribes, or as it is once said, "the high priest and all those who were with him, that is, the party of the Sadducees."[91] Pharisees, by contrast, oppose the aggressive policy of the high priest and his men.[92]

In Matthew, however, Pharisees do figure prominently in the passion narrative, in part even in association with the chief priests and scribes. In Matt. 21:45, "the chief priests and the Pharisees" get the message that the "vineyard" shall be taken away from them and given to "a people that produces the fruits of the kingdom."[93] Again, in Matt 27:62, chief priests and Pharisees ask Pilate for guards on the grave, which later leads to the rumor "among the Jews" about the theft of Jesus' body (28:11–15). The hostile distance voiced here gives reason to relegate this to the latest stratum of Matthew. In the Temple disputes in Matthew, it is the Pharisees who "come together" and take the hostile initiative (22:15, 34, 41). And, most significant, it is not against the greedy scribes (Mark 13:38ff.; Luke 20:45ff.) that Jesus directs his scathing criticism in the Temple compound but, extensively and explicitly, against "scribes and Pharisees, hypocrites!" (Matt. 23:13, 23, 25, 27, 29).

In John, even this anti-Pharisaic stage has been largely left behind. A total conflict with "the (chief priests and) Pharisees" that we associated with the war period is still heard beneath the narrative, but it has largely been painted over with the more general conflict with "the Jews." There is an additional element that is also visible in Luke and Matthew but less so in Mark: the transfer of responsibility for the crucifixion from Pilate to the Jewish authorities. Three times in Luke, Pilate addresses "the chief priests and the crowds" and explicitly states that he finds Jesus innocent, but they remain adamant about his guilt (Luke 23:4, 14, 22); yet in Luke, this does not lead to a generalized inculpation of the Jews. In Matthew, however, Pilate blatantly "washes his hands" from guilt of Jesus' blood, whereupon "the people as a whole" (πᾶς ὁ λαός) cry out, "His blood be on us and on our children!" (Matt 27:24f.). In John, the phenomenon takes on an even more sinister aspect. Pilate interrogates Jesus inside the praetorium, but the Jewish authorities, later identified as "the Jews," stand outside so as not to defile themselves on the eve of Passover (John 18:28)—consummate Johannine irony in this narrative setting, even though it may refer to an

91. Acts 5:17; cf. 4:1, 5f., 23; 6:12; 23:2, 6f.
92. Acts 5:34; 23:9. See Tomson, "Gamaliel's Counsel."
93. In the parallels in Mark and Luke, the parable is addressed against the chief priests and scribes only.

actual event. Thus Pilate is forced to move back and forth, here, too, three times, and the narrative contrast between the near-intimacy of the conversations within and the hostile shouting outside tends to generate a feeling of sympathy with him. The Johannine narrator even says Pilate is "afraid" when he hears the Jews' accusation that Jesus has "claimed to be the Son of God." He seems really moved, goes inside, and asks Jesus: "Where are you from?" (19:8f.). It is easy to imagine how later, apocryphal tradition would develop this into Pilate's sympathy for Jesus.

Any such sympathy is to no avail. "The Jews" have Jesus condemned. The climax of the story, and of the Gospel narrative as a whole, is probably found in the preceding verse: "The Jews answered him, 'We have a law, and according to that law he ought to die because he has claimed to be the Son of God.'" This is what the reader has been sensing ever since the initial scene with John the Baptist: "the Jews" and "their law" stand in fatal opposition to Jesus Christ.[94]

Johannine Texts with No "Jews"

We are left with the three sections in the Gospel where no "Jews" appear. The same is true of the Johannine letters, and it may be useful to address these texts together. Even though the prologue to John mentions no Jews, they are hinted at: unlike those who "believed" in the "true light," "his own people" did not receive him (1:11). The previous verse states even more generally that "the world did not know him." The reference to "the law . . . given through Moses" (1:17) is also relevant. But the adversaries are indicated only in these general terms; they are not identified, not yet. The longest stretch without "Jews" is the extended farewell discourse (14–17). Only once is a direct indication of the identity of the adversaries given, namely, when Jesus says, "They will put you out of the synagogues" (16:2). Otherwise, in this long, hortatory address to the disciples, opposition is said to come from "the world." The concluding chapter of the Gospel gives no hints of adversaries, apart from the "other one" (ἄλλος) who will be instrumental in Peter's death (21:18).

There seems to be no single answer to why no "Jews" occur in these sections. In all, three indications are found that they belong to a later text stratum: in the prologue, this is the singular expression λόγος and the hymn devoted to it that appears to underlie the section; in chapters 15–17, it is

---

94. Cf. "law" and "grace" opposed just before "the Jews" investigate John the Baptist, 1:17. The law "of the Jews" also in 7:19, 51; 8:17; 10:34; 15:25; 18:31.

the prolongation of the farewell address after the announced conclusion in 14:31; and as to the concluding chapter, it is the conclusion that already preceded (20:30f.) and the retrospective point of view (21:18f., 23–25). This could lead to the speculation that "Jews" do not occur because the real confrontation belonged to the past by the time these sections were written. But another observation concerns the various rhetorical settings of these sections. The prologue chants of the heavenly descent of "Jesus Christ" in intentionally general terms and exudes reluctance to give direct identifications. The farewell discourse is an exclusive exchange between Jesus and his disciples, which equally would exclude naming distinct opponents. And the last chapter also consists of intimate conversations between the Lord and the disciples, with general comments to the readers being added. By contrast, the ἀποσυνάγωγος in 16:2 and the rejection by the ἴδιοι in 1:11 remind us that this is only a temporary shift of focus. Quite likely, the passages where Jesus speaks of "Jews" to fellow Jews (13:33; 18:20) also date from the later stages of the Gospel.

Likewise, the complete absence of "Jews" in the Johannine letters is hard to interpret. It could indicate either a completely inner-Jewish or a fully non-Jewish situation. The fact that we hear nothing about a conflict with Jewish authorities may mean either that it was long past or that it had not broken out yet, but in any case, a similar conflict was not relevant to the occasion of the letters. Judith Lieu has warned us not to draw simple, one-way conclusions from differences between the Johannine Gospel and letters.[95] That applies here. Even if we could suppose the letters to be earlier than the extant Gospel,[96] the absence of "Jews" does not necessarily mean that anti-Jewish polemics did not exist in the writer's community.

The ἐθνικοί in 3 John 7 do not help us further at this point. The adjective occurs three times in the Judeo-Christian stratum of Matthew with a sharply negative ring—"heathen," that is, non-Jews,[97]—and the adverb appears once in Paul, equally sharp but with a tinge of irony.[98] In what amounts to the opposite sense, it occurs three times in Philo and Josephus

---

95. J. M. Lieu, *The Second and Third Epistles of John: History and Background* (Edinburgh, 1986), especially the final chapter about meaning of absence of anti-Jewish polemics (pp. 166–216, esp. p. 212).

96. As done by G. Strecker, "Die Anfänge der johanneischen Schule," *NTS* 32 (1986): 31–47; and U. Schnelle, *Antidocetic Christology in the Gospel of John: An Investigation of the Place of the Fourth Gospel in the Johannine School,* trans. L. M. Maloney (Minneapolis, 1992). J. Zumstein, "Zur Geschichte des johanneischen Christentums," *TLZ* 122 (1997): 417–28, gives no reasons when rejecting Strecker's theory without ado and assuming a linear development from the Gospel of John via 1 and 2 to 3 John.

97. Matt. 5:47; 6:7; 18:17.

98. Gal. 2:14, ἐθνικῶς καὶ οὐχὶ Ἰουδαϊκῶς.

meaning "ethnic, national," that is, "Jewish."[99] The Egerton papyrus seems to prove that the Johannine tradition was not exclusive of a Judeo-Christian stance.[100] But most commentators do not accept a Jewish meaning for 3 John 7;[101] rather, they assume the meaning of later Christian usage, ἐθνικός being equivalent to *paganus,* that is, non-Christian.[102] As we shall see, the word also occurs in the definitely non-Judeo-Christian *Gospel of Philip* (52:15), where it designates the lowest state of unbelief, below the "Hebrew." Here, too, it is the antonym of χριστιανός, but this is late third century. This remains a moot point, as does the absence of "Jews" in the Johannine letters.

"Jews" and "Israel" in Some New Testament Apocrypha

Within the canon, the Fourth Gospel is a "maverick" not only for its vehemence against "the Jews" but for its idiosyncratic language, Christology, and Gospel tradition.[103] This oddity vis-à-vis the Synoptic Gospels decreases if we take in the apocryphal Gospels—provided we avoid the mistake of comfortably relegating their import to the late second century and after.[104] It is instructive for us to compare the attitude to the Jews of the Fourth Gospel with that of the New Testament apocrypha.

Not all the apocrypha mention Jews, even if some relation to Jews or Judaism is often indicated. *The Gospel of Thomas,* for example, which is preserved in Coptic, gives an enigmatic encouragement to Sabbath observance (logion 27) and an equally ambiguous denial of the importance of circumcision (logion 53), while no "Jews" are signaled.[105] As in the Johannine

99. Philo, *De vita Mosis* 1:69; 1:188 (the ἔθνος follows directly); Josephus, *Ant.* 12:36. Similarly in Polybius; see LSJ, s.v.

100. If K. Erlemann, "Papyrus Egerton 2: 'Missing Link' zwischen synoptischer und johanneischer Tradition," *NTS* 42 (1996): 12–34, is right.

101. G. Strecker, *Die Johannesbriefe* (KEK 14; Göttingen, 1989), p. 363; R. E. Brown, *The Epistles of John* (AB 30; Garden City, N.Y., 1982), p. 742; M. De Jonge, *De brieven van Johannes (De prediking van het Nieuwe Testament)* (Nijkerk, 1986), p. 261. F. Vouga, *Die Johannesbriefe* (HNT 15/3; Tübingen, 1990), p. 90, leaves undecided whether it means "heathen," as in Matthew, or non-Johannine Christians. H. J. Klauck, *Der zweite und dritte Johannesbrief* (EKKNT 13/2; Zurich–Neukirchen, 1992), p. 92, thinks either of "Jews" as ἔθνος, following the suggestion by Lieu, *Second and Third Epistles of John,* p. 108, or of pagan individuals, but rejects the thought of "jüdische oder judenchristliche Berührungsängste," as is supposed by E. Delebecque, *Épîtres de Jean* (CahRB 25; Paris, 1988): the milieu of the Johannine letters was Judeo-Christian.

102. See LSJ and *PGL,* s.v.

103. Kysar, *John: The Maverick Gospel.*

104. Cf. the useful query of D. Moody Smith, "The Problem of John and the Synoptics in Light of the Relation between Apocryphal and Canonical Gospels," in A. Denaux, ed., *John and the Synoptics* (BETL 101; Leuven, 1992), pp. 147–62.

105. Logion 53, "their father" (translation as in J. M. Robinson, ed., *NHL,* designates the Jews and indicates distance.

letters, this indicates that real interaction with Jews was not an issue. The Greek *Acts of Andrew,* to quote another example, neither shows a relation to Judaism nor mentions any Jews.[106] But other texts present us with illuminating examples.

The Acts of John

It was proposed to view this composite document,[107] which is dated to the late second century and whose middle part shows a docetic or Gnostic Christology,[108] as a further stage of the Johannine trajectory.[109] The suggestion was even made that it was produced by an "ultra-Johannine group"[110] related to the adversaries of the Johannine letters, who deny that Christ really "came in the flesh."[111] The suggestion would be the more interesting if the adversaries were of pagan background and if—what we just left undecided—the letters issued from a Judeo-Christian community.[112] By contrast, the document, while giving prominence to John the apostle, draws on the Synoptic tradition as much as on that of the Fourth Gospel.[113] Moreover, it shares the apostolic recognition of "John" centered around Ephesus.[114] As to literary form, the apocryphal *Acts* show little of the singular homiletical style of the Johannine writings. Hence it seems that the group that created the *Acts* was not identical with the adversaries of the

106. See Prieur's edition, with exhaustive indexes: J.-M. Prieur, ed., *Acta Andrea* (CCSA 5; Turnhout, 1989).

107. Standard edition and commentaries: E. Junod and J.-D. Kaestli, eds., *Acta Ioannis. Praefatio, textus, textus alii, commentaria, indices,* 2 vols. (CCSA1; Turnhout, 1983). See also K. Schäferdiek, "Johannesakten," in W. Hennecke and W. Schneemelcher, eds., *Neutestamentliche Apokryphen in deutscher Übersetzung,* vol. 1: *Evangelien* (5th ed., Tübingen, 1987), pp. 138–90; and recently, P. J. Lalleman, *The Acts of John: A Two-Stage Initiation into Johannine Gnosticism* (Groningen, 1998).

108. On the Gnostic character of 94–102, see Junod and Kaestli, *Acta Ioannis,* pp. 581–632; Lalleman, *Acts of John,* chapter 2. The hypostasizing of λόγος versus κύριος and ἄνθρωπος in *Acts of John* 101, along with the ὀγδοὰς μία and the δωδέκατος ἀριθμός (*Acts of John* 95), seems to me typically Gnostic (cf. Junod and Kaestli, *Acta Ioannis,* pp. 589–93).

109. H. Koester, "Les Discours d'adieu de l'évangile de Jean. Leur trajectoire au premier et au deuxième siècle," in Kaestli, Poffet, and Zumstein, eds., *La communauté johannique et son histoire,* pp. 269–80; pp. 275–79 referring to Junod and Kaestli, *Acta Ioannis,* pp. 595–600.

110. Lalleman, *Acts of John;* cf. G. S. Sloyan, "The Gnostic Adoption of John's Gospel and Its Canonization by the Catholic Church," *BTB* 26 (1996): 125–32.

111. 1 John 4:2; 2 John 7; cf. John 1:14; 19:34. Cf. also 1 John 5:6, "by water and blood," with Lalleman's interesting explanation in *Acts of John,* pp. 22f.

112. Lalleman, *Acts of John,* taking up the suggestion by J. Painter, "The 'Opponents' in 1 John," *NTS* 32 (1986): 48–71.

113. Cf. Schäferdiek, "Johannesakten," pp. 152–55; Hengel, *Die johanneische Frage,* pp. 53–55. Jesus' visit with τίς ποτε τῶν φαρισαίων (in the Gnostic part; *Acts of John* 93) is striking in view of this exclusively Lukan item; see Luke 7:36; 14:1; and cf. Luke 11:37.

114. If we are to follow Hengel, *Johannine Question* and *Die johanneische Frage,* and accept John of Ephesus as the *auctor intellectualis* of the Fourth Gospel, this is of course no argument.

Johannine communities who, as 1 John 2:19 puts it, "went out from us."[115] The *Acts* must have issued from the wider audience the canonical Gospel was attracting during the second century, which also included apostolic Christians, first of all in Asia Minor.[116]

It seems, in fact, it was a Gentile Christian group that produced the document. It was correctly pointed out that the *Acts of John* as a whole "does not recognise the Old Testament as Scripture and has none of the characteristic traits of Jewish Christianity."[117] Indeed the docetic-Gnostic middle part contains a farewell scene of Jesus that opens on a violently anti-Jewish tone:

πρὶν δὲ συλληφθῆναι αὐτὸν ὑπὸ τῶν ἀνόμων καὶ ὑπὸ ἀνόμου ὄφεως νομοθετουμένων Ἰουδαίων συναγαγὼν πάντας ἡμᾶς ἔφη. Πρίν με ἐκείνοις παραδοθῆναι ὑμνήσωμεν (. . .)

Before he was arrested by the unlawful Jews—who accepted the law given by the unlawful snake—he called us all together and said: Before I am delivered up to those, let us sing.

(Acts of John 94)[118]

Again, this sentence carries both Johannine and Synoptic reminiscences.[119] As to the contents, the editors of the apocryphal *Acts* concluded that here we have a diabolization of the Jewish law that is without peer "even in the gnostic texts most hostile to the Old Testament God," and moreover, "it is not without reminiscence of the 'anti-Judaism' of the Gospel of John," especially John 8:44.[120] Quite unlike the canonical Gospel, however, this is the only occurrence of "Jews" in the apocryphal *Acts*. It reads like a brief flare-up of intense polemics that otherwise is not or no longer relevant to the author.[121]

115. The predestinational implications of this phrase (Hengel, *Die johanneische Frage*, pp. 163f.) do not exclude their social meaning.

116. Cf. J.-M. Poffet, "Indices de réception de l'évangile de Jean au IIe siècle, avant Irénée," in Kaestli, Poffet, and Zumstein, eds., *La communauté johannique et son histoire*, pp. 305–21; J.-D. Kaestli, "L'exégèse valentinienne du quatrième évangile" and "Remarques sur le rapport du quatrième évangile avec la gnose et sa réception au IIe siècle," in Kaestli, Poffet, and Zumstein, eds., *La communauté johannique et son histoire*, pp. 305–50; W. Bauer, *Rechtgläubigkeit und Ketzerei im ältesten Christentum* (BHT 10; Tübingen, 1934), pp. 205–15.

117. Lalleman, *Acts of John*, p. 31; cf. Junod and Kaestli, *Acta Ioannis*, pp. 680f.

118. Cf. the snake in 71–76.

119. Johannine: cf. John 18:36, παραδοθῶ τοῖς Ἰουδαίοις; Synoptic: Mark 14:26; Matt. 26:30, ὑμνήσαντες ἐξῆλθον. The intimate farewell scene recalls of the farewell discourse John 14–17 but also the Passover conversation in Luke 22:21–38—πρὸ τοῦ με παθεῖν, Luke 22:15. See Junod and Kaestli, *Acta Ioannis*, pp. 624, 643.

120. Ibid., pp. 643f.

121. *Acts of John* 94–102 is a farewell scene that seems to derive from a distinct source. It could be from a lost Gospel that contained more directly anti-Jewish language, but, just as in the Fourth Gospel, only sparsely in its farewell scene. Just so, the extant *Acts of John* has only this one reminiscence of anti-Jewish polemics.

Mainline "apostolic" Christianity was not free from anti-Judaism either, of course; after all, it was able to swallow the canonization of the Fourth Gospel. A mainline position is taken by the so-called *Acts of John at Rome*, a much later text that was once edited as chapters 1–17 of the *Acts of John*. Its author identifies the beloved disciple with John the apostle and with John of Patmos, whose "Revelation" he knows (14). He also adopts later Christian usage distinguishing between the Ἰουδαῖοι, who are Jesus" adversaries, and his friends, the noble Ἑβραῖοι.[122] Such downgrading of Ἰουδαῖοι before Ἑβραῖοι is also found in Eusebius,[123] and this coincides with strong indications of Eusebian influence on this stretch of text.[124]

The Gospel of Peter

This Greek fragment is variously placed somewhere in the second century. The extant text has no Gnostic slant at all. It uses Gospel traditions reminiscent of all canonical Gospels, so to say, "from memory."[125] "The Jews" play a most remarkable role in it.[126]

1:1   οἱ Ἰουδαῖοι do not want to wash hands along with Pilate (!) and accept full responsibility for Jesus" trial and death;

6:23   οἱ Ἰουδαῖοι rejoice over Jesus" death and give his corpse to Joseph of Arimathea;

7:25   οἱ Ἰουδαῖοι καὶ οἱ πρεσβύτεροι καὶ οἱ ἱερεῖς begin to understand they have sinned and wail over the imminent end (τέλος) of Jerusalem. Remorse is voiced by οἱ γραμματεῖς καὶ οἱ φαρισαῖοι καὶ πρεσβύτερες again in 8:28, but this time without "Jews" being added, which brings out the strangeness of their being there in 7:25;

12:50 Mary Magdalen comes to the grave φοβουμένη διὰ τοὺς Ἰουδαίους; and again,

12:52 she and her friends ἐφοβοῦντο μὴ ἴδωσιν αὐτὰς οἱ Ἰουδαῖοι.

All of this expresses "the very outspoken anti-Jewish character of this text."[127] It is striking that not only is Pilate largely exonerated, as in other

122. Ἰουδαῖοι, *Acts of John* 1, 3; Ἑβραῖοι, 3, 5.

123. Eusebius, *Demonstratio Evangelica* and *Praeparatio Evangelica* passim. See especially *Praeparatio* 7.6–8: the patriarchs were "Hebrews" who did not observe the "Jewish" laws of Moses, and the "Jewish nation" existed from Moses until Christ.

124. Junod and Kaestli, *Acta Ioannis*, pp. 854–56.

125. W. Schneemelcher, "Petrusevangelium," in Hennecke and Schneemelcher, *Neutestamentliche Apokryphen*, pp. 180–85.

126. Adduced also by Bauer, *Das Johannesevangelium*, p. 31; R. Schnackenburg, *Das Johannesevangelium* (HTKNT 4/1; Freiburg, 1967), p. 275.

127. M. G. Mara, ed., *L'évangile de Pierre. Introduction, texte critique, traduction, commentaire et index* (SC 201; Paris, 1973), p. 33, referring to the opinion of "presque tous les spécialistes."

canonical and apocryphal Gospels, but "the Jews" themselves perform the tasks of the Roman soldiers in torturing and executing Jesus.

It is even more remarkable to find "the Jews," in 2:7 and 4:11, referring to Jesus as βασιλεὺς τοῦ Ἰσραήλ. This glaringly contrasts with the inscription on the cross, βασιλεὺς τῶν Ἰουδαίων, which does not figure in the fragment. Moreover, this happens precisely while the Jews are doing their job as stand-ins for the Roman soldiers, who in the Synoptic account jeer Jesus as "King of the Jews"! The modern editor of the text notes the exceptional character of the appellation "King of Israel" and suggests it is "a divine and messianic title,"[128] without explaining why Ἰουδαῖοι fails to generate that meaning. A Judeo-Christian setting is out of the question in view of the replacement of the Roman soldiers with "the Jews."[129] Indeed, while at first the "Jews" cheerfully take the place of the Roman soldiers, they later have remorse over the execution. In 8:28 they even confess Jesus' innocence:[130] πόσον δίκαιός ἐστιν! They also evoke Jerusalem's destruction as a result of the crucifixion.

All this later became stock-in-trade Gentile Christian anti-Jewish polemics, and it seems the expression "King of Israel" must be understood in that light. Indeed, Melito's On Pascha expresses the same anti-Jewish use of "Israel": "The king of Israel has been put to death by an Israelite right hand."[131] A similar usage is found throughout the staunchly anti-Jewish Pseudo-Barnabas.[132] These texts apparently do not separate "the Jews" from "Israel," as do Justin and later church fathers, more subtly appropriating the latter name for the church.[133] This element would make for a dating of the Gospel of Peter earlier in the second century.

By contrast, this sets off once more the unspecific use of "Israel" in the canonical John. As documented especially in John 1:31, where the Baptist announces the Christ's revelation "to Israel" and in 3:1, where Jesus calls Nicodemus a leader "of Israel," this is a naive remnant within the extant text of inner-Jewish dual usage. Such a remnant is no longer found in the Gospel of Peter. Thus we must modify Walter Bauer's conclusion, correct in itself, that the Gospel of Peter "uses Ἰουδαῖοι quite in the style of the

128. Ibid., pp. 90f, 112f. In n. 2 on p. 113, he fails to remark that βασιλεὺς Ἰσραήλ occurs precisely in the mouth of Jews, as distinct from βασιλεὺς τῶν Ἰουδαίων.

129. Schneemelcher, "Petrusevangelium," p. 184, rejects a Judeo-Christian background on the grounds of the outspoken anti-Jewish polemics.

130. Again as the Roman soldier, Luke 23:47.

131. ὁ βασιλεὺς τοῦ Ἰσραήλ ἀνῄρηται ὑπὸ δεξιᾶς ἰσραηλίτιδος; Melito, On Pascha 96, trans. S. G. Hall (Oxford, 1979). Hall, p. 39 n. 40, notes the parallel with the Gospel of Peter here.

132. Pseudo-Barnabas 5:2, πρὸς Ἰσραήλ as opposed to πρὸς ἡμᾶς; passim.

133. Justin, Dialogue 11:5; 135:2; though an ἰσραηλιτικὸν πνευματικόν.

Gospel of John,"[134] to the extent that it differs in its bluntly Gentile-Christian polemical use of Ἰσραήλ.[135]

The Gospel of Philip

Found in Nag Hammadi, this full-blown Gnostic text features a spiritual marriage symbolizing the reentry of the soul into the salvific ascent of divine syzygies.[136] While it does not polemicize against the Jews, the text is explicit about a past connection with Judaism. The terminology is interesting insofar as the Coptic rendering has retained characteristic Greek and Aramaic terms.[137] In the context of our survey, it is remarkable that the name Jew appears only in the latter part, while the beginning uses the synonym *Hebrew.* The rise of this name is rather late,[138] which ties in with the dating of the document to the late third century. This also makes the latter part seem older. Let us examine some quotations:[139]

> A Hebrew [εβραιος] makes another Hebrew, and such a person is called proselyte [προσηλυτος]. A gentile [εθνικος] does not die, for he has never lived in order that he may die. He who has believed in the truth has found life. . . . When we were Hebrews we were orphans and had only our mother, but when we became Christians [χριστιανος] we had both father and mother. (51:29–52:24)

> Mary is the virgin whom no power defiled. She is the great anathema to the Hebrews, who are the apostles [αποστολος] and [the] apostolic men [αποστολικος. (55:23–31)

---

134. Bauer, *Das Johannesevangelium,* p. 31.

135. That this Gentile-Christian, anti-Jewish usage can be adopted by baptized Jews is apparently shown by the sixth-century liturgical poet Romanos. His Jewish descent is argued by P. Maas and C. A. Trypanis, eds., *Sancti Romani Melodi Cantica: Cantica Genuina* (Oxford, 1963), xv, xviii. To the arguments from language and vocabulary one can add γὴ Ἰσραήλ (no. 23, iV 8, p. 175) and υἱὸς πρωτότοκος ὁ Ἰσραὴλ ἐπεκέκλητο (no. 11, kV 5, p. 86). Yet he can also say, Λαὸς μὲν ὁ τοῦ Ἰσραὴλ ναοῦ ἀποστερεῖται / ἡμεῖς δὲ [!] ἀντ᾿ ἐκείνου / Ἀνάστασιν ἁγίαν καὶ τὴν Ζιὼν ἔχομεν νῦν / ἤνπερ Κωνσταντίνος καὶ Ἑλένη ἡ πιστή [!] / τῷ κόσμῳ ἐδωρήσαντο. This relinquishing of "Israel" identifies the former Jew with the Gentile church. Indeed, in hymn no. 21 (pp. 157–63), he has Βελίαρ and the διάβολος conspire with the Ἰουδαῖοι (6x) to crucify Jesus.

136. See the introduction in J. E. Ménard, *L'évangile selon Philippe: Introduction, texte, traduction, commentaire* (Paris, 1967); also the brief introduction in Robinson, ed., *NHL,* p. 131.

137. Aramaic: 56:8f., "In Syriac [συρος] it is Messiah, in Greek it is Christ"; 63:21–24, "The eucharist [ευχαριστια] is Jesus, for he is called in Syriac φαρισαθα, which is the one who is spread out" פרישתא, "spread"; but the author seems to play on Hebrew פרוס, "morsel," i.e., κλάσμα). That the author does know Hebrew appears in 62:13f., "Jesus in Hebrew is the redemption." Furthermore, the name Jew (see below) appears not in its Greek but in its prior Aramaic form: ιουδαι, i.e., יהודא.

138. See Tomson, "Names," p. 128.

139. I quote the translation from Robinson, ed., *NHL,* and follow the page and line indications given there.

The author makes a point of classifying humanity. His own group are no longer "Hebrews," that is, those who make "proselytes" and therefore seem to be identical with Jews. Even less are they "Gentiles," those without faith altogether. They have passed to the superior category of "Christians." The author seems to mean these terms also in an esoteric sense, following the well-known Gnostic distinction: εθνικος designating the "hylic" and εβραιος the "psychic."[140] It is interesting that at the same time he can identify the "Hebrews" with the "apostles" and their followers, the "apostolics."[141] As we know, the churches that called themselves apostolic insisted on retaining the Old Testament and the tradition of the apostles;[142] it suffices to point to Irenaeus's *Adversus haereses*. It seems the author put these in one category with the Jews, while surprisingly, he felt free to appropriate the name Christians.

The same happens in the two passages further on where "Jews" appear:

> If you say, I am a Jew [ιουδαι], no one will be moved. If you say, I am a Roman, . . . if you say, I am a Greek, a barbarian, a slave, [a] free man, no one will be troubled. [If] you [say], I am a Christian, the [world] will tremble. (62:26–32)

> No Jew [was ever born] to Greek parents [as long as the world[143]] has existed. And, [as a] Christian [people], we [ourselves do not[144] descend] from the Jews.[145] (75:30–34)

The first saying seems to allude to Pauline passages such as Col. 3:11 and Gal. 3:28. The second one is badly damaged and its reading uncertain. All we can do is conclude that "Jews" and elements from Judaism are well known to the author, but that he is conversant with the superior category of "Christians." He does not care about anti-Jewish polemics; his energy simply goes elsewhere.

Wirkungsgeschichte

Finally, let us throw a glance into the effective history of some other apocryphal Gospels—along with the canonical John. This will bring us well

140. See Ménard, *L'évangile selon Philippe*, p. 124.

141. Ménard (ibid.) recognizes this in his comment on p. 136 yet in his introduction on p. 23 identifies the 'αποστολικοί with the prototypical believers.

142. Cf. Bauer, *Rechtgläubigkeit und Ketzerei*, chapter 9.

143. Ménard (*L'évangile selon Philippe*) reconstructs "Loi."

144. Ménard (ibid.) proposes to read the opposite: "Et [nous-mêmes, nous fûmes engendrés] des Juifs."

145. In the badly damaged continuation, Robinson (*NHL*) reconstructs, "[There was] another [people and] these [blessed ones] are referred to as the chosen people." This contradicts the superior position of "Christians" in the other passages. Ménard (*L'évangile selon Philippe*) does not fill in the lacunae at the end of lines 34f.

into medieval England and Flanders. It concerns the old English versions of *Evangelium Nichodemi* and *Vindicta Salvatoris*. The former is a composition from late antiquity that combines various texts, among which are those known elsewhere as *Acta Pilati* and *Descensus ad Inferos*; the latter must have been produced in the early Middle Ages using material such as the Veronica legend.[146] The exoneration of Pilate at the expense of the Jews is here developed to the point of almost making him a Christian. Both narratives became popular in medieval England, as appears from a range of eleventh-century Old English versions. It was never known from what prior text these had been made until such was recently identified in a ninth-century Latin manuscript produced in Flanders and preserved in St.-Omer, near Calais in the Flemish part of modern France.[147] A recent handsome publication containing the parallel Latin and Old English texts, along with modern English translations, gives an impression of the "industry" of copying, recycling, and producing of apocryphal Gospel material in medieval western Europe.[148] It also suggests how the conceptions embodied in this material spread among the population. If it was not the St.-Omer manuscript, it must have been some other like it that is mentioned in a medieval book inventory as a *spelboc,* that is, a homiliary providing elaborations on the Gospel lessons for feast days.[149] We may infer that the function of these legends was analogous to and prefigured the passion plays and oratorios that became popular elsewhere in Europe, even to the present day.

One thing is clear at first glance in these documents: the stage setting of the Gospel of John has become paradigmatic. Jesus is pushed toward his execution by the ferocity of "the Jews," while Pilate is moderate and intimidated and even secretly warns "the Jews" for their mistake. Apart from novel legendary elements, such as the Roman legionary signs testifying to Jesus' divine authority, telling motifs from the canonical Gospels are used. As in Matt. 27:19, Pilate is warned by his wife because of a dream, though "the Jews" interpret this as proof of Jesus' malefic powers. Especially striking is a word-for-word quotation of John 18:30–38, not without vicious

---

146. See F. Scheidweiler, "Nikodemusevangelium," in Hennecke and Schneemelcher, *Neutestamentliche Apokryphen,* pp. 395–99; J. E. Cross, ed., *Two Old English Apocrypha and Their Manuscript Source: 'The Gospel of Nicodemus' and 'The Avenging of the Saviour'* (CSASE 19; Cambridge, 1996), pp. 36–81 [ed. and trans. T. S. Hall].

147. The decisive proof being one larger and two smaller corresponding gaps; see Cross, ed., *Two Old English Apocrypha,* pp. 5f. and 82.

148. Ibid.

149. Ibid., pp. 31–35 [ed. and trans. J. E. Cross and Julia Crick]; ibid., p. 58 [ed. and trans. T. S. Hall]: "popularity," "fertile industry."

explanatory glosses,[150] which may reflect the passion lesson concerned. By way of comment, this is followed by the scene in Matt. 27:24f., where Pilate washes his hands from guilt of Jesus' blood and "the Jews" respond in unison: "His blood be upon us and upon our children."[151] One might say that the anti-Jewish motifs in Matthew[152] are grafted onto the anti-Jewish stage setting of John.[153]

Concluding Theses

1. The dual usage typical of Judaism in the Greco-Roman period involves semantic equivalence but social differentiation of the two names, "Israel" being the self-appellation Jews use in inner-Jewish situations and "Jews" when including non-Jews among the intended hearers.

2. As well as other rabbinic writings, the Palestinian Talmud is an inner-Jewish document, that is, a text meant to communicate between Jewish authors and a Jewish audience. Accordingly, "Israel" is the appellation of Jews, except in intermezzi containing real or imaginary interaction with non-Jews. In two cases where no such interaction is implied, a saying ironically portrays the "Jews" from outside with a moralistic aim.

3. With three exceptions, the Synoptic Gospels retain the inner-Jewish speech situation that must have prevailed during the Judeo-Christian stage of their trajectory. In two cases, a neutral explanation is given to implied non-Jewish readers, which merely switches the narrative to a non-Jewish speech situation. In the remaining case, an anti-Jewish remark effectively breaks up the semantic equivalence and therefore abandons Jewish dual usage.

4. Quite differently, the Fourth Gospel

    a. not only as a whole is formulated in a non-Jewish setting, addressing non-Jews,

    b. but in large parts portrays "the Jews" as being hostile to Christianity and

---

150. Cf. ibid., pp. 156 and 158. When the Jews say: "Nobis non licet occidere neminem" (John 18:31), Pilate replies: "Vobis dixit Deus 'non occideris'—sed mihi?"

151. Ibid., pp. 156–60.

152. In my judgment, Matt. 27:25 has an anti-Jewish effect within the extant text, though probably not in earlier strata. See P. J. Tomson, *If This Be from Heaven . . . : Jesus and the New Testament Authors in Their Relationship to Judaism* (The Biblical Seminar 76; Sheffield 2001), p. 283f.

153. On another occasion, I hope to write on the extended passage in the *Gospel of Nicodemus* that features the frequent inner-Jewish use of the name Israel, while the overall narrative setting remains non-Jewish, as signaled by the name Jews.

   c. often projects this later **portrayal** into the originally inner-Jewish narrative about Jesus;

   d. to that extent it has abandoned the dual usage of its Judeo-Christian origins and has given the name Jew a very negative ring;

   e. though it has preserved some remnants of the prior inner-Jewish tradition,

   f. in effect, its extant text is predominantly anti-Jewish.

5. In their use of the name Jew, the apocryphal texts of the *Gospel of Peter* and the *Acts of John* display a similar anti-Jewish orientation but in further stages of development. The still-later *Gospel of Philip* shows only estrangement and a remote echo of former conflicts with Jews.

6. The Latin and Old English *Gospel of Nicodemus* and the *Avenging of the Savior* document the medieval *Wirkungsgeschichte,* the process whereby the anti-Jewish orientation of the canonical Fourth Gospel, in association with apocryphal traditions, struck deep roots in western European culture.

7. Exegetes and homilists should join efforts to make the *Wirkungsgeschichte* of the Fourth Gospel effectively progress in our day, so that while being read and expounded, its anti-Jewish orientation is effectively criticized and corrected within the perspective of Mark and especially Luke and in prudent comparison with ancient Jewish literature.

8. First and foremost, however, Christian exegetes and homilists need the living encounter with Jews in order to shatter the "spectralized" image of the Jews integral to their interpretive tradition and to learn that the name Jew—thank heavens—never leaves its flesh-and-blood meaning.

9. Once we are enabled to do all this, the treasures of insight and inspiration deposited in this most battered of canonical Gospels may again shine on us in their pristine radiance.

CHAPTER 10

"Jews" and Jews in the Fourth Gospel

Adele Reinhartz

It has become customary in recent years for New Testament scholars to clothe the Johannine Jews in quotation marks, that is, to write of "the Jews" rather than the Jews in the Fourth Gospel. These markings, though small, are not inconsequential. Rather, they convey a number of theological and historical presuppositions: that the Jews as presented in the Gospel of John are a construct of the text itself; that they represent the state of unbelief and symbolize the unbelieving world as a whole; that they are not to be identified with the historical Jewish nation that lived in the Greco-Roman empire in the first century of the common era, whom the modern-day Jewish people consider their historical and spiritual ancestors.[1] Underlying these points is the conviction that the Gospel as such is not anti-Jewish, since it speaks not of "real" Jews but only about "Jews" as symbol or metaphor.

As a Jewish student of this Gospel, and, perforce, of the vast literature that it has spawned, I confess my discomfort with the quotation marks around "the Jews" and all that they imply. This discomfort has its origin, no doubt, in my own initial encounters with this text, in which each Johannine usage of the term *Jew* felt like a slap in the face. Repeated readings of this text over many years have inured me to this effect to some degree; my own fascination with the literary aspects of this Gospel have often engaged me in exegetical problems in which "the Jews" did not figure greatly. Familiarity with the complex source and historical-critical issues and the slipperiness of the text itself cautioned me against taking any of its language, narrative, and theology at face value. Nevertheless, I have not entirely shed my sense that talking about "the Jews" rather than the Jews in this Gospel

---

1. R. Bultmann, *The Gospel of John: A Commentary,* trans. G. R. Beasley-Murray (Philadelphia, 1971), pp. 86–87. Cf. S. Sandmel, *Anti-Semitism in the New Testament?* (Philadelphia, 1978), pp. 117–18, for a critique of this view. See also J. Ashton, *Studying John: Approaches to the Fourth Gospel* (Oxford, 1994), p. 61; and J. Ashton, "The Identity and Function of the Ἰουδαῖοι in the Fourth Gospel," *NovT* 27 (1985): 40–75.

sweeps an important, if difficult problem, under the rug. Sometimes sweeping a problem under the rug is the right or perhaps the only thing to do, a convenient way of cleaning house when guests arrive at one's door earlier than expected. And so there are exegetical occasions when it is not necessary or appropriate to focus on the Jews, as, for example, in a study of textual variants or a philological discussion of a difficult term, such as μονογενής. But sooner or later, one must pull back the rug and clean up. The invitation to write an essay on the theme of "Anti-Judaism and the Fourth Gospel" was an opportunity to do precisely that: to take a close look at "the Jews" or the Jews and to consider, explicitly and carefully, the question of whether and to what extent the Gospel is anti-Jewish, that is, conveys negative attitudes toward the Jews as a group and carries the potential to inculcate such views in its audience.

In this contribution I argue that the Fourth Evangelist identifies the Jews as a historical people with the negative pole of his dualistic rhetoric, and that while later anti-Jewish interpretations have read the Gospel through the lens of a priori attitudes, these interpretations are not inconsistent with the rhetoric and tone of the Gospel itself. In the course of developing this argument, I address three main topics. I argue (1) that anti-Jewish elements are inherent in the texts themselves and not attributable solely to the interpretative tradition. For this reason, (2) the Christology of the Fourth Gospel does not include salvation for nonbelievers such as the Jews. I will also suggest (3) that the Fourth Evangelist was less concerned to present a historical conflict between Jesus and the Jews than to set them up as the two opposing poles of his Christology, his soteriology, and his narrative. That is, while the Evangelist may have believed that a conflict between Jesus and the Jews had occurred, his concerns were more literary and theological than historical.

The chapter begins by outlining the positive and negative poles around which Johannine Christology and soteriology are organized in order to argue that the Jews, not "the Jews," are identified with the negative poles. It then continues the argument by looking at the Johannine use of the term Ἰουδαῖοι and the historical situation of the Johannine community and concludes by considering briefly the implications of the discussion for the question of Johannine anti-Judaism.

The Two Poles of Johannine Theology

The Fourth Gospel frames its soteriology around contrasting states of being, such as light/darkness, life/death, from above/from below, being from God or not from God, and contrasting activities, such as believing/not believing, accepting/not accepting, doing good/doing evil, loving/hating. The first element of each pair is associated with Jesus. The second element of each pair is associated with the forces that oppose and reject Jesus, or, more precisely, that negate the claim that Jesus is the Messiah, the Son of God. These paired terms imply the existence of two types of people. One consists of those aligned with the positive elements in each pair (light, life, above, and so on). This alignment also brings them into association with Jesus, and thereby with God, since, for John, Jesus was God's Son, sent by God to do God's work in the world, and is thus the sole conduit for divine revelation, that is, the knowledge and love of God. The Gospel challenges and exhorts the readers to be part of this group, as indicated in the concluding verses of John 20. In 20:31, the narrator addresses the reader directly, using the second-person plural, and declares that this Gospel has been "written so that you may come to believe that Jesus is the Messiah, the Son of God, and that through believing you may have life in his name." The opposing group consists of those aligned against Jesus and therefore linked to darkness, death, and the other negative elements in each pair. Although these terms often appear in passages that have a general and universal tone, the Gospel consistently and directly associates the negative side of each pair with explicitly Jewish characters within the narrative. This point can be made through a brief overview of each of the pairs.

Basic to Johannine Christology is the claim that Jesus is the light of the world (1:4; 8:12). The light challenges the darkness, which has tried but not succeeded in overcoming it (1:4). The light, as Jesus, came into the world in order that believers not remain in darkness (12:46). Some, however, love darkness rather than light, because their deeds are evil (3:19). Though "darkness" is an abstract metaphor, it is associated at several points in the narrative with the Jews as a group or with individual Jewish characters. In 3:2, Nicodemus, a Pharisee and leader of the Jews (3:1), is said to have come to Jesus by night (3:2). In 8:12, Jesus promises the Jews, "Whoever follows me will never walk in darkness but will have the light of life." But their absolute rejection of Jesus leaves them out of this promise (12:37). A consequence as well as a cause of their being in darkness is their inability or unwillingness to see. Their blindness is contrasted with the newfound vision of the man born blind, who declares Jesus to be the Son of man (9:39–41).

Just as Jesus is the light, so also is he life (1:3; 8:12). Believing in Jesus assures the believer of eternal life (3:16; 10:28). The nonbeliever, by contrast, "will not see life, but must endure God's wrath" (3:36). The representatives of these nonbelievers are the Jews, who are destined to die in their sin (8:21). This is a destiny they share with their ancestors, who ate manna and died (6:49, 58), in contrast to believers, who eat the bread of life that is Jesus himself and live forever (6:27, 51, 53). Jesus and his followers who dwell in the light and experience eternal life are "from above" (1:1–18). Jews, by contrast, are "from below" (8:23) and therefore are cut off from heavenly things. As Jesus tells Nicodemus, "If I have told you about earthly things and you do not believe, how can you believe if I tell you about heavenly things?" (3:12). Finally, those who are reborn "from above" are the children of God (1:13), who hear and abide by God's words (8:47). The Jews, by contrast, are children of the devil (8:44). Evidence for their lineage includes their ongoing efforts to kill Jesus (8:39) and their inability or unwillingness to understand and accept the words of Jesus and of God (8:42–44). The two contrasting states of being, while described in universal terms at certain points within the Gospel, are therefore also made concrete in the form of Jesus' followers on the one hand and the Jews on the other hand.

A similar move occurs with respect to the range of paired activities associated with each state of being. The most fundamental of these pairs is believing and not believing. Belief in Jesus is evidence of faith in God (12:44); the one who sees Jesus also sees God (12:45). The Jews, by contrast, are those who do not believe and do not see God because they do not believe in Jesus as the Christ and Son of God (5:38). The same duality is expressed by the language of accepting (λαμβάνω) and not accepting. According to the prologue, the Word's own people did not accept him, but those who did accept him became children of God and thereby received grace upon grace (1:11–12, 16). This contrast is reiterated and made more specific in 3:32, which declares that the one from heaven testifies to what he has seen and heard, but no one accepts (λαμβάνει) his testimony. John 3:11 identifies the people who do not accept Jesus as Jews; in this verse, Jesus tells Nicodemus, and with him, other Jews, that "we speak of what we know and testify to what we have seen; yet you [plural] do not receive [οὐ λαμβάνετε] our testimony." Similarly, in 5:43–44, Jesus chides his Jewish listeners: "I have come in my Father's name, and you do not accept me [οὐ λαμβάνετε]; if another comes in his own name, you will accept him [λήμψεσθε]. How can you believe when you accept glory from one another and do not seek the glory that comes from the one who alone is God?"

Accepting Jesus demonstrates a love for God, Jesus, and fellow believers (15:12–17). Rejecting Jesus is tantamount to hating God. Jesus accuses the Jews of not having the love of God in them (8:42) and tells the disciples that his enemies have seen and hated both Jesus and his Father (15:23–24). Acceptance and rejection also become the measure of one's deeds. According to 3:19–21: "people loved darkness rather than light because their deeds were evil. For all who do evil hate the light and do not come to the light, so that their deeds may not be exposed. But those who do what is true come to the light, so that it may be clearly seen that their deeds have been done in God." The only violent, death-dealing, and therefore evil acts in the Gospel are executed by the Jews, who bear responsibility even for Jesus' death by crucifixion, a Roman form of execution. According to 5:16–18, the Jews began persecuting Jesus because he desecrated the Sabbath and called God his own Father and thereby made himself equal to or like God (ἴσον ἑαυτὸν ποιῶν τῷ θεῷ). Their machinations against Jesus demonstrate that they are not Abraham's children, nor God's, but rather the devil's (8:39–44). Not only Jesus but also his followers are in danger, as the chief priests' plan to kill Lazarus demonstrates (12:10–11). Jesus warns his disciples that they, too, will face persecution (15:20), expulsion from the synagogue, and death (16:2).

The Gospel therefore identifies the Jews who do not believe in Jesus with the negative pole of Johannine soteriology; that is, they possess the attitudes and engage in the actions that from a Johannine perspective will exclude them from salvation. The fact that abstract theological concepts are applied to players within the narrative indicates an intermingling of theological and historical modes of discourse. While the Gospel narrative is not historiography in our modern sense of the term, the Gospel makes historical claims (e.g., "His testimony is true"; 19:35; 21:24). The fact that theological claims are not abstracted from the ostensible historical situation therefore raises the possibility that the negative comments about Jews reflect not only a symbolic use of "the Jews" but also a negative assessment about the non-believing Jews as a historical group in the first century. The arguments for and against this possibility must take at least two factors into account: (1) the precise referent of the term Ἰουδαῖοι and (2) the historical relationship between the Johannine and Jewish communities at the time the Gospel was written.

The Johannine Usage of the Term Ἰουδαῖος

The term Ἰουδαῖος as used in John carries a variety of meanings and nuances, which can often be determined from the context. In passages that attribute a character's action or nonaction to his or her fear of the Jews (e.g.,

9:22; 19:38; 20:19), for example, the term denotes the feared rather than the fearful, though it is clear that both parties are Jewish. These passages support a translation of "Jewish leaders" or "Jewish authorities" for οἱ Ἰουδαῖοι, since it is the Jewish leadership that presumably has the power to strike fear into the hearts of other Jews. This is the route suggested by Urban von Wahlde, who argues that the term Ἰουδαῖοι most frequently denotes the Jewish authorities, in contrast to the Jewish people as a whole.[2] In his view, the term Ἰουδαῖος "does not refer to the nation as a whole in a way that can be called racially anti-Semitic."[3] At other points, the geographical meaning of Ἰουδαῖοι seems plausible, as throughout John 11, in which the geographical location of Bethany as a village just outside Jerusalem and therefore in Judaea is made clear (11:18). Malcolm Lowe argues that in first-century Judaea, the term *Israel* would have been used to denote the Jewish people as a whole, whereas Ἰουδαῖοι designated specifically the residents of Judaea.[4] Lowe interprets Ἰουδαῖοι primarily not as "Jews," a particular ethnic/religious group per se, nor as a subgroup such as the Jewish authorities, but rather as "Judaeans," the inhabitants of Judaea.[5] Lowe accuses the translators who render Ἰουδαῖος as "Jew" of committing a philological error with far-reaching consequences. By confusing "the Palestinian use of Ἰουδαῖος to distinguish Judaeans from Galileans, etc. with its wider meanings in the diaspora," these translators "provided . . . a constant excuse for antisemitism whose further existence cannot be permitted."[6]

It must be remembered, however, that, according to most scholars, the Gospel itself, while set in Judaea, Galilee, and Samaria, was written and circulated in the Diaspora, in which, as Lowe himself argues, the broader sense of Ἰουδαῖος as designating a national, religious, political group was already current.[7] Furthermore, as Shaye Cohen has shown, the meaning of Ἰουδαῖος, a complex term from its earliest attestations, changed over time. Before the mid- to late second century B.C.E., to be sure, Ἰουδαῖος was primarily an ethnic-geographic term, properly translated "Judaean";

---

2. Von Wahlde derives this definition from its usage throughout the Gospel, with the exception of 6:41 and 6:52, in which οἱ Ἰουδαῖοι denotes the Jewish audience of Jesus' "bread of life" discourse. U. C. von Wahlde, "The Johannine 'Jews': A Critical Survey," *NTS* 28 (1981–82): 54–74. Cf. also U. C. von Wahlde, "The Gospel of John and the Presentation of Jews and Judaism," in D. P. Efroymson et al., eds., *Within Context: Essays on Jews and Judaism in the New Testament* (Philadelphia, 1993), pp. 67–84.

3. von Wahlde, "Johannine 'Jews,'" p. 74.

4. M. Lowe, "Who Were the Ἰουδαῖοι?" *NovT* 18 (1976): 101–30, pp. 102–7.

5. Ibid., 101–30.

6. Ibid., 130.

7. Ibid., 104.

but by the second half of the second century B.C.E., the term was applied also to people who were not ethnic or geographic Judaeans but who affiliated either religiously by coming to believe in the God of the Judaeans or politically by joining the Judaean state as allies or citizens. In the Maccabean period, when the Judaean ἔθνος opened itself to incorporation of outsiders, the primarily ethnic-geographic self-definition was supplemented and eventually supplanted by religious or cultural and political definitions.[8] These points suggest that by the time the Fourth Gospel was written, toward the end of the first century C.E., the term was used to denote both an ethnic-geographic and a religious identity, and that even the former was not limited to Jews who lived in Judaea or who were born of Judaean parents.[9]

The Johannine usage supports an understanding of Ἰουδαῖος that includes ethnic-geographic, political, and religious elements. In places, the term is used in the context of religious customs and beliefs that extend beyond Judaea and are characteristic of Diaspora as much as Palestinian Jewry. For example, the Gospel narrative is punctuated by festivals designated as feasts of the Jews (2:13; 5:1; 6:4; 7:2; 11:55; cf. also 19:42). Although, as Lowe argues, these feasts required pilgrimage to the Temple located in Judaea,[10] they are not defined by their geographical location but by the identity of their celebrants. That is, they are not "feasts of Judaea" but rather "feasts of the Ἰουδαῖοι," many of whom come from other parts of Palestine and from the Diaspora. The term Ἰουδαῖος is also used in the narrator's explanations of particular Jewish customs. John 2:6 refers to the water and jars used in the Jewish rites of purification, in the context of a wedding taking place in Cana in Galilee; 19:40 refers to Jewish burial rites that do not seem to be specific to Judaea.

The term Ἰουδαῖος also occurs in the descriptions of specific claims and practices that are constitutive of Jewish identity in the land of Israel and the Diaspora. In John 8, Jesus' interlocutors claim to be children of Abraham and of God. The former is a common form of Jewish self-designation, while the latter refers to covenantal theology. In the course of Pilate's interrogation, Jesus says that he has spoken openly in synagogues and the Temple "where all Jews come together" (18:20). Although the latter phrase can be read as modifying the Temple only, it most naturally is read as modifying

---

8. S. J. D. Cohen, *The Beginnings of Jewishness: Boundaries, Varieties, Uncertainties* (Berkeley, 1999), p. 70.

9. Ibid., p. 73.

10. Lowe, "Who were the Ἰουδαῖοι?" p. 116.

"synagogues" (many of which were outside Judaea, as in Capernaum; cf. 6:59) and the Jerusalem Temple alike.

As a political designation, the term is also not limited to Judaea. Key here is the sign on the cross that reads "Jesus of Nazareth, the King of the Ἰουδαῖοι." Although the tone of this sign is no doubt mocking, it presumes that it is not implausible for a man from Nazareth, and hence a non-Judaean, to claim kingship of the Ἰουδαῖοι. This suggests that other references to Jesus as king of the Jews may also refer not to Judaeans specifically but to the Jewish nation as a whole. Most explicit is 18:35, in which Pilate declares, "I am not a Jew [Ἰουδαῖος], am I? Your own nation [ἔθνος] and the chief priests have handed you over to me."

These examples suggest that the Fourth Evangelist is not operating with a narrow and limited definition of Ἰουδαῖος. While some cases may permit a narrower translation according to the context, the sense in all cases is best met by the direct translation of Ἰουδαῖος as "Jew," with all its connotations of a national but not geographically limited religious, political, and cultural identity. This is particularly the case if we view the Gospel as having been written in the Diaspora, where, according to Lowe himself, the term was most commonly used for the Jewish nation as a whole.[11]

The fact that the same word occurs numerous times and in a variety of contexts tends, in my view, to blur the fine distinctions and nuances implied by these contexts and to generalize the meaning to its broadest possible referent, that is, the Jews as a nation defined by a set of religious beliefs, cultic and liturgical practices, and a sense of peoplehood. As R. A. Culpepper notes, "Even if the Greek term οἱ Ἰουδαῖοι once denoted Judaeans or Jewish authorities, the Gospel of John generalized and stereotyped those who rejected Jesus by its use of this term and elevated the bitterness and hostility of the polemic to a new level."[12] Given the ubiquity of the term Ἰουδαῖος, however, it is curious that while it is applied to Jesus (4:9), it is never used of a figure who is a believer; this despite the fact that almost all the followers of and believers in Jesus within the Gospel narrative, with the exception of the Samaritan woman, her compatriots, and, perhaps, the officer of John 4, are Jewish in the national and ethnic sense. This is true of the primary spokespersons for faith, namely, the first disciples, the man

11. The negative use of the term is not to be attributed to the pre-Johannine source. According to R. T. Fortna, *The Gospel of Signs* (Cambridge, 1970), p. 32 n. 6, the term almost always occurs as an expression of the writer.

12. R. A. Culpepper, "The Gospel of John as a Document of Faith in a Pluralistic Culture," in F. F. Segovia, ed., *"What Is John?"* vol. 1: *Readers and Readings of the Fourth Gospel* (SBLSymS 3; Atlanta, 1996), p. 114.

born blind, the Bethany siblings, Mary Magdalene, and the beloved disciple. The most explicit example is Nathanael, who is praised by Jesus not as a "true Jew" but as a "true Israelite" in whom there is no guile or deceit (1:47)—in contrast, perhaps, to the Jews themselves. Some of them, such as the Bethany siblings, the man born blind, and possibly the beloved disciple, are even Judaean in the narrower sense yet are not referred to as Ἰουδαῖοι.[13]

From this brief survey we conclude that the term Ἰουδαῖος does not refer narrowly to a resident of Judaea but rather denotes a member of a national, religious, cultural, and political group for whom the English word *Jew* is the best signifier. Hence the simple technique of using "Judaean" or "Jewish leader" as a translation of Ἰουδαῖος does not work except (perhaps) for a small number of specific verses and should not be used to explain, or to explain away, the Gospel's hostile remarks about Ἰουδαῖοι.

The Relationship between the Johannine and Jewish Communities

Another issue central to the question of Johannine anti-Judaism concerns the historical relationship between the Johannine and Jewish communities. Many scholars argue that the Gospel's negative comments about Jews are not a reflection of anti-Judaism but rather an expression of a prolonged and violent controversy between the Johannine community and the Jews in the wake of the community's traumatic expulsion from the synagogue.[14] J. L. Martyn, followed by many other scholars, argues that John 9:22; 12:42; and 16:2, which refer to the expulsion from the synagogue of those who confess Jesus to be the Christ, reflect a decision taken at Jamnia in the late first century to insert a "blessing" (understood as a euphemism for curse) on Jewish Christians and other heretics into the Twelfth Benediction of the 'Amidah, the central prayer of the Jewish liturgy.[15] The inclusion of this "blessing," referred to as *birkat ha-minim*, exposed Jewish Christians who continued to participate in synagogue services and hence claimed

---

13. The beloved disciple has friends in high places (18:15) and does not appear on the scene until chapter 13, set in Judaea. There is little exegetical basis for the idea that he is the unnamed disciple of chapter 1.

14. R. Kysar, "The Gospel of John in Current Research," *RelSRev* 9 (1983): 316. The classic statement of the expulsion theory is J. L. Martyn's *History and Theology in the Fourth Gospel*, 2d ed. (Nashville, 1979). See also R. Kysar, "The Promises and Perils of Preaching on the Gospel of John," *Di* 19 (1980): 3, 219.

15. Martyn, *History and Theology*, pp. 50–62.

continued membership in the Jewish community.[16] Suspected Christians were recruited as prayer leaders and then were watched closely to see whether they would recite *birkat ha-minim*. Failure to do so was interpreted as a sign of allegiance to Jesus and cause for expulsion. The strife mirrored in the Gospel therefore pertains to a period when the Johannine community still saw itself as a group within Judaism. For this reason, the conflict is better interpreted as an inner-family feud than a conflict between two religious groups.[17] In this construction of Johannine history, the Gospel of John can be seen as providing support for those Johannine Christians engaged in a struggle with the synagogue, but without intending that his words about "the Jews" be taken as a sweeping condemnation of the Jewish people as a whole.[18]

There are sound reasons, however, to question the historicity of the notion that Johannine Christians were expelled from the synagogue.[19] As Reuven Kimelman argued convincingly, there is no evidence that this prayer referred to Jewish Christians in the first century, that it was ever used as an instrument of exclusion, or that it played any role at all in the eventual parting of the ways between Judaism and Christianity.[20] Pieter van der Horst agrees: "The original Birkat ha-Minim, whatever its text may have been, was never intended to throw Christians out of the synagogues—that door always remained open, even in Jerome's time—but it was a berakah that served to strengthen the bonds of unity within the nation in a time of catastrophe by deterring all those who threatened that unity."[21] Stephen Katz argues that if the curse had the effect of gradual withdrawal of heretics from the Jewish community, this was the result of the dissidents' choice and was not due to a forceful exclusionary ban issued by the Jewish authorities.[22]

Although the views of Kimelman and others are widely conceded, the

16. Among the many scholars who express this view are J. Townsend, "The Gospel of John and the Jews: The Story of a Religious Divorce," in A. Davies, ed., *Antisemitism and the Foundations of Christianity* (New York, 1979), pp. 72–97, p. 87; S. Smalley, *John: Evangelist and Interpreter* (Greenwood, S.C., 1978), p. 143; C. K. Barrett, *The Gospel according to St. John*, 2d ed. (Philadelphia, 1978), p. 361; R. Schnackenburg, *The Gospel according to St. John* (New York, 1982), 2:239.

17. Kysar, "Promises and Perils," pp. 219–20.

18. Ibid.

19. For detailed discussion, see A. Reinhartz, "The Johannine Community and Its Jewish Neighbors: A Reappraisal," in F. F. Segovia, ed., *"What Is John?"* vol. 2: *Literary and Social Readings of the Fourth Gospel* (SBLSymS 7; Atlanta, 1998), pp. 111–38.

20. R. Kimelman, "*Birkat Ha-Minim* and the Lack of Evidence for an Anti-Christian Jewish Prayer in Late Antiquity," in E. P. Sanders et al., eds., *Jewish and Christian Self-Definition*, vol. 2: *Aspects of Judaism in the Greco-Roman Period* (Philadelphia, 1981), p. 226–44, 391–403.

21. P. van der Horst, "The Birkat Ha-Minim in Recent Research," *ExpTim* 105 (1994): 367–68.

22. S.T. Katz, "Issues in the Separation of Judaism and Christianity after 70 C.E.: A Reconsideration," *JBL* 103 (1984): 43–76, p. 74.

exclusion theory has not been abandoned.[23] Some scholars, however, have modified the theory and suggest, for example, that the ban may have been local to the Evangelist's community and not centrally decreed and enforced.[24] A second basis for rethinking the theory, however, comes not from extratextual evidence, or the absence thereof, but from the Gospel narrative itself. The expulsion theory emerges from interpreters' conviction that the Fourth Gospel tells two stories simultaneously: the story of Jesus in the first part of the first century C.E. and the story of the Johannine community some fifty or sixty years later. On this principle, the three passages that refer to the expulsion from the synagogue speak not of a situation in Jesus' own time, when such an expulsion would have been anachronistic, but of an experience of the historical Johannine community.

What complicates this picture and, in my view, undermines the expulsion theory itself is the presence of two passages that, when read on two levels according to this principle, imply a rather different relationship between the Jews and the Johannine Christians than that indicated in the expulsion theory. The first is John 11:1–44, which describes the sisters Mary and Martha in mourning for their brother Lazarus. In a two-level reading of the Gospel, these sisters would represent Johannine Christians. Though apparently known to be "beloved" of Jesus, these women have clearly not been excluded from the Jewish community, as evidenced by the fact that they are comforted in their mourning for Lazarus by "many of the Jews" (11:19). The second passage is John 12:11, which reports the chief priests' plan to execute Lazarus, as well as Jesus, "since it was on account of him that many of the Jews were deserting [ὑπῆγον] and were believing in Jesus." This desertion is not linked in this verse to an official Jewish policy of expulsion but implies an act of free will by the Jews themselves.

A two-level reading of the Gospel therefore implies at least three different models of the historical relationship between the Johannine and Jewish communities. The expulsion passages suggest that Johannine Christians were excluded or expelled from the Jewish community for confessing Jesus to be the Messiah. John 11 implies that known members of the Johannine community were comforted in their mourning by Jews who did not (as yet) believe Jesus to be the Messiah. John 12:11 suggests that some Jews were deserting their community in order to join the Johannine church.

23. See R. Kysar, "Anti-Semitism and the Gospel of John," in C. A. Evans and D. A. Hagner, eds., *Anti-Semitism and Early Christianity: Issues of Polemic and Faith* (Minneapolis, 1993), pp. 113–27, p. 120 n. 18.

24. Culpepper, "Gospel of John," p. 283. Cf. C. Setzer, *Jewish Responses to Early Christians: History and Polemics, 30–150 C.E.* (Minneapolis, 1994), p. 93. Martyn himself, somewhat reluctantly, recognizes this as a possible interpretation of 9:22. Cf. Martyn, *History and Theology,* p. 55 n. 69.

No doubt an elaborate historical and/or redactional theory that would take all three models into account could be constructed. But one can also question the specificity of the two-level reading strategy and of the expulsion theory as the backdrop for and justification of the Gospel's identification of the Jews with the negative pole of its theology. While the two-level reading as proposed by Martyn provides an avenue for imagining a history that is lost to us, we should also remember that the earliest audience would have seen this Gospel as a story of Jesus' life and may not have been as troubled by or knowledgeable about its anachronisms as we are.

Nevertheless, the two-level reading is not completely without its uses. Although it is difficult and possibly misguided to read a specific historical event out of the Fourth Gospel, the insight that the Gospel story would have had some relevance to the situation of the Johannine community that formed its original audience is helpful.[25] What draws the three models of Jewish-Christian relations that we have noted together is the underlying assumption, or perhaps knowledge, of a definitive separation between Judaism and Christianity, at least within the environment in which the Johannine community existed.[26] That is, the Gospel implies that a parting of the ways between the Johannine and the Jewish communities has already occurred at some point prior to the writing of the Gospel, even if we cannot tease out any specific information as to the circumstances under which the parting occurred. Knowledge of such a split provides plausible background to the expulsion passages, which attribute the parting to an act of expulsion occurring in Jesus' time; to the relationship between the Bethany siblings and their Jewish neighbors, which is warm but which also requires that Jews decide either to believe or not; and also to the high priests" fear that Jews were deserting their ancestral faith.

Such a reading also makes sense of the Johannine usage of the term Ἰουδαῖοι, and particularly the avoidance of this label for those who are Jewish in origin but who have become Jesus' disciples and followers. In following Jesus, Jews relinquish the ethnic and national categories that hitherto marked their lives. Believers are reborn from above (3:7), become children of God (1:13), and live in this world though they are not of this world (17:14). If, by the end of the second century C.E., the term Ἰουδαῖος

25. Of course, this too is an assumption—the existence of a Johannine community can be surmised only from the Johannine literature itself.

26. This is not to argue for a universal split between Judaism and Christianity by the end of the first century C.E.. As S. G. Wilson, *Related Strangers: Jews and Christians 70–170 C.E.* (Minneapolis, 1995), p. 143, notes, Jewish Christians and Gentile Judaizers continued to exist and to blur the boundaries between Judaism and Christianity for several centuries.

had already taken on religious connotations, as Cohen asserts, then it would seem that, from the Johannine perspective, those Jews who become believers cease being Jews. This does not mean that social contacts, such as would take place at a time of mourning, were not allowed, or that Jews were not sometimes interested in Christianity or vice versa, but that in becoming a follower of Jesus, one passed not only from death to life (5:24) but also from one religious/ethnic group to another. Johannine Christians did not maintain their activities in or ties to the synagogue as a place of worship; Jews by definition did not believe in or follow Jesus.

Conclusion

The Johannine use of the term Ἰουδαῖος and the possibility that, in John's historical context, being a follower of Jesus and being a Jew were mutually exclusive categories help account for the identification of the Jews with the negative terms in the contrasting pairs, such as light/darkness and believing/not believing, in which much of Johannine theology is couched. Against this background, I argue that the Fourth Gospel does not merely speak about "the Jews" as a symbol for the unbelieving world but also sees the historical community of Jewish nonbelievers as children of the devil and sinners destined for death. Further, the Evangelist does not distinguish between the Jews who, in his understanding, persecuted Jesus and led him to his death and those in his own time with whom his community may have had an uneasy relationship. While he was not specifically anticipating the impact that his writings might have on Jewish-Christian relations throughout the millennia, the universal tone of many of the discourses suggests the Evangelist did not exclude from his negative assessment those Jews in the future who would also reject the word of Jesus as conveyed in his Gospel, who would refuse to believe that Jesus is the Christ, Son of God, and, therefore, who would not attain life in his name.

I now return to the three main topics with which we began. I have argued that the anti-Jewish elements are present in the text itself. This claim does not exonerate the interpretative tradition, but it does suggest that anti-Jewish readings of this text are by no means distortions of the Gospel's meaning. This is not to say that the principal goal of the Gospel is to promote anti-Judaism. Rather, the Gospel's anti-Judaism is a by-product of the Evangelist's strong convictions regarding the identity and salvific role of Jesus, on the one hand, and his tendency to view not only attributes and actions but also communities in a polarized way, on the other.

But anti-Judaism, and its more recent corollary, anti-Semitism, are not simply intellectual positions that we may abhor or tolerate, depending on who we are. They are also powerful emotions, whether or not they lead to hostile behavior. It is common for us scholars to read sacred texts in a dispassionate and emotionally disengaged manner and to treat these texts as if they were written in the same vein.[27] But perhaps we should, at least for a moment, allow ourselves to engage with the text and to recognize the emotions that seethe beneath its surface.[28] The audience to whom the Gospel is addressed (cf. 20:30–31), like the disciples within the Gospel narrative, are not only to know and understand Jesus' relationship to the Father (10:38) and to believe the words of spirit and life (6:63–74) but also to love one another (13:34) and let their hearts rejoice (16:22). If so, are they not also to identify with Jesus and against those who hate, persecute, and kill Jesus, and who, Jesus warns, will threaten their own lives as well? Are we to imagine that they looked kindly upon those whom Jesus called children of the devil? The power of emotion is clearly seen in the fact that Easter, when the passion narratives were read, was a popular season for anti-Semitic pogroms in eastern Europe. While the Evangelist could not have foreseen and, I hope, would not have condoned the violence that some of his images and words have justified over the centuries, it strikes me as unlikely that he himself would have distinguished between the Jews in his narrative and those in the world outside the narrative.

The Fourth Evangelist believes in the historical truth of the narrative he is relating, including the elements of conflict between Jesus and the Jews. His main concern is not to encode the events experienced by his community into a cryptic narrative but to present his own understanding of Jesus in a way that may encourage others to become or to remain faithful. His strongly dualistic language provides the terms with which readers can define themselves—as believing in Jesus, coming to the light, having eternal life, and becoming children of God. The Gospel also constructs a (negative) role for those who do not make this life choice and thus helps define the relationship between the community and those outside it. This framework is built on the knowledge of the definitive split between the Johannine and Jewish communities and does not allow for salvation for nonbelievers. Jews, like all others, will have eternal life only if they believe

27. Recent exceptions are M. W. Newheart, "Toward a Psycho-Literary Reading of the Fourth Gospel," in Segovia, ed., "*What Is John?*" vol. 1: *Readers and Readings*, pp. 43–58; and J. L. Staley, *Reading with a Passion: Rhetoric, Autobiography, and the American West in the Gospel of John* (New York, 1995).

28. Cf. A. Reinhartz, "On Travel, Translation, and Ethnography: The Gospel of John at the Turn of the Century," in Segovia, ed., "*What Is John?*" vol. 2: *Literary and Social Readings*, pp. 249–56.

Jesus to be the Christ and Son of God, but in taking on this belief, they also leave behind their own community and Jewish identity.

If this is so, what are the implications in our own time? In his call for an ethically responsible interpretation of John, R. A. Culpepper suggests that "the Fourth Gospel's declaration of God's boundless love for the world undermines its polemic against the Jews."[29] My own, more pessimistic reading is that the Fourth Gospel's polemic against the Jews (minus the quotation marks) undermines its declaration of God's boundless love for the world. Surely a text that is so problematic in itself must be handled with care. The canonical status of the text, and hence the authority ascribed to it, makes it difficult to ignore. From my perspective, New Testament scholars' efforts to limit the meaning of Ἰουδαῖος and to explain John's comments on Jews and Judaism as a response to Jewish exclusion are not primarily dispassionate academic interpretations but rather attempts to defuse the Gospel's anti-Judaism and make its expressions more acceptable to a post-Holocaust audience without undermining its status as an authoritative and sacred text.[30] Although I have argued that these attempts are not convincing, at least not to me, I can see their usefulness in the pulpit and other venues in which the Gospel is encountered, particularly those that occur in a context in which the intricacies of the text cannot be explored at length. Nevertheless, my fear is that the effect of such interpretations, that is, of dressing the Johannine Jews in quotation marks, is to whitewash this text and absolve it of responsibility for the anti-Jewish emotions and attitudes it conveys.

29. Culpepper, "Gospel of John," p. 127.
30. Ibid.

PART THREE

CHAPTER 11

John and Judaism

C. Kingsley Barrett

Any contribution to this discussion should begin with the recognition that it stands in danger of the unforgivable exegetical sin, the sin of attempting to make a passage mean something other than the meaning intended by the author and conveyed by the words. If, in our text, there are passages that in the author's intention are untrue or unkind, and that have in consequence given hurt to some readers, it must be recognized that this is what they are and do. The exegete may say: "I disagree with these words; I dissociate myself from them, I wish they had not been written," but he may not twist or conceal their meaning. Some scholars have the ambition to develop an alternative interpretation of John 8:31–59. Alternative to what? Alternative to misinterpretations, on whatever ground these may be based? Yes, of course. We seek the true interpretation. But the context within which this aim is expressed suggests an interpretation of John's text that shall be less offensive. There are indeed interpretations of John 8 that have made the passage more offensive and damaging than a correct interpretation would be, and the question must be looked at from all sides, but in such a matter as this, the exegete must be more than ordinarily careful to employ no criterion but truth. As in all his or her work, the exegete must be prepared to ask questions that are only indirectly exegetical but are nevertheless important in the work. Such are historical questions: Were the words in our text spoken by Jesus himself, or did they arise within the postresurrection community of Christians? What background of thought and belief—theological, social, political—provides the raw material for work on them? I doubt whether questions of *Wirkungsgeschichte*, important though these are, have the same relevance. The *Wirkung* has too often been the result of mistaken exegesis.

This contribution falls into three main parts; each part contains an answer to a question. The three main questions discussed here are:

1. Is affinity of John's Gospel with Gnosticism a possible (partial) explanation for his anti-Jewish statements?
2. How does the Fourth Evangelist differ from the other so-called anti-Jewish New Testament writers?
3. Is canonicity of biblical texts still a basic criterion for their authority for theology today? Do theologians have the freedom or even the duty to practice *Sachkritik*?

If there is any connecting thread it must be found in the task of exegesis, which is approached from different angles.

Speaking about "affinity of John's Gospel with Gnosticism" the word *affinity* is well chosen because it leaves open a variety of interpretations. The two extremes, of wholesale borrowing and total rejection, are both mistaken. The "historicizing" or "Christianizing" of a Gnostic myth (terms I have myself on occasion used), often taken as expressing Bultmann's understanding of the literary and theological processes underlying the Fourth Gospel, are also unsatisfactory insofar as they suggest, if they do not actually assume, the existence of an established Gnostic redeemer myth as the basis of the Gospel, Christianized by the Evangelist. By contrast, the common but simplistic criticism of Bultmann that Gnosticism is a postapostolic, second-century development is invalid unless the word *Gnosticism* is defined as appropriate only to such developed systems as that of Valentinus. If a term such as *pre-Gnosticism* or *proto-Gnosticism* or *gnosis* is preferred, so be it; it is certain that thought of a Gnostic kind existed and was permeating Christian thought as early as Paul, a generation before John. Such thought was developing, in relation to both Judaism and Christianity, through the second half of the first Christian century, and it was a process by which John was influenced and which he in turn influenced. It is sufficient here to quote the Gnostic definition of eternal life in John 17:3 ("And this is eternal life, that they may know you, the only true God, and Jesus Christ whom you have sent"), which could be used in any Gnostic system with the substitution of an appropriate name for Jesus Christ, and the importance in John of the sending to earth of a heavenly being. This is a basic theme of the Gospel, where Jesus repeatedly claims that he has been sent by God (e.g., 3:17, ἀποστέλλειν; 4:34, πέμπειν, 3:31, ἔρχεσθαι) and that, after fulfilling his mission (of bearing witness to the truth; e.g., 18:37), he will return to heaven whence he came (e.g., 8:14).

There are touches of the Old Testament, if not of the New, in *Poimandres*, which in its earliest form is to be dated little, if at all, after John.[1] With John, *Poimandres* bears witness to a primitive development of Gnosticism toward the end of the first century.

A very important contribution to the study of this development is made in an article by N. A. Dahl.[2] This cannot be reviewed here, and it is doubtful whether it can be accepted *in toto*; the association of John 8:44 with Polycarp 7.1 is, however, important. This passage deals with Christian heretics: those who do not confess Jesus Christ to have come in the flesh (cf. 1 John 4:2; 2 John 7—Polycarp's connection with Johannine Christianity is clear); those who do not profess the mystery of the cross; those who pervert the Lord's oracles to suit their own desires and say there is no resurrection or judgment. It is clear that the heresy is (or heresies are) of a docetic kind and therefore presumably are Gnostic in origin. It is doubtful whether Polycarp would have distinguished sharply among the three things he predicates of his heretics: is antichrist, is of the devil, is the firstborn of Satan. It is doubtful also whether under πρωτότοκος τοῦ Σατανᾶ he is alluding to the tradition that Cain was born as the result of the seduction of Eve by Satan. First John 3:12 (Κάϊν ἐκ τοῦ πονηροῦ ἦν) could perhaps reflect this belief, but the context makes it clear that those who do not love one another fall into the same category, as a matter of resemblance rather than of descent.

It is, in fact, a moral, and to some extent doctrinal, line of descent, rather than a physical or metaphysical one. The epistle's ἐκ τοῦ πονηροῦ, used of Cain, the murderer of his brother, must be compared with its ἐκ τοῦ κόσμου (1 John 2:16; 4:5). Those who are described by this term are not thought of as related to the κόσμος by a process of generation. They have gone out from John's Christian community and learned to speak ἐκ τοῦ κόσμου (4:5). They have acquired the world's language (which is, indeed, Gnostic language) and accordingly have gained the world's ear; the world listened to them as it does not listen to John and his orthodox (but old-fashioned) colleagues. The suggestion that Cain was actually begotten by Satan seems to be late and is not required by the context of Polycarp's epistle, where the interest (in Polycarp 7) is, as we have seen, moral and doctrinal.

---

1. R. Reitzenstein, *Poimandres* (Leipzig, 1904), p. 36, holds that: "die Urform des Poimandres vor den Beginn des zweiten Jahrhunderts n. Chr. fällt." So perhaps for the *Urform*; most place the work as we have it in the second or third century.

2. N. A. Dahl, "Der Erstgeborene Satans und der Vater des Teufels (Polyk.7.1 und Joh 8.44)," in W. Eltester and F. H. Kettler, eds., *Apophoreta*, FS E. Haenchen (*BZNW* 30; Berlin, 1964), pp. 70–84.

This is further illustrated by Philo's tract on the posterity (ἔγγονοι) of Cain. Philo allegorizes the city that Cain was building (ἣν οἰκοδομῶν, Gen. 4:17; *Post.* 33); real cities are for many inhabitants, and in Cain's time there were at most only three persons available to inhabit the city. Hence (*Post.* 51) βέλτιον ἀλληγοροῦντας λέγειν ἐστιν ὅτι καθάπερ πόλιν τὸ αὑτοῦ δόγμα κατασκευάζειν ὁ Κάιν ἔγνωκε. "His inhabitants are the wise in their own conceit, devotees of impiety, godlessness, self-love, arrogance, false opinion, men ignorant of real wisdom. . . . His laws are various forms of lawlessness and injustice, unfairness, licentiousness, audacity, senselessness, self-will, immoderate indulgence in pleasures, unnatural lusts that may not be named."[3]

The Johannine affinity with Gnosticism emphasizes the meaning of John 8:44, which is in any case reasonably clear from the context. John's language points not so much to a necessary genetic relation as to moral resemblance. The devil is a figure matching that of the descending and ascending heavenly messenger—in John, the Son of man, who is also Word and Messiah. The coming of the Word meets with a twofold reception. He came to his own appointed place, and those who were his own people did not receive him; rather, some did not and some did, and to those who did receive him he gave the power to become children of God, to live as God's children (John 1:11, 12). What happened to those who did not receive him the prologue does not tell. It is in chapter 8 that we learn of their preference for the alternative supernatural visitant, the devil, whose children they now show themselves to be by their readiness to carry out his desires—murder and lying.

That their relation with the devil was a matter of imitation rather than of genetic descent was perceived by the church fathers. Thus already Irenaeus (*Haer.* 4.41.2), commenting on Matt. 13:38 but with John 8:44 clearly in mind, writes: "Filius enim, quemadmodum et quidam ante nos[4] dixit, dupliciter intellegitur: alius quidem secundum naturam, eo quod natus sit filius, alius autem secundum id quod factus est reputatur filius." A few lines later, Irenaeus refers explicitly to John 8:44: "qui autem non credunt[5] et non faciunt ejus voluntatem filii et angeli sunt diaboli, secundum id quod opera diaboli faciunt." Similarly, Augustine (*Tract. Ev. Jo.* 42.10)

3. *Post.* 52, see P. Alexandrinus, *Philo, with an English Translation* (*LCL* Greek Authors), trans. by F. H. Colson and G. H. Whitaker, vol. 2, London, 1968.

4. Who? This interpretation must go back a long way toward John's own time.

5. There is a problem here in relation to John 8:31: it seems that Jesus was addressing Jews who believed in him. If the solution of the problem is not to be found in careless editing, it must be sought in the theme of duality, discussed at the end of this essay. For the textual problems here, see SC 100.1.283–5. See also Clement of Alexandria, *Strom.* 1.1 (PG 8, col. 688).

uses his exposition of John 8 to rebut the Manicheans,[6] who take up the words "Vos a patre diabolo estis" and conclude that they mean "quod essent illi velut natura mali, ducentes originem de gente contraria tenebrarum." Augustine continues: "Sic errant, sic excaecantur. . . . Bona est enim omnis natura . . . unde ergo judaei filii diaboli? Imitando, non nascendo." This is proved by the quotation of Ezek. 16:3—"ille inobiendo et superbiendo lapsus est angelus et factus est diabolus."

It is John's affinity with the Gnostic myth of the descending and ascending redeemer-revealer that gives form to the language of John 8. It gives form to the language; it does not create the thought behind it. That the language should be (in part) derived from Gnostic mythology does not explain or justify (if justification is needed) that which the language expresses; and the language expresses uninhibited denunciation. This is what no exegetical acrobatics can remove from the verse before us. More important than the considerations hitherto adduced is the fact that John believed (rightly or wrongly) that he was describing persons who were engaged in plotting and, indeed, attempting the murder of Jesus (8:59). He also believed that they had, in the end, succeeded in their attempt, for (again, rightly or wrongly) his passion narrative tends on the whole to exonerate the Roman authorities and blame the Jews for the crucifixion. He was probably also affected by the belief (correct or incorrect) that in his own day Jews were plotting and perhaps securing the death of Christian believers (cf. John 16:2). If, therefore, the devil was a murderer from the beginning (8:44), they shared with him his major characteristic, and in the sense described (Augustine's *imitando*) might be described as derived from him.[7] Again, their action was based on assertions about Jesus: he had a demon; he was a Samaritan; he was born of fornication. These assertions (according to John) were not true; John probably believed that the persons who made them knew that they were not true. They were therefore lying, and about a matter of ultimate significance. Lying also was a characteristic of the devil.[8] What must be added to this is that nothing implies the belief that this damning charge applies to anyone other than those who were, at that time, contradicting the truth (as John believed it to be) about Jesus and seeking to bring about his death. These persons were indeed Jews, but they were a particular group of Jews, living at a particular time and place. Nothing is

---

6. Cf. *Acta Disputationis Archelai. . . et Manetis* 33 (M. J. Routh, *Reliquiae Sacrae* [Oxford, 1848], 5:122–26).

7. Cf. Origen, *Comm. Jo.*20.21(19).

8. This goes back to Gen. 3:4: "You will not die"—as in fact they did; both lying and murder were involved.

said about the Jewish people as a whole; and the question of race is not even remotely in mind. It is true, and the ground of infinite sorrow, that John's words have been understood to apply to the Jewish people as a whole. John is open to the charge of having written in a way that was capable of being misunderstood; he may serve as a dreadful warning to all writers to watch their language and guard against ambiguity. But it is fair to say in his defense that he was writing for Ephesus (say) in the years 80–100 and would hardly expect to be read in the 1930s and 1940s.[9]

There is, then, a Gnostic element in the way in which John expresses the necessary difference between Judaism and Christianity; it seems to contribute to the form of the provocative charge of 8:44: "You are from your father the devil." This element gives a distinctive color to Johannine polemic, but it is not the only constituent of it. There is, for example, a treatment of Torah, epigrammatically summed up in 1:17 (the Law was given through Moses, grace and truth came by Jesus Christ), that clearly echoes that of Paul, though there is little or no trace of any literary connection. For Paul, the Law is a good gift from God, abused when it is understood and used not in terms of faith, as was intended, but in terms of works. It is holy, righteous, good, spiritual; it sets forth the whole duty of man in the command to love one's neighbor. It contains hints and promises of the salvation that was to come. Yet not only is its glory inferior to that of the gospel, but it engenders passions of sin, and the only right course is to die to it. In John, the Law was given not *by* Moses but *through* Moses (1:17; but cf. 7:19), and the subject of the active verb implied by the passive ἐδόθη can only be God. The Law foretells the coming of Christ (1:46), but it is also invoked by those who would kill him (19:7) and treated as a mark of religious superiority. John repeats the command of love (13:34) but, so far from drawing it out of Torah, describes it as a new commandment. Judaism is not using its most precious possession as it ought.

Lacking in Paul[10] but present in John's criticism of Judaism is a political element. This is particularly apparent in John's passion narrative, where John shares the tendency of all the Evangelists to spare the Roman authorities and blame the Jews for the death of Jesus but in fact does more than this. The evidence may be quickly sketched. It is worth noting at the out-

---

9. See note 5, above. It is often held that not only 8:31 but 8:30–36 is a gloss. These verses, however, invoke the theme of freedom (here only in the chapter), which is the criterion of faith. The Jews in question profess to be in no need of the liberation Christ gives and thereby show that they do not understand the meaning of ultimate freedom, which is freedom from sin, the latter typified by murder and lying. Application of this criterion to their "faith" shows its unreality.

10. Rom. 13:1–7 may be an exception.

set that John describes the party that arrested Jesus as including a cohort and a tribune (18:12). The Romans were thus involved from the beginning. The interrogation of Jesus is conducted first by the high-priestly group (18:13–28), but after this, the most notable feature is a sequence of conversations between Jesus and Pilate. The first is contained in 18:30–38. It deals with the βασιλεία (that is, with the authority) of Jesus and his witness to the truth. Here the Jews seem to be forgotten (except in Pilate's rhetorical question "I am not a Jew, am I?" 18:35).[11] The Roman soldiers mock Jesus' kingship (19:1–5), and Pilate seeks to hand over responsibility for the trial to the Jews (19:6, 7). The second conversation ensues (19:8–11). Any authority Pilate may have is secondary and derivative—it comes from God and is a kind of subordinate executive authority, so that he is less guilty than he who handed Jesus over (ὁ παραδούς) to Pilate. Opinions differ regarding the identity of this person. Some think that the Jews, personified and represented by Caiaphas, are meant; more probably ὁ παραδούς is, as elsewhere in the tradition, Judas Iscariot (the devil— 6:70f.). The Jews now begin to put pressure on Pilate by bringing his loyalty into question: "If you release this man, you are no friend of the emperor" (19:12). Pilate retorts and provokes their avowal "We have no king but the emperor" (19:15), which represents the Jews as abdicating their position as the people whose king is God alone. Pilate has Jesus crucified under the title, "Jesus of Nazareth the King of the Jews." Jesus thus dies, according to John, as the king whom the Jews refuse, sacrificing their theological for their political security. In 8:44 they are theological apostates; here they are political traitors—at least, their most influential representatives are.

All this means that behind John's presentation of the matter is a good deal of theological and political thought. If we are to compare John with other parts of the New Testament, we turn naturally to the Synoptic Gospels, less sophisticated in their treatment of the historical tradition than John but showing in their passion narratives the same interest in blaming Jews and exonerating Romans—though it is fair to ask whether Roman authorities would have taken action against the Galilean teacher, or would even have noticed him, if he had not been brought to their attention by Jews. None of the three Synoptics has much regard for either the Jewish or the Roman

---

11. On this theme, here and below, I may refer not only to C. K. Barrett, *The Gospel according to St John: An Introduction with Commentary and Notes on the Greek Text* (London, 1955; 2d ed., 1978), but also to C. K. Barrett, "Johanneisches Christentum," in J. Becker, ed., *Johanneisches Christentum. Die Anfänge des Christentums* (Stuttgart, 1987), pp. 255–78 (ET: *Christian Beginnings* [Nashville, 1993], pp. 330–58.

authorities; indeed, it is hard to read the three accounts, especially Mark's, without feeling some sympathy for both parties. The Jews had some ground for thinking Jesus guilty of blasphemy, acting as he did with a more-than-human authority that he refused to explain or justify; yet he had not been guilty of blasphemy as understood in accordance with the rules.[12] The Romans had some ground for thinking Jesus guilty of *laesa maiestas*: he spoke of a kingdom, and if he did not proclaim himself its anointed king, others suggested it. Yet where was the army he had led against Rome? And had he not said, "Give to the emperor the things that are the emperor's?" (e.g., Mark 12:17). Both sides were in something of a quandary and may well have thought it best to enter into collusion to get rid of him. All this is not very different from John, though John handles the matter at a deeper level.

The Synoptic Gospels contain a good deal of controversial material before the Passion is reached. Though it is true that every occurrence in John of the word Ἰουδαῖος ought to be studied before any conclusions are reached, it is not far wrong to say that in the majority of cases, the word could well be rendered or paraphrased "the opposition." The Synoptic Gospels are nearer to history in mentioning separately (and, to a limited extent, understanding correctly) the different groups: Pharisees, Sadducees, scribes, (chief) priests, rulers, teachers of the Law, Herodians. This is not the place to conduct an analysis. There is in these Gospels a greater attempt to relate the polemical encounters to specific themes, as, for example, when the Sadducees debate with Jesus and his disciples on the theme of resurrection. Again, however, the essential question is that of authority, complicated no doubt by the still-disputed question of where authority lay in Judaism itself after the collapse of political structures in 70 C.E. The supplanting of Judaism by the church becomes clearest in Matthew, not only in the often-quoted verse 27:25 ("His blood be on us and on our children") but in such passages as 21:41, where, in the parable of the vineyard, Jesus makes the owner of the vineyard say, with clarity not found in Mark and Luke, that he will bring those evil men to an evil end and will let out the vineyard to other workers, who will deliver to him the fruit at the due seasons. Matthew presumably believed the saying of 27:25 to be an authentic utterance but even so should have been aware of the fact that those present at the crucifixion had neither right nor power to implicate their children in their misdeeds.[13]

12. See m. Sanh. 7:5.

13. Is it possible that Matthew knew the sentence was capable of a double meaning? Cf. the lines in Charles Wesley's hymn "O Jesus, My Hope": "Each moment applied / my weakness to hide, / Thy blood be upon me, and always abide."

The Pauline epistles bear witness to the existence in the early years of those who understood Christianity as a form—no doubt they would have said, the best form—of Judaism. They were Christians in the sense that they believed Jesus of Nazareth to have been the Messiah (not necessarily that he was the Son of God). Gentiles, they held, might join them only by becoming Jews, circumcised and observant of the Law. To Paul, this attitude was intolerable, not because he disliked Jews but because after his conversion Christ had taken a place in his theology and in his personal life that was incompatible with any alternative religious authority. The very term *Christ*, however, meant that Jesus had been, in Paul's belief, not inconsistent with but the fulfillment of Judaism, and Paul's theological language is rich in words—*law, sin, grace, righteousness*, for example—that it is impossible to understand without reference to their use (in Greek and in the underlying Hebrew) in the Old Testament, though this use was always given a new direction by the new figure of Christ crucified and risen. The same tension appears in Paul's understanding of himself. He never ceases to be a Jew (e.g., Rom. 11:1; 2 Cor. 11:22; Phil. 3:5f.); loyalty to the synagogue and its discipline brought him under the lash (2 Cor. 11:24). Yet he can write (1 Cor. 9:20), "To the Jews I became as a Jew"—which at least on the surface implies that he is not, in fact, a Jew.[14] He is a Jew who has been transferred into the messianic age.[15]

This ambiguity of personal existence may go some little way toward explaining the problems that arise when Paul's attitude to Jews and Judaism is considered. Two passages are always discussed; they appear to point in opposite directions.

In 1 Thess. 2:14–16, Paul speaks of the way in which Christians in Judaea have suffered at the hands of their fellow Jews, "who killed both the Lord Jesus and the prophets, and drove us out; they displease God and oppose everyone by hindering us from speaking to the Gentiles so that they may be saved. Thus they have constantly been filling up the measure of their sins; but God's wrath has overtkaen them at last." The other passage is much longer and cannot be summarized here: Romans 9–11. In this passage, Paul twice (9:1–5; 10:1) affirms his affection and concern for the Jews; in fact, his ministry to the Gentiles, to which he has been called by God, is for their benefit (11:13), for the salvation of the Gentiles will lead to the salvation of the Jews. God does not go back on his gracious acts and his call (11:29), and in the end, all Israel will be saved.

14. I have used only the epistles here in order not to be hampered by historical problems in Acts. For the attitude of Acts to the Jews, see below.

15. Cf. H. J. Schoeps, *Paulus* (Tübingen, 1959), pp. 95–110: "Paulus als Denker der postmessianischen Situation."

The two passages are so different from each other that they constitute a considerable problem. It is impossible to doubt that the passage in Romans (much longer and more detailed and in a later epistle) represents Paul's mature thought; that in 1 Thessalonians may mean less than on the surface it appears to mean, may be a gloss inserted after 70 C.E., may come from a moment of thoughtless anger as Paul is moved by undeserved suffering. One may think of 1 Thessalonians as a reaction to persecution, Romans as a reaction to unbelief.[16] In Romans, it is impossible to question Paul's devotion to his own people; his belief that they have mistaken and misused their greatest treasure, the Torah; and his conclusion that God has not cast off God's own people. Yet Paul could not escape the fact that while Gentiles all over the world were accepting the gospel, Jews were rejecting it. His explanation is cast not in terms of Gnostic mythology but of grace. The gospel can be understood only as the free mercy, grace, of God, and this can be grasped only by those who are in *and know that they are in* a state of disobedience. Only those who know that they have been disobedient can know that they have been forgiven. But God's calling remains, though it remains as calling, and a positive response to it is not guaranteed. God's ultimate purpose is the salvation of all Jews. But Paul does not say that God's intention will meet with universal acceptance or that Jews can dispense their own saving Messiah.

It is natural to turn from Paul to Acts, where most of the evidence is focused on Paul. Before he appears, it seems that the Jews are accepting the gospel (but this need mean little more than that they are accepting the messiahship of Jesus) in large numbers: three thousand (Acts 2:41), even five thousand (Acts 4:4). After the conversion of Saul, there is no further indication of such large numbers (except at Acts 21:20, πόσαι μυριάδες), and the narrative supports the impression given by Romans 9–11: the majority of Jews do not believe. There is already in the early chapters a move against Stephen (Acts 6 and 7), and Stephen's speech makes a sharp attack on his fellow Jews, who (he says) have rejected the word God spoke to them through the prophets, preferring the institutionalized religion of the Tem-

---

16. I am drawn to the explanation given long ago by J. A. Bengel, *Gnomon Novi Testamenti,* 8th ed. (Stuttgart, 1887), p. 812: "Sub Herode Agrippa res Judaica refloruerat; sed eo mortuo (Act. 12,23), rediere procuratores Romani Cumanus et Felix eorumque successores magis magisque Judaeos vexabant. Scripta est haec epistola AD 48, et circa id tempus, in paschali festo, ingens multitudo Hierosolymis, orto tumultu, oppressa est. Nonnulli plus 30 millia narrant." See Josephus, *J. W.* 2.224–7; *Ant.* 20, 105–111. For the number, cf. Eusebius, *Hist. eccl.* 2.19.1. If reports such as this, perhaps further exaggerated, reached Paul at the time he was writing to Thessalonica (still better if we think of 50 C.E. rather than 48), he might well have thought that total war between Rome and Israel was about to break out. He would have been mistaken by no more than sixteen years.

ple. It is, however, incorrect to say that the book ends by writing off the mission of the Jews.[17] It is Paul's insistence that his is the true version of Judaism that most incenses the Jews. It is clear, however, that in general it is (in Acts; cf. 2 Cor. 11:24, 26) the Jews who constitute the threat to Paul's life; the Romans rarely do more than see fair play. But Luke understands Paul as, like Stephen, a representative of Diaspora Judaism. This is hardly correct; it is, however, part of what lies behind Acts as the essential question: What do you mean by a Jew? It is Luke's conviction that true Judaism is represented by Paul, though he is attacked by those who think of themselves as the authorized exponents of Judaism.

Notwithstanding this and the general opposition to Paul's mission by Jews, Luke insists that Jews—especially, of course, Christian Jews—have their rights. They must not be expected to compromise their Judaism by eating with Gentiles unless the Gentiles observe basic regulations about food (Acts 15:19–21) and may reasonably expect to be convinced that Paul is not an apostate (21:20–25). According to Luke, Paul himself teaches only what is contained in the Law and the Prophets (26:22), together with the messiahship of Jesus, and is astonished that he should be accused by Jews (26:2), though he is eventually obliged to call to mind the words of Isaiah (Isa. 6:9, 10; Acts 28:26, 27) and to recognize in his turning to the Gentiles the intention of God.

The question "What do you mean by a Jew?" or "Who is a true Jew?" recurs in Revelation, probably, in its present form, roughly contemporary with Acts, and full of Old Testament imagery and of Semitic syntax.[18] The question arises explicitly in the seven letters (Rev. 2, 3). In 2:9 and 3:9 we hear of those who say that they are Jews and are not, but constitute in fact a "synagogue of Satan." These blaspheme and probably persecute the readers of the book; they recall the scene that J. L. Martyn finds behind John 9[19] and Satan's attack on believers (Rev. 20:2–7; cf. the other evil characters in Revelation—the devil, the snake, the dragon, the beast, the false prophet). The Great City, which as the scene of the crucifixion must be Jerusalem, is spiritually called Sodom and Egypt (11:8), the place of wickedness and oppression—which now, paradoxically, are made to appear

---

17. Chapter 28 ends with Paul receiving all who came to him. This cannot exclude Jews, and the point of the quotation from Isaiah (Acts 28:26, 27) is that Paul's mission is not to be regarded as a failure; its outcome was foretold in scripture.

18. See, inter alia, R. H. Charles, *The Revelation of St John* (ICC; Edinburgh, 1920), 1:cxvii–clix; G. Mussies, "The Morphology of Koine Greek, as Used in the Apocalypse of St John," (NovTSup 27; Leiden, 1971); S. Thompson, *The Apocalypse and Semitic Syntax* (SNTSMS 52; Cambridge, 1985); S. E. Porter, "The Language of the Apocalypse," *NTS* 35 (1989): 582–603.

19. J. L. Martyn, *History and Theology in the Fourth Gospel,* 2d ed. (Nashville, 1979), pp. 24–36.

as the work of Jews. The Christians are the true Israel, the true people of God. Their capital is the New Jerusalem (21:2, 10); they are now the twelve tribes of the sons of Israel (21:12). These are matters of eschatological conviction; they have not yet appeared on the level of history.

In comparison with John's Gospel, John's Revelation (they cannot be the same John) contains little argument; it is essentially assertion, the defiant assertion of a persecuted group, and it must be remembered that persecution is by no means the work of Jews only; it comes also from the heathen, and they (for example, the Roman emperors) are at least equally regarded as agents of the powers of evil. But there is fierce conflict between Jewish and Christian groups. It is not hard to imagine a cross-street shouting match between the synagogue (of Satan!) and the church, each convinced that it is the true people of God. And probably brickbats are being thrown, as well as words. There is, it seems, less mutual understanding, less attempt to achieve understanding, than in John and Acts. We may perhaps see the effect (perhaps also, at a different date, the cause) of the *birkat ha-minim.*

Other early Christian writings must be treated very briefly. The author (or authors) of the pastoral epistles stands within the Pauline tradition, from which he has learned that Paul was frequently in trouble with persons of Jewish origin. The references, however, are more than a cloak of pseudonymity; Jews were still a problem when the epistles were written, but the Judaism then current was neither the Judaism nor the Judaizing Christianity of Paul's time but a blend of Judaism and Gnosticism. Both elements constitute, in the author's mind, perils for the Christian faith. The strongest language directed against Jews personally occurs in 1 Tim. 1:7–11: they are ignorant people who represent themselves as teachers of law (νομοδιδάσκαλοι) yet do not know how to use the law (itself a good thing) properly (νομίμως).[20] This is a relatively mild form of *odium theologicum,* and for us, the main importance of the pastorals is that they support the view that a blend of Judaism and Gnosticism, with varying support and opposition from Christians, was in existence when John wrote. Other parts of the New Testament must be passed over; this is unfortunate, but study of the catholic epistles would contribute little of first importance. The same is true of the Didache and *1 Clement.* We must look briefly at Ignatius and Polycarp.

---

20. See C. K. Barrett, *The Pastoral Epistles* (Oxford, 1962), p. 10–17; also on 1 Tim. 1:7–11, 13; Titus 1:10, 14; 3:9.

"Jews and Judaizers in the Epistles of Ignatius" I have discussed else-where.[21] I confine myself here to quotation of the concluding sentence of that essay:[22] "As most more recent students have recognized, Lightfoot was wrong in identifying Ignatius" attack on Judaizing with Paul's and part of the difficulty in defining the Judaizers' beliefs . . . is due to the fact that Ignatius himself finds the Judaizers easier to define sociologically than the-ologically. The Hellenistic world in general had noted the existence of the Jews as an ethnic group with strange sociological characteristics, to be hated and scorned, or, it may be, tolerated; it is one of the tragedies of Jewish-Christian relations that the church, which had at first, in the person of Paul, dealt with the relationship theologically, so soon fell out of theology and into sociology, adopting the common Hellenistic attitude."

The tendency observable in Ignatius reappears in Polycarp. The Jews are represented as playing a leading part in securing Polycarp's martyrdom. (See the Martyrdom 12:2; 13:1 [ὡς ἔθος αὐτοῖς]; 17:2; 18:1.) Little love seems to be lost on either side.

After this, it is a relief to encounter the relatively amiable discussion or debate in Justin's *Dialogue with Trypho*. This is far too large a work to be seriously discussed here,[23] but its existence and temperate tone, in the mid-dle of the second century, make it a phenomenon of great importance, unfortunately without any real parallel in early Christian literature.

Behind these matters lies a historical question so difficult (because of the paucity of the evidence) that in this setting it can only be mentioned and not discussed; it must, however, be mentioned, because it is bound up with the question of the relations that obtained between Jews and Christians in what may be termed the Johannine period, say, 80–100 C.E. J. Jervell[24] has maintained that in the closing decades of the first century the conservative Jewish Christian group, though numerically a minority, exercised an in-fluence on developing Christianity (including books of the New Testa-ment) that was out of proportion to their numbers. This is a serious and

21. In C. K. Barrett, "Jews and Judaizers in the Epistles of Ignatius," in R. Hamerton-Kelly and R. Scroggs, *Jews, Greeks and Christians: Essays in Honor of W. D. Davies* (Leiden, 1976), pp. 220–44.
22. Ibid., p. 244.
23. H. M. Gwatkin, *Early Church History to A.D. 313,* 2d ed. (London, 1927), p. 17: "In the end Trypho declares himself greatly edified by the discussion, politely wishes him (Justin) a prosperous voy-age, and asks to be remembered as a friend. But Trypho was an exceptional Jew." Perhaps also Justin was an exceptional Christian. See also E. F. Osborn, *Justin Martyr* (BHT 47; Tübingen, 1973), index, "Jews and Judaism."
24. In several works, but especially J. Jervell, "The Mighty Minority," *ST* 34 (1980): 13–38 (reprinted in J. Jervell, *The Unknown Paul: Essays on Luke-Acts and Early Christian History* [Minneapolis, 1984], pp. 26–51).

important suggestion, which (as Jervell himself points out) goes back to A. Hilgenfeld,[25] and calls for detailed consideration. I have myself sought to modify it[26] in the sense that it was not Jewish Christians of Palestinian background but their counterparts of Hellenistic origin who were influential in this period. The sort of picture painted by J. L. Martyn[27] as the background of John 9, which is of great importance in the study of the Johannine attitude to Jews and Judaism, must be reconsidered in the light of these suggestions.

This discussion, which shows that the early Christian attitude to Jews and Judaism was not uniform, leads to the question of canonicity, which I shall not approach directly, and to *Sachkritik,* which is as much an obligation for the exegete and biblical student as literary and historical criticism. There is, however, an important distinction. In practicing literary criticism, the critic will draw parallels and contrasts from literature at large in order to illuminate, describe, analyze, and clarify the piece of literature with which he or she is directly concerned. Similarly, the historical critic, whose task is to consider the contribution to historical knowledge made by his or her text, will use historical data drawn from any relevant source. In comparison with these, *Sachkritik* is an internal operation. The reader of a text is, of course, at liberty to say, I disagree with what I read in my text; the truth is to be found in a different text, or perhaps in my own thought. The reader then has to make a straightforward decision, which could—perhaps must—involve the denial of any claim for canonical authority made on behalf of the original text. This is a valid, if controversial, operation, but it is not (what I mean by) *Sachkritik.* This process puts side by side two (or more) passages within one text (or a group of related texts viewed as a unit) that differ, or appear to differ, from one another. Again, the process may turn out to be a simple one. The critic may conclude that the author is a stupid man who cannot recognize that he is contradicting himself. Or the critic may say, "These contradictory statements are a mark of literary compilation. The editor, drawing material from different sources, has inadvertently included contradictory passages. Or it may be that one of them has been introduced by textual corruption." These, however, are dangerous conclusions to draw, and the critic must always ask himself or herself

25. A. Hilgenfeld, *Die Ketzergeschichte des Urchristentums* (Leipzig, 1884; reprint, Hildesheim, 1963); to which may be added A. Hilgenfeld, *Judenthum und Judenchristenthum: Eine Nachlese zu der Ketzergeschichte des Urchristenthums* (Leipzig, 1884; reprint, Hildesheim, 1966).

26. C. K. Barrett, "What Minorities?" in D. Hellholm, H. Moxnes, and T. K. Seim, eds., *Mighty Minorities? Minorities in Early Christianity: Positions and Strategies,* FS Jacob Jervell (Oslo–Copenhagen–Stockholm–Boston, 1995), pp. 1–10.

27. See n. 19, above.

whether there is some underlying unity that the reader has failed to observe.[28]

John 4:22 and 8:44 are outstanding examples of apparent contradiction. Salvation comes from the Jews; the Jews come from the devil. Is there a sense in which John may consciously intend both propositions, in which both may be true? What light does the one throw on the other? In what sense (one must ask) does salvation come from the Jews? In what sense are the Jews children of the devil? Are "the Jews" who are referred to the same in each verse? Augustine was well aware of this question:[29] "Nos adoramus quod scimus. Ex persona quidem judaeorum dictum est, sed non omnium judaeorum, non reproborum judaeorum: sed de qualibus fuerunt apostoli, quales fuerunt prophetae, quales fuerunt illi omnes sancti, qui omnia vendiderunt, et pretia rerum suarum ad pedes apostolorum posuerunt." The distinction is valid, though perhaps superficial. The two verses, expressing positive and negative views of the Jewish people, do not stand alone.

The Jewishness of the Fourth Gospel has been frequently described and assessed, and there is no need here to cover the ground in detail.[30] The Old Testament is frequently quoted, and in a perceptive way.[31] There are allusions to Jewish feasts and to customs associated with them, and it is clear that Jesus is himself a Jew (e.g., 4:9; 18:35). Other passages, however, are critical of Jews and Judaism. Nicodemus, the teacher of Israel, does not know what he ought to know (3:10); the Jews misunderstand and seek to kill Jesus (e.g., 5:18; 7:19, 25; 10:31); they do not have the love of God in them (5:42); many even of Jesus' disciples turn their backs on him (6:66); the chief priests and Pharisees seek to seize him (7:32, 45–49); their sin remains (9:41); they allege that Jesus has a demon and is mad (10:20); the chief priests and Pharisees plot Jesus' death (11:45–53). They fulfill the prophecy of Isaiah 6:10 (12:39, 40). So much—and more—can be quoted without use of the passion narrative or chapter 8. It is impossible after reading John to conclude in unqualified terms that the Jews are bad or that the Jews are good. Life is not so simple. In the New Testament, duality enters into the estimate of the good institutions of Judaism. Thus, in Acts, the Temple is contrary to God's will and ought not to exist (7:47–50); yet apostles and other Christians use it for prayer, for their gatherings, and for

28. See C. K. Barrett, *The Dialectical Theology of St John* (New Testament Essays; London, 1972), pp. 49–69; and C. K. Barrett, *Paradox and Dualism: Essays on John* (London, 1982), pp. 98–115.

29. Augustine, *Tract. Ev. Jo.* 15.26 (on 4:22).

30. I refer to my lectures, C. K. Barrett, *Das Johannesevangelium und das Judentum* (Stuttgart, 1970)—ET: *John and Judaism* (London, 1975); and to Barrett, *Gospel according to John*, pp. 27–34 (see n. 11, above).

31. See C. K. Barrett, "The Old Testament in the Fourth Gospel," *JTS* 48 (1947): 155–69.

liturgical, sacrificial purposes (3:1; 5:12; 21:26).[32] At an even deeper level, we may note Paul's treatment of Torah; his conviction that the Law is holy, righteous, and good (Rom. 7:12); and his recognition that passions of sins operate through it (7:5).[33]

This duality is not a matter of saying, for example, that the Law is partly good and partly bad. All depends on the way in which the Law is approached, accepted, and practiced. According to the New Testament, this must be by faith, not by works (Rom. 9:32)—a faith not impossible for the saints of the Old Testament but now to be directed through Christ, crucified and risen (cf. Rom. 4:23–25).

New Testament duality (I avoid the word *dualism*) is to be found in John in relation to the world (κόσμος). The world has a ruler who is inimical to Christ (14:30); the world will hate the disciples as it hated Christ (15:18, 19); Christ's kingdom is not of this world (18:36). Yet the world, though it did not recognize him, was made by the Word (1:10); it was loved beyond measure by God (3:16), and Christ came into it as its light (8:12; 12:43). The key to this duality may be said to lie in the apparent contradiction: it was for judgment that Christ came into the world (9:39; cf. 3:19; 12:31; 16:8–11), yet he did not come to judge (3:17f.; 12:47). And Israel is the religious element in the world, the religious aspect of the world, the world viewed in the light of religion. This is where judgment and love both come to their sharpest focus. The duality, which is of the essence of revelation as the New Testament understands it, lies behind both those verses that appear to be favorable and those that appear to be unfavorable to Jews.

---

32. See C. K. Barrett, "Attitudes to the Temple in the Acts of the Apostles," in W. Horbury, ed., *Templum Amicitiae: Essays on the Second Temple,* FS Ernst Bammel (Sheffield, 1991), pp. 345–67.
33. Cf. supra; also C. K. Barrett, *Paul: An Introduction to His Thought* (London, 1994), pp. 74–87.

CHAPTER 12

The Gospel of John: Exclusivism Caused by a Social Setting Different from That of Jesus (John 11:54 and 14:6)

James H. Charlesworth

The following study is intended for scholars and advanced students of the New Testament.[1] Sometimes we need to write for scholars so that together we may obtain a better perspective on some perplexing issues that may not be easy to communicate to nonspecialists. Some publications are intended to bubble up from the nonscholarly community to the scholarly academy; this one is intended to filter down from scholars to others.

I think this is the proper approach, since some readers may neither perceive nor understand what is meant by anti-Judaisms or anti-Semitisms in the New Testament. Two colleagues offered a course at Princeton Theological Seminary in the fall of 1999. They were astounded by the ignorance and then the horror of the theological students when they confronted the anti-Jewish problems in the translations of the New Testament. Devotion to the New Testament is good, but it must not camouflage the fact that some passages in the New Testament are problematic and seem anti-Jewish (a better term for ancient phenomena than *anti-Semitic,* which is a relatively recent term).[2]

Some people advise that we simply cut such passages out of the New Testament. That method is impossible, since it violates the integrity of New Testament research, is faithless to traditions that must be honored, and creates a modern construct out of an ancient, though not antiquarian, text. Therein lies the problem. If the text were antiquarian, it would be easy to leave it alone, perhaps even ignore it (like the hatred of the Canaanites in

---

1. The notes are selected and focused on publications not well known to specialists. In addition, I include references to my published thoughts on the New Testament and anti-Judaism. (This may serve to substantiate some dubious points or to provide some insight into the development of my own thought.)

2. See J. H. Charlesworth, "Neologisms: Their Origins—'Anti-Semitism,'" *Expl.* 1 (1987): 1, p. 4. Also, see J. H. Charlesworth, "Is the New Testament Anti-Semitic or Anti-Jewish?" *Expl.* 7 (1993): 2, pp. 2–3.

the Hebrew Bible; they are no longer extant, and so there is no problem of anti-Canaanitism). But the New Testament remains arguably the most influential collection of writings in global culture, so misuse or misinterpretations of them are causes for alarm.

The problem now before us was succinctly phrased by D. J. Harrington, S.J.:

> The basic problem before us is that John's gospel says nasty things about a group that it calls "the Jews." When twentieth-century people hear such negative talk about "the Jews," they may assume a direct relation between "the Jews" of the Fourth Gospel and their Jewish neighbors who attend the local synagogue. Thus the Fourth Gospel can become a vehicle for increasing anti-Semitism.[3]

I think we would all agree that we must endeavor to make it certain that it is no longer easy to use the Gospel of John to increase anti-Semitism.

Perhaps the four most jarring examples of alleged anti-Judaism in the New Testament are found in Revelation and our two most Jewish Gospels, Matthew and John (two times).

The first example is that some Jews "are a synagogue of Satan" (συναγωγὴ τοῦ σατανᾶ, Rev. 2:9). This passage is obviously a composition by the second generation of Jesus' followers. I would have no difficulty translating the Greek as "the assembly of Satan" and thus remove any reference to "synagogue." This translation is also justifiable, since if most of us were to find συναγωγὴ τοῦ σατανᾶ in an early (pre–100 C.E.) papyrus, we would not translate it "synagogue of Satan," because we are leery about positing "synagogues" in early times.

The second example is from the First Gospel. Matthew reports that "[all] the people," probably Israel, shouted, "His blood be on us and our children" (Matt. 27:25). This is also clearly a second-generation expansion of the Marcan passion narrative. It is a subject of another study but clearly is an addition—a corruption—of the primary stratum, which is available in Mark.

Thus, we scholars can claim that the corruption occurred only in the second generation; but it is not clear how we can communicate this in translations. The Greek text cannot be changed, and translations must be faithful to it.[4] K. Stendahl warns us that there are anti-Semitisms in the New Testament, and there is "no single way to get at the problem of translation."[5]

3. D. J. Harrington, "The Problem of 'the Jews' in John's Gospel," *Expl.* 8 (1994): 1, p. 3.

4. For more of my own reflections on Matthew and anti-Judaism, see J. H. Charlesworth, "Is the Gospel of Matthew Anti-Jewish?" *Hor.* 9 (1996): 10–11.

5. K. Stendahl, "Anti-Semitism and the New Testament," *Expl.* 7 (1993): 2, p. 7.

The third and fourth examples are found in the Gospel of John and constitute the focus of the present essay; that is, we soon focus on John 11:54 and 14:6. It is not immediately clear that these are later expansions and corruptions of Jesus' life and essential message, and each needs to be studied in its literary and sociological contexts. The results of my research suggest that both passages in the Gospel of John are later expansions and corruptions in the development of Jesus traditions.[6] Clearly, in the process of obtaining a normative self-definition, especially between 70 and 200 C.E.,[7] both Jews and "Christians" lost much that was pure and fecund for the future.[8]

Translating Ἰουδαῖοι in the Gospel of John

Observation: Translations Almost Always
Represent Ἰουδαῖοι as "Jews"

In most translations of the New Testament, Ἰουδαῖοι is translated, regardless of context, as "Jews." It is clear that many passages in John portray the Ἰουδαῖοι as "Jews" and that sometimes the Jews represent the cosmos that is hostile to Jesus.[9]

What is the meaning of John 11:54? This verse has been used to inflame anti-Semitisms. Does it mean that "Jews" were seeking to kill Jesus? That conclusion seems odd when it is clear that according to 11:45 only a few verses earlier, "many of the Jews" (πολλοὶ οὖν ἐκ τῶν Ἰουδαίων) believed (ἐπίστευσαν) in Jesus. Among the Jews there were different groups and opposite reactions to Jesus, as we know from John 10:19: "Again the Jews were divided because of these words [of Jesus]." These reflections make it apparent that to translate Ἰουδαῖοι, or other plural nouns related to it, always as "Jews" does violence to the flow of the Johannine narrative and ignores the search for the intention of the implied author. One should

6. One of the shared insights found in the articles published in *Anti-Judaism and Early Christianity* is that the anti-Judaisms in the New Testament are frequently from post-70 communities. The first volume of this work was edited by P. Richardson, with D. Granskou, and the second by S. G. Wilson. They were published in Waterloo, Ontario, Canada, by Wilfrid Laurier University Press, 1986.

7. See A. Paul, *Leçons paradoxales sur les juifs et les chrétiens* (Paris, 1992).

8. See the formative studies published in E. P. Sanders, A. J. Baumgarten, and A. Mendelson, eds., *Jewish and Christian Self-Definition*, 3 vols. (Philadelphia, 1980–82).

9. See my comments made in the 1960s and 1970s: J. H. Charlesworth, ed., *John and the Dead Sea Scrolls* (1972; reprint, New York, 1991), pp. 90–96. I would now avoid the use of the word *Jews*. Also see G. Theissen, "Aporien im Umgang mit den Antijudaismen des Neuen Testaments," in E. Blum, C. Macholz, and E. W. Stegemann, eds., *Die hebräische Bibel und ihre zweifache Nachgeschichte*, FS R. Rendtorff (Neukirchen-Vluyn, 1990), pp. 535–53, esp. p. 541.

not forget that Jesus says to the Samaritan woman that "salvation is from the Jews" (John 4:22); and this plural noun (ἐκ τῶν Ἰουδαίων) cannot be translated otherwise than "Jews."[10]

Methodology: Words Have Meaning in Literary Contexts

Does the plural Greek noun Ἰουδαῖοι always mean "Jews"? Most scholars, even if they usually or almost always do translate it as "Jews," would probably reply that a noun's meaning depends on the context. While that advice is correct, it is far too seldom followed; that is, almost always Ἰουδαῖοι (or other forms of this plural noun) is translated, regardless of context, simply as "Jews."

Most of us would agree that it is inappropriate to translate a word with eyes only on a lexicon. Words have no meanings in such contexts; they obtain meaning only from a context with other words that are united by an intent. A word thus obtains meaning within a literary context. Since most words have more than one meaning (that is, are multivalent), the meaning intended can be discerned by studying the word in its context and observing grammar, syntax, literary forms, and flow of a document. That Ἰουδαῖοι can mean "Jews" in some contexts does not control the meaning it might have in other contexts.

A Parade Example of Mistranslating Ἰουδαῖοι

What is the most important example of this philological phenomenon for the discussion on anti-Judaism and the Gospel of John? It is found in John 11:54:

> Jesus therefore no longer walked about openly among the Jews [ἐν τοῖς Ἰουδαίοις], but went from there [ἐκεῖθεν] to a town called Ephraim in the region near the wilderness; and he remained there [κἀκεῖ] with the disciples.

According to this translation, Jesus leaves a certain unnamed place with his disciples, goes to a town called Ephraim, and "no longer walked about openly among the Jews." This translation inflames anti-Jewish sentiment. The reader is told, or at least given the impression, that Jesus removes himself from the Jews. He is thus portrayed in such a way that he appears not

---

10. U. Schnelle argues that the Gospel of John is not anti-Jewish, and in it, the "Jews" are sometimes portrayed as those who bear the promises. See U. Schnelle, "Die Juden im Johannesevangelium," in C. Kähler et al., eds., *Gedenkt an das Wort*, FS Werner Vogler (Leipzig, 1999), pp. 217–30.

to be a Jew. The translation also suggests that Jesus' disciples also cannot be Jews, and that Ephraim is not a Jewish town, because they have gone to it from "among the Jews." Perhaps the difficulty in understanding the noun Ἰουδαῖοι in John 11:54 may explain the numerous variants in this verse.

Translation and Jesus' Jewishness

Is not the regnant translation misleading, because Jesus was a deeply devout Jew? Surely, the answer is yes, as I have shown in *Jesus' Jewishness*,[11] in *Jesus within Judaism*,[12] and in *Jesus and the Dead Sea Scrolls*;[13] as David Flusser has clarified in his masterful *Jesus*;[14] and as Paula Fredriksen[15] and Bruce Chilton[16] clarify in their recent books on Jesus.

Is not the translation of Ἰουδαῖοι as "Jews" also misleading, because each of the Twelve was a Jew? We need to be alert to the old, and now discarded, claim by some Jewish leaders that Jews did not follow Jesus.[17] They did follow him; all his chosen disciples were Jews. As Carlo Maria Martini, the cardinal of Milan, states, "Jesus is fully Jewish; the apostles are Jewish; and one cannot doubt their attachment to the traditions of their forefathers."[18] Thus, any translation that implies otherwise is to be suspect and should be corrected.

Translation and Topography

Have not archaeological work and topographical studies indicated that Ephraim is a Jewish town? In favor of an affirmative answer is the fact that it is a very Jewish name.[19] It is not a Greek city in the decapolis; it is a Jewish town in the hills northeast of Jerusalem. Jesus goes from among the

11. J. H. Charlesworth, ed., *Jesus' Jewishness: Exploring the Place of Jesus within Early Judaism* (Shared Ground Among Jews and Christians 2; New York, 1991).

12. J. H. Charlesworth, *Jesus within Judaism: New Light from Exciting Archaeological Discoveries* (ABRL 1; New York, 1988).

13. J. H. Charlesworth, *Jesus and the Dead Sea Scrolls* (ABRL; New York, 1993; reprint, 1995).

14. D. Flusser, *Jesus in Selbstzeugnissen und Bilddokumenten* (RoMo 140; Hamburg, 1968).

15. P. Fredriksen, *Jesus of Nazareth: King of the Jews* (New York, 1999; reprint, 2000).

16. B. Chilton, *Rabbi Jesus: An Intimate Biography* (New York, 2000).

17. It is difficult to agree with Y. Kaufmann, for example, when he claims that "Jewish intellectuals" were "not drawn" to Christianity, and that "to the Jewish intellectuals," Christianity seemed both "foolishness" and a "stumbling block." He seems to be misunderstanding Paul, and such a claim fails to realize that many of Jesus' followers were intellectuals and Jews, namely, Paul and the implied authors of Matthew, John, Hebrews, and Revelation. See Y. Kaufmann, *Christianity and Judaism: Two Covenants*, trans. C. W. Efroymson (Jerusalem, 1988), p. 203.

18. C. M. Martini, "A Historical View," *Expl.* 2 (1988): 2.

19. See Y. Tsafrir, "Apharaema: Ephraim," in Y. Tsafrir, L. D. Segne, and J. Green, eds., *Tabula Imperii Romani: Iudaea Palestina. Eretz Israel in the Hellenistic, Roman and Byzantine Periods. Maps and Gazetteer* (Publications of the Israel Academy of Sciences and Humanities, Section of Humanities; Jerusalem, 1994), p. 64.

'Ιουδαῖοι to Ephraim, which is a village (πόλιν)[20]—and also a territory—northeast of Jerusalem.[21] The claim that Jesus leaves "the Jews" is impossible, since Ephraim was a thoroughly Jewish village or district in a Jewish area. This name, Ephraim, is genuinely Jewish. It often denotes the Northern Kingdom of Israel.

The key to the meaning of 'Ιουδαῖοι in John 11:54 is provided by the two adverbs of place "from there" (ἐκεῖθεν) and "there" (κἀκεῖ). The context seems clear: Jesus leaves a place; "he went" from where the 'Ιουδαῖοι are to be found. Jesus went from there, where the 'Ιουδαῖοι were, to another place. That means the plural noun should be understood in terms of a place or region. Two places are contrasted: Ephraim and where the 'Ιουδαῖοι are located.

Perhaps an attempt to implicate all Jews and not Judaeans helps explain the omission of ἐκεῖθεν in some early manuscripts of the Gospel of John, in Greek (e.g., P[45vid] D Γ), Syriac (Syrus Sinaiticus), and Latin (the Vulgate and some Old Latin witnesses). That omission would bring the altered text into line with the anti-Judaism that is so rampant in the composition of the apocryphal works,[22] but it does not explain why the same scribes (or textual traditions) kept the adverb of place "there" (κἀκεῖ). The issue of omission and possible anti-Jewish sentiment is complex. The problem is also reflected in the complex mixture of positive and negative attitudes to Jews and Judaism by the early scholars of the church.[23] What, then, could be the meaning of this noun 'Ιουδαῖοι?

The 'Ιουδαῖοι and Sociological Problems in Judaea and Jerusalem

Does a sociological study of Jesus' time not reveal the "institution" of banditry and the internecine struggles within Judaism?[24] And is not Jerusalem

20. Some early manuscripts (P[66*] and Syrus Sinaiticus) omit the word *town*.

21. The exact location is disputed, but it is clearly very Jewish. See H. O. Thompson, "Ephraim," in *ABD* 2:556. The location is discussed neither in *The New Encyclopedia of Archaeological Excavations in the Holy Land* nor in *The Oxford Encyclopedia of Archaeology in the Near East*. Still full of valuable information are the two entries in W. Smith, *A Dictionary of the Bible* (1893), 1.2.972–75.

22. See J. H. Charlesworth and C. A. Evans, "Jesus in the Agrapha and Apocryphal Gospels," in B. Chilton and C. A. Evans, eds., *Studying the Historical Jesus* (NTTS 19; Leiden, 1994), pp. 479–533. Also see J. R. Mueller, "Anti-Judaism in the New Testament Apocrypha," in C. A. Evans and D. A. Hagner, eds., *Anti-Semitism and Early Christianity* (Minneapolis, 1993), pp. 253–68.

23. See D. Rokeah, "Behind the Appearances: 'Appreciation' of the Jews in the Writings of the Church Fathers," *Expl.* 3 (1989): 3–4. Also see R. S. MacLennan, "Were the Second-Century *Adversus Judaeos* Preachers Anti-Jewish?" *Expl.* 5 (1991): 1 and 4. MacLennan says no.

24. See esp. R. A. Horsley, *Archaeology, History, and Society in Galilee: The Social Context of Jesus and the Rabbis* (Harrisburg, Pa., 1996); K. C. Hanson and D. E. Oakman, *Palestine in the Time of Jesus: Social Structures and Social Conflicts* (Minneapolis, 1998); and E. W. Stegemann and W. Stegemann, *The Jesus Movement: A Social History of Its First Century*, trans. O. C. Dean Jr. (Minneapolis, 1999).

often the center of the struggle? From the second century B.C.E., at least, until the demise of Ancient Israel in 136 C.E., priests were struggling for power, prestige, and purse. The rivalry centered in Jerusalem, as we know from so many sources, including John 11. The study of Qumran origins and history and of the Samaritans brings into high relief the importance of priestly power that was centered in Jerusalem.

According to the Johannine narrative, the opposition to Jesus originated in Jerusalem. Note these representative passages. During the feast of Dedication in Jerusalem (John 10:22), some "Jews ['Ιουδαῖοι] took up stones again to stone him [Jesus]" (John 10:31; cf. 11:8). Later, they try to arrest him (John 10:39). Jesus subsequently leaves Jerusalem and goes to a place "across the Jordan" where John the Baptizer had first baptized (John 10:40). When Jesus decides to return to the area of Jerusalem, Thomas advises, "Let us also go, that we may die with him" (John 11:16).[25] Thus, the implied author of the Gospel of John wants his readers to know that Jerusalem and its vicinity are a dangerous place for Jesus. The Fourth Evangelist also makes it clear that this Jerusalem was a dangerous area for Jesus long before his crucifixion there by the Roman soldiers. According to John 11:37–53, the opposition to Jesus is localized in the chief priests and the Pharisees in Jerusalem: "the chief priests and the Pharisees called a meeting of the council, and said, 'What are we to do?'. . . So from that day on they·planned to put him to death" (John 11:47, 53). This verse, John 11:53, is the verse prior to and contiguous to John 11:54; this passage helps define 'Ιουδαῖοι in 11:54.

Also note the verses that follow 11:54, especially 11:57: "Now the chief priests and the Pharisees had given orders that anyone who knew where Jesus was should let them know, so that they might arrest him." Not "Jews" but some chief priests (and not Caiaphas; cf. 11:49)[26] and some Pharisees, near the end of Jesus' life, were committed to finding a way to put him to death. That is at least the thrust of the Johannine narrative. Hence, 'Ιουδαῖοι seems not to denote "Jews"; perhaps it denotes "some Judaean leaders."[27]

This claim did not originate with the author of the Gospel of John. It also appears in the Synoptic Gospels (Matthew, Mark, and Luke). They

---

25. For a fuller discussion of John 11:16, see J. H. Charlesworth, *The Beloved Disciple: Whose Witness Validates the Gospel of John?* (Valley Forge, Pa., 1995).

26. See J. H. Charlesworth, "Caiaphas, Pilate, and Jesus' Trial," *Expl.* 7 (1993): 3–4.

27. Long ago, S. Sandmel suggested that words too easily translated "Jews" in the Gospel of John really denoted "Judaeans" or "Jewish leaders." See S. Sandmel, *Anti-Semitism in the New Testament?* (Philadelphia, 1978), p. 101.

indicate that Jesus was opposed by authorities based in Jerusalem. According to Mark, the opposition to Jesus originated with scribes and spies who came from Jerusalem: "And the scribes [οἱ γραμματεῖς] who came down from Jerusalem [οἱ ἀπὸ Ἰεροσολύμων] said, 'He has Beelzebul, and by the ruler of the demons he casts out the demons" (Mark 3:22). Jesus was at "home" (John 3:20), which is presumably Capernaum (cf. Mark 2:1). Thus, the Jerusalem scribes found him at Capernaum.

Such scenes as these have been miscast by scholars. They claimed that Galilee was a backwater part of Palestine, that Jews were sparse there, and that Torah observance was lax. Thanks to the research of G. Alon,[28] A. Büchler,[29] and massive excavations in Galilee,[30] we now know, as S. Safrai states, that "Galilee was a place where Jewish cultural life and a firm attachment to Judaism flourished well before the destruction of the Second Temple."[31] These new insights reveal that Jesus was no marginal Jew, and that there were close ties between Galilee and Judaea.

When Jesus is challenged about the laws of purity, he is questioned by some why he and his disciples do not follow the "tradition of the elders" (Mark 7:3). Those who oppose Jesus at this time are some of the Pharisees and scribes—and they are "from Jerusalem" (Mark 7:1).

Jesus' precursors had been martyred. The Galilean miracle worker named Honi had been stoned outside the walls of Jerusalem. Jesus' teacher John the Baptizer had been beheaded by a Herodian ruler. According to the early tradition, and also the Johannine narrative, Jesus' life was the way of a martyr. The opposition to him was constant, and it seems almost always to emanate from the metropolis called Jerusalem.

The Gospel of John, Christology, and Expulsion from the Synagogue

There can be no doubt that the Gospel of John comes to us, in the form it reached at the end of the first century C.E., from a community that consisted of people with a mixed background, including non-Jews and Jews

28. G. Alon, *Toledot ha-Yehudim be-Eretz Yisrael bi-Tekufat ha-Mishnah we-ha-Talmud* (Tel Aviv, 1953). The Hebrew title means "The History of the Jews in the Land of Israel during the Mishnaic and Talmudic Periods."

29. A. Büchler, *Am ha-Aretz ha-Galili* (Jerusalem, 1964). The Hebrew means "The Galilean Am ha-Aretz."

30. See the numerous publications by E. M. Meyers and J. Strange, and the summaries of their discoveries, especially in Sepphoris, found in C. L. Meyers and E. M. Meyers, "Sepphoris," in *OEANE*; and in *NEAEHL*.

31. See S. Safrai, *The New Testament and Christian-Jewish Dialogue* (Immanuel 24/25; Jerusalem, 1990), p. 149.

(including Samaritans and Essenes).[32] As R. Kysar reported, "Most scholars now agree that the Gospel [of John] was written in response to the expulsion of the Johannine church from the synagogue and the subsequent dialogue between these two religious parties."[33] It seems evident, if the Gospel of John reflects more than one level in the transmission of Jesus' sayings,[34] that Ἰουδαῖοι (or similar plural nouns) has moved from a descriptive to a polemical denotation or connotation. As members of the Johannine community or school were cast out of—or barred from—their former synagogues that they wished to attend, then the concept of Ἰουδαῖοι would take on negative connotations.[35] It is impossible to date such expulsion, since synagogues existed before 70 (in Jericho, Gamla, Masada, the Herodian, and Jerusalem),[36] and Jesus' followers, especially Stephen and Paul—not to mention Jesus himself—were often "expelled" from a synagogue.

It is apparent how an early favorable tradition about the "Jews" would have evolved to a pejorative one; that is, under the stringent social setting, the same collection of words would have taken on a new connotation. Agreeing with U. C. von Wahlde and M. Lowe that the Greek noun Ἰουδαῖοι can denote Jewish authorities[37] and those centered in Judaea,[38] we also concur with J. Ashton[39] and R. A. Culpepper.[40] If passages such as John 11:54 denote a group that is hostile to Jesus and labeled Ἰουδαῖοι, then this plural Greek noun colors other passages elsewhere in the Johannine narrative. Eventually learning that Ἰουδαῖοι are those who seek to kill Jesus, readers of the Gospel of John could easily have shifted from a neutral attitude or even philo-Judaism to some form of anti-Judaism. It is most unfortunate that the author of the Gospel of John used Ἰουδαῖοι to denote both "Jews" as in 4:22 (and elsewhere) and "some Judaean

32. See R. E. Brown, *The Community of the Beloved Disciple* (New York–London, 1979); and J. H. Charlesworth, "The Dead Sea Scrolls and the Gospel according to John," in R. A. Culpepper and C. C. Black, eds., *Exploring the Gospel of John: In Honor of D. Moody Smith* (Louisville, 1996), pp. 65–97.

33. R. Kysar, "The Gospel of John and Anti-Jewish Polemic," *Expl.* 6 (1992): 2, 3–4.

34. The first scholar to illustrate the two levels of the Gospel of John was J. L. Martyn. See his *History and Theology in the Fourth Gospel,* 2d ed. (Nashville, 1979).

35. I am, of course, influenced by the historical and sociological studies by J. L. Martyn and R. E. Brown; see Martyn, *History and Theology*; and Brown, *Community of the Beloved Disciple.*

36. J. S. Kloppenborg clarifies that the Theodotos inscription antedates 70 C.E. See his "Dating Theodotus (CIJ II 1404)," *JJS* 51 (2000): 243–80.

37. U. C. von Wahlde, "The Johannine 'Jews': A Critical Survey," *NTS* 28 (1982): 33–60.

38. M. Lowe, "Who Were the Ἰουδαῖοι? *NovT* 18 (1976): 101–30, pp. 106–7.

39. J. Ashton, "The Identity and Function of the Ἰουδαῖοι in the Fourth Gospel," *NovT* 27 (1985): 40–75, pp. 55–57.

40. R. A. Culpepper, "The Gospel of John as a Threat to Jewish-Christian Relations," in J. H. Charlesworth with F. X. Blisard and J. L. Gorham, eds., *Overcoming Fear between Jews and Christians* (Shared Ground among Jews and Christians 3; New York, 1993), pp. 21–43, p. 27.

authorities" in 11:54 (and elsewhere). In the Greek text, the pejorative and polemical use of this noun discolored the other places in which it appeared; the result is a masterpiece marred by a disturbing imperfection.

D. Moody Smith rightly points out that Israel has a positive meaning in the Gospel of John, and that terms usually translated "Jews" sometimes have a positive connotation. He suggests that we should endeavor, in translating Ἰουδαῖοι and similar nouns in the Gospel of John, to denote "a group of Jewish leaders who exercise great authority among their compatriots and are especially hostile to Jesus and his disciples."[41]

Thus, it is imperative to translate Ἰουδαῖοι, wherever possible, as "some Judaean leaders" and not the equivalent of "Jews."[42] Not only is "Jews" sometimes inaccurate within the Johannine narrative and the historical context of the book, but—unlike Canaanites—there are Jews living in our communities. The same word, *Jews*, has been employed indiscriminately to denote two different groups of people—those in the first century and those contemporaneous with us—who are separated by much more than two millennia. This observation warns translators against choosing *Jews* to translate some sections of ancient texts.

Summary

Thus, Ἰουδαῖοι in John 11:54 should not be translated "Jews." Because Jesus and his disciples were Jews, they cannot be portrayed as leaving "Jews." Since Jesus left the region of Judaea for Ephraim, one possible rendering of Ἰουδαῖοι is "Judaeans."[43] Since it was the leaders with whom Jesus was having some problems, the rendering "Judaean leaders" seems even better. Once again, we must be informed of the consensus among us; during the time of Jesus, Judaism was deeply divided. It is unwise to conclude that "Judaean leaders" were united in opposing Jesus. Jews seem never to have been united, not even when the Roman soldiers encircled the city in the summer of 70 C.E.. Then, the "Jews" under John of Gis-

41. D. M. Smith, "Judaism and the Gospel of John," in J. H. Charlesworth with F. X. Blisard and J. S. Siker, eds., *Jews and Christians: Exploring the Past, Present, and Future* (Shared Ground among Jews and Christians 1; New York, 1990), pp. 76–99, p. 82.

42. E. Haenchen rightly saw that "the Jews" denoted those "within Judaea." E. Haenchen, *John: A Commentary on the Gospel of John: Chapters 7–21*, trans. R. W. Funk (Philadelphia, 1984), p. 76.

43. N. A. Beck suggests in John 11:54 the rendering "his enemies" or "the Judaeans." The former loses the etymological link with the Greek. The latter misses that only some Judaean leaders were seeking to stop Jesus. Yet Beck was on the right track. See N. A. Beck, *Mature Christianity in the Twenty-first Century: The Recognition and Repudiation of the Anti-Jewish Polemic in the New Testament* (New York, 1994), p. 263.

chala and those under Simon bar Giora fought against each other and, at times, apparently among themselves. Moreover, the Gospel of John clarifies that Caiaphas was not categorically opposed to Jesus and that Nicodemus and Joseph of Arimathea admired or were "secret" followers of Jesus (John 3:1–2; 19:38). Each of these three was an influential Judaean leader. Thus, "some Judaean leaders" seems to be the best rendering of Ἰουδαῖοι in some places.[44] It seems best for John 11:54. Hence, here is my translation:

> Jesus therefore no longer went about openly among some Judaean leaders, but went from there [Judaea] to the country near the wilderness, to a town called Ephraim; and there he remained with his disciples.

I am relatively certain this is an improvement over previous translations, especially those that simply replace Ἰουδαῖοι with "Jews." The translation is sensitive to the text, to the flow of the Johannine narrative, and to the literary and sociological contexts. There is even more. If you are a Jew—or Jewish in commitment—it makes a big difference when Christian preachers and missionaries cease claiming that "Jews" were those whom Jesus fled and begin observing that, according to the Gospel of John, only some Judaean leaders based in Jerusalem were seeking his death. One translation did help produce the Holocaust, during which, as Elie Wiesel reminds us, Jews "lose their minds before they find their death."[45] The translation offered now may make it possible for all of us to live in a more tolerant and peaceful world.

Elsewhere in the Gospel of John, the noun Ἰουδαῖοι is also inaccurately translated as "Jews." In some of these cases it also has a local coloring. Note these examples:

> Jesus is in Jerusalem (John 5:1) and heals a man by the Sheep Gate on the Sabbath; "And that is why some Judean leaders [οἱ Ἰουδαῖοι] persecuted Jesus, because he did these things on the Sabbath" (John 5:16).

> He would not go about in Judaea (ἐν τῇ Ἰουδαίᾳ) because some Judaean leaders (οἱ Ἰουδαῖοι) sought to kill him (John 7:1).

> Jesus is in Jerusalem (John 8:58), and he heals a man who had been blind from birth. His parents subsequently "feared some Judaean leaders [τοὺς Ἰουδαίους]" (John 9:22).

---

44. For some of my earlier reflections on this issue, see J. H. Charlesworth, "Discussing Anti-Judaism in the New Testament with Hans Küng," *Expl.* 6 (1992): 1–2.
45. E. Wiesel, "Why Should People Care?" *Expl.* 1 (1987): 2, 1.

Jesus says to Pilate in Jerusalem, "If my kingship were of this world, my servants would fight, that I might not be handed over to some Judaean leaders [τοῖς 'Ιουδαίοις]" (John 18:36).[46]

The Judaean aristocrat and most likely also a leader, Joseph of Arimathea, remains a "secret" follower of Jesus "because of fear of some Judaean leaders [τῶν 'Ιουδαίων]" (John 19:38).

Jesus' eleven disciples hide in Jerusalem after the crucifixion "because of fear of some Judaean leaders [τῶν 'Ιουδαίων]" (John 20:19).

By including in our view the flow of the Johannine narrative and seeing the Judaean setting of these verses, it becomes clear that almost always the most appropriate meaning of the problematic Greek plural noun is "some Judaean leaders." These exegetical moves are also in harmony with the geography of John; it is the Gospel that centers Jesus' ministry in Judaea.

To the above research it is important to add a note about textual variants. As the Gospel tradition was copied, more anti-Judaisms were added. For example, in John 5:16, some important early witnesses have the following: "And that is why the 'Ιουδαῖοι persecuted Jesus, and sought to kill him" (τὸν 'Ιησοῦν οἱ 'Ιουδαῖοι καὶ ἐζήτουν αὐτόν ἀποκτεῖναι; cf. esp. E F H 2* A K M N U θ).[47]

Martin Buber, in "On Concluding the Translation of the Bible," stressed two points that are appropriate to mention now. First, in translating the Bible, we must avoid the vulgarization that turns the Creator who is open to his creation into "a God of strict justice and not of love." Second, both Jews and Christians have a missionizing task. It is in sharing the "primal truth" that we may join together to revitalize the translations of scripture and so help ensure "the future of both" Jews and Christians. "Scripture does the missionizing."[48] As R. J. Zwi Werblowsky informs us, Buber may have regretted the implications of calling Jesus his "great brother";[49] yet Buber lived out the knowledge that it is not Jesus but the Christian who is the brother of the Jew. Such a vision, as Buber emphasized, is grounded in a

46. Clearly, the portrait of Pilate evolves so that he is "Christianized" and the "Jews" demonized. One major publication in this area of research that is too often ignored is by N. Willert, *Pilatus-billedet in den antike jødedom og kristendon* (Århus, 1989).

47. See R. J. Swanson, ed., *New Testament Greek Manuscripts: Variant Readings Arranged in Horizontal Lines against Codex Vaticanus:* John (Sheffield–Pasadena, Calif., 1995), p. 57.

48. M. Buber, "On Concluding the Translation of the Bible," in F. A. Rothschild, ed., *Jewish Perspectives on Christianity* (New York, 1996), pp. 154–55.

49. R. J. Zwi Werblowsky, "Reflections on Martin Buber's Two Types of Faith,"*JJS* 39 (1988): 92–101, p. 95.

deeper perception of the Judaism of Jesus and his followers. This viewpoint is canonized—I am convinced—in the Gospel of John.

Exclusivism and John 14:6

One text in the Gospel of John is an exceptional embarrassment to Christians who are seeking a fruitful dialogue with persons of other religions, especially Jews. Yet little research has been focused on trying to explain it in the light of the contemporary need to relate "in a Christian way" to those in other religions. Here is the verse: "Jesus said to him [Thomas], "I am the way, and the truth, and the life; no one comes to the Father except through me." Here is the Greek text:

ἐγώ εἰμι ἡ ὁδὸς καὶ ἡ ἀλήθεια καὶ ἡ ζωή·
οὐδεὶς ἔρχεται πρὸς τὸν πατέρα εἰ μὴ δι᾽ ἐμοῦ
(14:6)

Since there are virtually no textual variants, and no textual reason to remove this verse or any portion of it from the Gospel of John, the only avenues are to keep it as preserved or to see if it may have been affected by the redactional activity that has reshaped the Gospel of John. Thus, the focal question becomes: Is the verse composed of two strata, and can one be assigned accurately to a later stratum of tradition? We cannot let the wish become the father of the thought; that is, we cannot simply seek to improve the theology of the Gospel of John by removing words unattractive or bothersome to us (as some critics claim that R. Bultmann tended to do in his magisterial commentary).

Observation

This verse states that Jesus is the one and only way to God. Such an exclusivistic claim has been at the center of the use of the Gospel of John to initiate or to inflame hatred of Jews. In a world in which more and more Christian leaders are conceiving a global ethic (e.g., H. Küng), the text is an embarrassment. Is it misrepresentative of the fundamental message of Jesus?

Misconception

Is not John 14:6 unified and structured with an inclusio? That is, does the sentence not begin with the first-person pronoun and then end with it? And if so, is it then not the product of one author, the implied author of the Gospel of John? The sentence begins with "I" and ends with "me." Do these pronouns not create an inclusio?

The answer seems to be no. An inclusio would be evident if the author had written, as he easily might have, "Through me is the way, the truth, and the life; no one comes to the Father except through me." The sentence is not an example of an inclusio. Even if it were, a redactor could have created such a sentence by expanding an earlier tradition. Hence, there is no philological reason to assume that the whole verse comes from one scribal hand.

Are There Two Layers in John 14?

John 14:6 seems to consist of two sections. That is, it is really two grammatically independent sentences. The first sentence is 14:6a, "I am the way, and the truth, and the life." The second sentence is 14:6b, "No one comes to the Father except through me." John 14:6a has only one minor variant; "and the truth" is missing in MS 157. John 14:6b is almost unique in the New Testament; there is not one variant.[50] That may signify that it was a later addition to the developing traditions and in harmony with the "Christianity" congenial to the scribes who later copied and helped shape the Greek New Testament. It is prima facie apparent that 14:6b may be an addition (perhaps to the first edition of John), but that needs to be studied carefully, and our own desires must not dictate what might be found.

The differences between the two sentences need to be clarified. The first is positive: "I am the way and the truth and the life." It is directed to those in the community, and there is no demand to think that there is no other way. The second sentence is negative: "No one comes to the Father except through me." It is directed to those outside the community, and it clearly denies any other way to God. An implicit exclusivism in v. 6a becomes explicit in v. 6b. Finally, v. 6a is in harmony with, and v. 6b discordant with, the Fourth Evangelist's universalistic claim that Jesus is "the light of the world" (8:12; 9:5; cf. 1:4–5 and 11:10). As we shall see, 14:6a could have been said by many early Jews, but 14:6b is clearly inconceivable to nonbelieving Jews—indeed, it is anathema to them. This sentence, 14:6b, seems to me to represent the struggles against either other nonbelieving Jews or

---

50. See the attractive list of Greek words found in Swanson, ed., *New Testament Greek Manuscripts,* p. 199.

the so-called Docetists who caused the Johannine schism. It is thus redactional and misrepresents Jesus' purpose.[51]

Methodology: Texts Have Meaning Only within Historical and Social Contexts

Two different methodologies are essential: a taxonomy of interpolation methods, with special attention to John, and sociological insights, especially into the shaping of the Gospel. Modern scholars have presented us with two solid conclusions that will aid our search for answers to the question focused on John 14:6. These illustrate the conclusion that the Gospel of John has been edited and reedited. Here is a brief synopsis of a strong consensus (of course, there will always be scholars who prove a consensus by disagreeing with it):

	virtually certain additions to the Gospel of John
1:1–18	the Logos Hymn
21:1–25	the Appendix (20:30–31 is an ending)

	probable additions to the Gospel of John
15:1–17:26	an insertion (14:31 leads into 18:1)

	possible additions to the Gospel of John
4:2	an interpolation (it contradicts 4:1 and 3:22)

	certain additions to the Gospel of John
7:53–8:11	an interpolation by a later scribe (not in early manuscripts)

In light of the research that reveals virtually certain, probable, and possible reediting of the Gospel of John, one may ponder if 14:6b could also be an interpolation.

Redaction-Analysis Methodology

One reason some distinguished scholars, such as M. Hengel,[52] are not persuaded by theories of redactional alterations of the Gospel of John is the unified thought so evident in it. This unity of language, rhetoric, and

---

51. See also M. Rissi's comments on the "Endredaktion" of the Gospel in "'Die Juden' im Johannesevangelium," *ANRW* 2.26.3 (1996): 2099–141.

52. M. Hengel, *Die johanneische Frage* (WUNT 67; Tübingen, 1993). An earlier, and smaller, version was presented in English: *The Johannine Question*, trans. J. Bowden (London–Philadelphia, 1989).

theology in the Gospel of John could be the result of the author's continuing work over decades or the result of a school of Johannine thinkers and authors (cf. also the epistles of John, Revelation, and the Odes of Solomon).

There is another reason that redactional activity has not been fully persuasive. It is that a methodology for proving the redaction of the Gospel of John has not been refined. Thus, it is necessary to summarize succinctly the redactional activity by scribes and a proper method for discerning them. One should include the full range of scribal redactional activity, both within and outside the canon.[53]

Sensitivity. How does one perceive a possible redaction? Any word, phrase, sentence, paragraph, or chapter that seems odd may be redactional and a later addition. One needs also to balance with this observation the fact that ancient authors were not systematic and consistent. Their love of repetition and circular thought opens them up for inconsistencies that are often unattractive to individuals influenced by the post-Enlightenment. For example, it is not wise to follow L. Gry and conclude that 4 Ezra 7:118 is an interpolation by a Christian because an early Jew would not have held both the concept of free will and that of sin inherited from Adam.[54] Especially during the time when the Johannine community was still aligned with the synagogue and in dialogue—obviously polemical—with the Jewish group who controlled the local synagogue, Jews did not seek to be consistent or systematic. They rather admired the both–and of a theological position.

Evidence of redaction may be the following:

1. A specificity that is out of character with the contiguous passages or the character of the document.
2. A circumscribed section of a text that has a vocabulary that is distinct from the rest of the document.
3. Words, even a word, that seem odd and reflect a different thought or a social setting that is incongruent with the rest of the document or corpus (thus, the pastorals are post-Pauline but not non-Pauline).
4. Words that explain the means of an action or supply the meaning of a previous ambiguous collection of words; the words are probably redactional if they are so focused that they look out of context.
5. Words that are grammatically free from the context (they can be removed without disturbing the grammar or syntax; hence, they may have been added).

53. This is only a summary of a much more detailed aspect of my present research.
54. See M. E. Stone, *Fourth Ezra,* ed. F. M. Cross (Minneapolis, 1990), p. 258.

Degree of Certainty. Redaction is relatively uncertain when only one of these peculiarities is observed and it is only apparent and not really impressive. Redaction is relatively certain if a scholar observes some words that are uncharacteristically specific, contain vocabulary distinct from the rest of the document, represent a thought that diverges from that of the implied author, indicate a social setting from a later time, and form an explanatory gloss that is grammatically free from the contiguous words.

Proof. An addition is revealed when a passage reads better grammatically, rhetorically, or thematically when it is removed—or when the theology of the document then becomes clearer. (Yet we must avoid the temptation to improve a text in our own eyes.) The best proof of redaction is when a manuscript is discovered that is closer to the putative original than the manuscript with the alleged interpolation, and the purer text does not have the passage or word. Some examples follow:

Second Cor. 6:14–7:1 appears to be an interpolation. It contains *termini technici* atypical of Paul in Romans and his other nondisputed epistles. The following concepts and terminology are not found in Paul's genuine letters: "righteous," "light," and "Christ" versus "iniquity," "darkness," and "Belial." In fact, these terms and concepts are typical of the Essenes. Thus, this section of 2 Corinthians seems to be an interpolation by one who was not Paul.

John 7:53–8:11 is intrusive and interrupts the flow of thought. It is certain these verses are a later addition to the Gospel of John. They are self-contained; that is, they preserve *in toto* the pericope concerning the woman caught in the act of adultery. Proof that the passage is later is the observation that it is not extant in the earliest manuscripts of the Gospel of John. This example is rare, since we have manuscript evidence to prove a theory; that is, the suspicion of a redactional addition is proved by manuscripts that are the earliest ones and do not contain the passage.

Caution. Errors have been committed by those trained in ancient texts. It is usually easy to improve a text by omitting apparent flaws or inconsistencies. This task is rather simple when we have access to grammars, concordances, and lexicons. An inconsistency, however, is not evidence of redaction. Authors are inconsistent and redundant. We need to avoid the errors committed by the luminaries R. H. Charles, in his commentary on Revelation, and R. Bultmann, in his commentary on the Gospel of John. Both tended to think the extant text on which they were working resulted from an ecclesiastical redactor who was either stupid or did not comprehend the author's original work.

Now we may more carefully examine John 14:6. Is 14:6b a later addition to 14:6a? In favor of this suggestion is the recognition that, as with other redactions (e.g., chapter 21), it comes at the end of a passage. The scribes have put a minor stop before and a major stop after 14:6b. Hence, the sentence 14:6b is textually isolated.

The sentence under suspicion is the following: οὐδεὶς ἔρχεται πρὸς τὸν πατέρα εἰ μὴ δι' ἐμοῦ. Since the vocabulary of John is unified and the implied author always rephrases his sources, it is not promising to seek evidence of redaction by an appeal to vocabulary. Nevertheless, an attempt should be made to discern how these words are related to other passages in the Gospel of John.

While οὐδείς is found frequently in chapters 1, 15–17, and 21 it is not necessarily, in itself, evidence of redactional activity. This Greek noun is found frequently throughout the Gospel of John. While οὐδεὶς δύναται is typical of the author (3:2; 6:44, 65; 9:4; 10:29), οὐδεὶς ἔρχεται is found only in 14:6b (cf. 7:27). This unique occurrence could be evidence of an addition.

Is πρὸς τὸν πατέρα the work of a redactor or an addition by the author? Since chapter 16 is probably an addition to the first edition of the Gospel, it is at first exciting evidence of redaction to note that the same accusative phrase also appears in 16:10, 17, and 28. But this phrase is also found elsewhere, in what is indubitably the original core of the Gospel of John (13:1; 14:6, 12, 28; and 20:17). Thus, the phrase is not evidence of redaction. One could argue that the phrase was typical of the redactor's work, but the reply is also impressive: the phrase is found in the core of the Gospel of John.

The phrase εἰ μὴ δι' ἐμοῦ may be the work of the redactor. It is found only in John 14:6b; that is, it is not found elsewhere in the core or in an allegedly redactional passage in the Gospel of John.

Perhaps one of the strongest arguments for redactional expansion of 14:6 is the observation that the words οὐδεὶς ἔρχεται πρὸς τὸν πατέρα εἰ μὴ δι' ἐμοῦ are grammatically free from the context. Since they can be removed without disturbing grammar or syntax, they may have been inserted at this place. Thus, without this sentence, the passage would read as follows:

> Thomas said to him, "Lord, we do not know where you are going. How can we know the way?" Jesus said to him, "I am the way, and the truth, and the life. If you had known me, you would have known my Father also. From now on you do know him and have seen him." (John 14:5–7, NRSV note at 7a)

When 6b is removed, the passage reads better and the flow is improved. One moves from Thomas's "we do not know" (οἴδαμεν) and "how can we know" (infinitive of οἶδα, a perfect used as a present) to Jesus' "If you had known [ἐγνώκατέ] me, you would have known [γνώσεσθε][55] my Father" and "From now on you do know [γινώσκετε] him." The thrust of this passage is about knowing; and—as is well known—these two verbs that mean "to know" are typical of the Gospel of John. The verb οἶδα appears twenty-five times in Matthew, twenty-two in Mark, twenty-five in Luke, but eighty-five in John. The verb γινώσκω appears twenty times in Matthew, twelve in Mark, twenty-eight in Luke, but fifty-six in John.[56]

The concept "No one comes to the Father except through me" seems intrusive to this strain of thought. It thus is not only grammatically free from the context but also intrusive conceptually.[57] Verse 16b appears to be a later addition to the Gospel of John, perhaps by the author of the "second edition" (who is conceivably the same as the author of the first edition). As we consider the force of this argument, it is helpful to note that U. C. Von Wahlde concluded that 8:31 and 10:19, which respectively contain the nouns Ἰουδαίους and Ἰουδαίοις, were redactional expansions to the Gospel of John.[58]

Contextuality and *Entwicklungslinie*

As we seek to discern later accretions to the Jesus traditions, we need to be aware of the difference between the sociology of Jesus and the sociology of the Johannine group. In *Judas Iscariot and the Myth of Jewish Evil,* H. Maccoby highlights the developed and negative portrayal of Judas in the Gospel of John: "John's chief addition to the story is to turn Judas Iscariot into the treasurer of Jesus' movement. Being thus soiled by contact with money, Judas can more credibly turn to evil."[59]

It seems more likely to me that the first edition contained the tradition that Judas was the treasurer of Jesus' group (13:29). That would be a

55. This future verb is changed in some manuscripts to a pluperfect of οἶδα, esp. B C*, or a pluperfect of γινώσκω, esp. A and C³.

56. See R. Morgenthaler, *Statistik des neutestamentlichen Wortschatzes* (Stuttgart, 1973).

57. I have enjoyed fruitful conversations with Prof. B. Klappert, who urges me to explore to what extent 14:6b should be understood in terms of eschatology; that is, does it mean "no one shall come to the Father except by me"? It is obvious that some members of the Johannine school may have understood it to denote an eschatological wish, similar to the one articulated by Paul in Romans 9–11.

58. Von Wahlde, "Johannine 'Jews,'" pp. 53–54.

59. H. Maccoby, *Judas Iscariot and the Myth of Jewish Evil* (New York, 1992), p. 63.

positive evaluation of Judas, and there is nothing intrinsically evil about being in charge of the money for Jesus' group. Also, when Judas leaves the Last Supper, according to chapter 13, everyone in the room—including the beloved disciple—assumes he is going out to do something positive. This seems quite remarkable, since the episode begins with the editorial comment that "the devil had already" persuaded Judas to betray Jesus (13:2). It thus appears that a later redactor added the negative innuendoes that Judas stole from the money pouch; 12:6 is clearly an editorial comment: "He [Judas] said this not because he cared for the poor, but because he was a thief; he kept the common purse and used to steal what was put into it." If this passage is redactional, then Judas appears in a negative light only in the later strata. As we know from Hegesippus, the hatred of Judas grew as the tradition developed.

While Paul and the Synoptic Gospels contrast Jesus with Greeks, the Gospel of John and Acts differentiate between Jesus' group and "the Jews."[60] This is clearly a later development.

Another later development is the concept that Jesus and the early members of the Palestinian Jesus movement did not speak about those outside of a closed group as "Jews." The study of Mark 4:11 has revealed that "those outside" (ἐκείνοις δὲ τοῖς ἔξω)[61] is a Marcan redaction, indeed, not only an alteration but a perversion of Jesus' message. That is, in the attempt to explain the meaning of Jesus' parables and to make it clear that Jesus was coherent and that his disciples understood them, Mark added that "those outside" did not understand them, and that this was Jesus' intent. To bolster the point, Mark paraphrases Isa. 6:9–10.[62] Many more passages than this Marcan redaction indicate that Jesus and his followers were seeking to reach others; they neither conceived "those outside" nor rejected them. Hence, the strong social barriers between Jesus and "the Jews" reflect a post-30 development of the Jesus traditions.

The concept that there are some outside of Jesus' group and that they cannot come to God except through Jesus is a later development in the flow of traditions from Jesus' own traditions to the traditions attributed to him. That is, the negative portrayal of "the Jews" and the exclusives in the Gospel seem not to be from Jesus but are most likely later alterations of what Jesus had said.[63]

60. See Smith, "Judaism," pp. 76–99.
61. Cf. the variant εζωθεν in MSS. B and Σ.
62. Mark's Greek does not follow the LXX, and it is different from the *Biblia Hebraica*.
63. For an explanation of the flow from Jesus' traditions to the Jesus traditions, see J. H. Charlesworth and W. Weaver, eds., *Jesus Two Thousand Years Later* (Valley Forge, Pa., 2000).

Contextuality and Sociology

If it appears that the historical Jesus did not think about those "outside" his group and, moreover, judge them to be lost, the same does not apply to the Johannine community. Johannine Christians, like the members of the Qumran community (יחד), did think about those out side as lost and damned.

Who were those outside? For the members of the Johannine community, they were the other Jews who had expelled from the synagogue Jews who openly believed in Jesus and also wished to continue to celebrate Sabbaths and festivals in the synagogue. As we know, the Johannine Jews who believed in Jesus and who thought of themselves as Jewish[64] were being expelled from a synagogue.

The adjective αφπο ἀπογυνάγωγος appears three times in the New Testament, each time only in the Gospel of John. This adjective mirrors a major sociological crisis for the Johannine Christians. There appear to be three sociological groups: some Johannine Christians obviously were not Jews and had no interest in frequenting the synagogue; others were Jews who had been expelled from the synagogue; and most likely others continued to attend synagogal services—but hiding, as did Joseph of Arimathea (John 19:38), their commitment to Jesus.

The reason some Jews were being expelled from the synagogue was their commitment to Jesus and their belief in him as the Messiah and One who was identified with God.[65] Note the explanation in the Gospel of John for being cast out of the synagogue: "some Judaean leaders had already agreed that if any one should confess him [Jesus] to be the Christ, that one was to be put out of the synagogue" (John 9:22 J.H.C.).

Messianology is not Christology. As Bishop E. Lohse has shown, for Jews the Messiah never became the ground of meaning or the content of salvation. Jews did not direct their eschatological expectations to a person or a Messiah; they directed them "to the messianic age which he will inaugurate and to the work he will accomplish under God's commission."[66]

---

64. See J. T. Sanders's argument regarding the Jewish consciousness of the followers of Jesus in Jerusalem and the reason other Jews found them offensive. J. T. Sanders, *Schismatics, Sectarians, Dissidents, Deviants: The First One Hundred Years of Jewish-Christian Relations* (Valley Forge, Pa., 1993), esp. pp. 67–81.

65. See J. Painter, *The Quest for the Messiah: The History, Literature and Theology of the Johannine Community*, 2d ed. (Nashville, 1993).

66. E. Lohse, "The Christ of the Jews and the Messiah of the Christians," *Expl.* 9 (1995): 2, 1.

Thus, not only members of the Palestinian Jesus movement but also many Jews held messianic beliefs, and some of Jesus' followers may have thought that *when he returned* he would be the Messiah and fulfill the expectations sometimes associated with this eschatological figure (cf. especially Acts 2:36).

The obvious reason for expulsion was exclusivistic theology and Christology. Messianology or Christology was tolerated within Judaism,[67] but what would have been abhorrent was the claim that Jesus was God's Messiah and that the crucified one was to be equated with God.[68] That belief was volatile within Judaism, and the Johannine community was still on the fringes of Judaism. Exclusivistic Christology causes divisiveness, and it shapes the later layers of the Gospel of John. A prime example is 14:6b.

Thus, we have come to perceive that the author of the Gospel of John lived at a time or place in which the tensions with Jews had increased, for example, beyond that experienced by the author of Luke-Acts. As D. Juel states, the trial of Paul provides the author of Luke–Acts the "opportunity to refute charges that Paul is a Jewish heretic."[69] The noun *heretic* may seem anachronistic, but its use helps make the point that, according to some— maybe most—Jews, Paul had moved beyond the borders of acceptable behavior and belief. That is, more than the Jewish authorities had concluded that Paul had ceased to be a faithful and accepted Jew. His future damnation was at stake, and as E. E. Urbach has shown,[70] the Jews stoned other Jews to purify them from demons and other impurities. Jews stoned other Jews to cleanse them so that they could remain within Israel in "the world to come," to quote 4 Ezra, an apocalypse composed at about the same time as the editing of the Gospel of John (cf. 4 Ezra 8:1).[71]

For the Jews near the Johannine community, the unthinkable had occurred. Those Jews in the Johannine community espoused views that were seen by other Jews as unacceptable within the Judaism that was taking shape between 70 and 132 C.E.. The rift was far more severe than the

67. See the contributions in J. H. Charlesworth et al., eds., *The Messiah: Developments in Early Judaism and Christianity* (Minneapolis, 1992); and in J. H. Charlesworth, H. Lichtenberger, and G. S. Oegema, eds., *Qumran-Messianism* (Tübingen, 1998).

68. See further J. H. Charlesworth, "From Jewish Messianology to Christian Christology: Some Caveats and Perspectives," in J. Neusner, W. S. Green, and E. Frerichs, eds., *Judaisms and Their Messiahs at the Turn of the Christian Era* (Cambridge–New York, 1987), pp. 225–64.

69. D. Juel, *Luke-Acts: The Promise of History* (Atlanta, 1983), p. 77.

70. I am indebted to E. E. Urbach for numerous lengthy conversations; he is now deceased, but see his monumental *The Sages*, 2 vols. (Jerusalem, 1979).

71. "Et respondit ad me et dixit: Hoc saeculum fecit Altissimus propter multos, futurum autem propter paucos" (4 Ezra 8:1). See A. F. J. Klijn, ed., *Der lateinische Text der Apokalypse des Esra* (TUGAL 131; Berlin, 1983), p. 56.

implied author of Luke-Acts knew, but not so severe and shattered as the
implied author of Matthew seems to experience. For the Johannine community there was still some contact with Jews. Barriers were rapidly going
up, and the reason was an exclusivistic claim about Jesus being the only way
to God the Father.

How do these reflections impact on the understanding of John 14:6b?
Since the adjective ἀποσυνάγωγος appears in the early stratum of John
(9:22; 12:42; 16:2), it cannot be judged to be a redactional addition to
John.

The concept represented by this Greek adjective is not entirely clear. If
"being cast out of the synagogue" is a generic term, then the concept can
fit into the life of Jesus, since there are traditions that he was expelled from
a synagogue (Luke 4:16–30). If the Greek adjective is a *terminus technicus,*
as many exegetes conclude, then it denotes an institutional rejection of
believers in Jesus by some official synagogue, obviously the one in the setting of the Johannine community. The term then takes on meaning only
in the second generation of Jesus' followers. It thus appears in the early stratum of John (not the elusive sources) and apparently denotes a sociological rejection not experienced by Jesus or Paul.

These reflections help us comprehend that the exclusivism of John 14:6b
cannot be traced back to Jesus and is an accretion to the early traditions.
Thus, I agree with D. M. Smith, who notes "the radical claim of Johannine
Christology" and sees John 14:6b in light of the "bitter polemic between
Christ-confessing and Christ-denying Jews, in which confessors are being
expelled from synagogues for their belief."[72] As L. T. Johnson has shown,
we must seek to understand the hostile words in the New Testament, especially in the Gospel of John, in light of what we have learned about the
rhetoric of polemics in antiquity.[73]

Contextuality and Narrative Exegesis

What is the literary type of the statement "No one comes to the Father
except through me"? It is an answer. Then what was the question, and how
does it help us approximate the work of editing by the author(s) of the
Gospel of John? The question was posed by Thomas, who responded to
Jesus' statement to the disciples "And you know the way to the place where
I am going" (14:5). Thomas then asks, "Lord, we do not know where you

72. D. M. Smith, *John* (Nashville, 1999), p. 269.
73. See L. T. Johnson, "The New Testament's Anti- Jewish Slander and the Conventions of Ancient
Polemic," *JBL* 108 (1989): 419–41.

are going. How can we know the way?" (John 14:5). Jesus' answer is clear: "I am the way, and the truth, and the life." The rest of the verse looks like an addition, since it is not an answer but a pronouncement that is not related to the specific question raised by Thomas.

Thomas did not ask, "Are there other ways to the Father except through you?" Thus, the statement in John 14:6b does not fit the narrative and looks like a later addition.[74]

John 14:6 and Johannine Theology

Does a study of the theology of the Gospel of John help answer the question of whether John 14:6 is composite? That is, is 14:6 a mixture of early tradition (v. 16a) with an expansion that derives from a later situation (v. 16b)? I do not think that John 14:6b is similar to 10:9, in which Jesus depicts himself as "the gate" (or "door"). John 14:6b is blatantly exclusivistic, but in 10:9 we do not find a claim that one can reach God only through Jesus, or that Jesus is the only door.[75] Hence, my comments are limited to three observations.

1. Jesus' saying is an "I am" pronouncement: ἐγώ εἰμι ἡ ὁδὸς καὶ ἡ ἀλήθεια καὶ ἡ ζωή. The "I am" sayings in the Gospel of John serve narratively as a recognition formula for the disciples and for the implied reader; they also indicate Jesus' consciousness. John 14:6a is clearly related to numerous "I am" declarations found elsewhere in the Gospel of John.[76] This "I am" formula is part of the earliest stratum in the Gospel of John. It appears infrequently in the Synoptics (five times in Matt, three in Mark, four in Luke) but twenty-nine times in the Gospel of John. Thus, the author of John did not create the formula. As R. Schnackenburg concluded, the "I am" sayings "certainly antedate the gospel."[77] It is obvious that the symbols that appear as predicates with the formula "I am" in the Gospel of John (namely, bread, light, door, shepherd, way, truth, and life) are well known in early Jewish texts. Each of these symbols was well known to the Palestinian Jews who produced the Old Testament Apocrypha and

74. For reflections on the individual eschatology found in 14:6, see J. Frey, *Die johanneische Eschatologie,* 2 vols. (WUNT 96 and 110; Tübingen, 1997–98), 1:172.

75. Contrast R. E. Brown, who thinks that in John 14:6 "Jesus is presenting himself as the only avenue of salvation, in the manner of x 9: 'I am the gate.'" (*The Gospel according to John* [AB; New York, 1970], p. 630).

76. See J. Becker, "Die Ich-bin-Worte," in *Das Evangelium nach Johannes,* 2 vols. (Würzburg, 1979–81; 3d ed., 1991), 1:249–69.

77. R. Schnackenburg, *The Gospel according to St John,* 3 vols., trans. K. Smyth (New York, 1987), 2:80.

Pseudepigrapha and the Dead Sea Scrolls. Thus, John 14:6a seems to belong to at least the earliest stratum of John; it contrasts with what we have learned about 14:6b.

2. The "Love Commandment," found only in John 13:34 (only a few verses before 14:6), may have once been intended to be inclusive. The disciples are to love "one another" as Jesus had loved them. It is tempting to see this exhortation as inclusive, but the setting is the Last Supper, and Jesus says to his disciples that they are to love "one another." The exhortation is markedly dissimilar to the one in the Sermon on the Mount: "Love your enemies and pray for those who persecute you" (Matt. 5:44).

As has been known for decades, the Johannine "Love Commandment" is even more restricted in the Johannine epistles. There love seems limited to a fellow Christian: "Whoever loves a brother or sister lives in the light, and in such a person there is no cause for stumbling. But whoever hates another believer is in the darkness, walks in the darkness, and does not know the way to go, because the darkness has brought on blindness" (1 John 2:10–11). This is an exclusive concept of love that is now restricted to a fellow Christian. The symbolic dualism and the *termini technici,* and surely the exclusion of others, raise the question of some Essene influence.

If this passage in 1 John postdates the core of the Gospel of John, it then throws light on the secondary nature of the exclusiveness of John 14:6b. Perhaps the general command to "love one another" of John 13:34, which is not necessarily delimited to those only in Jesus' group, has become even more restricted in John 15:12. In this verse, love of one another seems colored by love for one's friends (John 15:13). If so, since chapter 15 is an addition to the core of John, then it looks more likely that 14:6b may also be a later addition. Both are exclusivistic. That is, to exclude others from love is in harmony with the claim that those who do not come to God through Jesus are damned.

3. Does the incipient Docetism apparent in the Gospel of John and the schism clear in the later stages of the Johannine tradition help clarify if John 14:6 is composite? Perhaps it does, since the cause of the schism was a Docetic type of Christology and the concern of 14:6b is an exclusivistic Christology. Both are related to a social and ideological distancing from Judaism, for as D. Bonhoeffer saw (and F. H. Littell later affirmed), Docetism is a heresy coming from paganism.[78] As Bonhoeffer stated, "The docetic heresy is the typical heresy of Greek thought. It is pagan thought par excellence. It has one opponent: Jewish thought."[79]

78. F. H. Littell, *The Crucifixion of the Jews* (Macon, Ga., 1975), p. 50.
79. D. Bonhoeffer, *Christ the Center* (New York, 1966), p. 79.

The final emphasis on "Jewish thought" has not been sufficiently developed by the commentators on the Gospel of John. That is, not only Docetism but the offensive Christology of John 14:6b may help us understand the schism within the Johannine community, which is obvious from 1 John 2:19. That is, a crisis Christology is typical of the later stages of the Gospel of John, and John 14:6b would be explosively controversial within the development of Jesus' sayings.

R. Schnackenburg concluded that John 14:6b is "a culminating point in Johannine theology." He was convinced that "it forms a classical summary of the Johannine doctrine of salvation that is based entirely on Jesus Christ."[80] This is misleading, even if we see 14:6b in light of the redactional sections. John 14:6b is similar to the theology in John 1:1–18, which is clearly a later addition to the Gospel. The verse is also similar to the thoughts found in chapters 15–17 (especially John 1:11–13) that follow chapter 14 and are also an expansion to the core of John.

But there is more to be said. In my judgment, explicit exclusivistic theology that denies salvation, a way to God, except through Jesus is found in the Gospel of John only in 14:6b.[81] Elsewhere it is certainly implied, but there is a paradigmatic difference between implied and explicit exclusivism, and usually the concern of Johannine exclusivism is knowing and not salvation.[82] To claim that Jesus Christ is "the way, and the truth, and the life" does not mean all who do not believe in Jesus are damned. John 14:6a does not remove God's free salvific mission and imply that all previous means of reaching him, all previous covenants, are now null and void.

John 14:6b states unequivocally that no one can come to God "except through" Jesus Christ. That violates much of biblical theology, especially Paul's theology in Romans 9–11, which, as K. Stendahl has shown, is the climax and not an appendix to Paul's thought in Romans.[83] John 14:6b also betrays the fundamental thrust and message of biblical theology.[84] John 14:6b adumbrates the horrific jettisoning of sacred scriptures (the Old Testament) that Marcion advocated in the middle of the second century C.E.

---

80. Schnackenburg, *Gospel according to St. John*, 3:65.

81. In contrast, B. Lindars thought that John 14:6 contained "no narrow exclusivism." Cf. B. Lindars, *The Gospel of John* (London–Grand Rapids, 1972), p. 473.

82. See J. Neusner, *A Rabbi Talks with Jesus* (New York, 1993), p. 72.

83. K. Stendahl, *Paul among Jews and Gentiles* (Philadelphia, 1976). Also see J. G. Gager, "Has Christ Abrogated the Torah? Has God Rejected His People?" in J. G. Gager, *The Origins of Anti-Semitism: Attitudes toward Judaism in Pagan and Christian Antiquity* (Oxford–New York, 1983), pp. 213–29.

84. See the special issue of the *Princeton Seminary Bulletin,* supplementary issue (1990) 1, which contains reflections on Romans 9–11, under the focused theme "The Church and Israel," by D. L. Migliore, P. M. van Buren, O. Hofius, J. C. Beker, A. F. Segal, B. J. Brooten, D. Satran, M. P. Engel, and M. Welker.

Clearly, the author of the Gospel of John was no Marcion, since he emphasized the Jewishness of Jesus (who was portrayed going up to Jerusalem to celebrate the Jewish festivals), and that Jesus was the Messiah of the Jews.[85]

Thus, John 14:6b looks intrusive and misrepresentative of the early core of the Fourth Gospel. The thought is reminiscent of the chilling *extra ecclesia nulla salus est* and the anti-Jewish hermeneutic of some "church fathers."[86] There is exclusivism in the Gospel of John, but such an explicit exclusivism that damns all who are not of the same mind is typical of Qumran but not of the core of Johannine theology.

These short forays into Johannine theology, in light of John 14:6b, all lead in the same direction. The evidence suggests that exclusivism appears only in the redactional stratum of the Gospel of John. Thus, John 14:6b seems to be redactional.

Johannine Theology and Jewish Theology

In what ways, if at all, does Johannine theology—when seen in light of Jewish theology—help solve the problem with 14:6? The appeal to "way," "truth," and "life" links John 14:6a with Jewish Wisdom traditions (especially Wisdom of Solomon and Sirach) and only to a minor extent with apocalypticism (e.g., *1 Enoch*). The claim on exclusivism in John 14:6b has more ties with Qumran sectarianism and with some forms of apocalypticism. Perhaps a case can be made that these observations help us see a difference between the two grammatically independent sentences in 14:6, but even so, this cannot be used, by itself, as an argument for 14:6 being a later addition. As we know from recent research on apocalypticism, the apocalypses are indebted not only to prophecy but also to Wisdom.

Thinking about early Jewish theology, however, does make it clear how different John 14:6a is from 14:6b. John 14:6a is harmonious with ideas found within Second Temple Judaism. At Qumran, for example, the members of the Community called themselves "the perfect of the Way" (1QS 7.10) and "Sons of Truth" (1QS 4.5). They believed that they had "living water" (1QH 8.16)[87] and would thus have "perpetual life" (1QS 4.7). Concern for the "way," "truth," and "life" is also found in works

85. See further J. T. Townsend, "The Gospel of John and the Jews," in A. Davies, ed., *Antisemitism and the Foundations of Christianity* (New York, 1979), p. 81.

86. See G. Stemberger, *Juden und Christen im Heiligen Land: Palästina unter Konstantin und Theodosius* (Munich, 1987).

87. "Living water," of course, is well known in Johannine theology. For creation motifs and this metaphor, see M. A. Daise, "'Rivers of Living Water' as New Creation and New Exodus: A Traditio-Historical Vantage Point for the Exegetical Problems and Theology of John 7:37–39" (Ph.D. diss., Princeton Theological Seminary, 1999).

more representative of established Judaism in Jerusalem and can be found in *Jubilees,* Sirach, the Wisdom of Solomon, the *Testaments of the Twelve Patriarchs,* and elsewhere.

In light of Jewish theology, however, John 14:6b is unattractive theology. To claim that "no one comes to the Father" except through one person is anathema to Judaism. It is not even easy to attribute such ideas to the authors of the Qumranic *Pesharim,* in which "the Righteous Teacher" is celebrated as the only one to whom God has given the key to the mystery of prophecy (1QpHab 7). Within Judaism, John 14:6b would have been unthinkable and horrific, because it impinges on God's freedom and implies that God has broken his covenant with the Jews.[88] The latter thought, of course, was anathema to Paul, who argued assiduously against it (Rom. 11:1): "Has God rejected his people? μὴ γένοιτο."

Summary

As I have suggested previously, "We need to 'indwell' the social setting that gave rise to the words chosen, and then attend to the narrative and rhetorical thrust of the author and the type of literature he (or she) has produced."[89] Indwelling the social setting of the Gospel of John reveals some reasons why these Johannine Christians would feel compelled to alter some of Jesus' traditions. We have already seen how the narrative and rhetorical thrust of chapter 14 is altered by the statement that "no one comes to the Father except through me." The Gospel of John is not a polemic treatise, although there are polemical passages in it. It is a Gospel, and the only one that contains a new commandment. As just mentioned, it is the commandment attributed to Jesus: "I give you a new commandment, that you love one another. Just as I have loved you, you also should love one another" (John 13:34).

This new commandment anchors the Gospel of John in the Hebrew scriptures in which ten commandments are given by God, through Moses, to Israel. The very first words—"In the beginning"—in the Gospel of John are a deliberate attempt to link the new with the old. Moreover, as P. Borgen has shown, many words in the prologue are taken from Genesis 1, and the whole hymn is influenced by targumic exegesis.[90] While some scholars argue that the relation between the Old and New Testaments is one of

88. God's covenant with the Jews is just as important and unbreakable as his covenant with others, especially those who would be called Christians (a term that is anachronistic in the first century). See P. O'Hare, *The Enduring Covenant* (Valley Forge, Pa., 1997).

89. J. H. Charlesworth, "Faith Grounded in History," in E. J. Fisher, *Faith without Prejudice* (New York, 1993), p. 11.

90. P. Borgen, *Logos Was the True Light* (Relieff 9; Trondheim, 1983).

promise and fulfillment, I am persuaded that this is a dangerous model. It tends to feed Christian supersessionism. Much more accurate is the concept of expanded scripture; that is, the Christian Bible reveals the continuing activity of God, always seen as moving toward his people on earth, reflected upon and set down in writing. Thus, far better is the paradigm of "expectation-proclamation," the perception of a relation of typology, and an experience of God's awe.[91]

We have discovered that a case—perhaps only a conceivable case—can be made for the possibility that John 14:6b is a later addition to the Gospel of John. In summation, John 14:6a has the character of tradition; that is, it may derive ultimately from Jesus—or may be a restating of his original message. In contrast, John 14:6b is redactional. It cannot be traced back to Jesus. It seems to reflect and thus derive from the problems and perspectives of the second generation of Jesus' followers.

Conclusion

Paradigmatic Difference: Jews Did Not Kill Jesus

Many of the verses in which Ἰουδαῖοι or similar plural nouns appear have been translated so that hatred of Jews and Judaism is fostered or inflamed. We have shown that in some places, especially in John 11:54, the word does not single out "the Jews." It specifies some of the Judaean leaders who were jealous of Jesus, who were upset by some of his teachings, who feared his threat to the security of their powerful position, or who were concerned with problems he might cause from the ruling Romans. While we cannot change the Greek text of the New Testament, we can be more attentive when we translate so that the original contexts of texts inform us of translations and possible misinterpretations. Translating the New Testament is not similar to translating the Dead Sea Scrolls or Old Testament Pseudepigrapha. With the New Testament, we must be alert to how the texts are being read by the masses; that is, as if they were this morning's news from God.

The Problematic of John 14:6

At the beginning of this research, I was convinced that John 14:6 was an insurmountable problem for the scholar. Now I can imagine that many

---

91. For further reflections, see J. H. Charlesworth, "What Has the Old Testament to Do with the New?" in J. H. Charlesworth and W. P. Weaver, eds., *The Old and the New Testaments: Their Relationship and the "Intertestamental" Literature* (Valley Forge, Pa., 1993), pp. 39–87.

scholars will see that John 14:6 consists of two grammatically independent sentences. The ancient Greek scribes have shown us that by their punctuations; in English, the first probably indicates a semicolon and the second a period. John 14:6b looks redactional. It mirrors the struggles of two Jewish communities who, in their attempt to establish and defend their own existences, spewed out invectives upon others (thus following the earlier lead of the Qumranites). Thus, John 14:6b is a relic of the past. It is not the Word of God for our time. This conclusion will be shared by many others, including those who are not convinced that it is supported by disinterested philological, redactional, and historical research.

Communication

I am not sure how we can communicate the insights regarding John 11:54 and 14:6 to a wider audience. I have learned that scholars are viewed with suspicion in some circles, and these are the very ones from which hatred of Jews often evolves. As scholars, our medium is writing, but today most people obtain information from visuals and television. We should make some changes: we need to write what others besides scholars are reading, and we should contemplate communicating through media other than writing.

Remaining Problems

Some problems with the explicit exclusivism in the Gospel of John may be discarded or exposed as later accretions in the transmission of traditions.[92] John 14:6b seems to represent a second-generation crisis. Yet some of the later concept of exclusivism may derive fundamentally from Jesus and the unparalleled claims he placed on those who heard him. It was costly to follow Jesus. He demanded all. He redefined families and what was God's will. Like Hillel, Jesus had an exalted concept of himself and made exclusive claims.[93] Being honest and scholars with integrity does not preclude us from being alert against errors such as translations and interpretations that foster Christian heresy, anti-Judaism, and supersessionism.[94]

---

92. Contrast G. Lüdemann, who thinks that the Gospel of John is strongly anti-Jewish (*Das Unheilige in der Heiligen Schrift: Die andere Seite der Bibel* [Stuttgart, 1996], p. 107).

93. See D. Flusser, "Hillel and Jesus: Two Ways of Self- Awareness," in J. H. Charlesworth and L. L. Johns, eds., *Hillel and Jesus: Comparative Studies of Two Major Religious Leaders* (Minneapolis, 1997), pp. 71–107.

94. See especially R. T. Osborn, "The Christian Blasphemy: A Non-Jewish Jesus," in J. H. Charlesworth, ed., *Jews and Christians: Exploring the Past, Present, and Future* (Shared Ground Among Jews and Christians 1; New York, 1990), pp. 211–39.

Hope and Promise

By studying the Greek of the Gospel of John with the literary context and social setting in mind, we may be able to remove some of the problems with this masterpiece.[95] Before focusing our research on the Gospel of John in light of anti-Judaism, we may have agreed with R. R. Ruether that in this Gospel the "Jews" are "the very incarnation of the false, apostate principles of the fallen world, alienated from its true being in God."[96] Now we know that some of the hatred poured into Greek terms that have been translated as "Jews" is focused on "some Judaean leaders (or authorities)" and can often be explained by the tension between the followers of Hillel and the followers of Jesus, in a world in which Israel has been defeated and the house of God burned by infidels. While Christians have a Greek New Testament that has been canonized, they are not bound by anti-Judaism in its translations—or in its Greek text.

We scholars must follow the lead of the Vatican and make a break with our past practices. Some of our way may be indicated in the words of *Nostra Aetate* 4:

> Even though the Jewish authorities and those who followed their lead pressed for the death of Christ (cf. John 19:6), neither all Jews indiscriminately at that time, nor Jews today, can be charged with the crimes committed during his passion.[97]

It is encouraging and enlightening to note that from the Vatican comes not the word *Jews* but "Jewish authorities." One step ahead for us will be to recognize that οἱ Ἰουδαῖοι in John 19:6 denotes "some Judaean leaders" who are debating with Pilate in Jerusalem. As other professors and scholars once endorsed and gave credibility to the Nazis, so we must, in our own countries and in the global community, dedicate ourselves so "that those who died will not be forgotten and that never again will the brutality of those unspeakably horrible acts be repeated."[98]

---

95. Contrast M. Brumlik, "Johannes. Das judenfeindliche Evangelium," in D. Neuhaus, ed., *Teufelskinder oder Heilsbringer: Die Juden im Johannes-Evangelium* (Arnoldshainer Texte 64; Frankfurt-am-Main, 1990; 2d ed., 1993), pp. 6–21).

96. R. R. Ruether, "The Philosophizing of Anti-Judaism in Paul, Hebrews, and the Gospel of John," in *Faith and Fratricide: The Theological Roots of Anti-Semitism* (New York, 1974), pp. 95–116, 113.

97. J. H. Charlesworth, "The Vatican's Lead against Anti-Semitism and Anti-Judaism," in S. Wiesenthal, *Every Day Remembrance Day* (Philadelphia, 1992), pp. vii–ix.

98. J. H. Charlesworth, "Expressing the Inconceivable," in I. J. Borowsky, ed., *Artists Confronting the Inconceivable* (Philadelphia, 1992), p. 9.

As scholars, we need to emphasize that we need Jews thriving in our communities.[99] Maybe some of the past problems were because the two groups that evolved out of early Judaism (or Second Temple Judaism) shared so much and needed to obtain self-definition by relating polemically with the other Jewish interpretation of Torah.[100] We need Jews in our communities, because they keep us honest and provide different and enlightening perspectives. God has given gifts to the Jews.[101] Both Christians and Jews inherit the faith of Abraham and are Rebecca's children.[102] As Jack Neusner states,

> The ancient rabbis of Judaism teach important lessons to believing people today. . . . The ancient rabbis show us how to read Scripture in a way that we can follow. They show us ways of responding to Scripture that we may not have imagined. They also teach us dimensions of scriptural meaning that we may not otherwise grasp. We Jews and Christians, together revering Scripture . . . do well to seek in our encounter with the teachings of the living God the wisdom, imagination, and insight of the ages.[103]

A new millennium has dawned as I have written this essay. Surely, as Father J. J. Petuchowski states, Jews and Christians may find hope in asking if we are "all recipients of the same divine revelation." Certainly, by improving our translation of John 11:54 and our understanding of the secondary nature of 14:6b, we come much closer to agreeing with Petuchowski "that such an assent may ultimately be given."[104] Is not H. Cox right that we need to move from tendencies toward abstractions from life to actualizing in our own being God's reign? Is this not becoming a disciple of Jesus, to eschew the fantasy of emulating or mimicking him and to live "in our era the same way he lived in his—as a sign and servant of the reign of God"? That is, "to take up his life project—making the coming of God's reign of Shalom real and immediate—our own."[105]

---

99. B. Klappert rightly shows that scholars must be familiar with Jews if they intend to understand the gospel. See his "Man muss die Juden kennen, wenn man das Evangelium verstehen will," in F. Grubauer and W. Lenz, eds., *Protestantisch—weltoffen—streitbar* (Bad Boll, 1999), pp. 139–69.

100. For a discussion of the many ideas shared by Jews and "Christians," see K. H. Rengstorf, ed., *Kirche und Synagoge,* 2 vols. (Stuttgart, 1968–70).

101. See T. Cahill, *The Gifts of the Jews* (New York, 1998).

102. See the informative and encouraging thought by A. F. Segal, *Rebecca's Children: Judaism and Christianity in the Roman World* (Cambridge, Mass., 1986). Also see M. R. Wilson, *Our Father Abraham: Jewish Roots of the Christian Faith* (Grand Rapids, 1989). In a wider context, I want to stress that Arabs, as well as Jews and Christians, are spiritual descendants of Abraham. See F. E. Peters, *Children of Abraham: Judaism, Christianity, Islam* (Princeton, N.J., 1982); and B. Klappert, "Abraham eint und unterscheidet," *Rhein Reden* 1 (1996): 21–64.

103. J. Neusner, "Christian Faith and the Bible of Judaism," *Expl.* 2 (1988): 3, p. 4.

104. J. J. Petuchowski, "Toward a Jewish Theology of Christianity," in V. A. McInnes, ed., *Renewing the Judeo-Christian Wellspring* (New York, 1987), p. 52.

105. H. Cox, *Many Mansions* (Boston, 1988), p. 11.

CHAPTER 13

"Synagogues of Satan" (Rev. 2:9 and 3:9):
Anti-Judaism in the Book of Revelation

Jan Lambrecht

No doubt the main enemy of the Christians[1] in the book of Revelation is the surrounding omnipresent paganism. Concretely speaking, behind the actions of Satan and the two beasts that appear on the scene in chapters 12 and 13 is the emperor cult, with its political, economic and religious propaganda and its menacing oppression.[2] Christians in western Asia Minor are suffering; persecution, even to death, could be imminent. Some Christians are tempted to adapt to a pagan lifestyle and "to compromise with trade guilds and their patron deities."[3] In the church of Sardis, Christ, "who has the seven spirits of God and the seven stars," does not find the Christians' "works perfect" (3:1–2); in Laodicea, Christ, who is "the Amen, the faithful and true witness, the origin of God's creation," addresses Christians as follows: "You are neither cold nor hot. . . . Because you are lukewarm . . . I am about to spit you out of my mouth" (3:14–16). Visibly, there is in more than one community lack of ardor, even of perseverance.

Moreover, the Christians of Ephesus as well as those of Pergamum are warned against the sect of the Nicolaitans, "who hold to the teaching of

---

1. Most probably the majority of the Christians in the churches of Revelation were Jewish Christians who still considered themselves "Jews." In this essay, the term *Christians* points to all believers in Jesus Christ in western Asia Minor.

2. See, e.g., S. R. F. Price, *Rituals and Power: The Roman Imperial Cult in Asia Minor* (Cambridge, 1984). T. Söding, "Heilig, heilig, heilig. Zur politischen Theologie der Johannes-Apokalypse," *ZTK* 96 (1999): 49–76, provides a brief and balanced description on pp. 50–54. Cf. A. Yarbro Collins, "Vilification and Self-Definition in the Book of Revelation," *HTR* 79 (1986): 308–20, p. 315: "The receptive audience of Revelation would reject the symbolic universe held by many around them which had the emperor at the center."

3. G. K. Beale, *The Book of Revelation* (NIGTC; Grand Rapids–Cambridge, 1999), p. 30. On the same page Beale writes: "Homage to the emperor as divine was included along with worship of such local deities. . . . After all, the patron gods of the guilds together with the imperial god of Rome were purportedly responsible for the social and economic blessings that the culture had enjoyed."

Balaam, who taught Balak to put a stumbling block before the people of Israel, so that they would eat food sacrificed to idols and practice fornication" (2:14; see 2:15 and 2:6). The Christians of Thyatira appear to be tolerating "that woman Jezebel, who calls herself a prophet and is teaching and beguiling my servants to practice fornication and to eat food sacrificed to idols" (2:20; cf. 2:21–24). Notwithstanding the Old Testament comparison with Balaam and the Old Testament name Jezebel, the people referred to are or represent heretic Christians, not Jews.

Yet, in two letters (according to the author of Revelation, the early Christian prophet John), the risen Lord speaks of "those who say that they are Jews and are not, but are a synagogue of Satan" (2:9b; cf. 3:9a). In the author's opinion, not the Jews but the Christians are the real Jews. Corroborative evidence is found in the way in which John identifies the Christian community with Israel and depicts the eschatological future of the church as the "new Jerusalem." Because of this negative mention of the Jews, as well as in view of John's almost matter-of-course presentation of the church's identity, the question of whether there is not a degree of anti-Judaism in the book of Revelation cannot be avoided.

This brief contribution first analyzes the immediate literary context of 2:9 and 3:9 and tries to determine the activity of the inimical Jews.[4] Second, the counterattack of John the prophet is investigated. Finally, a critical reflection must lead us to some hermeneutical conclusions.[5]

The Jews in Revelation 2:9 and 3:9
Revelation 2:8–11: Smyrna

8	a	And to the angel of the church in Smyrna write:
	b	These are the words of the first and the last, who was dead and came to life:
9	a	I know your affliction and your poverty, even though you are rich.
	b	I know the slander on the part of those who say that they are Jews and are not, but are a synagogue of Satan.

4. In this study there is no analysis of the clause "where also their Lord was crucified" in 11:8, probably not a reference to Jerusalem. See also n. 30, below.

5. For extensive bibliographies, see Beale, *Book of Revelation,* pp. xxviii–lxiv; and D. E. Aune, *Revelation* (WBC; Dallas, 1997), vol.1, particularly pp. 106 and 238 for 2:8–11 and 3:7–13, respectively.

10 a Do not fear what you are about to suffer.

   b Beware, the devil is about to throw some of you into prison
      so that you may be tested,

   c and for ten days you will have affliction.

   d Be faithful until death, and I will give you the crown of
      life.

11 a Let anyone who has an ear listen to what the Spirit is say-
      ing to the churches.

   b Whoever conquers will not be harmed by the second
      death.

The first occurrence of the name Ἰουδαῖοι is to be found in the letter
or message to the church of Smyrna, the second in the series of seven:
2:8–11. One immediately notes the correspondence between verses 8 and
10–11. The opposition of death and life on the one hand and eschatological life and death on the other is present at the beginning and the end of
the letter. The theme referred to in the clause "the words of the first and the
last, ὃς ἐγένετο νεκρὸς καὶ ἔζησεν" (v. 8b; cf. 1:17–18) is taken up in "Be
faithful ἄχρι θανάτου, and I will give you τὸν στέφανον τῆς ζωῆς"[6]
(v. 10d) and equally in "Whoever conquers will not be harmed ἐκ τοῦ
θανάτου τοῦ δευτέρου" (v. 11b). Obviously, this inclusion referring to
both Christ and Christians is by no means accidental.

It would seem that the clauses of verses 9 and 10 together constitute a
unity; they explain one another. Although the reference to "poverty" in
verse 9a may be partly due to the social and economic situation of Christians in Smyrna, the "affliction" in the same clause should almost certainly
be connected with the slander of the Jews in verse 9b, as well as with
the suffering, the prison, the testing,[7] and the "affliction" (same term:
θλῖψις) mentioned in verse 10abc. Moreover, although the vocabulary
varies, the "devil" in verse 10b can hardly be different from "Satan" at the
end of verse 9b. (See the identification of the dragon in 12:9, who is called
"the Devil and Satan"; cf. also 20:2.)

---

6. The last expression is not found outside the New Testament. Cf. R. H. Charles, *The Revelation
of St. John* (ICC; Edinburgh, 1920), 1:56; W. Schrage, "Meditation zu Offenbarung 2,8–11," *EvT* 48
(1988): 388–402, pp. 391–92.

7. Cf. Charles, *Revelation*, p. 58: "πειράζειν and πειρασμός in iii. 10 refer to the demonic
attacks which are to befall all the unbelievers on the earth, but which cannot affect those who
have been sealed. . . . But in the present verse πειράζειν is used in the sense of testing by persecution."

It has been claimed that the term *Jews* in 2:9b (and 3:9a) does not refer to non-Christian Jews but to "heretical" Christians such as the Nicolaitans or the followers of Jezebel: they claim to be "spiritual" Jews, but in fact they are not.[8] Since specific warnings against such "spiritual" Jews are lacking, however, it is better to take the name Jews in its normal meaning, that is, in its non-Christian sense and not as pointing to Jewish Christians.[9]

The Christians" affliction and suffering, their being in prison and being tested, appear to be caused by the βλασφημία of the Jews of Smyrna. Elsewhere in the book of Revelation, this term, as well as the verb βλασφημέω, signifies the insult of God and hence plausibly also the denial of Jesus as his Messiah.[10] In view of the connection between verse 9 and verse 10, however, especially the mention of prison (v. 10b), the term here most likely means "slander," not "blasphemy." The context makes that it probably points here to the denunciation of Christians before Roman or civic authorities.[11] Jewish Christians in Smyrna may have tried to avoid the obligations

---

8. Schrage, "Meditation," pp. 390–91 and 394–95, seems to prefer this identification. See H. Kraft, *Die Offenbarung des Johannes* (HNT; Tübingen, 1974), pp. 60–61: "Johannes ist nicht an den Juden, sondern an den Christen interessiert. Eine Satanssynagoge in seinem Sinn ist eine jüdisch-christliche Gruppe, deren Kult von ihm als Götzendienst, d.i. Satansdienst angesehen wird. Ihre 'Lästerungen' sind ihre Behauptungen über Tod und Auferstehung Christi, die sie entweder völlig, oder wenigstens in ihren Heilswert leugnen. . . . Da jene Gruppe sich ausdrücklich als Juden bezeichnet, ist nicht nur zu folgern, dass den Juden in der bevorstehenden Verfolgung keine Gefahr droht, sondern auch vor allem, dass die Gruppe eben dadurch, dass sie sich als Juden bezeichnet, sich der Verfolgung entzieht" (p. 61); see also pp. 81–82.

9. See Collins, "Vilification," esp. pp. 310–16; and cf. E. Lohse, "Synagogue of Satan and Church of God: Jews and Christians in the Book of Revelation," *SEÅ* 58 (1993): 105–23, esp. pp. 106–7; H. Giesen, *Die Offenbarung des Johannes* (RNT; Regensburg, 1997), p. 107; Aune, *Revelation*, p. 164; P. Borgen, "Polemic in the Book of Revelation," in C. A. Evans and D. A. Hagner, eds., *Anti-Semitism and Early Christianity: Issues of Polemic and Faith* (Minneapolis, 1993), pp. 119–211, esp. p. 200.

10. So, e.g., Lohse, "Synagogue of Satan," pp. 119–20: "it is the most probable assumption that the controversy about the problem of the Messiah and the Christian confession of the church has caused refusal and contradiction from the side of the synagogues." Cf., e.g., Acts 18:5–6 and 26:11. In Rev. 13:1, 5, 6; 16:9, 11, 21; and 17:3, the terminology is employed in the usual sense of blaspheming against God, cursing (the name of) God.

11. Cf. J. Lambrecht, "Jewish Slander: A Note on Revelation 2,9–10," *ETL* 75 (1999): 421–29. For the procedure of denunciation, reference is very often made to the well-known letter of Pliny the Younger (*Ep. Tra.* 10.96.1–10) and the answer by Emperor Trajan (*Ep. Tra.* 10.97.1–2). See, however, H. Lichtenberger, "Überlegungen zum Verständnis der Johannes-Apokalypse," in C. Landmesser, H.-J. Eckstein, and H. Lichtenberger, eds., *Jesus Christus als die Mitte der Schrift. Studien zur Hermeneutik des Evangeliums*, FS O. Hofius (BZNW 86; Berlin–New York, 1997), pp. 603–18, esp. pp. 611–18 on Rev. 2:8–11: "βλασφημία/-μεῖν bedeutet in der Johannes-Apokalypse nie die Denunziation (gegenüber Behörden o.ä), sondern immer die Lästerung Gottes oder Jesu Christi als des Messias und Heilands der Welt. Damit entfallen all die Vermutungen und Konstruktionen, die eine jüdische Beteiligung an . . . den kleinasiatischen Gemeinde postulieren" (pp. 613–14). Cf. also Aune, *Revelation*, p. 166: "There is no explicit connection between the βλασφημία of the Jews mentioned in v 9 and impending imprisonment, though the work of Satan or the Devil is seen behind both." Schrage, "Meditation," p. 391, is hesitant: "Ob speziell die "Blasphemie" der Joudaioi das Leiden der Gemeinde ausgelöst hat und einige der Gemeindeglieder dadurch ins Gefängnis geworfen werden, lässt sich nicht sagen." Cf. also p. 394; and, already, W. Bousset, *Die Offenbarung Johannis* (KEK; Göttingen, 1906), p. 209.

of emperor worship by emphasizing their Jewish birth, but non-Christian Jews must have denounced them to authorities who therefore persecuted Christians and threw some of them into prison in order to "test" them, that is, to force them publicly to honor the emperor. Slander thus contains Jewish accusation or denunciation; in this sense it contains active participation of some Jews in causing affliction, suffering, and imprisonment to Christians.[12]

Revelation 3:7–13: Philadelphia

7	a	And to the angel of the church in Philadelphia write:
	b	These are the words of the holy one, the true one, who has the key of David, who opens and no one will shut, who shuts and no one opens:
8	a	I know your works.
	b	Look, I have set before you an open door, which no one is able to shut.
	c	I know that you have but little power, and yet you have kept my word and have not denied my name.
9	a	I will make those of the synagogue of Satan who say that they are Jews and are not, but are lying—
	b	I will make them come and bow down before your feet, and they will learn that I have loved you.
10	a	Because you have kept my word of patient endurance,
	b	I will keep you from the hour of trial that is coming on the whole world to test the inhabitants of the earth.

12. Cf., e.g., Charles, *Revelation*, pp. 55–56; Beale, *Book of Revelation*, pp. 29–32; 239–41; H.-J. Klauck, "Das Sendschreiben nach Pergamon und der Kaiserkult in der Johannesapokalypse," *Bib 74* (1992): 153–82, esp. pp. 162–64. See also Collins, "Vilification," pp. 312–14: "This juxtaposition [of the reference to the Jews with the prediction of detention in prison] suggests that the 'synagogue of Satan' are instigators of legal action against the persons whom John is addressing. Their blasphemy or slander then would be the charge or accusation which they made to initiate legal proceedings. The attribution of the detention to the work of the devil (2:10) links that event to the synagogue of Satan (2:9)" (p. 313). M. Hengel, *Die johanneische Frage. Ein Lösungsversuch* (WUNT 67; Tübingen, 1993), p. 292, writes: "Dass es von jüdischer Seite zu Klagen gegen die missionarisch aktiven Christen (vgl. Apk 3,9) kam, ist nur zu gut verständlich: Die Juden mussten diese enthusiastisch-missionarische Lehre als eine gefährliche Konkurrenz betrachten, durch die sie selbst bei den staatlichen Organen in Misskredit kommen konnten." Jews who persecute Christians are, of course, mentioned in Acts and the Pauline letters. In Acts 17:5–8 and 18:12–17, Jews accuse Christians before pagan authorities. Mention must also be made of the so-called *birkat ha-minim* at the end of the first century, the Jewish curse against the heretics, Jewish Christians included (cf. Justin, *Dial.* 16.4; 17.6; 96.2). Cf., however, Lichtenberger, "Überlegungen," p. 615: "ob der 'Ketzersegen' auch in Kleinasien üblich war, wissen wir freilich nicht" and "Die Birkat ha-Minim war nicht die Wasserscheide zwischen Judentum und Christentum, zu der sie gerne gemacht wird. Sie ist eher ein Dokument als die Ursache des Auseinandergehens."

11   a   I am coming soon;

       b   hold fast to what you have, so that no one may seize your
             crown.

12   a   If you conquer, I will make you a pillar in the temple of
             my God; you will never go out of it.

       b   I will write on you the name of my God, and the name of
             the city of my God, the new Jerusalem that comes down
             from my God out of heaven, and my own new name.

13   Let anyone who has an ear listen to what the Spirit is say-
             ing to the churches.

The sixth letter, that to the church of Philadelphia (3:7–13), is longer
than the second. Besides parts of 3:9, which are very much like 2:9, one
may see a reminder of that second letter in the mention of "crown" at the
end of 3:11b (cf. 2:10) and perhaps also in the clause "you have but little
power" in 3:8c (cf. "poverty," 2:9a). Moreover, these two letters are the only
ones in which no word of blame is uttered.[13]

Elements of the christological predication of verse 7b (the one "who has
the key of David, who opens and no one will shut, who shuts and no one
opens") are carried over into verse 8b: "an open door, which no one is able
to shut."[14] The expression "my name" at the end of verse 8c corresponds
with "my own new name" at the end of verse 12b; both expressions thus
constitute an inclusion.

Just as in 2:9b, the mention of the Jews in 3:9a cannot be isolated from
its immediate context. The Christians in Philadelphia have proven their
faithful obedience to Christ's word (vv. 8c and 10a), most probably during
the affliction and sufferings that the Jews brought about. The hypothesis
of the Jewish denunciation as well as the announcements of 2:9–10 has to
be supplied. The sentence in verse 9a is incomplete. A verb in the infinitive
(or a purpose clause) is missing after ἰδοὺ δίδῶ;[15] the sentence remains

13. It must strike the reader of the *Martyrium Policarpi* 19.1 that Philadelphia is mentioned as the
place where, as in Smyrna, Christians have been martyred. In this writing (12.2; 13.1; 17.2; 18.1), Jews
are said to have participated in Polycarp's execution in Smyrna (circa 155). Aune, *Revelation,* p. 162,
warns: "This account, however, is historically tendentious as well as strikingly anti-Jewish, consciously
formulated in an attempt to replicate the Gospel narratives of the passion of Jesus." For a recent critical edition and discussion of the *Martyrdom,* see B. Dehandschutter, *Martyrium Polycarpi. Een literair-
kritische studie* (BETL 52; Leuven, 1979).

14. The expression "open door" probably refers to favorable opportunities for missionary work. Cf.
Charles, *Revelation,* p. 87.

15. M. Zerwick and M. Grosvenor, *A Grammatical Analysis of the Greek New Testament* (Rome,
1981), p. 748, explain the two words as follows: a "literal Hebrew construction 'behold me granting,
that . . .'; i.e. 'I will bring it about that. . .'" The present tense points to the future; cf. the future tense

incomplete but is further taken up by means of the new introduction ἰδοὺ ποιήσω in verse 9b[16] and completed by what follows. In contrast to 3:8–10, however, nothing explicit is said here about the activity of the Jews. Christ announces the final outcome; he will make Jews prostrate before Christians, and they will learn that he has loved[17] the Christians of Philadelphia (v. 9). In verse 10 he adds that because of the Christians' faithfulness he will keep them out of the hour of trial (for both vocabulary and thought, cf. John 17:6, 11–12, 15). In verse 10b, however, the horizon is suddenly widened: a "trial that is coming on the whole world to test the inhabitants of the earth."[18]

In verse 12 it is also announced that the conquerors will be made pillars in God's eschatological temple[19] and will receive God's name, the name of "the new Jerusalem" and also the new name of the risen Christ himself. By mentioning "the new Jerusalem that comes down from my God out of heaven," John the prophet anticipates his depiction of 21:1–22:5. The readers should interpret the symbol of that city as a reference to the eschatological future of the church universal. One cannot but ask how non-Christian Jews could react to such a Christian self-perception.

The Counterattack of John

Like John's statements of what the Jews are doing, so also his counterattack in 2:9 and 3:9 consists of words spoken by the risen Lord (cf. 2:8 and 3:7) and, at the same time, by the Spirit (cf. 2:11a and 3:13). In both letters, those words contain a negative and a positive content. The Jews who

---

of the second verb. The positive comment on 3:9 by Beale, *Book of Revelation*, pp. 286–88, can hardly be correct: "behold, I will give" of v. 9a echoes "behold I have given" of v. 8b; "Christ will continue to empower his church to witness by opening the door of salvation for the unbelieving Jews in their community" (p. 286).

16. Cf. Bousset, *Offenbarung*, p. 227: "erklärende Wiederaufname."

17. An aorist indicative with a perfective value. Cf. G. Mussies, *The Morphology of Koine Greek as Used in the Apocalypse of St. John: A Study in Bilingualism* (NovTSup 27; Leiden, 1971), p. 338. W. J. Harrington, *Revelation* (SP; Collegeville, Minn., 1993), p. 72, comments: "here, for the first time in these messages, in relation to this little but faithful Church, we find explicit mention of the love of Christ."

18. For the πειράζω terminology ("to try, trial"), cf. note 7, above.

19. Notwithstanding the fact that John is directly dependent on Ezekiel 40–48 (new Temple) for his description of the new Jerusalem, he explicitly states in 21:22: "I saw no temple in the city, for its temple is the Lord God the Almighty and the Lamb." Yet in 3:12, as well as in 11:1–2, passages that are equally influenced by Ezekiel, the temple is mentioned. See, for an excellent discussion, J. M. Vogelgesang, "The Interpretation of Ezekiel in the Book of Revelation" (unpublished Ph.D. Diss., Harvard University, 1985), pp. 39–40 and 76 ("each utilization represents a different interpretation of the Ezekiel-traced material"). Cf. also p. 113.

slander and denounce Christians are not true Jews; on the contrary, they belong to the synagogue of Satan. Moreover, from this counterattack, and also from 3:12, it appears that John considers the Christians as the genuine Jews.

They Are Not (Real) Jews

In 2:9b the text reads ἐκ τῶν λεγόντων Ἰουδαίους εἶναι ἑαυτοὺς καὶ οὐκ εἰσὶν ἀλλά . . . 3:9a has ἑαυτοὺς after λεγόντων. The καί here possesses an adversative sense: but, in reality, they are not Jews. Then, in 2:9b, the even stronger adversative ἀλλά clause indicates what they really are, "the synagogue of Satan." In 3:9a this expression stands at the beginning of the sentence. An ἀλλά clause is equally present; it stresses the Jews' insincerity: but, as a matter of fact, they lie.[20] This qualification applies, it would seem, to all Jews in Smyrna and Philadelphia, not only to those who slander Christians.

One should also note that in 3:9 the partitive ἐκ construction manifests that not all Jews in Philadelphia are involved. The indefinite pronoun τινες must be mentally supplemented before the ἐκ construction : "[certain ones] of the synagogue of Satan."[21] This construction, however, does not imply that *not* all Jews belong to the synagogue of Satan. In 2:9 the ἐκ construction grammatically depends on τὴν βλασφημίαν: I know the slander "proceeding from" those who say. . . Here the preposition ἐκ most probably indicates the agents, those who slander. One may refer to 2:11b in the same pericope for a similar ἐκ after a passive verb: "Whoever conquers will not be harmed *by* the second death." Yet, notwithstanding these different grammatical functions of the preposition, the nuance of "certain ones" can be assumed to be present in 2:9 as well: not all those in Smyrna who say that they are Jews, but only some of them, are denouncing the Christians.

Synagogues of Satan

Almost certainly the genitive "of Satan" in 2:9b and 3:9a is subjective. For the expression "the synagogue of Satan,"[22] reference is often made to the

---

20. For the complex expression, compare 2:2: "you cannot tolerate evildoers; you have tested those who claim to be apostles but are not, and have found them to be false [ψευδεῖς]"; see also 2:20: "the woman Jezebel, who calls herself a prophet." For the grammar of such clauses, see Mussies, *Morphology,* p. 327.

21. According to Mussies, *Morphology,* p. 96 n. 1, such a partitive ἐκ, is found in 2:7, 10; 3:9; 5:9; and 11:9.

22. In Num. 16:3; 20:4; 26:9 (variant); and 31:16, the expression συναγωγὴ κυρίου is found.

parallel Qumran phrases "the congregation of Belial" (1QH 2.22 and 1QM 4.9). One thinks, of course, also of John 8:44, where Jesus says to the Pharisees that the devil is their father: ὑμεῖς ἐκ τοῦ πατρὸς τοῦ διαβόλου ἐστέ. These expressions and other Qumran passages show how bitter inner fights among Jews could lead to abuse with such dualistic pronouncements.[23] In Revelation, the tension is perhaps still somewhat intramural; there is still a Jewish context. Yet the boundaries between Jews and Christians are breaking down almost completely.[24] It should be noticed that, in the second part of his work, John demonizes non-Christian Gentiles to the extreme. For the mention of Satan in the letter to Pergamum, see 2:13—twice.[25] This datum, of course, tends to make a parallel between Jews and Gentiles.

In both messages, John appears to refer concretely to the local communities of Jews. In Smyrna, they are not Jews "but are a synagogue of Satan" (2:9b: no article). In Philadelphia, John uses the article: in a more literal translation, "Behold, I will make [certain ones] out of *the* synagogue of Satan . . ." (3:9a), yet by means of the article he points to the Jewish community in that city.

In contrast to Rev. 3:9a, where the expression "the synagogue of Satan" occurs almost at the beginning of the sentence, in 2:9b the expression is found at the very end. Then, immediately afterward, one reads in 2:10a: "Do not fear what you are about to suffer. Beware, the devil is about to throw some of you into prison." The close connection of these clauses suggests in its own way that at the root of the suffering as well as in the activity of the devil one must most probably see the involvement of Jews. They are instigators; they cause the suffering and are the instruments in the persecuting work of the devil. The question cannot but be asked whether that is not the main reason the Jews are called "the synagogue of Satan."[26]

23. Cf., e.g., Borgen, "Polemic," pp. 204–5, 209–10. The expression τὰ βαθέα τοῦ σατανᾶ in Rev. 2:24 is used for the teaching of other (heretical) Christians. See also 2 Cor. 11:14–15.

24. Cf. Borgen, "Polemic," pp. 206–11; Collins, "Vilification," pp. 113–14; Aune, *Revelation*, p. 164: "This phrase ('synagogue of Satan') may reflect the beginning of separation of the church from the synagogue." Not so much later, Ignatius of Antioch would emphasize the Christian identity as different from that of the Jews. Christianity was no longer "Judaism." Cf. Collins, "Vilification," pp. 311–12.

25. Twice: "I know where you are living, *where Satan's throne is* [ὅπου ὁ θρόνος τοῦ σατανᾶ]. Yet you are holding fast to my name and you did not deny your faith in me even in the days of Antipas, my witness, my faithful one, who was killed among you, *where Satan lives* [ὅπου ὁ σατανᾶς κατοικεῖ]." See Klauck, "Sendschreiben," esp. pp. 156–64.

26. Cf. also the different approach by J.N. Kraybill, *Imperial Cult and Commerce in John's Apocalypse* (JSNTSup 132; Sheffield, 1996), pp. 169–72: "Vituperative language about a 'synagogue of Satan' might stem from a belief that Jews helped persecute Christians. John's larger use of symbolism, however, suggests that he mentions Satan here as a way of highlighting commercial or political relationships some Jews had with Rome. . . . By using the epithet 'synagogue of Satan' in his letter to Smyrna and

In 2:10c, the risen Lord states that the affliction will last only ten days. If the Christians are faithful unto death, he will give them "the crown of life" (v. 10d). In 2:11b, moreover, it is said that the one who conquers will not be hurt "by the second death" (cf. 20:6 and 21:8). In 3:9b, however, the reversal of the Jews' situation is indicated: "I will make them come and bow down before your feet, and they will learn that I have loved you." It would seem that John refers here to the Isaian motif that announces the homage of the Gentiles: "The descendants of those who oppressed you shall come bending low to you, and all who despised you shall bow down at your feet" (Isa. 60:14; cf. 45:14; 49:23). In the same way as the Gentiles will honor Israel, the so-called Jews will humble themselves before the Christians, the true Jews.[27] Perhaps John mentally adds the rest of Isa. 60:14: the Jews "shall call you the City of the LORD, the Zion of the Holy One of Israel" (cf. Rev. 3:12b).

The Christians Are the True Jews

The term *Jews* in 2:9b and 3:9a is certainly to be understood positively.[28] The fact that John so strongly denies that the Jews are genuine Jews implicitly proves that, in his opinion, the Christians are the true Jews. This seizure of the Jewish identity, its denial to the Jews and use for themselves, must have appeared to the Jews as "anti-Judaistic" to the extreme.[29]

Philadelphia, John implies that certain Jews in those cities are in the same category as Rome—that is, in league with Satan" (p. 170).

Still another hypothesis is proposed by Lichtenberger, "Überlegungen," p. 618: Since in Revelation there is "die Übertragung von Gottesprädikate auf Jesus Christus," one can understand "dass die 'Schmähungen' gegen das Bekenntnis zu Christus vom Verfasser der Apokalypse wie der Gemeinden in Analogie zur Lästerung Gottes verstanden werden mussten. Und auch nur so ist die Heftigkeit des Vorwurfs, 'Synagoge Satans' zu sein, begreifbar, macht sich doch die jüdische Gemeinde durch die Ablehnung, d.h. Lästerung Christi, in den Augen des Verfassers der Gotteslästerung schuldig und verwirkt damit den Anspruch auf den Ehrentitel 'Jude.'" Yet see Lambrecht, "Jewish Slander."

27. Cf. Charles, *Revelation,* p. 89: "The homage that the Jews expected from the Gentiles, they were themselves to render to the Christians." See also M. Rissi, "Das Judenproblem im Lichte der Johannesapokalypse," *TZ* 13 (1957): 241–59 ("eine merkwürdige Umkehrung," p. 258); Lohse, "Synagogue of Satan," p. 122; Aune, *Revelation,* p. 238. Recently G. K. Beale, *John's Use of the Old Testament in Revelation* (JSNTSup 166; Sheffield, 1998), pp. 122–23, and *Book of Revelation,* p. 288, calls this procedure an "inverted" use of the Old Testament. John here shows an "ironic understanding" of a major theme in Isaiah 40–66.

28. Borgen, "Polemic," p. 198; P. Tomson, "The Names Israel and Jew in Ancient Judaism and in the New Testament," *Bijdr* 47 (1986): 120–40, 266–89, esp. p. 286. Rissi, "Das Judenproblem," p. 242, writes: it is evident "dass Ἰουδαῖος für den christlichen Apokalyptiker [= the author John the prophet] höchstes Ehrenprädikat bedeutet." Cf. also Charles, *Revelation,* p. 57: "The fact that our author attaches a spiritual significance of the highest character to the name Ἰουδαῖος shows that he is himself a Jewish Christian. In such a connection the Fourth Evangelist would have used the term Ἰσραηλίτης (cf. i. 47), whereas he represents the Ἰουδαῖοι as specifically and essentially the opponents of Christianity." Cf. already Bousset, *Offenbarung,* pp. 209 and 227.

29. Cf. Rom. 2:28–29; 9:6–9; and Phil. 3:3: ἡμεῖς γάρ ἐσμεν ἡ περιτομή.

That our making explicit what remains inherent in 2:9 and 3:9 is correct is already corroborated by what is stated in 3:12. The conquering Christians will be part of the new Jerusalem[30] that comes down out of heaven; they have the name of that city written on them. From 21:1–22:5, it becomes evident that this city is nothing other than the eschatological church, "the bride, the wife of the Lamb" (21:9). The Christians are that city. The same appears from 7:4–8. In John's self-perception, the Christians are the "one hundred forty-four thousand, sealed," the twelve tribes of Israel.[31] They are the new, true Israel (cf. 14:3 and 21:12–14).

Thus, throughout the whole book of Revelation, those who believe in Jesus are to be considered at the same time as the real Jews, the new Jerusalem, and the true Israel. This third aspect of John's counterattack is by no means the least severe and the least damaging to the Jews' honor and what would seem to be their righteous pride.

Critical Reflection

The language of the author of Revelation in 2:9 and 3:9 is not moderate, not objective. It is a language of aggression and vilification. Much has been written about the sad and dreadful *Wirkungsgeschichte* that expressions such as "the synagogue of Satan" have had. We may give one poignant example:

> In 1988 in Germany we had to draw the attention of our people to the awful events that had taken place fifty years ago. On November 9 in 1938 hundreds of synagogues all over Germany were burnt and destroyed, many Jewish people were arrested, some of them were killed—a terrible foreboding symptom of the holocaust which took place some years later. In 1988 we had to explain what had been done at that time, we had to show how dreadful the consequences of antisemitism are. . . . Accidentally it happened to be that the pericope given for the following Sunday service was Revelation 2:8–11. . . . All of you who will look to the text will be frightened finding

---

30. Can a somewhat hidden but scathing counterattack also be assumed in 11:8, where the unnamed Jerusalem would be pointed to by the clause "where also their Lord was crucified"? Like Rome, the old historical Jerusalem then is "the great city that is prophetically called Sodom and Egypt." Cf. Borgen, "Polemic," p. 205. Rissi, "Das Judenproblem," pp. 244–50, detects Jerusalem (and Israel) polemic in the whole of Revelation 11. But see, e.g., Beale, *Book of Revelation*, pp. 591, 592: "the 'great city' where the bodies lie is best identified as the ungodly world and not the earthly city of Jerusalem"; that world-city "is spiritually like Jerusalem, which had become like other ungodly nations, and even worse, by killing Christ."

31. On Rev. 7:1–8 (*ecclesia in via*) and 7:9–17 (*ecclesia triumphans*)—not two different groups!—see J. Lambrecht, "The Opening of the Seals (Rev. 6,1–8,6)," *Bib* 79 (1998): 198–220, esp. pp. 210–12. This church consists of Jewish Christians and Gentile Christians. Cf. Borgen, "Polemic," p. 209.

the sentence: that the Jews from whom the congregation was separated are in fact the Synagogue of Satan (Rev 2:9).[32]

To redress the anguish caused by the content of these verses, it would seem that three hermeneutical considerations should be made.

Generalization

In defense of John the prophet and his view of the Jews, many commentators emphasize that the Jews are mentioned in only two of the seven churches. Therefore, it is said, the Jewish anti-Christian activity appears to have been limited locally. Moreover, the ἐκ construction in 3:9 points to "some," and not all, of the Jews living in Philadelphia. The direct object of ἰδοὺ διδῶ, contained in the ἐκ expression (3:9a) and taken up by αὐτούς after ἰδοὺ ποιήσω (3:9b), restricts their number in Philadelphia. The limiting nuance of the partitive ἐκ ("some") should be fully recognized. Furthermore, as already stated, one is allowed to suppose that a similar restriction applies to Smyrna, although the ἐκ construction in 2:9 is grammatically different.

There certainly is, however, a generalization in John's attack. We must assume that, according to John, not some but all Jews in Smyrna and Philadelphia say that they are Jews but are not, and that not some but all Jews in both cities belong to the synagogue of Satan. Exceptions are not mentioned and should not be imported into the text.

It may also be questioned if John would qualify the Jews of other cities in the province Asia differently.[33] If pressed, he might even have included not only those in western Asia Minor but all non-Christian Jews. Local synagogues then become "the synagogue of Satan." One can hardly escape the conclusion that John is generalizing, indeed.

Demonization

As has been explained above, the twofold sharp outburst against "the synagogue of Satan"[34] should most probably not be interpreted in isolation from its context in 2:8–10. It is because of vile, presumably denouncing actions

32. This is the beginning of Lohse's conference; see "Synagogue of Satan," p. 105. Cf. Schrage, "Meditation," esp. pp. 388–89 and 397.

33. Aune, *Revelation,* p. 162, writes: in Rev. 2:9 and 3:9, "the author is not condemning Jews generally but only those associated with synagogues in Smyrna and Philadelphia." As a matter of fact, this statement may be too exclusive as far as John is concerned.

34. Bousset, *Offenbarung,* p. 209, notes: "Das Wort συναγωγή (nicht ἐκκλησία) ist wohl mit Absicht gewählt."

of some Jews that the Jewish community is called "the synagogue of Satan" by John the prophet.[35] In 3:9b, it is stated that, by way of retribution, the risen Lord will prostrate the persecuting Jews before the feet of the Christians, and thus the Jews will learn that Christ has loved the Christians. The author of Revelation detects Satan as the instigator behind the Jewish accusing slander. This is part of what can be called "the sad overkill of polemic."[36]

Of course, this sample of identification of Satan is but a part of the major demonization in the book of Revelation. The persecution of the church that manifests itself through forms of imperial worship and an idolatrous trade system is, for John, in the last analysis the work of the dragon, "that ancient serpent, who is called the Devil and Satan, the deceiver of the whole world" (12:9). The dragon gives authority to the first (political) beast (cf. 13:4), and the first beast gives authority to the (religious) second, the false prophet (cf. 13:12). To John, diabolizing the Jews is but a detail of that worldwide scenery that seems to be governed by demonic forces. Confronted with such a deep conviction, one can hardly accuse John of lack of love of the human enemy.

Christian Minority

It is rightly held that the author of Revelation is a Jewish Christian. The major part of the church in western Asia Minor must have been Jewish Christian. The Jewish Christians considered themselves still to be ethnic Jews; they were the heirs of the promises to Israel and the legitimate owners of the Jewish traditions. But the separation of the church from the synagogue by that time had almost become an irreversible fact.

Guesses about numbers are extremely tentative. At the end of the first century, the Roman empire is estimated to have had a population of sixty million; there may have been four to five million Jews and presumably not many more than fifty thousand Christians.[37] Not only in the midst of a

35. One should perhaps point out a more profound theological reason. See, e.g., J. Roloff, *Die Offenbarung des Johannes* (ZBK NT 18; Zurich, 1984), p. 52: since the Jews reject Christ, they no longer belong to God's people. "Wer sich . . . der Herrschaft Jesu Christi und damit Gottes nicht unterstellt, der gibt sich, gemäss der zum Dualismus tendierenden Geschichtsschau der Apokalypse, der Herrschaft des dämonischen Widersachers Gottes anheim."

36. So Harrington, *Revelation*, p. 58.

37. Aune, *Revelation*, p. 164; Lohse, "Synagogue of Satan," p. 108; P. W. van der Horst, "Jews and Christians in the Light of Their Relations in Other Cities of Asia Minor," *NThT* 43 (1989): 106–21. With particular attention to Aphridisias and Sardis, the last author deals with the impressive position of Judaism in Asia Minor, especially in the fourth and fifth centuries C.E. For the Diaspora Jews in Asia, see now P. R. Trebilco, *Jewish Communities in Asia Minor* (SNTSMS 69; Cambridge, 1991); Kraybill, *Imperial Cult*; J. M. G. Barclay, *Jews in the Mediterranean Diaspora: From Alexander to Trajan (323 B.C.E.–117 C.E.)* (Edinburgh, 1996), esp. pp. 259–81, "The Province Asia." In note 50 (p. 279), Barclay remarks: "It is possible to interpret . . . the opposition of the synagogues to the churches in Rev 2:9 . . . and 3:9 . . . as attempts to dissociate the Jews from the more socially subversive Christians."

Gentile society but confronted with the unbelieving Jews, the followers of Christ could not have failed to grasp how small a minority they were.

One should try to realize the painful experience of vulnerable minority Christians who, lost as they were in a pagan society, happened some times to be accused by fellow Jews. They must have felt betrayed. Therefore, one can hardly be surprised at their fierce reaction. Those Jews who are accusing us, they say, and all the non-Christian Jews are not true Jews; they are the synagogue of Satan. More and more, as days go on, that counterattack is being founded in their own conviction and claim: we are the true Israel and new Jerusalem; we are the real Jews.[38]

This type of anti-Judaism, to be sure, took its origin in people who as Christians were for the most part still Jews, and who as weak and poor minority people were persecuted not only by Gentiles but eventually also by fellow Jews. In the message to the church in Philadelphia, Jesus says: "I am coming soon" (3:11a; cf. 22:7, 12, 20). This cannot be understood in a directly temporal way. The parousia is delayed, and the situations later in history have been very different. Christian majorities persecuted Jewish minorities. It is extremely sad that New Testament texts, including Rev. 2:9 and 3:9, have been used to justify what in no way could or can be justified.[39]

38. Cf. Collins, "Vilification," pp. 319–20: "John's polemic was part of the struggle of Christians in western Asia Minor to survive physically and to establish an identity as legitimate heirs to the heritage of Israel. Christians were an extreme minority and in a very precarious position."

39. After the completion of this essay, I read the excellent monograph by P. Hirschberg, *Das eschatologische Israel. Untersuchungen zum Gottesvolkverständnis der Johannesoffenbarung* (WMANT 84; Neukirchen-Vluyn, 1999). The author devotes a substantial part of his work to Rev. 2:9 and 3:9 (pp. 31–127) and two major sections to chapters 7 and 21–22. In Hirschberg's opinion, the expression "synagogue of Satan" most probably is "eine Reaktion auf die jüdischen Distanzierungsmassnahmen . . . , die für Christen verhängnisvolle Folgen hatten. In der Sicht des Sehers werden die Synagogen zu Handlangern des gottfeindlichen Rom" (p. 123). The accusation of βλασφημία refers to "das konkrete gesellschaftliche Verhalten der Juden den Christen gegenüber," as well as to "die darin implizierte Gotteslästerung." John, a Jew who believes in Jesus, blames other Jews. Hirschberg stresses that the separation between Jews and Christians was not yet definitive. Part of historical Israel (i.e., Jewish Christians) as well as Gentile believers belong to God's eschatological people. "Heilsgeschichtlich unterscheidet der Seher also zwischen Juden und Heiden, soteriologisch ist jeder Unterschied aufgehoben" (p. 194). Therefore, the later theological category of the substitution of Jews by Christians should be avoided with regard to the book of Revelation. John's emphasis on the twelve tribes of Israel— "die eschatologische Fülle"—may even point to an "eschatologische Hoffnung für Israel" (pp. 286–87).

SELECT BIBLIOGRAPHY

This select bibliography is based on the bibliographical information given in the contributions to this volume as well as on information made available by Frederique Vandecasteele-Vanneuville and Urban C. von Wahlde. It does not include references to commentaries or lexicon entries.

Alexander, P. S. "'The Parting of the Ways' from the Perspective of Rabbinic Judaism." In J. D. G. Dunn, ed., *Jews and Christians: The Parting of the Ways AD 70 to 135*, pp. 1–25. WUNT 66, Tübingen, 1992.

Allen, E. L. "The Jewish Christian Church in the Fourth Gospel." *JBL* 74 (1955): 88–92.

Alon, G. *The Jews in Their Land in the Talmudic Age*. 2 vols. Jerusalem, 1980–84.

"Antijudaismus." *BK* 44, 2 (1989).

Ashton, J. "The Identity and Function of the Ἰουδαῖοι in the Fourth Gospel." *NovT* 27 (1985): 40–75.

Atal, D. "'Die Wahrheit wird euch frei machen' (Joh 8,32)." In J. Gnilka, ed., *Neues Testament und Kirche: Für Rudolf Schnackenburg*, pp. 283–99. Freiburg, 1974.

Augenstein, J. "'Euer Gesetz'—Ein Pronomen und die johanneische Haltung zum Gesetz." *ZNW* 88 (1998): 311–13.

Baarda, T., H. J. de Jonge, and M. J. J. Menken, eds. *Jodendom en vroeg christendom: Continuïteit en discontinuïteit*. Kampen, 1991.

Barrett, C. K. *Das Johannesevangelium und das Judentum*. Stuttgart, 1970. ET: *The Gospel of John and Judaism*. Philadelphia; London, 1975; 3d ed., 1983.

Barth, M. "Die Juden im Johannes-Evangelium: Wiedererwägungen zum Sitz-im-Leben, Datum und angeblichen Anti-Judaismus des Johannes-Evangeliums." In D. Neuhaus, ed., *Teufelskinder oder Heilsbringer: Die Juden im Johannes-Evangelium*, pp. 39–94. Arnoldshainer Texte 64. Frankfurt, 1990; 2d ed., 1993.

Bassler, J. M. "The Galileans: A Neglected Factor in Johannine Community Research." *CBQ* 43 (1981): 243–57.

Bauer, W. *Das Johannesevangelium*. HNT 6. Tübingen, 1933.

———. *Rechtgläubigkeit und Ketzerei im ältesten Christentum*. BHT 10. Tübingen, 1934. Reprinted with supplement by G. Strecker in 1963.

Baum, G. *The Jews and the Gospel: A Re-examination of the New Testament*. London, 1961. German translation: *Die Juden und das Evangelium: Eine Überprüfung des Neuen Testaments*. Einsiedeln, 1963.

———. *Is the New Testament Anti-Semite? A Re-examination of the New Testament*. New York, 1965.

Baumbach, G. "Abraham unser Vater: Der Prozeß der Vereinnahmung Abrahams durch das frühe Christentum." In J. Rogge and G. Schille, eds., *Theologische Versuche* 16 (1986): 37–56.

Beck, N. A. *Mature Christianity in the 21st Century: The Recognition and Repudiation of the Anti-Jewish Polemic in the New Testament.* Rev. and expanded. Shared Ground among Jews and Christians 51; New York, 1994. (See especially chapter 9: "Anti-Jewish Polemic in John and in the Johannine Epistles," pp. 285–312).

Beilner, W. *Christus und die Pharisäer: Exegetische Untersuchung über Grund und Verlauf der Auseinandersetzungen.* Vienna, 1959.

Beker, J. C. "The New Testament View of Judaism." In J. H. Charlesworth, ed., *Jews and Christians: Exploring the Past, Present, and Future,* pp. 60–69. Shared Ground among Jews and Christians 1. New York, 1990.

Ben-Chorin, S. "Antijüdische Elemente im Neuen Testament." *EvT* 40 (1980): 203–14.

Betz, O. "'To Worship God in Spirit and Truth': Reflections on John 4:20–26." In A. Finkel and L. Frizzell, eds., *Standing before God: Studies on Prayer in Scriptures and Tradition with Essays,* pp. 53–72. FS J. M. Oesterreicher. New York, 1981.

———. *Jesus, der Messias Israels: Aufsätze zur biblischen Theologie.* Vol. 1. WUNT 42. Tübingen, 1987.

Betz, O., M. Hengel, and P. Schmidt, eds. *Abraham unser Vater: Juden und Christen im Gespräch über die Bibel.* FS Otto Michel. AGSU 5; Leiden–Cologne, 1963.

Beutler, J. "Die 'Juden' und der Tod Jesu im Johannesevangelium." In H. H. Henrix and M. Stöhr, eds., *Exodus und Kreuz im ökumenischen Dialog zwischen Juden und Christen: Diskussionsbeiträge für Religionsunterricht und Erwachsenenbildung,* pp. 75–93. ABPB 8. Aachen, 1978.

Bieringer, R. "'My Kingship Is Not of This World' (John 18,36): The Kingship of Jesus and Politics." In T. Merrigan and J. Haers, eds., *The Myriad Christ: Plurality and the Quest for Unity in Contemporary Christology,* pp. 159–175. BETL 152. Leuven, 2000.

Bieringer, R., D. Pollefeyt, and F. Vandecasteele-Vanneuville, eds. *Anti-Judaism and the Fourth Gospel: Papers of the Leuven Colloquium, 2000.* Jewish and Christian Heritage 1. Assen, 2001.

Billings, J. S. "Judas Iscariot in the Fourth Gospel." *ExpTim* 51 (1939–40): 156–57.

Bittner, W. J. *Jesu Zeichen im Johannesevangelium: Die Messias-Erkenntnis im Johannesevangelium vor ihrem jüdischen Hintergrund.* WUNT 2/26. Tübingen, 1987.

Bloth, P. C. "'... denn das Heil kommt von den Juden' (Joh 4,22). Zur Bedeutung eines Bibelwortes für den Religionsunterricht vor fünfzig Jahren." *BTZ* 4 (1987): 228–30.

Böcher, O. *Der johanneische Dualismus im Zusammenhang des nachbiblischen Judentums.* Gütersloh, 1965.

Boers, H. *Neither on This Mountain nor in Jerusalem: A Study of John 4.* SBLMS 35. Atlanta, 1988.

Bornhäuser, K. B. *Das Johannesevangelium, eine Missionschrift für Israel.* Gütersloh, 1928.

Botha, F. J. "The Jews in the Fourth Gospel." *Theologia Evangelica* 2 (1969): 40–45.

Bowman, J. *The Fourth Gospel and the Jews: A Study in R. Akiba, Esther and the Gospel of John.* Pittsburgh, 1975.

Bratcher, R. J. "'The Jews' in the Gospel of John." *BT* 26 (1975): 401–9.

Braun, F.-M. "L'arrière-fond du quatrième évangile." In M.-É. Boismard, F.-M. Braun, and L. Cerfaux, eds., *L'évangile de Jean. Études et problèmes,* pp. 179–96. RechBib 3. Bruges, 1958.

————. *Jean le théologien.* Vol. 2: *Les grandes traditions d'Israël et l'accord des écritures selon le quatrième évangile.* ÉBib. Paris, 1964.

Broer, I. "Die Juden im Johannesevangelium: Ein beispielhafter und folgenreicher Konflikt." *Diakonia* 14 (1983): 332–41.

————. "The Jews in John's Gospel." *TD* 32 (1985): 41–44.

————. "Die Juden im Urteil der Autoren des Neuen Testaments: Anmerkungen zum Problem historischer Gerechtigkeit im Angesicht einer verheerenden Wirkungsgeschichte." *TGl* 82 (1992): 2–33.

Brown, R. E. *The Qumran Scrolls and the Johannine Gospel and Epistles.* NTE. Garden City, N.Y., 1965.

————. *The Gospel according to John.* AB 29. Garden City, N.Y., 1966.

————. "Johannine Ecclesiology—The Community's Origins." *Int* 31 (1977): 379–93.

————. "'Other Sheep Not of This Fold': The Johannine Perspective on Christian Diversity in the Late First Century." *JBL* 97 (1978): 5–22.

————. *The Community of the Beloved Disciple: The Life, Loves, and Hates of an Individual Church in New Testament Times.* New York–London, 1979.

————. *The Epistles of John.* AB 30. Garden City, N.Y. 1982.

————. "Not Jewish Christianity and Gentile Christianity, but Types of Jewish/Gentile Christianity." *CBQ* 45 (1983): 74–79.

————. "The Narratives of Jesus' Passion and Anti-Judaism." *America* 172 (April 1995): 8–12.

Brown, S. "John and the Resistant Reader: The Fourth Gospel after Nicea and the Holocaust." *Journal of Literary Studies* 5 (1989): 252–61.

Brumlik, M. "Johannes. Das judenfeindliche Evangelium." In D. Neuhaus, ed., *Teufelskinder oder Heilsbringer: Die Juden im Johannes-Evangelium,* pp. 6–21. Arnoldshainer Texte 64. Frankfurt, 1990; 2d ed., 1993. (= "Johannes. Das judenfeindlichste Evangelium." *Kirche und Israel* 4 [1989]: 102–13)

Bultmann, R. *Das Evangelium des Johannes.* KEK 2. Göttingen, 1941; 21st ed., 1986.

————. "Die Bedeutung der neuerschlossenen mandäischen und manichäischen Quellen für das Verständnis des Johannesevangeliums." In R. Bultmann and E. Dinkler, ed., *Exegetica. Aufsätze zur Erforschung des Neuen Testaments,* pp. 55–104. Tübingen, 1967.

Burke, D. G. "Translating *hoi Ioudaioi* in the New Testament." *Expl.* 9 (1995): 1–7.

Busse, U. "Die Bewertung der 'Juden' in der Auslegungsgeschichte und in der Metaphorik des vierten Evangeliums." Paper presented at the Fifty-fourth General Meeting of the SNTS, Pretoria, South Africa, August 1999.

Callan, T. *Forgetting the Root: The Emergence of Christianity from Judaism.* New York, 1986.

Camarero, M. L. "Derás cristologico en Juan 8,12–59." Diss., Madrid, 1993.

Caron, G. "Exploring a Religious Dimension: The Johannine Jews." *SR* 24 (1995): 159–71.

————. "The Lifting Up of the Human One and the Johannine Jews." *EgT* 26 (1995): 319–29.

————. *Qui sont les "juifs" dans l'évangile de Jean?* Recherches 35. Quebec, 1997.

Carroll, K. L. "The Fourth Gospel and the Exclusion of Christians from the Synagogues." *BJRL* 40 (1957–58): 19–32.

Casabó Suqué, J. M. "Los Judíos en el evangelio de Juan y el antisemitismo." *RB* 35 (1973): 115–29.

Casey, M. *Is John's Gospel True?* London–New York, 1996.

Cazeaux, J. "Concept ou mémoire? La rhétorique de Jean. chap. 8, v. 12–59." In A. Marchadour, ed., *Origine et postérité de l'évangile de Jean*, pp. 277–308. LD 143. Paris, 1990.

Charlesworth, J. H. "Exploring Opportunities for Rethinking Relations among Jews and Christians." In J. H. Charlesworth, ed., *Jews and Christians: Exploring the Past, Present, and Future*, pp. 35–53. Shared Ground among Jews and Christians 1. New York, 1990.

———, with F. X. Blisard and J. S. Siker, eds. *Jews and Christians: Exploring the Past, Present, and Future*. Shared Ground among Jews and Christians 1. New York, 1990.

———, ed. *Jesus' Jewishness: Exploring the Place of Jesus within Early Judaism.* Shared Ground among Jews and Christians 2. New York, 1991.

———, with F. X. Blisard and J. L. Gorham, eds. *Overcoming Fear between Jews and Christians.* Shared Ground among Jews and Christians 3. New York, 1993.

Chave, P. "The Jews." *ExpTim* 93 (1981–82): 176–77.

Chilton, B. *Judaic Approaches to the Gospels.* International Studies in Formative Christianity and Judaism 2. Atlanta, 1994.

Chilton, B., and J. Neusner. *Judaism in the New Testament: Practice and Beliefs.* New York–London, 1995.

———. *Trading Places: The Intersecting Histories of Judaism and Christianity.* Cleveland, 1997.

Cook, M. J. "Jesus and the Pharisees: The Problem as It Stands Today." *JES* 15 (1978): 441–60.

———. "Anti-Judaism in the New Testament." *USQR* 38 (1983): 125–38.

———. "The Gospel of John and the Jews." *RevExp* 84 (1987): 259–71.

———. "The New Testament and Judaism: An Historical Perspective on the Theme." *RevExp* 84 (1987): 183–99.

Cory, C. "Wisdom's Rescue: A New Reading of the Tabernacles Discourse (John 7:1–8:59)." *JBL* 116 (1997): 95–116.

Cothenet, E. "L'arrière-plan vétéro-testamentaire du IVe évangile." In A. Marchadour, ed., *Origine et postérité de l'évangile de Jean,"* pp. 43–69. LD 143. Paris, 1990.

Cross, J. E., ed. *Two Old English Apocrypha and Their Manuscript Source: 'The Gospel of Nichodemus' and 'The Avenginging of the Saviour.'* CSASE 19. Cambridge, 1996.

Crossan, D. M. "Anti-Semitism and the Gospel." *TS* 26 (1965): 189–214.

Crossan, J. D. *Who Killed Jesus? Exposing the Roots of Anti-Semitism in the Gospel Story of the Death of Jesus.* San Francisco, 1995.

Cullmann, O. "L'évangile johannique et l'histoire du salut." *NTS* 11 (1964–65): 111–22.

———. *Der johanneische Kreis: Sein Platz im Spätjudentum, in der Jüngerschaft Jesu und im Urchristentum. Zum Ursprung des Johannesevangeliums.* Tübingen, 1975. French ed.: *Le milieu johannique: Étude sur l'origine de l'évangile de Jean.* Neuchâtel–Paris, 1975. ET: *The Johannine Circle.* Translated by J. Bowden. Philadelphia, 1976.

Culpepper, R. A. "The Gospel of John and the Jews." *RevExp* 84 (1987): 273–88.

———. "The Gospel of John as a Threat to Jewish-Christian Relations." In J. H. Charlesworth, with F. X. Blisard and J. L. Gorham, eds., *Overcoming Fear between Jews and Christians*, pp. 21–43. Shared Ground among Jews and Christians 3. New York, 1992.

———. "The AMHN AMHN Sayings in the Gospel of John." In R.B. Sloan and M. C. Parsons, eds., *Perspectives on John: Methods and Interpretation in the Fourth Gospel*, pp. 57–102. NABPR Special Studies Series 11. Lewiston–Queenston–Lampeter, 1993.

———. "The Gospel of John as a Document of Faith in a Pluralistic Culture." In F. F. Segovia, ed., *"What Is John?"* vol. 1: *Readers and Readings of the Fourth Gospel*, pp. 107–27. SBLSymS 3. Atlanta, 1996.

Cuming, G. J. "The Jews in the Fourth Gospel." *ExpTim* 60 (1948–49): 290–92.

Dahl, M. "'Das Heil kommt von den Juden'." *LuthBei* 4 (1999): 234–40.

Dahl, N. A. "The Johannine Church and History." In W. Klassen and G. F. Snyder, eds., *Current Issues in New Testament Interpretation: Essays in Honor of Otto A. Piper*, pp. 124–42. London, 1962.

———. "Der Erstgeborene Satans und der Vater des Teufels (Polyk. 7.1 und Joh. 8.44)." In W. Eltester and F. H. Kettler, eds., *Apophoreta*, pp. 70–84. BZNW 30. Berlin, 1964.

Daly-Denton, M. *David in the Fourth Gospel: The Johannine Reception of the Psalms.* AGJU 47. Leiden–Boston–Cologne, 2000.

Davies, A. T., ed. *Antisemitism and the Foundations of Christianity.* New York, 1979.

Davies, W. D. "Reflections on Aspects of the Jewish Background of the Gospel of John." In R. A. Culpepper and C. C. Black, eds., *Exploring the Gospel of John: In Honor of D. Moody Smith*, pp. 43–64. Louisville, Ky., 1996.

de Boer, M. C. "L'évangile de Jean et le christianisme juif (nazoréen)." In D. Marguerat, ed., *Le déchirement: Juifs et chrétiens au premier siècle*, pp. 179–204. Le Monde de la Bible 32. Geneva, 1996.

———. "The Nazoreans: Living at the Boundary of Judaism and Christianity." In G. N. Stanton and G. G. Stroumsa, eds., *Tolerance and Intolerance in Early Judaism and Christianity*, pp. 239–62. Cambridge, 1998.

———. "The Narrative Function of Pilate in John." In G. J. Brooke and J.-D. Kaestli, eds., *Narrativity in Biblical and Related Texts: La narrativité dans la Bible et les textes apparentés*, pp. 141–58. BETL 149. Leuven, 2000.

Dehn, G. *Jesus und die Samariter: Eine Auslegung von Johannes 4,1–42.* BibS(N) 13. Neukirchen-Vluyn, 1956.

De Jonge, H. J. "Jewish Arguments against Jesus at the End of the First Century C.E. according to the Gospel of John." In P. W. van der Horst, ed., *Aspects of Religious Contact and Conflict in the Ancient World*, pp. 45–55. UTR 31. Utrecht, 1995.

de Jonge, M. "Jewish Expectations about the 'Messiah' according to the Fourth Gospel." *NTS* 19 (1972–73): 246–70.

———. "Jesus as Prophet and King in the Fourth Gospel." *ETL* 49 (1973): 160–77. Reprinted in M. de Jonge, *Jesus: Stranger from Heaven and Son of God: Jesus Christ and the Christians in Johannine Perspective*, pp. 49–76. SBLSBS 11. Missoula, Mont., 1977.

———. "The Conflict between Jesus and the Jews, and the Radical Christology of the Fourth Gospel." *PRSt* 20 (1993): 341–56.

———. *L'évangile de Jean Sources, rédaction, théologie.* BETL 44. Gembloux, 1977.

De Lange, C. C. M. "Het dieptepunt in de controverse tussen Jezus en de joden (Johannes 8,31–59)." In G. Van Belle, ed., *Het Johannesevangelie: Woorden om van te leven,* pp. 87–101. Leuven, 1993.

de la Potterie, I. "'Nous adorons, nous, ce que nous connaissons, car le salut vient des juifs.' Histoire de l'exégèse et interprétation de Jn 4,22." *Bib* 64 (1983): 74–115.

Delebecque, É. "Autour du verbe *eimi,* 'je suis,' dans le quatrième évangile. Note sur Jean VIII,25." *RThom* 86 (1986): 83–89.

———. "Jésus contemporain d' Abraham selon Jean 8,57." *RB* 93 (1986): 85–92.

———. *Epîtres de Jean.* CahRB 25. Paris, 1988.

Denaux, A., ed. *John and the Synoptics.* BETL 101. Leuven, 1992.

Derrett, J. D. M. "Exercitations on John 8." *EstBíb* 52 (1994): 433–51.

De Ruyter, B. W. J. *De gemeente van de evangelist Johannes: Haar polemiek en haar geschiedenis.* Delft, 1998.

Devillers, L. "La lettre de Soumaïos et les Ioudaioi johanniques." *RB* 105 (1998): 556–81.

"Die christlichen Wurzeln des Antijudaismus." *BL* 71, 1 (1998).

Dietzfelbinger, C. "Aspekte des Alten Testaments im Johannesevangelium." In H. Cancik, H. Lichtenberger, and P. Schäfer, eds., *Geschichte—Tradition—Reflexion,* vol. 3, pp. 203–18. FS Martin Hengel. Tübingen, 1996.

Dodd, C. H. "A l'arrière-plan d'un dialogue johannique (Jo 8,33–58)." *RHPR* 37 (1957): 5–17.

Dozemann, T. B. "*Sperma Abraam* in John 8 and Related Literature: Cosmology and Judgment." *CBQ* 42 (1980): 342–58.

Dunn, J. D. G. "Let John Be John: A Gospel for Its Time." In P. Stuhlmacher, ed., *Das Evangelium und die Evangelien: Vorträge vom Tübinger Symposium 1982,* pp. 309–39. WUNT 28. Tübingen, 1983

———. *The Partings of the Ways between Christianity and Judaism and Their Significance for the Character of Christianity.* London–Philadelphia, 1991.

———. "The Question of Anti-Semitism in the New Testament Writings of the Period." In J. D. G. Dunn, ed., *Jews and Christians: The Parting of the Ways A.D. 70 to 135,* pp. 177–212. WUNT 66. Tübingen, 1992.

———. "Judaism in the Land of Israel in the First Century." In J. Neusner, ed., *Judaism in Late Antiquity.* Vol. 2: *Historical Syntheses,* pp. 229–61. HO 1: Der Nahe und der Mittlere Osten, 17.2. Leiden, 1995.

———. "Jesus and Factionalism in Early Judaism: How Serious Was the Factionalism of Late Second Temple Judaism?" In J. H. Charlesworth and L. L. Johns, eds., *Hillel and Jesus: Comparative Studies of Two Major Religious Leaders,* pp. 156–75. Minneapolis, 1997.

———. "Who Did Paul Think He Was? A Study in Jewish-Christian Identity." *NTS* 45 (1999): 174–93.

———, ed. *Jews and Christians: The Parting of the Ways A.D. 70 to 135.* WUNT 66. Tübingen, 1992.

Eckert, W. P., N.P. Levinson, and M. Stöhr, eds. *Antijudaismus im Neuen Testament? Exegetische und systematische Beiträge.* Munich, 1967.

Edwards, M. J. "'Not Yet Fifty Years Old': John 8.57." *NTS* 40 (1994): 449–54.

Efroymson, D. P. "Jesus, Opposition and Opponents." In E. J. Fisher and L. Klenicki, eds., *Within Context: Essays on Jews and Judaism in the New Testament,* pp. 85–103. Philadelphia, 1993.

———. "Let Ioudaioi be Ioudaioi: When Less Is Better." *Expl.* 11 (1997): 5.

Efroymson, D. P., E. J. Fisher, and L. Klenicki, eds. *Within Context: Essays on Jews and Judaism in the New Testament.* Philadelphia, 1993.

Epp, E. J. "Anti-Semitism and the Popularity of the Fourth Gospel in Christianity." *CCARJ* 22 (1975): 35–57.

Erlemann, K. "Papyrus Egerton 2: 'Missing Link' zwischen synoptischer und johanneischer Tradition." *NTS* 42 (1996): 12–34.

———. "1 Joh und der jüdisch-christliche Trennungsprozess." *TZ* 55 (1999): 285–302.

Evans, C. A., and D. A. Hagner, eds. *Anti-Semitism and Early Christianity: Issues of Polemic and Faith.* Minneapolis, 1993.

Falk, H. *Jesus the Pharisee: A New Look at the Jewishness of Jesus.* New York, 1985.

Farmer, W. R., ed. *Anti-Judaism and the Gospels.* Harrisburg, Pa., 1999.

Feldmann, L. H. "Is the New Testament Anti-Semitic?" *HCC* 21 (1987): 1–14.

Flannery, E. H. "Anti-Judaism and Anti-Semitism: A Necessary Distinction." *JES* 10 (1973): 581–88.

Flesseman-Van Leer, E. "Antisemitisme in het Nieuwe Testament." In *Ontmoeting tussen joden en christenen,* pp. 78–83. Nijkerk, s.d.

Flusser, D. *Judaism and the Origins of Christianity.* Jerusalem, 1988.

Fortna, R. T. *The Gospel of Signs: A Reconstruction of the Narrative Source Underlying the Fourth Gospel.* SNTSMS 11. Cambridge, 1970

———. "From Christology to Soteriology: A Redaction-Critical Study of Salvation in the Fourth Gospel." *Int* 27 (1973): 31–47.

———. *The Fourth Gospel and Its Predecessor: From Narrative Source to Present Gospel.* Edinburgh, 1989.

Franke, A. H. *Das Alte Testament bei Johannes: Ein Beitrag zur Erklärung und Beurtheilung der johanneischen Schriften.* Göttingen, 1885.

Frankemölle, H. "'Pharisäismus' in Judentum und Kirche. Zur Tradition und Redaktion in Matthäus 23." In *Biblische Handlungsanweisungen: Beispiele pragmatischer Exegese,* pp. 133–90. Mainz, 1983.

———. "Antijudaismus im Matthäusevangelium?" In R. Kampling, ed., *"Nun steht aber diese Sache im Evangelium . . .". Zur Frage nach den Anfängen des christlichen Antijudaismus,* pp. 73–106. Paderborn, 1999.

Fredriksen, P. *From Jesus to Christ: The Origins of the New Testament Images of Jesus.* New Haven, Conn., 1988.

Freed, E. D. "Who or What Was before Abraham in John 8:58?" *JSNT* 17 (1983): 52–59.

Freudmann, L. C. *Antisemitism in the New Testament.* Lanham, Md., 1994.

Freyne, S. "Vilifying the Other and Defining the Self: Matthew's and John's Anti-Jewish Polemic in Focus." In J. Neusner and E. S. Frerichs, eds., *"To See Ourselves as Others See Us": Christians, Jews, "Others" in Late Antiquity,* pp. 117–43. Scholars Press Studies in the Humanities. Chico, Calif, 1985.

Fuller, R. "The 'Jews' in the Fourth Gospel." *Di* 16 (1977): 31–37.

Gager, J. G. *The Origins of Anti-Semitism: Attitudes toward Judaism in Pagan and Christian Antiquity.* New York, 1983.

García Moreno, A. "Libertad del hombre en Jn 8,32." In A. Aranda, J. M. Yanguas, and A. Fuentes, eds., *Dios y el hombre: VI Simposio internacional de teologia de la Universidad de Navarra*, pp. 641–58. Universidad de Navarra, Coleccion teologica 43. Pamplona, 1985.

Getty, M. A. "The Jews and John's Passion Narrative." *Liturgy* 22 (1977): 6–10.

Geyser, A. S. "Israel in the Fourth Gospel." *Neot* 20 (1986): 13–20.

Gielen, M. *Der Konflikt Jesu mit den religiösen und politischen Autoritäten seines Volkes im Spiegel der matthäischen Jesusgeschichte.* BBB 115. Bonn–Cologne, 1998.

Goodblatt, D. "From Judeans to Israel: Names of Jewish States in Antiquity." *JSJ* 29 (1998): 1–36.

Goodwin, M. "Response to David Rensberger: Questions about a Jewish Johannine Community." In W. R. Farmer, ed., *Anti-Judaism and the Gospels*, pp. 158–71. Harrisburg, Pa., 1999.

Goppelt, L. *Christentum und Judentum im ersten und zweiten Jahrhundert: Ein Aufriß der Urgeschichte der Kirche.* BFCT 2/55. Gütersloh, 1954.

Granskou, D. "Anti-Judaism in the Passion Accounts of the Fourth Gospel." In P. Richardson and D. Granskou, eds., *Anti-Judaism in Early Christianity.* Vol. 1: *Paul and the Gospels*, pp. 201–16. Studies in Christianity and Judaism 2. Waterloo, 1986.

Grässer, E. "Christen und Juden. Neutestamentliche Erwägungen zu einem aktuellen Thema." In *Der Alte Bund im Neuen: Exegetische Studien zur Israelfrage im Neuen Testament*, pp. 271–89. WUNT 35. Tübingen, 1985.

———. *Der Alte Bund im Neuen: Exegetische Studien zur Israelfrage im Neuen Testament.* WUNT 35. Tübingen, 1985.

———. "Die antijüdische Polemik im Johannesevangelium." *NTS* 11 (1964–65): 74–90 = *Der Alte Bund im Neuen: Exegetische Studien zur Israelfrage im Neuen Testament*, pp. 135–53. WUNT 35, Tübingen, 1985.

———. "Die Juden als Teufelssöhne in Johannes 8,37–47." In W. P. Eckert, N. P. Levinson, and M. Stöhr, eds., *Antijudaismus im Neuen Testament? Exegetische und systematische Beiträge*, pp. 157–70. ACJD 2. Munich, 1967 = *Der Alte Bund im Neuen: Exegetische Studien zur Israelfrage im Neuen Testament*, pp. 154–67. WUNT 35. Tübingen, 1985.

———. "Jesus und das Heil Gottes. Bemerkungen zur sog. 'Individualisierung des Heils.'" In *Der Alte Bund im Neuen: Exegetische Studien zur Israelfrage im Neuen Testament*, pp. 183–200. WUNT 35. Tübingen, 1985.

———. "Zwei Heilswege? Zum theologischen Verhältnis von Israel und Kirche." In *Der Alte Bund im Neuen: Exegetische Studien zur Israelfrage im Neuen Testament*, pp. 212–30. WUNT 35. Tübingen, 1985.

Grelot, P. "Jean 8,56 et Jubilés 16,16–29." *RevQ* 13 (1988): 621–28.

———. *Les juifs dans l'évangile selon Jean: Enquête historique et réflexion théologique* CahRB 34. Paris, 1995.

Grundmann, W. *Jesus der Galiläer und das Judentum.* Leipzig, 1940; 2d ed., 1941.

Guilding, A. *The Fourth Gospel and Jewish Worship: A Study of the Relation of St. John's Gospel to the Ancient Jewish Lectionary System.* Oxford, 1960.

Haacker, K. *Die Stiftung des Heils: Untersuchungen zur Struktur der johanneischen Theologie.* AzTh 1/47. Stuttgart, 1972.

———. "Gottesdienst ohne Gotteserkenntnis. Joh 4.22 vor dem Hintergrund der jüdisch-samaritanischen Auseinandersetzung." In B. Benzig, O. Böcher, and G. Mayer, eds., *Wort und Wirklichkeit: Studien zur Afrikanistik und Orientalistik*, vol. 1. FS Eugen Ludwig Rapp. Meisenheim am Glan, 1976.

Haenchen, E. "History and Interpretation in the Johannine Passion Narrative." *Int* 24 (1970): 198–219.

Hahn, F. "'Das Heil kommt von den Juden.' Erwägungen zu Joh 4,22b." In C. Breytenbach, ed., *Die Verwurzelung des Christentums im Judentum: Exegetische Beiträge zum christlich-jüdischen Gespräch*, pp. 99–118. Neukirchen-Vluyn, 1996 = B. Benzig, O. Böcher, and G. Mayer, eds., *Wort und Wirklichkeit: Studien zur Afrikanistik und Orientalistik*, vol. 1, pp. 67–84. FS Eugen Ludwig Rapp. Meisenheim am Glan, 1976.

———. "'Die Juden' im Johannesevangelium." In C. Breytenbach, ed., *Die Verwurzelung des Christentums im Judentum: Exegetische Beiträge zum christlich-jüdischen Gespräch*, pp. 119–129. Neukirchen-Vluyn, 1996 = in P.-G. Müller and W. Stenger, eds., *Kontinuität und Einheit*, pp. 430–38. FS Franz Mußner. Freiburg–Basel–Vienna, 1981.

———. *Die Verwurzelung des Christentums im Judentum: Exegetische Beiträge zum christlich-jüdischen Gespräch*. Edited by C. Breytenbach. Neukirchen-Vluyn, 1996.

Hanson, A. T. "John's Technique in Using Scripture." In *The New Testament Interpretation of Scripture*, pp. 157–76. London, 1980.

———. *The Prophetic Gospel: A Study of John and the Old Testament*. Edinburgh, 1991.

———. "John's Use of Scripture." In C. Evans and W. Stenger, eds., *The Gospels and the Scriptures of Israel*, pp. 358–79. JSNTSup 104. Sheffield, 1994.

Hare, D. "The Rejection of the Jews in the Synoptic Gospels and Acts." In A. Davies, ed., *Anti-Semitism and the Foundations of Christianity*, pp. 27–47. New York, 1979.

Hare, D. R. A., *The Theme of Jewish Persecution of Christians in the Gospel according to Matthew*. Cambridge, 1967.

Harrington, D. J. "The 'Jews' in John's Gospel." *Bible Today* 27 (1989): 203–9.

———. "The Problem of 'the Jews' in John's Gospel." *Expl.* 8 (1994): 3–4.

———. "Is the New Testament Anti-Jewish? The Need to Develop a Sense of History." *ITQ* 63 (1998): 123–32.

Harvey, G. *The True Israel: Uses of the Names Jew, Hebrew and Israel in Ancient Jewish and Early Christian Literature*. AGJU 35. Leiden, 1996.

Hemelsoet, B. "Een vader had twee zonen. De verhalen van het zaad van Abraham, op het Loofhuttenfeest (Joh 8,30–37)." *Amsterdamse Cahiers* 13 (1994): 97–112.

Hengel, M. "Die Schriftauslegung des 4. Evangeliums auf dem Hintergrund der urchristlichen Exegese." *JBTh* 4 (1989): 249–88.

———. *The Johannine Question*. London–Philadelphia, 1989.

———. *Die johanneische Frage: Ein Lösungsversuch*. WUNT 67. Tübingen, 1993.

———. "The Old Testament and the Fourth Gospel." In C. Evans and W. Stegner, eds., *The Gospels and the Scriptures of Israel*, pp. 380–95. JSNTSup 104. Sheffield, 1994.

Herford, R. T. *Judaism in the New Testament Period*. London, 1928.

Hickling, J. A. "Attitudes to Judaism in the Fourth Gospel." In M. de Jonge, ed., *L'évangile de Jean: Sources, rédaction, théologie*, pp. 347–54. BETL 44. Leuven, 1977.

Hollander, H. W. "'Vrijheid' en 'slavernij' in Johannes 8:31–36." *NedTTs* 48 (1994): 265–74.

Horbury, W. "The Benediction of the Minim and Early Jewish-Christian Controversy." *JTS* 33 (1982): 19–61. Reprinted in W. Horbury, *Jews and Christians in Contact and Controversy*, pp. 67–110. Edinburgh, 1998.

Hurtado, L. W. "First-Century Jewish Monotheism." *JSNT* 71 (1998): 3–26.

Idinopulos, T. A., and R. B. Ward. "Is Christology Inherently Anti-Semitic? A Critical Review of Rosemary Ruether's *Faith and Fratricide*." *JAAR* 45 (1977): 193–214.

Jansen, H. *Christelijke Theologie na Auschwitz*. Part 1: *Theologische en kerkelijke wortels van het antisemitisme*. Part 2: *Nieuwtestamentische wortels van het antisemitisme*. The Hague, 1981, 1985.

———. "'Anti-Semitic Potential' in het evangelie van Johannes." In D. van Arkel et al., eds., *Veertig jaar na '45: Visies op het hedendaagse antisemitisme*, pp. 75–116, 303–14. Amsterdam, 1985.

Jocz, J. "Die Juden im Johannesevangelium." *Judaica* 9 (1953): 129–42.

———. *The Jewish People and Jesus Christ: A Study in the Controversy between Church and Synagogue*. London, 1954.

Johnson, L. T. "The New Testament's Anti-Jewish Slander and the Conventions of Ancient Polemic." *JBL* 108 (1989): 419–41.

Junod, E., and J.-D. Kaestli, eds., *Acta Ioannis: Praefatio, textus, textus alii, commentarius, indices*. 2 vols. CCSA 1. Turnhout, 1983.

Kaestli, J.-D. "L'exégèse valentinienne du quatrième évangile" and "Remarques sur le rapport du quatriéme évangile avec la gnose et sa réception au IIe siècle." In J.-D. Kaestli, J.-M. Poffet, and J. Zumstein, eds., *La communauté johannique et son histoire*, pp. 305–50. Le Monde de la Bible. Geneva, 1990.

Kaestli, J.-D., J.-M. Poffet, and J. Zumstein, eds. *La communauté johannique et son histoire*. Le Monde de la Bible. Geneva, 1990.

Kampling, R., ed. *"Nun steht aber diese Sache im Evangelium . . .": Zur Frage nach den Anfängen des christlichen Antijudaismus*. Paderborn, 1999.

Katz, S. T. "Issues in the Separation of Judaism and Christianity after 70 C.E.: A Reconsideration." *JBL* 103 (1984): 43–76.

Kaufman, P. S. "Anti-Semitism in the New Testament: The Witness of the Beloved Disciple." *Worship* 63 (1989): 386–401.

———. *The Beloved Disciple: A Witness against Anti-Semitism*. Collegeville, Minn., 1991.

Keck, L. E. "Derivation as Destiny: 'Of-ness' in Johannine Christology, Anthropology, and Soteriology." In R. A. Culpepper and C. C. Black, eds., *Exploring the Gospel of John: In Honor of D. Moody Smith*, pp. 274–88. Louisville, Ky., 1996.

Kee, H., and I. Borowsky, eds. *Removing the Anti-Judaism from the New Testament*. Philadelphia, 1998.

Kern, W. "Der symmetrische Gesamtaufbau von Joh 8,12–58." *ZKT* 78 (1956): 451–54.

Kimelman, R. "*Birkat Ha-Minim* and the Lack of Evidence for an Anti-Christian Jewish Prayer in Late Antiquity." In E. P. Sanders, with A. I. Baumgarten and

A. Mendelson, eds., *Jewish and Christian Self-Definition.* Vol. 2: *Aspects of Judaism in the Graeco-Roman Period,* pp. 226–44. London, 1981.

Klappert, B. "'Moses hat von mir geschrieben. . . .'" In E. Blum, R. Rendtorff, C. Macholz, and E. W. Stegemann, eds., *Die hebräische Bibel und ihre zweifache Nachgeschichte,* pp. 619–40. FS R. Rendtorff. Neukirchen-Vluyn, 1990.

———. "Fellow Heirs and Partakers of the Promise: An Alternative for Christian Substitution Theology and Christology." In D. Pollefeyt, ed., *Jews and Christians: Rivals or Partners for the Kingdom of God? In Search of an Alternative for the Theology of Substitution,* pp. 38–61. LTPM 21. Leuven, 1997.

———. "Die Öffnung des Israelbundes für die Völker: Karl Barths Israeltheologie und die Bundestheologie der reformierten Reformation." In K. Wengst, G. Sass, T. Kriener, and R. Stuhlmann, eds., *Ja und nein: Christliche Theologie im Angesicht Israels,* pp. 331–48. FS W. Schrage. Neukirchen-Vluyn, 1998.

Klassen, W. "Anti-Judaism in Early Christianity: The State of the Question." In P. Richardson and D. Granskou, eds., *Anti-Judaism in Early Christianity.* Vol. 1: *Paul and the Gospels,* pp. 1–19. Studies in Christianity and Judaism 2. Waterloo, 1986.

———. *Judas: Betrayer or Friend of Jesus?* Minneapolis, 1996.

Klauck, H.-J. *Der zweite und dritte Johannesbrief.* EKKNT 13. Zurich–Neukirchen-Vluyn, 1992.

Knight, G. A. F. "Antisemitism in the Fourth Gospel." *RTR* 27 (1969): 81–88.

Koenig, J. *Jews and Christians in Dialogue: New Testament Foundations.* Philadelphia, 1979.

Koester, H. "Gnostic Sayings and Controversy Traditions in John 8,12–59." In C. Hedrick and R. Hodgson, eds., *Nag Hammadi, Gnosticism, and Early Christianity,* pp. 97–110. Peabody, Mass., 1986.

———. "Les Discours d'adieu de l'évangile de Jean: Leur trajectoire au premier et au deuxième siècle." In J.-D. Kaestli, J.-M. Poffett, and J. Zumstein, eds., *La communauté johannique et son histoire,* pp. 269–80. Le Monde de la Bible. Geneva, 1990.

Kotila, M. *Umstrittener Zeuge: Studien zur Stellung des Gesetzes in der johanneischen Theologiegeschichte.* AASF.DHL 48. Helsinki, 1988.

Kraemer, R. S. "On the Meaning of the Term 'Jew' in Graeco-Roman Inscriptions." *HTR* 82 (1989): 35–53.

Krauss, S. *Griechische und lateinische Lehnwörter in Talmud, Midrasch und Targum.* 2 vols. 1898–99; reprinted with additions by I. Löw, Hildesheim, 1964.

Kriener, T. *"Glauben an Jesus"—ein Verstoß gegen das zweite Gebot? Die johanneische Christologie und der jüdische Vorwurf des Götzendienstes.* NTDH 29. Neukirchen-Vluyn, 2000.

Kuhn, K. G. "Israel, Ioudaios, Hebraios in der nach-at.lichen jüdischen Literatur." *TWNT* 3 (1938): 360–70.

Kümmel, W. G. "Die Weherufe über die Schriftgelehrten und Pharisäer (Matthäus 23,13–36)." In W. P. Eckert, N. P. Levinson, and M. Stöhr, eds., *Antijudaismus im Neuen Testament? Exegetische und systematische Beiträge,* pp. 135–47. Munich, 1967.

Kysar, R. "The Gospel of John and Anti-Jewish Polemic." *Expl.* 2 (1992): 2–4.

———. "Anti-Semitism and the Gospel of John." In C. A. Evans and D. A. Hagner, eds., *Anti-Semitism and Early Christianity: Issues of Polemic and Faith,* pp. 113–27. Minneapolis, 1993.

———. "Coming Hermeneutical Earthquake in Johannine Interpretation." In F. F. Segovia, ed., *What Is John?* Vol. 1: *Readers and Readings of the Fourth Gospel*, pp. 185–89. SBLSymS 3. Atlanta, 1996.

Lalleman, P. J. "The Acts of John: A Two-Stage Initiation into Johannine Gnosticism." Diss., Groningen, defended 1998.

———. "The Adversaries Envisaged in the Johannine Epistles." *NedTTs* 53 (1999): 17–24.

Lambrecht, J. "Jewish Slander: A Note on Revelation 2,9–10." *ETL* 75 (1999): 421–29.

Landier, J. "Antijudaïsme de l'évangile de Jean? Étude d'une parole. 'Vous êtes de votre père, du diable!' Jn 8,44." *Chemins de dialogue* 10 (1997): 113–28.

Langbrandtner, W. *Weltferner Gott oder Gott der Liebe: Der Ketzerstreit in der johanneischen Kirche. Eine exegetisch-religionsgeschichtliche Untersuchung mit Berücksichtigung der koptisch-gnostischen Texte aus Nag-Hammadi.* BBET 6, Frankfurt–Bern–New York, 1977.

Lataire, B. "Jesus' Equality with God: A Critical Reflection on John 5,18." In T. Merrigan and J. Haers, eds., *The Myriad Christ: Plurality and the Quest for Unity in Contemporary Christology,* pp. 179–90. BETL 152. Leuven, 2000.

Lategan, B. C. "The Truth That Sets Man Free: John 8:31–36." *Neot* 2 (1968): 70–80.

Lea, T. D. "Response to David Rensberger." In W. R. Farmer, ed., *Anti-Judaism and the Gospels,* pp. 172–75. Harrisburg, Pa., 1999.

Leibig, J. E. "John and 'the Jews': Theological Antisemitism in the Fourth Gospel." *Christian Jewish Relations* 16 (1983): 27–38 = *JES* 20 (1983): 209–34.

Leistner, R. *Antijudaismus im Johannesevangelium? Darstellung des Problems in der neueren Auslegungsgeschichte und Untersuchung der Leidensgeschichte.* TW 3. Bern–Frankfurt, 1974.

Levenson, J. D. "Is There a Counterpart in the Hebrew Bible to New Testament Antisemitism?" *JES* 22 (1985): 242–60.

Lieu, J. M. *The Second and Third Epistles of John: History and Background.* Edinburgh, 1986.

———. "Blindness in the Johannine Tradition." *NTS* 34 (1988): 83–95.

———. "'The Parting of the Ways': Theological Construct or Historical Reality?" *JSNT* 56 (1994): 101–19.

———. *Image and Reality: The Jews in the World of the Christians in the Second Century.* Edinburgh, 1996.

———. "Temple and Synagogue in John." *NTS* 45 (1999): 51–69.

Lincoln, A. T. "Trials, Plots and the Narrative of the Fourth Gospel." *JSNT* 56 (1994): 3–30.

Lindars, B. "Slave and Son in John 8:31–36." In W. C. Weinrich, ed., *The New Testament Age: Essays in Honor of Bo Reicke,* vol. 1, pp. 269–86. Macon, Ga., 1984.

Locher, C. "Die Johannes-Christen und 'die Juden'." *Orien.* 48 (1984): 223–26.

Loewe, R. "'Salvation' Is Not of the Jews." *JTS* 32 (1981): 341–68.

Lohse, E. "Synagogue of Satan and Church of God: Jews and Christians in the Book of Revelation." *SEÅ* 58 (1993): 105–23.

Lona, H. E. *Abraham in Johannes 8: Ein Beitrag zur Methodenfrage.* EHS.T 65. Frankfurt, 1976.

Lowe, M. "Who Were the Ἰουδαῖοι?" *NovT* 18 (1976): 101–30.

Lowe, M. F. "'The Jews' according to John." *Christian Attitudes on Jews and Judaism* 62 (1978): 9–11.

Lowry, R. "The Rejected-Suitor Syndrome: Human Sources of New Testament 'Anti-Semitism.'" *JES* 14 (1977): 219–32.

Lüdemann, G. *Das Unheilige in der Heiligen Schrift: Die andere Seite der Bibel.* Stuttgart, 1996.

Luz, U. "Das Matthäusevangelium und die Perspektive einer biblischen Theologie." In O. Hofius and P. Stuhlmacher, eds., *'Gesetz' als Thema Biblischer Theologie,* pp. 233–48. *JBTh* 4. Neukirchen-Vluyn, 1989.

———. "Anti-Judaismus im Matthäusevangelium als historisches und theologisches Problem." *EvT* 53 (1993): 310–27.

Macina, M. R. "L'antijudaïsme' néotestamentaire: Entre doctrine et polémique." *NRT* 118 (1996): 410–16.

MacLennan, R. S. *Early Christian Texts on Jews and Judaism.* BJS 194. Atlanta, 1990.

Manns, F. "L'arrière-fond judaïque de Jean 8,31–59." Diss., Jerusalem, 1976.

———. *"La vérité vous fera libres": Étude exégétique de Jean 8,31–59.* SBFA 11. Jerusalem, 1976.

———. "L' évangile de Jean, réponse chrétienne aux décisions de Jabne: Note complémentaire." *SBFLA* 32 (1982): 85–108.

———. *L'évangile de Jean à la lumière du Judaïsme.* SBFA 33. Jerusalem, 1991.

———. *Une approche juive du Nouveau Testament.* Initiations Bibliques. Paris, 1998.

Mara, M. G., ed. *L'évangile de Pierre: Introduction, texte critique, traduction, commentaire et index.* SC 201. Paris, 1973.

Marchadour, A. "Les juifs dans l'évangile de Jean." In S. Légasse, A. Marchadour, and D. Marguerat, eds., *Le Nouveau Testament est-il anti-juif?* pp. 37–47. Cahiers Évangile 108; Paris, 1999.

Marguerat, D., ed. *Le déchirement. Juifs et chrétiens au premier siècle.* Le Monde de la Bible 32. Geneva, 1996.

Martyn, J. L. *History and Theology in the Fourth Gospel.* New York, 1968. 2d ed. Nashville, 1979.

———. "Glimpses into the History of the Johannine Community." In M. de Jonge, ed., *L'évangile de Jean: Sources, rédaction, théologie,* pp. 149–79. BETL 44, Leuven, 1977.

———. *The Gospel of John in Christian History: Essays for Interpreters.* Theological Inquiries. New York, 1978.

———. "A Gentile Mission That Replaced an Earlier Jewish Mission?" In R. A. Culpepper and C. C. Black, eds., *Exploring the Gospel of John: In Honor of D. Moody Smith,* pp. 124–44. Louisville, Ky., 1996.

Mason, S. "Chief Priests, Sadducees, Pharisees and Sanhedrin in Acts." In R. Bauckham, ed., *The Book of Acts in Its Palestinian Setting,* pp. 115–77. Carlisle–Grand Rapids, 1995.

McCaffrey, J. *The House with Many Rooms: The Temple Theme of John 14,2–3.* AnBib 114. Rome, 1988.

McHugh, J. "'In Him Was Life': John's Gospel and the Parting of the Ways." In J. D. G. Dunn, ed., *Jews and Christians: The Parting of the Ways A.D. 70 to 135,* pp. 123–58. WUNT 66. Tübingen, 1992.

Meeks, W. A. *The Prophet-King: Moses Traditions and the Johannine Christology.* NovT-Sup 14. Leiden, 1967.

———. "The Man from Heaven in Johannine Sectarianism." *JBL* 91 (1972):44–72.

———. "'Am I a Jew?' Johannine Christianity and Judaism." In J. Neusner, ed., *Christianity, Judaism and Other Graeco-Roman Cults: Studies for Morton Smith at Sixty,* pp. 163–86, SJLA 12. Leiden, 1975.

———. "Breaking Away: Three New Testament Pictures of Christianity's Separation from the Jewish Communities." In J. Neusner and E.S. Frerichs, eds., *"To See Ourselves as Others See Us": Christians, Jews, "Others" in Late Antiquity,* pp. 93–115. Scholars Press Studies in the Humanities. Chico, Calif., 1985.

Meeks, W. A., and R. L. Wilken. *Jews and Christians in Antioch in the First Four Centuries of the Common Era.* Missoula, Mont., 1978.

Mees, M. "Realer oder irrealer Konditionalsatz in Joh 8:39?" In E. J. Epp and G. D. Fee, eds., *New Testament Textual Criticism: Its Significance for Exegesis. Essays in Honour of Bruce M. Metzger,* pp. 119–30. Oxford, 1981. = M. Mees, *Die frühe Rezeptionsgeschichte des Johannesevangeliums am Beispiel von Textüberlieferung und Väterexegese.* Edited by G. Scheuermann and A. P. Alkofer. FB 72. Würzburg, 1994, pp. 29–37.

Mehlmann, J. "John 8,48 in Some Patristic Quotations." *Bib* 44 (1963): 206–9.

Menken, M. J. J. "Jezus tegenover de Farizeeën in het vierde evangelie: Joh 8, 12–20." In T. Baarda, H. J. de Jonge, and M. J. J. Menken, eds., *Jodendom en vroeg christendom. Continuïteit en discontinuïteit,* pp. 103–117. Kampen, 1991.

———. *Old Testament Quotations in the Fourth Gospel: Studies in Textual Form.* CBET 15. Kampen, 1996.

———. "Observations on the Significance of the Old Testament in the Fourth Gospel." *Neot* 33 (1999): 125–43.

Merkel, F. "Johannes 4,19–26." *GPM* 37 (1982–83): 268–74

Merklein, H. "'Die Wahrheit wird euch frei machen' (Joh 8,32)." In J. J. Degenhardt, ed., *Die Freude an Gott—unsere Kraft,* pp. 145–49. FS Otto Bernhard Knoch. Stuttgart, 1991.

Metzner, R. *Das Verständnis der Sünde im Johannesevangelium.* WUNT 122. Tübingen, 2000.

Michaels, J. R. "Alleged Anti-Semitism in the Fourth Gospel." *Gordon Review* 11 (1968): 12–24.

Modras, R. "Addressing the Demonic in Sacred Texts: The Next Step in Catholic-Jewish Relations after the Holocaust." In J. K. Roth and E. Maxwell-Meynard, eds., *Remembering for the Future: The Holocaust in an Age of Genocide.* Vol. 2, pp. 437–54. Hampshire, 2001.

Mollat, D. *Études johanniques:* Paris, 1979.

Morgen, M. "Le salut dans la littérature johannique." *DBSup* 11 (1991): 720–40.

———. *Afin que le monde soit sauvé: Jésus révèle sa mission de salut dans l'évangile de Jean.* LD 154. Paris, 1993.

Motyer, S. *Your Father the Devil? A New Approach to John and 'the Jews.'* PBTM. London, 1997.

———. "Is John's Gospel Anti-Semitic?" *Themelios* 23, 2 (1998): 1–4.

Müller, K. *Das Judentum in der religionsgeschichtlichen Arbeit am Neuen Testament.* Frankfurt, 1983.

Muñoz Bolivar, O. ΜΑΘΗΤΗΣ. *Estudio exegético-teológico del término en el cuarto evangelio a la luz de Jn 8,31–32.* Rome, 1988.

Neuhaus, D., ed. *Teufelskinder oder Heilsbringer: Die Juden im Johannes-Evangelium.* Arnoldshainer Texte 64. Frankfurt, 1990; 2d ed., 1993.

Neusner, J., and E. S. Frerichs, eds. *"To See Ourselves as Others See Us": Christians, Jews, "Others" in Late Antiquity.* Scholars Press Studies in the Humanities. Chico, Calif. 1985.

Neyrey, J. H., "Jesus the Judge: Forensic Process in John 8,21–59." *Bib* 68 (1987): 509–42.

———. *An Ideology of Revolt: John's Christology in Social-Science Perspective.* Philadelphia, 1988.

Nickelsburg, G. W. E. "Revealed Wisdom as a Criterium for Inclusion and Exclusion: From Jewish Sectarianism to Early Christianity." In J. Neusner and E. S. Frerichs, eds., *"To See Ourselves as Others See Us": Christians, Jews, "Others" in Late Antiquity,* pp. 73–91. Scholars Press Studies in the Humanities. Chico, Calif., 1985.

Nothomb, P. "Nouveau regard sur "les juifs" de Jean." *FoiVie* 71 (1972): 65–69.

Obermann, A. *Die christologische Erfüllung der Schrift im Johannesevangelium: Eine Untersuchung zur johanneischen Hermeneutik anhand der Schriftzitate.* WUNT 2/83. Tübingen, 1996.

O'Day, G. R. "A Study of John 8: Cultural Assumptions." *Candler Connection* (1994–95): 8–9.

O'Neill, J. C. "The *Jews* in the Fourth Gospel." *IBS* 18 (1996): 58–74.

Overman, J. A. *Matthew's Gospel and Formative Judaism: The Social World of the Matthean Community.* Minneapolis, 1990.

Painter, J. "The 'Opponents' in 1 John." *NTS* 32 (1986): 48–71.

Pancaro, S. "'People of God' in John's Gospel." *NTS* 16 (1969–70): 114–29.

———. "The Relationship of the Church to Israel in the Gospel of John." *NTS* 21 (1974–75): 396–405.

———. *The Law in the Fourth Gospel: The Torah and the Gospel, Moses and Jesus, Judaism and Christianity according to John.* NovTSup 42. Leiden, 1975.

Pedersen, S. "Anti-Judaism in John's Gospel: John 8." In J. Nissen and S. Pedersen, eds., *New Readings in John: Literary and Theological Perspectives. Essays from the Scandinavian Conference on the Fourth Gospel in Århus 1997,* pp. 172–93. JSNTSup 182. Sheffield, 1999.

Pietrantonio, R. "Los 'Ioudaioi' en el Evangelio de Juan." *RB* 47 (1985): 27–41.

Pilch, J. J. "Are There Jews and Christians in the Bible?" *HvTSt* 53 (1997): 119–25.

———. "No Jews or Christians in the Bible." *Expl.* 12 (1998): 3.

Pippin, T. "'For Fear of the Jews': Lying and Truth-Telling in Translating the Gospel of John." *Semeia* 76 (1996): 81–97.

Pitta, A. "La funzione 'eufonica' dell'articulo in Gv 8,39b.c; Gal 3,14.29" *RivB* 35 (1987): 321–25.

Poffet, J.-M. "Indices de réception de l'évangile de Jean au IIe siècle, avant Irénée." In J.-D. Kaestli, J.-M. Poffet, and J. Zumstein, eds., *La communauté johannique et son histoire: La trajectoire de l'évangile de Jean aux deux premiers siècles,* pp. 305–21. Le Monde de la Bible. Geneva, 1990.

Pollefeyt, D. "Jewish and Christian Theology Confronting the Holocaust: Theological Perspectives on the Evil of Auschwitz." In E. Talmor and S. Talmor, eds.,

Memory, History and Critique: European Identity at the Millennium. Proceedings of the Fifth Conference of the International Society for the Study of European Ideas (ISSEI) 1996. On CD-ROM. U.S.A., 1997.

———. "In Search of an Alternative for the Theology of Substitution" and "Jews and Christians after Auschwitz: From Substitution to Interreligious Dialogue." In D. Pollefeyt, ed., *Jews and Christians: Rivals or Partners for the Kingdom of God? In Search of an Alternative for the Christian Theology of Substitution,* pp. 1–9 and 10–37. LTPM 21. Leuven, 1997.

———. "Victims of Evil or Evil of Victims? Towards a Hermeneutic to Understand the (Un)Ethical Behavior of Victims of the Holocaust." In H. J. Cargas, ed., *Problems Unique to the Holocaust,* pp. 67–82. Lexington, Ky., 1999.

———. "Christology after the Holocaust: A Catholic Perspective." In M. Meyer and C. Hughes, eds., *Jesus Then and Now: Images of Jesus in History and Christology,* pp. 229–47. Harrisburg, Pa., 2001.

Porsch, F., "'Ihr habt den Teufel zum Vater' (Joh 8,44). Antijudaismus im Johannesevangelium." *BK* 44 (1989): 50–57.

Porter, S. E. "Can Traditional Exegesis Enlighten Literary Analysis of the Fourth Gospel? An Examination of the Old Testament Fulfillment Motif and the Passover Theme." In C. Evans and W. Stegner, eds., *The Gospels and the Scriptures of Israel,* pp. 396–428. JSNTSup, 104. Sheffield, 1994.

Pöttner, M. "Dynamische Offenbarung: Erwägungen zur johanneischen Rede vom 'Geist der Wahrheit' in Joh 15,1–16,15." In Wilfried Härle, ed., *Im Kontinuum: Annäherungen an eine relationale Erkenntnistheorie und Ontologie,* pp. 127–45. MTSt 54. Marburg, 1999.

Pratscher, W. "Die Juden im Johannesevangelium." *BL* 59 (1986): 177–85.

———. "Tiefenpsychologische Erwägungen zur Rede von 'den Juden' im Johannesevangelium." Paper presented at the Fifty-fourth General Meeting of the SNTS, Pretoria, South Africa, August 1999.

Preiss, T. *Life in Christ.* Translated by Harold Knight. SBT 13. London, 1957.

Prieur, J.-M., ed. *Acta Andrae.* CCSA 6. Turnhout, 1989.

Reim, G. *Studien zum alttestamentlichen Hintergrund des Johannesevangeliums.* SNTSMS, 22. Cambridge, 1974.

———. "Joh. 8,44—Gotteskinder/Teufelskinder: Wie antijudaistisch ist 'die wohl antijudaistischste Äusserung des NT'?" *NTS* 30 (1984): 619–24 = G. Reim, *Jochanan: Erweiterte Studien zum alttestamentlichen Hintergrund des Johannesevangeliums,* pp. 352–58. Erlangen, 1995.

———. *Zugänge zum Evangelium des Johannes.* Erlangen, 1994.

Reinhartz, A. "A Nice Jewish Girl Reads the Gospel of John." *Semeia* 77 (1997): 177–93.

———. "The Johannine Community and Its Jewish Neighbors: A Reappraisal." In F. F. Segovia, ed., *"What Is John?"* Vol. 2: *Literary and Social Readings of the Fourth Gospel,* pp. 111–38. SBLSymS 7. Atlanta, 1998.

———. "On Travel, Translation, and Ethnography: The Gospel of John at the Turn of the Century." In F. F. Segovia, ed., *"What Is John?"* Vol. 2: *Literary and Social Readings of the Fourth Gospel,* pp. 249–56. SBLSymS 7. Atlanta, 1998.

———. "John 8:31–59 from a Jewish Perspective." In J. K. Roth and E. Maxwell-Meynard, eds., *Remembering for the Future: The Holocaust in an Age of Genocide.* Vol. 2, pp. 787–97. Hampshire, 2001.

———. *Befriending the Beloved Disciple: A Jewish Reading of the Gospel of John.* New York; London, 2001.

Rendtorff, R. "Die neutestamentliche Wissenschaft und die Juden." *EvT* 36 (1976): 191–200.

———. "The Jewish Bible and Its Anti-Jewish Interpretation." *Christian Jewish Relations* 16 (1983): 3–20.

Rensberger, D. *Johannine Faith and Liberating Community.* Philadelphia, 1988.

———. "Anti-Judaism and the Gospel of John." In W. R. Farmer, ed., *Anti-Judaism and the Gospels,* pp. 120–57. Harrisburg, Pa., 1999.

Richardson, P., and D. Granskou, eds. *Anti-Judaism in Early Christianity.* Vol. 1: *Paul and the Gospels.* Studies in Christianity and Judaism 2. Waterloo, 1986.

Riedl, J. "Wenn ihr den Menschensohn erhöht habt, werdet ihr erkennen (Joh 8,28)." In R. Pesch and R. Schnackenburg, eds., *Jesus und der Menschensohn,* pp. 355–70. FS Anton Vögtle. Freiburg–Basel–Vienna, 1975.

Rissi, M. "Das Judenproblem im Lichte der Johannesapokalypse." *TZ* 13 (1957): 241–59.

———. "Die 'Juden' im Johannesevangelium." *ANRW* 2.26.3 (1996): 2099–2141.

Robert, R. "Le malentendu sur le nom divin au chapître VIII du quatrième évangile." *RThom* 88 (1988): 278–87.

———. "Étude littéraire de Jean VIII, 21–59." *RThom* 89 (1989): 71–84.

Ruether, R. R. "Theological Anti-Semitism in the New Testament." *ChrCent* 85 (1968): 191–96.

———. *Faith and Fratricide: The Theological Roots of Anti-Semitism.* New York, 1974.

———. "The *Faith and Fratricide* Discussion: Old Problems and New Dimensions." In A. T. Davies, ed., *Antisemitism and the Foundations of Christianity,* pp. 230–56. New York, 1979.

Russo, G. "Libertà nella filiazione: Riflessioni teologico-etiche su Gv 8,31–59." *Asprenas* 39 (1992): 179–98.

Sanders, J. A. "'Nor Do I . . .': A Canonical Reading of the Challenge to Jesus in John 8." In R. T. Fortna and B. R. Gaventa, eds., *The Conversation Continues: Studies in Paul and John in Honor of J. Louis Martyn,* pp. 337–47. Nashville, 1990.

Sanders, J. T. *Schismatics, Sectarians, Dissidents, Deviants: The First One Hundred Years of Jewish-Christian Relations.* Valley Forge, Pa., 1993.

Sandmel, S. *Anti-Semitism in the New Testament?* Philadelphia, 1978.

Santagada, O. D. "Los adversarios de Jesús en el evangelio de San Juan." *Criterio* 47–48 (1975): 371–74.

Schein, B. E. "'The Seed of Abraham'—John 8:31–59." *Abstracts of SBL Meeting* 159 (1971): 83–84.

Schenke, L. "Der Dialog Jesu mit den Juden im Johannesevangelium. Ein Rekonstruktionsversuch." *NTS* 34 (1988): 573–603.

———. "Das johanneische Schisma und die 'Zwölf' (Johannes 6.60–71)." *NTS* 38 (1992): 105–21.

Schiffman, L. H. *Who Was a Jew? Rabbinic and Halakhic Perspectives on the Jewish-Christian Schism.* Hoboken, N.J., 1985.

Schnelle, U. *Antidocetic Christology in the Gospel of John: An Investigation of the Place of the Fourth Gospel in the Johannine School.* Translated by L. M. Maloney. Minneapolis, 1992.

————. "Die Juden im Johannesevangelium." In C. Kähler, M. Böhm, and C. Bött-rich, eds., *Gedenkt an das Wort*, pp. 217–30. FS W. Vogler. Leipzig, 1999.

Scholtissek, K. "Antijudaismus im Johannesevangelium? Ein Gesprächsbeitrag." In R. Kampling, ed., *"Nun steht aber diese Sache im Evangelium . . .": Zur Frage nach den Anfängen des christlichen Antijudaismus*, pp. 151–81. Paderborn, 1999.

Schoon, S. "'Het heil is uit de Joden' (Joh. 4:22). Enkele consequenties voor de missi-ologie." In A. G. Honig, ed., *Heil voor deze wereld*, pp. 23–35. FS A. G. Honig. Kampen, 1984.

Schram, T. L. "The Use of IOUDAIOS in the Fourth Gospel: An Application of Some Linguistic Insights to a New Testament Problem." Diss., Utrecht, 1974.

Schuchard, B. G. *Scripture within Scripture: The Interrelationship of Form and Function in the Explicit Old Testament Citations in the Gospel of John*. Atlanta, 1992.

Segal, A. F. *Two Powers in Heaven: Early Rabbinic Reports about Christianity and Gnos-ticism*. Leiden, 1977.

————. "Judaism, Christianity, and Gnosticism." In S. Wilson, ed., *Anti-Judaism in Early Christianity*. Vol. 2: *Separation and Polemic*, pp. 133-61. Studies in Chris-tianity and Judaism 2. Waterloo, 1986.

————. *Rebecca's Children: Judaism and Christianity in the Roman World*. Cambridge, Mass., 1986.

Segovia, F. F. "The Love and Hatred of Jesus and Johannine Sectarianism." *CBQ* 43 (1981): 258–72.

Setzer, C. *Jewish Responses to Early Christians: History and Polemics, 30–150 C.E.* Min-neapolis, 1994.

Sevenster, J. N. *The Roots of Pagan Anti-Semitism in the Ancient World.* NovTSup 41. Leiden, 1975.

Sevrin, J.-M. "Le prince de ce monde: La fonction christologique du diable dans le qua-trième évangile." In M. Lagrée, H. Couzel, and J.-M. Sevrin, *Figures du démo-niaque, hier et aujourd'hui*, pp. 63–81. Publications des Facultés Universitaires Saint-Louis 55. Brussels, 1992.

————. "Le paradoxe de la foi dans le quatrième évangile." In A. Gesché and P. Sco-las, eds., *La foi dans le temps du risque*, pp. 55–78. Paris, 1997.

Shepherd, M. H. "The Jews in the Gospel of John: Another Level of Meaning." ATR.SS 3 (1974): 95–112.

Siker, J. S. *Disinheriting the Jews: Abraham in Early Christian Controversy.* Louisville, Ky., 1991.

Sikes, W. W. "The Anti-Semitism of the Fourth Gospel." *JR* 21 (1941): 23–30.

Simon, M. *Verus Israel: A Study of the Relations between Christians and Jews in the Roman Empire, 135–425.* Translated by H. McKeating. Littman Library of Jew-ish Civilization. New York, 1986.

————. "La Bible dans les premières controverses entre juifs et chrétiens." In C. Mondésert, ed., *Le Monde grec ancien et la Bible*, pp. 107–25. Bible de tous les temps 1. Paris, 1984. ET: "The Bible in the Earliest Controversies between Jews and Christians." In P. M. Blowers, ed., *The Bible in Greek Christian Antiquity*, pp. 49–68. The Bible Through the Ages 1. Notre Dame, Ind., 1997.

Sloyan, G. S. "The Gnostic Adoption of John's Gospel and Its Canonization by the Catholic Church." *BTB* 26 (1996): 125–32.

Smiga, G.M. *Pain and Polemic: Anti-Judaism in the Gospels.* New York–Mahwah, N.J., 1992.

Smith, D. M. *The Gospel of John and Judaism.* London, 1975; 2d ed., 1980.

———. "The Life Setting of the Gospel of John." *RevExp* 85 (1988): 433–44.

———. "Judaism and the Gospel of John." In J. H. Charlesworth, with F. X. Blisard and J. S. Siker, eds., *Jews and Christians: Exploring the Past, Present, and Future,* pp. 76–96. Shared Ground among Jews and Christians 1. New York, 1990.

———. "The Problem of John and the Synoptics in Light of the Relation between Apocryphal and Canonical Gospels." In A. Denaux, ed., *John and the Synoptics,* pp. 147–62. BETL 101. Leuven, 1992.

———. "Prolegomena to a Canonical Reading of the Fourth Gospel." In F. F. Segovia, ed., *"What Is John?"* Vol. 1: *Readers and Readings of the Fourth Gospel,* pp. 169–82. SBLSymS 3. Atlanta, 1996.

Söding, T. "'Was kann aus Nazareth schon Gutes kommen?' (Joh 1.46). Die Bedeutung des Judeseins Jesu im Johannesevangelium." *NTS* 46 (2000): 21–41.

Solin, H. "Excursus 'Iudaeus.'" In *ANRW* 2.29.2: 648–51.

Sproston, W. E. "Satan in the Fourth Gospel." In E. A. Livingstone, ed., *Studia Biblica 1978.* Vol. 2: *Papers on the Gospels,* pp. 307–11. JSNTSup 2. Sheffield, 1980.

Stanton, G. N., and G. G. Stroumsa, eds., *Tolerance and Intolerance in Early Judaism and Christianity.* Cambridge, 1998.

Stegemann, E. "Die Tragödie der Nähe: Zu den judenfeindlichen Aussagen des Johannesevangeliums." *Kirche und Israel* 4 (1989): 114–22.

Stern, M. "Aspects of Jewish Society: The Priesthood and Other Classes." In S. Safrai and M. Stern, eds., *The Jewish People in the First Century: Historical Geography, Political History, Social, Cultural and Religious Life and Institutions,* pp. 561–630. CRINT 1/2. Assen, 1976.

Stiassny, J. "Development of the Christian's Self-Understanding in the Second Part of the First Century." *Imm* 1 (1972): 32–34.

Strecker, G. "Die Anfänge der johanneischen Schule." *NTS* 32 (1986): 31–47.

———. *Die Johannesbriefe.* KEK 14. Göttingen, 1989.

Swetnam, J. "The Meaning of πεπιστευκότας in John 8,31." *Bib* 61 (1980): 106–9.

Tanzer, S. "Salvation is *for* the Jews: Secret Christian Jews in the Gospel of John." In B. A. Pearson, ed., *The Future of Early Christianity. Essays in Honor of Helmut Koester,* pp. 285–300. Minneapolis, 1991.

Taylor, M. S. *Anti-Judaism and Early Christian Identity: A Critique of the Scholarly Consensus.* Leiden–New York–Cologne, 1995.

Theissen, G. "Aporien im Umgang mit den Antijudaismen des Neuen Testaments." In E. Blum, C. Macholz, and E. W. Stegemann, eds., *Die hebräische Bibel und ihre zweifache Nachgeschichte,* pp. 535–53. FS R. Rendtorff. Neukirchen-Vluyn, 1990.

Theobald, M. "Die Entdeckung des Juden Jesus von Nazareth." In F. Mussner, ed., *Jesus von Nazareth im Umfeld Israels und der Urkirche,* pp. 1–10. Tübingen, 1999.

Thoma, A. "Das Alte Testament im Johannesevangelium." *ZWT* 22 (1879): 18–66.

Thoma, C. *Kirche aus Juden und Heiden: Biblische Informationen über das Verhältnis der Kirche zum Judentum,* pp. 79–91. Konfrontationen 8. Vienna–Freiburg–Basel, 1970.

Thomas, J. C. "The Fourth Gospel and Rabbinic Judaism." *ZNW* 82 (1991): 159–82.

Thyen, H. "'Das Heil kommt von den Juden.'" In D. Lüdemann and G. Strecker, eds., *Kirche.* pp. 163–84. FS G. Bornkamm. Tübingen, 1980.

―――. "Exegese des Neuen Testaments nach dem Holocaust." In R. Rendtorff and E. Stegemann, eds., *Auschwitz: Krise der christlichen Theologie. Eine Vortragsreihe,* pp. 140–58. ACJD 10. Stuttgart, 1980.

―――. "Ich bin das Licht der Welt." JAC 35 (1992): 19–46.

Tolmie, F. "The IOUDAIOI in the Fourth Gospel: A Narratological Perspective." Paper presented at the Fifty-fourth General Meeting of the SNTS, Pretoria, South Africa, August 1999.

Tomson, P. J. "The Names 'Israel' and 'Jew' in Ancient Judaism and the New Testament." *Bijdr* 47 (1986): 120–40, 266–89.

―――. *'Als dit uit de Hemel is . . .' Jezus en de schrijvers van het Nieuwe Testament in hun verhouding tot het Jodendom.* Hilversum, 1997. ET: *If This Be from Heaven . . . : Jesus and the New Testament Authors in Their Relationship to Judaism.* The Biblical Seminar 76. Sheffield, 2001.

Townsend, J. T. "The Gospel of John and the Jews: The Story of a Religious Divorce." In A. T. Davies, ed., *Antisemitism and the Foundations of Christianity,* pp. 72–97. New York, 1979.

Trachtenberg, J. *The Devil and the Jews.* Meridian Books: The Jewish Publication Society of America 22. Cleveland, 1961.

Trilling, W. "Gegner Jesu—Widersacher der Gemeinde—Repräsentanten der 'Welt'. Das Johannesevangelium und die Juden." ThJb (1980): 222–38 = H. Goldstein, ed., *Gottesverächter und Menschenfeinde? Juden zwischen Jesus und frühchristlicher Kirche,* pp. 190–211. Düsseldorf, 1979.

Trocmé, É. "Les juifs d'après le Nouveau Testament." *FoiVie* 90 (1991): 3–22.

Trumbower, J. A. "Origen's Exegesis of John 8:19–53: The Struggle with Heracleon over the Idea of Fixed Natures." *VC* 43 (1989): 138–54.

Van Belle, G. *Johannine Bibliography 1966–1985: A Cumulative Bibliography of the Fourth Gospel.* BETL 82. Leuven, 1988.

―――. *The Signs Source in the Fourth Gospel: Historical Survey and Critical Evaluation of the Semeia Hypothesis.* BETL 116. Leuven, 1994.

Vandecasteele-Vanneuville, F. "Johannine Theology of Revelation, Soteriology, and the Problem of Anti-Judaism." *SNTU* 26, in press.

Van der Horst, P. W. "The Birkat Ha-Minim in Recent Research." *ExpTim* 105 (1994): 367–68.

Van der Watt, J. G. "Seine blindes? Kantaantekeninge oor de 'Jode' en die 'Jodendom' in die Johannesevangelie." *NGTT* 37 (1996): 193–207.

Van Duyne, H. M. J. "Jezus en de "joden" in het evangelie van Johannes." *Ter Herkenning* 7 (1979): 112–22.

Van Henten, J. W. "Christenen binnen en buiten het jodendom." In T. Baarda, H. J. de Jonge, and M. J. J. Menken, eds., *Jodendom en vroeg christendom. Continuïteit en discontinuïteit,* pp. 137–61. Kampen, 1991.

Vasholz, R. T. "Is the New Testament Anti-Semitic?" *Presb* 11 (1985): 118–23.

Vawter, B. "Are the Gospels Anti-Semitic?" *JES* 5 (1968): 473–87.

Vignolo, R. "Gv 8,31–59. La paternità di Satana e il Figlio di Dio." *Ambrosius* 70 (1994): 387–410.

von Henze, D., C. Janssen, S. Müller, and B. Wehn. *Antijudaismus im Neuen Testament? Grundlagen für die Arbeit mit biblischen Texten.* Kaiser Taschenbücher 00149. Gütersloh, 1997.

von Wahlde, U. C. "The Johannine 'Jews': A Critical Survey." *NTS* 28 (1982): 33–60.

———. "Literary Structure and Theological Argument in Three Discourses with the Jews in the Fourth Gospel." *JBL* 103 (1984): 575–84.

———. *The Earliest Version of John's Gospel: Recovering the Gospel of Signs.* Wilmington, Del., 1989.

———. "The Gospel of John and the Presentation of Jews and Judaism." In D. P. Efroymson, E. J. Fisher, and L. Klenicki, eds., *Within Context: Essays on Jews and Judaism in the New Testament,* pp. 67–84. Philadelphia, 1993.

———. "Community in Conflict: The History and Social Context of the Johannine Community." *Int* 49 (1995): 379–89.

———. "The Relationships between Pharisees and Chief Priests: Some Observations on the Texts in Matthew, John and Josephus." *NTS* 42 (1996): 506–22.

———. "'The Jews' in the Gospel of John: Fifteen Years of Research (1983–1998)." *ETL* 76 (2000): 30–55.

Vouga, F. *Die Johannesbriefe.* HNT 15/3. Tübingen, 1990.

———. "Antijudaismus im Johannesevangelium?" *TGl* 83 (1993): 81–89.

Wander, B. *Trennungsprozesse zwischen Judentum und Christentum im 1. Jahrhundert n. Chr.: Datierbare Abfolgen zwischen der Hinrichtung Jesu und der Zerstörung des Jerusalemer Tempels.* Texte und Arbeiten zum neutestamentlichen Zeitalter 16. Tübingen, 1994; 2d ed., 1997.

Watson, A. *Jesus and the Jews: The Pharisaic Tradition in John.* Athens, Ga.–London, 1995.

Wengst, K. *Bedrängte Gemeinde und verherrlichter Christus: Der historische Ort des Johannesevangeliums als Schlüssel zu seiner Interpretation.* BThSt 5. Neukirchen-Vluyn, 1981; 3d ed., 1983; 4th ed., 1992. New ed.: *Bedrängte Gemeinde und verherrlichter Christus: Ein Versuch über das Johannesevangelium.* Munich, 1990.

———. "Die Darstellung 'der Juden' im Johannes-Evangelium als Reflex jüdischjudenchristlicher Kontroverse." In D. Neuhaus, ed., *Teufelskinder oder Heilsbringer: Die Juden im Johannes-Evangelium,* pp. 22–38. Arnoldshainer Texte 64. Frankfurt, 1990; 2d ed., 1993.

Westermann, C. *Das Johannesevangelium aus der Sicht des Alten Testaments.* AzTh 77. Stuttgart, 1994.

Whitacre, R. A. *Johannine Polemic: The Role of Tradition and Theology.* SBLDS 67. Chico, Calif., 1982.

White, M. C. *The Identity and Function of the Jews and Related Terms in the Fourth Gospel.* Ann Arbor, Mich., 1972.

Wiefel, W. "Die Scheidung von Gemeinde und Welt im Johannesevangelium auf dem Hintergrund der Trennung von Kirche und Synagoge." *TZ* 35 (1979): 213–27.

Wilckens, U. "Das Neue Testament und die Juden." *EvT* 34 (1974): 602–11.

Williams, M. H. "The Meaning and Function of IOUDAIOS in Graeco-Roman Inscriptions." *ZPE* 116 (1997): 249–62.

Wilson, M. R. *Our Father Abraham: Jewish Roots of the Christian Faith.* Grand Rapids, 1989.

Wilson, S. G. "Anti-Judaism in the Fourth Gospel? Some Considerations." *IBS* 1 (1979): 28–50.

———, ed. *Anti-Judaism in Early Christianity.* Vol. 2: *Separation and Polemic.* Studies in Christianity and Judaism 2. Waterloo, 1986.

———. *Related Strangers: Jews and Christians 70–170 C.E.* Minneapolis, 1995.

Windisch, H. "Das johanneische Christentum und sein Verhältnis zum Judentum und zu Paulus." *Christliche Welt* 47 (1933): 98–107.

Wylen, S. M. *The Jews in the Time of Jesus: An Introduction.* Mahwah, N.J., 1995.

Yee, G. A. *Jewish Feasts and the Gospel of John.* Zacchaeus Studies, New Testament. Wilmington, Del., 1989.

Zeitlin, S. "The Names Hebrew, Jew and Israel: A Historical Study." *JQR* 43 (1952–53): 365–79.

Zumstein, J. "La communauté johannique et son histoire." In J.-D. Kaestli, J.-M. Poffet, and J. Zumstein, eds., *La Communauté johannique et son histoire: La trajectoire de l'évangile de Jean aux deux premiers siècles,* pp. 359–74. Le Monde de la Bible. Geneva, 1990.

———. "Zur Geschichte des johanneischen Christentums." *TLZ* 122 (1997): 417–28.

SCRIPTURE INDEX

AUTHOR INDEX

SUBJECT INDEX